D1196503

WITHDRAWN

ATLA BIBLIOGRAPHY SERIES
edited by Dr. Kenneth E. Rowe

1. *A Guide to the Study of the Holiness Movement,* by Charles Edwin Jones. 1974.
2. *Thomas Merton: A Bibliography,* by Marquita E. Breit. 1974.
3. *The Sermon on the Mount: A History of Interpretation and Bibliography,* by Warren S. Kissinger. 1975.
4. *The Parables of Jesus: A History of Interpretation and Bibliography,* by Warren S. Kissinger. 1979.
5. *Homosexuality and the Judeo-Christian Tradition: An Annotated Bibliography,* by Thom Horner. 1981.
6. *A Guide to the Study of the Pentecostal Movement,* by Charles Edwin Jones. 1983.
7. *The Genesis of Modern Process Thought: A Historical Outline with Bibliography,* by George R. Lucas, Jr. 1983.
8. *A Presbyterian Bibliography,* by Harold B. Prince. 1983.
9. *Paul Tillich: A Comprehensive Bibliography . . .,* by Richard C. Crossman. 1983.
10. *A Bibliography of the Samaritans,* by Alan David Crown. 1984.
11. *An Annotated and Classified Bibliography of English Literature Pertaining to the Ethiopian Orthodox Church,* by Jon Bonk. 1984.
12. *International Meditation Bibliography, 1950 to 1982,* by Howard R. Jarrell. 1984.
13. *Rabindranath Tagore: A Bibliography,* by Katherine Henn. 1985.
14. *Research in Ritual Studies: A Programmatic Essay and Bibliography,* by Ronald L. Grimes, 1985.
15. *Protestant Theological Education in America,* by Heather F. Day. 1985.
16. *Unconscious: A Guide to Sources,* by Natalino Caputi. 1985.
17. *The New Testament Apocrypha and Pseudepigrapha,* by James H. Charlesworth. 1987.
18. *Black Holiness,* by Charles Edwin Jones. 1987.
19. *A Bibliography on Ancient Ephesus,* by Richard Oster. 1987.
20. *Jerusalem, the Holy City: A Bibliography,* by James D. Purvis. 1988.
21. *An Index to English Periodical Literature on the Old Testament and Ancient Near Eastern Studies,* by William G. Hupper. Vol. I, 1987; Vol. II, 1988; Vol. III, 1990.
22. *John and Charles Wesley: A Bibliography,* by Betty M. Jarboe. 1987.
23. *A Scholar's Guide to Academic Journals in Religion,* by James Dawsey. 1988.
24. *The Oxford Movement and Its Leaders: A Bibliography of Secondary and Lesser Primary Sources,* by Lawrence N. Crumb. 1988.
25. *A Bibliography of Christian Worship,* by Bard Thompson. 1989.
26. *The Disciples and American Culture: A Bibliography of Works by Disciples of Christ Members, 1866-1984,* by Leslie R. Galbraith and Heather F. Day. 1990.

D THE ISCIPLES AND AMERICAN CULTURE

A Bibliography of Works by Disciples of Christ Members 1866-1984

by
LESLIE R. GALBRAITH
and
HEATHER F. DAY

ATLA Bibliography Series, No. 26

The Scarecrow Press, Inc.
Metuchen, N.J., & London
1990

British Library Cataloguing-in-Publication data available

Library of Congress Cataloging-in-Publication Data

Galbraith, Leslie R., 1941-
    The Disciples and American culture : a bibliography of works by Disci-
ples of Christ members, 1866-1984 / by Leslie R. Galbraith and Heather F.
Day.
        p.   cm. -- (ATLA bibliography series ; no. 26)
    Includes index.
    ISBN 0-8108-2361-6 (alk. paper)
    1. Christian Church (Disciples of Christ)--Bibliography.   2. Christian
Churches and Churches of Christ--Bibliography.   3. Churches of Christ--
Bibliography.   4. United States--Civilization--19th century--Bibliography.
5. United States--Civilization--20th century--Bibliography.   I. Day, Heather
F.   II. Title.   III. Series.
Z7845.D6G35   1990
[BX7321.2]
016.2866--dc20   90-44838

CONTENTS

The American Theological Library Association Bibliography Series is designed to stimulate and encourage the preparation of reliable bibliographies and guides to the literature of religious studies in all its scope and variety. Compilers are free to define their field, make their own selections, and work out internal organization as the unique demands of the subject require. The ATLA Publication Committee is pleased to publish <u>The Disciples and American Culture: A Bibliography of Works by Disciples of Christ Members, 1866-1984</u> by Leslie R. Galbraith and Heather F. Day as number 26 in our series.

Following undergraduate and theology studies at Phillips University in Enid, Oklahoma, Mr. Galbraith took a library science degree at the University of Texas at Austin and postgraduate study at Indiana University. In 1972, Mr. Galbraith became director of the library at Christian Theological Seminary in Indianapolis. Heather Day did her undergraduate work at Taylor University, took a master's degree in church history at Butler University, and a library science degree at Indiana University. She served as librarian at the Lilly Endowment from 1974 to 1980. Her <u>Protestant Theological Education in America: A Bibliography</u> was published as number 15 in this series in 1985.

Kenneth E. Rowe
Series Editor
Drew University Library
Madison, New Jersey

INTRODUCTION

How do you study the impact of a religious group on American culture or the influences of that culture on the life and thought of that religious tradition? One way is to identify the publications of persons related to that tradition from all the professions and disciplines represented by members of that church.

That is the approach we have taken in this bibliography. We have attempted to identify persons related to the Christian Church (Disciples of Christ) and the two religious bodies which share their origins in the Restoration Movement of Thomas and Alexander Campbell and Barton W. Stone. Those churches are the Churches of Christ and the Independent Christian Churches known as the Christian Churches and Churches of Christ.

The inclusive dates for this bibliography are 1866 and 1984. Alexander Campbell, the last of the first generation of leaders of the Restoration Movement, died in 1866. As the American culture began to recover from the devastation of the Civil War, religious bodies became more involved in that recovery and both church and society became more interdependent. The date of 1984 was chosen because that represented the end of President Ronald Reagan's first term in office. This allowed us to include material on all three presidents who have been associated with the Christian Church (Disciples of Christ). The other Disciple presidents were James Garfield and Lyndon Johnson.

Although we have tried to be comprehensive, we know that there are persons we missed or publications we failed to identify as having Disciple authors. However, we are confident that the scope of this bibliography and our research methodology has provided a representative listing of materials to provide an adequate basis for any investigation of the Disciples and American culture.

The following pages will give the researcher an understanding of the scope of this project and an outline of the arrangement of the citations.

Arrangement of the Bibliography

A. Periodical and General Literature Section

This section covers literature about the Disciples of Christ by non-Disciple authors, as well as periodical articles by both Disciple and non-Disciple authors, and is the only section of the bibliography that covers periodical articles. It was compiled by searching the following data bases, indexes, catalogs and bibliographies using terms such as Disciples of Christ, Christian Church, Church(es) of Christ (through 1906), Restoration Movement and Campbellites.

Computer Searches.

America: History and Life (1963 to present)

Arts and Humanities Citation Index (1980 to present)

Books in Print (current)

Catalyst Resource on the Workforce and Women (1963 to present)

Dissertation Abstracts Online (1861 to present)

Education Index (1983 to present)

ERIC (Educational Resources Information Center, 1966 to present)

Essay and General Literature Index (1985 to present)

Family Resources Database (1970 to present)

LC MARC (Library of Congress Machine-Readable Cataloging, 1968 to present)

Magazine Index (1959-1970, 1973 to present)

National Newspaper Index (includes <u>Christian Science Monitor</u>, <u>Los Angeles Times</u>, <u>New York Times</u>, <u>Wall St. Journal</u>, <u>Washington Post</u>, 1979 to present)

Philosopher's Index (1940 to present)

Popular Magazine Review Online (1984 to present)

Psychological Abstracts (1967 to present)

PSYCINFO (1967 to present)

PAIS (Public Affairs Information Service, 1976 to present)

Religion Index (1949 to present)

REMARC database (Retrospective Machine-Readable Cataloging, i.e., all books cataloged by the Library of Congress, 1897-1978)

Social Sciences Citation Index (1972 to present)

Social Scisearch (1972 to present)

Sociological Abstracts (1963 to present)

U.S. Political Science Documents Database (1975 to present)

Manual Searches.

Bibliography of Religion in the South (c1985)

Catholic Periodical and Literature Index (1930 to present)

Combined Retrospective Index to Journals in History (1838-1974)

Education Index (1929-1983)

Education Literature (1907-1932)

Essay and General Literature Index (1900-1985)

Historical Abstracts (not indexing U.S. after 1963; 1955-1963)

Humanities Index (1974 to present)

Index to Periodicals by and about Blacks (1950-1983)

International Index to Periodicals (later Social Sciences and Humanities Index, 1907-1974)

Literature of American History (c1902)

Magazine Subject-Index (1907-1949)

New York Public Library. Dictionary Catalog of the Schomburg Collection of Negro Literature and History

Peabody Institute Library. First and Second Catalogues

Poole's Index to Periodical Literature (1802-1906)

Protestant Theological Education in America: A Bibliography (c1984)

Reader's Guide to Periodical Literature (1890 to present)

Religion and Society in North America: An Annotated Bibliography (c1983)

Religion in Indiana: A Guide to Historical Resources (c1986)

Religious and Theological Abstracts (1958 to present)

Religious Books, 1876-1982

Social Sciences Index (1974 to present)

Writings on American History (1902-1940; 1962-1976)

B. Name Section

A substantial file of names of Disciples who have played a significant role in the life of the church or who have achieved prominence in their own fields of endeavor was compiled at Christian Theological Seminary. The Vertical File at the seminary was searched, as well as the <u>Higher Education Directory</u> published annually since 1972 by the Disciples Board of Higher Education; <u>Journey in Faith: A History of the Christian Church (Disciples of Christ)</u> by McAllister and Tucker; and the <u>Disciples Theological Digest</u>.

Wherever possible, the individual's birth and death dates were noted as well as his/her profession to aid in identifying the individual. However, there were many cases where the bibliographers had to do further searching through biographical sources to find more complete information to place the name correctly. Intelligent guessing was necessary on occasion when it was not completely clear which was the correct individual. Professions are listed under most names to aid the user in identifying the authors with their areas of interest. No attempt was made to gather comprehensive biographical data about each person; rather, our main effort was toward finding all the works each person had produced.

Some of the people whose names appear in the bibliography
may not currently be members of the Disciples of Christ, but
they are included because they formerly were members, or
because they are affiliated with Disciple institutions. Their
denominational affiliations are noted whenever possible.

1. Works Included in the Name Section.

This section includes books, doctoral theses and reports
longer than 50 pages or so for each author, regardless of
field. No periodical articles are included in this section.
Shorter works by authors appearing in the Theology section have
also been included because of their probable significance to
any study of the Disciples of Christ.

2. How the Works in the Name Section Were Identified.
There were thousands of names given to the bibliographers to
search, many of which do not appear in the bibliography because
the search did not turn up any works by them.

The names which could be found in The Biography and
Genealogy Master Index (published by Gale Research Company,
1980-), which includes birth and death dates, were given to the
Computer-Based Information Services at Purdue University to be
searched through the LC MARC and REMARC databases. These
databases, produced by Carrollton Press (Arlington, Va.), claim
to have citations to all works in the Library of Congress shelf
list from 1897 to 1980 (REMARC - Retrospective Machine Readable
Cataloging) and from 1968 to the present (LC MARC - Library of
Congress Machine Readable Cataloging). The REMARC database

also includes citations cataloged by other libraries and organizations whose records were not included in the LC MARC database.

However, upon comparing the computer searches with manual searches of the same names, the manual searches often turned up works which did not appear on the computer printouts. But, due to the time-consuming nature of manual searching and the cost of the computer searches, it was decided not to do manual searches on all of the names which had already been searched by computer. Thus, those searched only on LC MARC or REMARC have been starred (*) to indicate that the list of works following the starred names may not be complete.

Manual searches were conducted on the names which could not be found in The Biography and Genealogy Master Index. Searching was done through the National Union Catalog, published by the Library of Congress, beginning with Pre-1956 Imprints (Mansell) and continuing with the National Union Catalog up to the present, as well as Books in Print (published by R.R. Bowker) for current works.

Some of the names were also searched at Christian Theological Seminary on the OCLC (Online Computer Library Center) database, with records of over 10,000 participating libraries since 1973. Where the names were searched on OCLC and also manually as a spot check, OCLC proved to turn up as many works since 1973 as did manual searching through the National Union Catalog.

Format

Turabian format (Kate E. Turabian. <u>A Manual for Writers of Term Papers, Theses and Dissertations</u>. 5th ed., 1987) has been followed in the "Periodical and General Literature" section. However, this format is abbreviated in the "Name" section so as to shorten this lengthy section. The place of publication has usually been omitted unless there is no publisher.

Acknowledgements

We owe a special thanks to Lilly Endowment for their financial support of this project. The bibliography is only one portion of the research generated by a grant to Christian Theological Seminary for the study of the Christian Church (Disciples of Christ). Dr. D. Newell Williams served as the grant director and is preparing a book of essays as well as a history of the Disciples in relation to American culture.

The librarians at Purdue University were most helpful to the bibliographers in handling requests for information, especially Katherine Markee of the Computer-Based Information Services, who took a particular interest in the project.

Two students from Christian Theological Seminary, Karen Binford and Kimberly Wheeler, served as research assistants. They were primarily involved in the process of gathering the names to be checked.

Claire Clemens and April Tubbs typed the manuscript on the word processor. Their task of having to take information from hand-written cards, typed sheets and computer printouts and ensuring that every "jot and tittle" was in place so that the information would be consistent and accurate, was a difficult one. A special word of thanks must be given to Judith Foster, Library Secretary at Christian Theological Seminary, for the valuable assistance she provided in preparing this manuscript in its final form.

The support of all of these people helped to bring the bibliography to the place where it can be used by researchers to better understand the Christian Church (Disciples of Christ) and its influence upon American culture.

Leslie R. Galbraith
Indianapolis, Indiana

Heather F. Day
West Lafayette, Indiana

1. Adams, H. "Baptists, Disciples Confer." Christian Century 67 (August 2, 1950):931-2.

2. Adams, J. E. "Brotherhood and Blandness; General Assembly." Christianity Today 23 (December 7, 1979):42-3.

3. "Alexander Campbell, Liberal." Christian Century 55 (September 21, 1938):1119-21.

4. Allen, C. L. "Baconianism and the Bible in the Disciples of Christ, Lamar, James S. and the 'Organon of Scripture.'" Church History 55, no. 1 (1986):65-80.

5. Allen, Charles R. "Disciples Ministers and the Mature Character." Encounter (CTS) 39 (Summer 1978):321-30.

6. Allen, Charles R. "Unprofessional Brotherhood and the Professional Brother." Lexington Theological Quarterly 12 (July 1977):69-80.

7. "Annual Convention, 1894, Richmond, Va." Outlook 50 (November 3, 1894):730.

8. "Another Church Union." Literary Digest 110 (July 18, 1931):19-20.

9. Arnold, Charles Harvey. "The Illuminati: The Origins of Liberalism among the Disciples of Christ, 1866-1909." Encounter (CTS) 43, no. 1 (1982):1-25.

10. Arnold, Charles Harvey. "A Religion That Walks the Earth: Edward Scribner Ames and the Chicago School of Theology." Encounter (CTS) 30 (Fall 1969):314-39.

11. Ash, Anthony L. "Old Testament Scholarship and the Restoration Movement." Restoration Quarterly 25, no. 4 (1982):213-22.

12. Ash, Anthony L. "Old Testament Studies in the Restoration Movement." Restoration Quarterly 9, no. 4 (1966):216-28; 10 (1967):25-39, 89-98, 149-60.

13. Association for the Promotion of Christian Unity, Faith, Order Committee. "A Response to Lund: The Status of This Document [Response to Report of the Third World Conference on Faith and Order, Lund, 1952]." Shane Quarterly 14 (July 1953):91-110.

14.   Association of Disciples for Theological Discussion. *Papers Presented October 14, 1960, Thompson Retreat House, Webster Groves, Mo.* St. Louis, 1961.

15.   Association of Disciples for Theological Discussion. *Papers Presented Nov. 13-15, 1959.* St. Louis, 1959.

16.   Atwater, Amzi. "Indiana University Forty Years Ago." *Indiana Magazine of History* 1, no. 3 (1905):140-9.

17.   Bailey, Fred A. "Woman's Superiority in Disciple Thought, 1865-1900." *Restoration Quarterly* 23, no. 3 (1980):151-60.

18.   "Baptist Joke." *Christian Century* 47 (June 11, 1930):744-6.

19.   "Baptists and Disciples and Baptism." *Christian Century* 43 (February 25, 1926):247-9.

20.   "Baptists and Disciples Discuss Union." *Christian Century* 66 (June 1, 1949):668.

21.   "Baptists Explore Church Union." *Christian Century* 80 (June 5, 1963):734.

22.   Bates, M. Searle. "Disciples' Missions in the Ecumenical Framework Address." *Shane Quarterly* 16 (April 1955):69-78.

23.   Beckelhymer, Paul Hunter. "Representative Preaching about Jesus: Two Generations of Disciples of Christ." *Encounter* (CTS) 19 (Spring 1958):193-207.

24.   Bedford, A. Goff. "Social Impressions of a Country Pastor in the Kentucky Bluegrass Region." *Lexington Theological Quarterly* 15 (January 1980):6-18.

25.   Bennett, Weldon. "J. W. McGarvey's Concept of the Ministry." *Restoration Quarterly* 24, no. 3 (1981):167-74.

26.   Benton, Allen Richardson. "Early Educational Conditions and Founding of a Denominational College [North Western Christian University, later Butler University]." *Indiana Magazine of History* 4 (March 1908):13-17.

27.   Berry, Charles. "The History of the Oldest Christian Church in Texas [On the First Christian Church of

Palestine, Texas, 1846-1947]." <u>Junior Historian</u>
(Texas) 9, no. 4 (January 1948 or 9):9-11.

28. Berry, Stephen P. "Room for the Spirit: The
     Contribution of Robert Richardson [Stone-Campbell
     Movement]." <u>Lexington Theological Quarterly</u> 21
     (July 1986):83-90.

29. Best, Thomas F. "Survey of Church Union Negotiations
     1981-1983." <u>Ecumenical Review</u> 36 (October 1984)
     :404-20.

30. Bicha, Karel D. "Prairie Radicals: A Common Pietism."
     <u>Journal of Church and State</u> 18, no. 1 (1976):79-94.

31. Bird, John. "Lyndon Johnson's Religion." <u>Saturday</u>
     <u>Evening Post</u> 238 (March 27, 1965):80+.

32. Black, W. F. [What Makes a Disciple.] <u>Chautauquan</u> 19
     (1894):174+.

33. Blake, Eugene Carson. "A United Church: Evangelical,
     Catholic and Reformed." <u>Thought</u> 41 (1966):52-60.

34. Blizzard, Samuel W. "The Suburban Movement and Church
     Programming." <u>Shane Quarterly 15</u> (October
     1954):169-86.

35. Board of Higher Education. <u>Education for the</u>
     <u>Ministry: Seminaries of the Disciples of Christ.</u>
     Indianapolis: Board of Higher Education, 195?

36. Board of Higher Education. <u>Higher Education for</u>
     <u>Disciples of Christ.</u> Indianapolis: Board of Higher
     Education, 19?

37. Boren, Carter E. "The History of Disciples of Christ
     in Texas, 1824-1906." <u>Church History</u> 23 (December
     1954):358-9.

38. Bower, William Clayton. "Church Membership: A
     Disciple Point of View." <u>College of the Bible</u>
     <u>Quarterly</u> 35 (1958):16-30.

39. Boyd, Robin. "Disciples of Christ - Roman Catholic
     Dialogue: 5th Session in Ireland [1981]." <u>Mid-</u>
     <u>Stream</u> 21 (October 1982):571-7.

40. Brinson, Marion B., ed. <u>A Century with Christ. A</u>
     <u>Story of the Christian Church in Richmond.</u>
     Richmond, Va.: Whittet & Shepperson, Printers,
     1932.

41.   Britton, Rollin J. "Disciples of Christ in Kansas
      City, Missouri, 1924." In The Annals of Kansas
      City. Vol. 1, no. 4. Kansas City, Mo.: Missouri
      Valley Historical Society, October 1924.

42.   Bro, M. H. "Problem for the Pope." Christian Century
      67 (February 8, 1950):170-2.

43.   Broadus, Loren A., Jr. "Three Years of Dedication
      [College of the Bible, Lexington]." College of the
      Bible Quarterly 40 (January 1963):53-8.

44.   Broadus, Loren A., Jr. "What in the World Does
      Theology Have To Do with Leadership." Lexington
      Theological Quarterly 11(July 1976):73-84.

45.   "Brotherhood Limited." Time 59 (June 2, 1952):60.

46.   Brown, Caroline. "Dr. Ryland Thomas Brown." Indiana
      Magazine of History 23 (March 1927):92-106.

47.   Brown, G. "Promotional Conference of Colleges of the
      Disciples of Christ." Christian Education 14
      (October 1930):26-7.

48.   Brown, Genevieve. Growing Edges in Home Missions for
      Disciples of Christ. Indianapolis: United
      Christian Missionary Society, 1956.

49.   Brown, Sterling Wade. The Changing Function of
      Disciple Colleges... Chicago, 1939.

50.   Browning, Don S. "The Disciples Divinity House and
      the University." Criterion 17 (Autumn 1978):4-7.

51.   Bunce, C. M. "Christian Churches Become a Church."
      Christianity Today 13 (October 25, 1968):41.

52.   Burnham, F. W. "Disciples Stirred By World Events;
      International Convention Calls Traffic in Arms
      Unchristian." Christian Century 56 (November 8,
      1939):1384-5.

53.   Burnham, F. W. "What Is Disturbing the Disciples?"
      Christian Century 61 (May 17, 1944):616-18.

54.   Butler, J. W. [Restoration in the 19th Century.]
      Christian Quarterly Review 2 (1883):389+.

55.   Butler University. School of Religion. "This Name
      'Encounter.' Retrospect, Introspect, Prospect. An
      Editorial." Encounter (CTS) 17 (January 1955 or
      6):72-9.

56. Campbell, G. A. "Convention, 1929, Seattle."
     Christian Century 46 (August 28, 1929):1070-1.

57. Campbell, K. "Old-Time Religion." _American Mercury_
     42 (December 1937):427-35.

58. [Campbellites, or Disciples.] _Penn Monthly_ 11
     (1880):547+.

59. Cardwell, Sue W. "Reflections on Religion and the
     Vital Balance." _Journal of Religion and Health_ 10
     (April 1971):138-59.

60. Carmon, J. N. [Church of Disciples.] _Baptist_
     Quarterly 9 (1875): 188+.

61. Carpe, William D. "Baptismal Theology and Practice of
     the Disciples of Christ." _Mid-Stream_ 18 (October
     1979):444-68.

62. Carpe, William D. "Baptismal Theology in the
     Disciples of Christ." _Lexington Theological_
     Quarterly 14 (October 1979):65-78; _Review and_
     Expositor (Winter 1980):89-100.

63. Carpe, William D. "Some Observations on Tradition as
     a Theological Issue for Disciples of Christ." _Mid-_
     Stream 20 (July 1981):243-50.

64. Carr, A. [The Name Christian.] _Expositor_ 3 (1897-
     98?):538+.

65. Cartwright, Colbert S. "The Christian Churches
     (Disciples of Christ): As Racial Ferment
     Accelerates, Pastors and Congregations Take Divided
     Stand on Issue." _Christianity and Crisis_ 18, no. 3
     (1958):20-2.

66. Casey, Mike. "An Era of Controversy and Division: The
     Origins of the Broadway Church of Christ, Paducah,
     Kentucky." _Restoration Quarterly_ 27, no. 1
     (1984):3-22.

67. Cassell, R. B. [Post Oak-Springs Christian Church,
     Tennessee.] _Daughters of the American Revolution_
     Magazine 71 (1937):518+.

68. "Centennial of the Disciples of Christ." _Independent_
     (New York) 67 (October 7, 1909):833-4.

69. Challen, James. "John Allen Gano." _Lexington_
     Theological Quarterly 17, no. 1 (1982):29-33.

70. Chambers, W. [Restoration Movement.] Chamber's
     Edinburgh Journal 57 (1880):81, 209, 417+.

71. Chandler, R. "Deferred Income: Financial Problems of
     the Churchman's Foundation." Christianity Today 20
     (March 12, 1976):49-51.

72. Christian Church (Disciples of Christ). "A World to
     the Church: 1980." Mid-Stream 20 (April 1981):191-
     8.

73. "Church Inaugurates Historical Society." Hobbies 47
     (July 1942):47.

74. "Church Statistics." Christian Century 101 (June 27,
     1984):625+.

75. "Church to Foster Black Composers and Writers." Jet
     61 (October 29, 1981):30+.

76. Clague, James G. "Current Thinking of Disciples of
     Christ." Shane Quarterly 16 (October 1955):177-84.

77. Clark, Elmer Talmage. "Legalistic Sects - Part Two."
     In Small Sects in America, pp. 238-68. Abingdon-
     Cokesbury, 1937.

78. Clark, Sara Graves. "'Macedonia.' 'The Church of Our
     Ancestors.'" Kentucky State Historical Society
     Register 36 (October 1938): 291-305.

79. Coffey, Carole. "Disciples of Christ - Going Their
     Way." Saturday Evening Post 256 (May - June
     1984):70+.

80. Coggins, James Caswell. Christian Philosophy and
     Science; A Vindication of Bible Teaching. Boston:
     Christopher Pub. House, 1950.

81. Cole, Myron C. "Church Councils and Federations as a
     Method of Cooperation and a Means toward Unity."
     Shane Quarterly 16 (April 1955):91-5.

82. "Complete Church Union." Christian Century 48 (June
     10, 1931):781.

83. "Concerning the Disciples." Christian Century 40
     (September 27, 1923):1222-3.

84. "Conflict Over Unity." Independent (New York) 54
     (November 27, 1902):2849.

85. Consultation on Church Union. _An Order of Worship for
     the Proclamation of the Word of God and the
     Celebration of the Lord's Supper._ Cincinnati:
     Forward Movement Publications, 1968.

86. "Convention, 1928, Columbus." _Christian Century_ 45
     (May 3, 1928): 561-3, 584-5.

87. Cook, G. M. "Disciples of Christ." _National Council
     Outlook_ 3 (June 1953):3-5.

88. Cory, A. E. "Progress of the Disciples." _Missionary
     Review of the World_ 39 (October 1916):764-6.

89. Council on Christian Unity. Commission on Theology.
     Christian Unity. "Issues of Ecclesiology for
     Disciples: An Interim Report." _Mid-Stream_ 19 (July
     1980):334-7.

90. Cox, Claude. "The Division between Disciples and
     Church of Christ in the Disciples Church at
     Meaford, Ontario." _Restoration Quarterly_ 27, no. 1
     (1984):23-36.

91. Craddock, Fred B. "The Bible in the Pulpit of the
     Christian Church: The Forrest F. Reed Lectures,
     1981 [Three Lectures: Principles of Clarity,
     Harmony, Finality]." _Impact_ (Claremont) Special
     Issue (1982):1-39.

92. Craig, J. E. "Who Are the Disciples of Christ?" _Look_
     18 (November 30, 1954):103-6+.

93. "Creed Row at Butler University." _Newsweek_ 18
     (October 6, 1941):57.

94. Crow, Paul A., Jr. "The Anatomy of a 19th Century
     Church: The Mingling of the Christians and the
     Disciples." _Impact_ (Claremont) 9 (Fall 1982):19-
     37.

95. Crow, Paul A., ed. "The Church - Created To Be One
     [Christian Church (Disciples of Christ), Anaheim,
     Calif. 1981 General Assembly]." _Mid-Stream_ 21
     (January 1982):1-69.

96. Crow, Paul A. "Disciples of Christ amid the Churches'
     Search for Global Wholeness." _Mid-Stream_ 19 (April
     1980):132-41.

97. Crow, Paul A., Jr. "Growing in Ministry: Landmarks for
     the Disciples of Christ on Their Ecumenical
     Future." _Impact_ (Claremont) 10 (1983):22-32.

98.   Crow, Paul A.   "Impulses toward Christian Unity in 9th
      Century America." Mid-Stream 22 (July - October
      1983):419-40.

99.   Crow, P. A., Jr.   "Ministry and the Sacraments in the
      Christian Church (Disciples of Christ)." Encounter
      (CTS) 41 (Winter 1980): 73-89.

100. Crow, Paul A., ed.   "Papers from the Disciples of
      Christ - Roman Catholic International Commission
      for Dialogue, 1979-80." Mid-Stream 20 (July
      1981):217-324.

101. Crow, Paul A., ed.   "Papers, Reports from Disciples of
      Christ - Roman Catholic International Commission
      for Dialogue, Venice, Italy." Mid-Stream 23
      (October 1984):335-409.

102. Crow, Paul A., Jr.   "Three Dichotomies and a Polar
      Star [Address, General Assembly, Christian Church
      (Disciples of Christ), Anaheim, Calif., Ag. 1,
      1981]." Mid-Stream 21 (January 1982): 21-30.

103. Crow, Paul A., ed.   "Your Kingdom Come: Mission and
      Unity in a Global Perspective [Disciples Ecumenical
      Consultative Council, 1979]." Mid-Stream 19 (April
      1980):129-256.

104. Cummins, D. Duane.   "The Christian Church (Disciples
      of Christ) Where From Here? The Institutional
      Church Tomorrow." Lexington Theological Quarterly
      16, no. 1 (1981):18-25.

105. Cummins, D. Duane.   "From Buffalo to Claremont: On the
      Occasion of the 23rd Anniversary Celebration of the
      Disciples Seminary Foundation." Impact (Claremont)
      11 (1983):5-13.

106. Cunningham, Agnes.   "Confirmed in Hope: Disciples and
      Roman Catholics in International Dialogue." Mid-
      Stream 17 (January 1978):81-3.

107. Cunningham, Agnes.   "A Continuing Pilgrimage:
      Disciples - Roman Catholics in Dialogue [Rome,
      Italy, Dec. 9-14, 1978]." Mid-Stream 18 (April
      1979):186-8.

108. Cunningham, Agnes.   "Disciples - Roman Catholics
      International Commission for Dialogue [Abbeylands
      Retreat House, Ardfert, Ireland, September 10-17,
      1981; News]." Mid-Stream 21 (April 1982):272-3.

109. A Curious Church Case. "A Star Chamber" Church
      Investigation Elder Robert Christie, Aided by
      Deacon Francis M. Applegate, Induced the Official
      Organization of the Congregation of the First
      Church of Disciples of Christ, in New York City, to
      "Withdraw the Right Hand of Fellowship" from
      Elizabeth B. Grannis, etc. New York, 1910.

110. Daniel, W. H. [Christian Association.] Virginia
      Magazine of History and Biography 69 (1961):93+.

111. Darst, Emma Delle Railsback. "Planting the Church of
      the Disciples at Little Mackinaw, 1833 - 1927,
      Mackinaw Township, Tazewell County, Illinois."
      Illinois State Historical Society. Journal 20
      (October 1926 or 7):411-21.

112. DeGroot, A. T. "The Communion - Richest Heritage of
      the Disciples of Christ." Shane Quarterly 12
      (January 1951):13-57.

113. Delloff, Linda-Marie. "C. C. Morrison: Shaping a
      Journal's Identity [A Century of the Century, part
      1]." Christian Century 101 (January 18, 1984):43+.

114. "Demilitarize the Chaplaincy!" Christian Century 53
      (October 28, 1936):1416-18.

115. "Denominational Quarrel Ends." Christian Century 42
      (February 5, 1925):181-2.

116. "Dietze, C. E. "Seven Years of Development." College
      of the Bible Quarterly (Lexington) 40 (January
      1963):42-5.

117. "Disciples: Accommodating COCU." Christianity Today
      19 (September 12, 1975):63-4.

118. "Disciples and Their Convention." Christian Century
      40 (August 23, 1923):1063-4.

119. "Disciples' Assembly." Christian Century 92
      (September 17, 1975): 784.

120. "Disciples at the Crossroads." Christian Century 42
      (December 17, 1925):1565-6.

121. "Disciples' Centennial." Outlook 93 (November 6,
      1909):525-6.

122. "Disciples Church Acts on Union." Christian Century
      74 (January 30, 1957):124.

123. "Disciples Convention." *Christian Century* 40
      (September 20, 1923):1189-90.

124. "Disciples Convention: An Interpretation." *Christian
      Century* 43 (December 2, 1926):1479-81.

125. "Disciples Decide; Homosexuality Issue." *Christianity
      Today* 22 (November 18, 1977):56-7.

126. "Disciples Face Year-Book Facts." *Christian Century*
      40 (November 22, 1923):1524.

127. "Disciples Favor Aid To Schools." *Christian Century*
      69 (June 4, 1952):676+.

128. "Disciples Get into the Act; Church Names of Disciples
      of Christ." *Christian Century* 87 (April 29,
      1970):551.

129. "Disciples Hold Huge Convention at the Nation's
      Capital." *Christian Century* 47 (November 5,
      1930):1333.

130. "Disciples in Congress Stress Social Gospel."
      Christian Century 43 (May 20, 1926):657.

131. "Disciples' Mission Board Interprets Rule." *Christian
      Century* 42 (December 17, 1925):1582-4.

132. "Disciples Missions." *Independent* (New York) 52
      (October 25, 1900): 2540.

133. Disciples of Christ. *Survey of Service: Organizations
      Represented in International Convention of
      Disciples of Christ.* William R. Warren, General
      Editor. St. Louis: Christian Board of Publication,
      1928.

134. Disciples of Christ. International Convention.
      Columbus, Ohio. 1937. *International Convention.
      Disciples of Christ. Columbus, Ohio, October 26-31,
      1937; Story of the Convention. Pictures and Short
      Biographies of the Speakers. Addresses. Convention
      Sermon. Resolutions.* St. Louis: Christian Board of
      Publication, 1938.

135. Disciples of Christ. International Convention. Dallas,
      1966.
      *In Christ...Fullness of Life: International
      Convention of Christian Churches (Disciples of
      Christ Dallas Assembly, Sept. 23-28.* St. Louis,
      Mo.: Christian Board of Publication, 1966.

136. Disciples of Christ. International Convention. Denver,
     1938. _International Convention. Disciples of_
     Christ. Denver. Colorado. October 16-21. 1938. St.
     Louis: Christian Board of Publication, 1938.

137. Disciples of Christ. International Convention. Des
     Moines, 1934. _International Convention. Disciples_
     of Christ. Des Moines. Iowa. October 16-21. 1934:
     Sermons and Addresses. St. Louis: Christian Board
     of Publication, 1935.

138. Disciples of Christ. International Convention. Kansas
     City, Mo., 1936. _International Convention._
     Disciples of Christ. Kansas City. Missouri. October
     12-18. 1936: Story of the Convention. Pictures and
     Short Biographies of the Speakers. Addresses.
     Convention Sermon. Resolutions. St. Louis:
     Christian Board of Publication, 1937.

139. Disciples of Christ. International Convention.
     Richmond, 1939. _International Convention. Disciples_
     of Christ. Richmond. Virginia. October 19-25. 1939.
     St. Louis: Christian Board of Publication, 1939.

140. Disciples of Christ. International Convention. San
     Antonio, 1935. _International Convention. Disciples_
     of Christ. San Antonio. Texas. October 15-20. 1935:
     Sermons. and Addresses. St. Louis: Christian Board
     of Publication, 1936.

141. Disciples of Christ. Study Commission on Ministerial
     Education. _The Imperative Is Leadership: A Report_
     on Ministerial Development in the Christian Church
     (Disciples of Christ). St. Louis: Bethany, 1973.

142. "Disciples of Christ and Christian Unity." _Christian_
     Century 46 (September 11, 1929):1111-13;
     "Discussion" 46 (October 2, 1929): 1221.

143. "Disciples of Christ - Catholic Dialogue: Insights
     along Unity's Path." _Origins_ 12 (June 24,
     1982):91-6.

144. "Disciples of Christ Elect First Woman to Head Group
     [Cynthia L. Hale]." _Jet_ 62 (August 30, 1982):24+.

145. Disciples of Christ Historical Society. "Academic
     Research: Theses and Dissertations." _Harbinger and_
     Discipliana 17 (Feb.-Aug. 1956 or 7):12, 23, 47.

146. Disciples of Christ Historical Society. "The Campbell
     Home: Its Growth, Importance, and Present Status."
     Harbinger and Discipliana 14 (July 1954):96-8.

147. Disciples of Christ Historical Society. "The
      Controversial [Jacob] Creath, Jr. [1779-1886]."
      Harbinger and Discipliana 16 (October 1955 or
      6):63-7.

148. Disciples of Christ Historical Society. Hampton
      Adams: A Register of His Papers in the Disciples of
      Christ Historical Society. Nashville, 1969.

149. Disciples of Christ Historical Society. Preliminary
      Guide to Black Materials in the Disciples of Christ
      Historical Society. Nashville, 1971.

150. Disciples of Christ Historical Society. "Report of
      Progress since 1941: Ten Year Program Outlined."
      Discipliana 10 (July 1950): 9-13.

151. Disciples of Christ, Illinois. Disciples in Illinois,
      1850-1950. Jacksonville, Ill.: Centennial
      Convention, Disciples of Christ in Illinois, 1950.

152. "Disciples of Christ in the United States and Canada
      [Excerpts from the Responses to the Lund Report]."
      Ecumenical Review 6 (January 1954):169-74.

153. "Disciples Message on Peace." Mid-Stream 21 (January
      1982):75-7.

154. "Disciples Set an Example." Christian Century 63
      (September 18, 1946):1109-11.

155. "Disciples To Study Union with Two Other Churches."
      Newsweek 14 (November 6, 1939):36.

156. "Disciples vs. Liquor." Newsweek 20 (August 10,
      1942):51.

157. "Disciples, Which Way?" Christian Century 66
      (November 16, 1949):1351-3.

158. "Disciplined Disciples." Time 92 (October 11,
      1968):49.

159. "Dr. Griggs Scourges Disciple Vote." Christian
      Century 42 (November 12, 1925):1423.

160. Doyle, B. "Disciples: Middle Americana."
      Christianity Today 18 (November 23, 1973):58-9.

161. Drake, Ralph. "What If--?" In From Clergy to
      Convert, pp. 55-60. Edited by S. Gibson. 1983.

162. "Drake Conference on the Church and the New World
     Mind." Christian Century 61 (February 16,
     1944):211+.

163. Duke, James O. "An Ecclesiological Inventory." Mid-
     Stream 19 (July 1980):263-71.

164. "Education and Its Money; School of Religion, Butler
     University, and Its Support from the Christian
     Foundation." Christian Century 58 (September 17,
     1941):1136-7.

165. "Elect Montgomery To Head Disciples." Christian
     Century 71 November 24, 1954):1421.

166. Eller, David B. "Hoosier Brethren and the Origins of
     the Restoration Movement." Brethren Life and
     Thought 27 (Winter 1982):35-54. Indiana Magazine
     of History 76 (March 1980):1-20.

167. Ellis, William E. "The Fundamentalist - Moderate
     Schism over Evolution in the 1920's." Register of
     the Kentucky Historical Society 74, no. 2
     (1976):112-23.

168. England, Stephen J. "Disciples' Thinking within the
     Ecumenical Movement." Shane Quarterly 16 (October
     1955):185-94.

169. Ethridge, F. Maurice. "Sect-Denominational Evolution:
     A Dialectical Model of Organizational Change."
     Ph.D. diss., University of Texas, 1973.

170. Ethridge, F. Maurice and Joe R. Feagin. "Varieties of
     'Fundamentalism': A Conceptual and Empirical
     Analysis of Two Protestant Denominations."
     Sociological Quarterly 20 (Winter 1979):37-48.

171. Evangelical Restorationist. Troy, N.Y.: B. Streeter &
     D. Skinner, 1899.

172. "Evangelism and Heresy." Christianity Today 14
     (February 27, 1970): 26.

173. Ewers, J. R. "Disciples Take Strong Stand for Peace,
     Temperance, Social Justice, at Pittsburgh
     Convention." Christian Century 50 (October 25,
     1933):1342+.

174. "Faith of the President [Lyndon B. Johnson]."
     Newsweek 62 (December 9, 1963):90.

175. Farnham, J. E. [Campbellism and Saving Baptism.]
      Baptist Quarterly Review 11 (1877):477+.

176. Favorite Recipes from Women of the Christian Church:
      Casseroles, Including Breads: 2000 Favorite Recipes
      from Christian Women's Fellowships (Disciples of
      Christ). Montgomery, Ala.: Favorite Recipes Pr.,
      1970.

177. Fey, H. E. "Disciples at Des Moines." Christian
      Century 73 (October 17, 1956):1191-3.

178. Fey, H. E. "Disciples Change Course; International
      Convention of Christian Churches." Christian
      Century 83 (October 19,1966):1266-7.

179. Fey, H. E. "Disciples Cool to Social Evils; 1935
      International Convention, San Antonio, Texas."
      Christian Century 52 (November 6, 1935):1432-3.

180. Fey, H. E. "Disciples Debate Church and State."
      Christian Century 64 (August 13, 1947):976-7+.

181. Fey, H. E. "Disciples Dialogize." Christian Century
      77 (November 16, 1960):1334-5.

182. Fey, H. E. "Disciples For Merger Talks." Christian
      Century 78 (October 18, 1961):1230-1.

183. Fey, H. E. "Disciples in Denver." Christian Century
      76 (September 16-23, 1959):1047, 1077.

184. Fey, H. E. "Disciples in Detroit; International [U.S.
      and Canada] Convention of Christian Churches."
      Christian Century 81 (October 28, 1964):1327-8.

185. Fey, H. E. "Disciples in Louisville: Democracy at
      Work." Christian Century 88 (December 1,
      1971):1426-8.

186. Fey, H. E. "Disciples Launch Basic Change; 118th
      Assembly of the International Convention of
      Christian Churches." Christian Century 84
      (November 8, 1967):1421-3.

187. Fey, H. E. "Disciples Meet in Oklahoma." Christian
      Century 67 (November 1, 1950):1300-1+.

188. Fey, H. E."Disciples Now Christians." Christian
      Century 71(October 30, 1957):1278-80.

189. Fey, H. E. "Disciples on Civil Rights; International
      Convention of Christian Churches." Christian
      Century 80 (October 30, 1963):1326-7.

190. Fey, H. E. "Disciples Oppose Drift toward War."
      Christian Century 58 (May 14, 1941):667-8.

191. Fey, H. E. "Disciples Revamp Church; International
      Convention of Christian Churches." Christian
      Century 85 (October 30, 1968):1362-3.

192. Fey, H. E. "Disciples Scorn War Armaments."
      Christian Century 51 (October 31, 1934):1389-90.

193. Fey, H. E. "Disciples Vote To Resume Union Talks with
      UCC." Christian Century 94 (November 9,
      1977):1021-2.

194. Fey, H. E. "God and Mammon; International
      Convention." Christian Century 71 (November 10,
      1954):1358-60.

195. Fey, H. E. "International Convention at Columbus."
      Christian Century 54 (November 10, 1937):1404-6.

196. Fey, H. E. "International Convention of Christian
      Churches." Christian Century 75 (November 19,
      1958):1350.

197. Fey, Harold E. "Is the Christian Church Able and
      Willing for Union?" Lexington Theological
      Quarterly 7, no. 2 (1972):341-51.

198. Fey, H. E. "Northern Baptists Seen Favoring Proposed
      Union with Disciples; Annual Meeting of the
      Northern Baptist Convention." Christian Century 65
      (June 16, 1948):602-3.

199. Fey, H. E. "Power Struggle among Disciples."
      Christian Century 86 (September 17, 1969):1187-9.
      Bayer, C. H. "Reply."   Christian Century 86
      (October 29, 1969):1402-3.

200. Fey, Harold E. "Seventy Years of the Century."
      Christian Century 95 (October 11, 1978):950-4.

201. Flowers, Ronald B. "The Bible Chair Movement: An
      Innovation of the Disciples of Christ."
      Discipliana 26 (March 1966):8-13.

202. Ford, Harold Warner. A History of the Restoration
      Plea...Being a History of the Statements of the
      Plea of the Churches of Christ for Christian Unity

upon the Basis of a Restoration of the Church of the New Testament Oklahoma City: Semco Color Pr., 1952.

203.   "Forward Step [Disciples of Christ - United Church of Christ]." Christian Century 101 (October 31, 1984):1008+.

204.   Fowler, Newton B.   "LTS as a Graduate Professional School." Lexington Theological Quarterly 13 (October 1978):125-8.

205.   Francisco, Noel. "Sketch of a Master Teacher [Gardner, Frank Nelson, 1907-1981]." Lexington Theological Quarterly 16, no. 4 (1981):142-5.

206.   Freudenberger, C. Dean.   "Seminar: From Story to Screen Play: Our Vision of the Future [Edited Transcription] [Church and Social Justice]." Impact (Claremont) 6 (1981):17-29.

207.   "From Churches To Church." Christian Century 83 (October 12, 1966): 1266-7. Huston, R. W. "Reply." Christian Century 83 (November 23, 1966):1446.

208.   "From Resolution 'Concerning Ending the Arms Race,' Adopted 1979." In Nuclear Disarmament, pp. 245-47. Edited by R. Heyer. 1982.

209.   Front Rank. St. Louis: Christian Bd. of Publication.

210.   Garnett, Leroy. The Stone-Campbell Movement: An Anecdotal History of Three Churches. Joplin, Mo.: College Pr. Pub. Co., 1981.

211.   Garrison, W. E.   "Conception of the Church As Held By Disciples of Christ." Christendom 9 (1944), no. 3:433-6.

212.   Garrison, W. E.   "Disciples Meet, Listen, Adjourn; Indianapolis Convention." Christian Century 49 (October 26, 1932):1317.

213.   Garrison, W. E.   "Disciples Urge That Federal Council Call a Conference to Consider Unity." Christian Century 63 (August 21, 1946):1018-19.

214.   Garrison, W. E."Response of Disciples of Christ in the United States and Canada to the Report of Section I [Assembly of the World Council of Churches, Amsterdam, 1948.]" Shane Quarterly 11 (1950):164-76.

215. Garrison, W. E. "Why I Am a Disciple." _Forum_ 77
     (April 1927): 626-7.

216. Gilpin, W. Clark. "Common Roots, Divergent Paths: The
     Disciples and the Churches of Christ." _Christian_
     Century 95 (December 20, 1978):1234-8.

217. Gilpin, W. Clark. "The Doctrine of the Church in the
     Thought of Alexander Campbell and John W. Nevin."
     Mid-Stream 19(October 1980):417-27.

218. Gilpin, W. C. "Issues Relevant to Union in the
     History of the Christian Church (Disciples of
     Christ)." _Encounter_ (CTS) 41 (Winter 1980):15-23.

219. Graham, Ronald W., ed. "The J. W. McGarvey
     Sesquicentennial Lecture Series." _Lexington_
     Theological Quarterly 16 (January 1981):3-52.

220. Gray, James. "The Authority of Scripture and
     Tradition. 3 Lectures: Living Tradition and
     Scripture; Essentials of Apostolic Christianity."
     Shane Quarterly 14 (April 1953):35-85.

221. Greisch, J. R. "Key: Epidemic, '74?" _Christianity_
     Today 18 (March 29, 1974): 45.

222. Gresham, Perry E. "Lordship of Christ: Spiritual and
     Ecumenical Implications of a Central Christian
     Doctrine." _Encounter_ (CTS) 17(Winter 1956):64-71.

223. Griffeth, Ross J. "The National Rural Church
     Commission of the Disciples of Christ [1928-39]."
     Shane Quarterly 12 (October 1951):155-69.

224. Griffin, D. R. "Ordination for Homosexuals? Yes."
     Encounter (CTS) 40 (Summer 1979):265-72.

225. Hall, Colby Dixon. "Climbing out of the Valley."
     Harbinger and Discipliana 15 (December 1954 or
     55):149-55.

226. Hamilton, Fannie Frazee. "Ephraim Samuel Frazee,
     1824-1896." _Indiana Magazine of History_ 24
     (September 1928):186-97.

227. Hamlin, Griffith A. "Educational Activities of the
     Disciples of Christ in North Carolina, 1852-1902."
     North Carolina Historical Review 33 (July
     1956):310-31.

228.   Hardy, Kenneth R. "Social Origins of American
        Scientists and Scholars." Science 185 (August 9,
        1974):497-506.

229.   Harms, John W. "Comity as an Ecumenical Opportunity
        for the Disciples of Christ." Shane Quarterly 16
        (April 1955):85-90.

230.   Harper, Charles L. and Kevin Leicht. "Religious
        Awakenings and Status Politics: Sources of Support
        for the New Religious Right." Sociological
        Analysis 45 (Winter 1984):339-53.

231.   Harper, W. A. "Educational Program of the Christian
        Church." Religious Education 21 (February
        1926):51-4.

232.   Harrell, David Edwin, Jr. "The Agrarian Myth and the
        Disciples of Christ in the Nineteenth Century."
        Agricultural History 41, no.2 (1967):181-92.

233.   Harrell, D. E., Jr. [The Disciples and Christian
        Pacifism in 19th Century Tennessee.] Tennessee
        Historical Quarterly 21(1961): 263+.

234.   Harrell, D. E., Jr. [Disciples of Christ.]
        Agricultural History 41(1967):181+.

235.   Harrell, David Edwin, Jr. "The Disciples of Christ
        and Social Forces in Tennessee, 1865-1900." East
        Tennessee Historical Society's Publications 38
        (1966):48-61.

236.   Harrell, David Edwin. "The Disciples of Christ and
        the Single Tax Movement, 1880-1900." Encounter
        (CTS) 26, no. 1 (1965):39-47.

237.   Harrell, David E., Jr. "James Shannon: Preacher,
        Educator, and Fire-Eater." Missouri Historical
        Review 63 (January 1969):135-70.

238.   Harrell, David Edwin. "Pardee Butler: Kansas
        Crusader." Kansas Historical Quarterly 34, no. 4
        (1968):386-408.

239.   Harrell, D. E., Jr. "Sectional Origins of the
        Churches of Christ." Journal of Southern History
        30 (August 1964):261-77.

240.   Harrell, David E., Jr. "The Sectional Pattern: The
        Divisive Impact of Slavery on the Disciples of
        Christ." Discipliana 21(1961):26+.

241. Harrell, David Edwin, Jr. "The Significance of Social
       Forces in Disciples History." Integrity 9
       (1977):67+.

242. Harrell, David Edwin, Jr. "Sin and Sectionalism: A
       Case Study of Morality in the Nineteenth-Century
       South." Mississippi Quarterly 19, no. 4
       (1966):157-70.

243. Harrison, Richard L. "Westward - Why: The Stone-
       Campbell Churches on the Pacific Slope." Impact
       (Claremont) 12 (1984):92-115.

244. Hartley, Shirley Foster. "Marital Satisfaction among
       Clergy Wives." Review of Religious Research 19
       (Winter 1978):178-91.

245. Hartley, Shirley F. and Mary G. Taylor. "Religious
       Beliefs of Clergy Wives." Review of Religious
       Research 19 (Fall 1977):63-73.

246. Hatch, Nathan O. "Christian Movement and the Demand
       for a Theology of the People." Journal of American
       History 67 (December 1980): 545-67.

247. Hatch, Nathan O. "Millennialism and Popular Religion
       in the Early Republic." In The Evangelical
       Tradition in America, pp. 113-30. Edited by L.
       Sweet. 1984.

248. Hatfield, E. F. [Alexander Campbell and His
       Disciples.] Presbyterian Review 3 (1884):529+.

249. Hawley, Monroe E. "Controversy in St. Louis."
       Restoration Quarterly 27, no. 1 (1984):49-64.

250. Haymes, Don. "Hall Calhoun and His 'Nashville
       Brethren,' 1897-1935." Restoration Quarterly 27,
       no. 1 (1984):37-48.

251. Haynes, Nathaniel Smith. "The Disciples of Christ in
       Illinois and Their Attitude toward Slavery."
       Illinois State Historical Society. Transactions
       (1913):52-9.

252. Hearthstone for the Christian Home. St. Louis:
       Christian Bd. of Publication, n.d.

253. Hensley, Carl Wayne. "The Death of a Rhetorical
       Vision: Disciples of Christ and Social Change."
       1978. (ERIC Document 165207).

254. Hensley, Carl Wayne. "The Rhetoric of Rationalism
        versus the Rhetoric of Emotionalism on the American
        Frontier." 1984. (ERIC Document 254892).

255. Hensley, Carl W. "Rhetorical Vision and the
        Persuasion of a Historical Movement: The Disciples
        of Christ in Nineteenth Century American Culture."
        Quarterly Journal of Speech 61 (October 1975):250-
        64.

256. Higdon, E. K. "Ecumenical Emphasis Pervades Disciples
        of Christ Convention in San Francisco." Christian
        Century 65 (October 20, 1948):1115+.

257. Historical Anniversary Booklet of the Christian
        Churches of Indianapolis and Marion County.
        Prepared for the Fiftieth Anniversary of the
        Christian Church Union of the Marion County Area of
        the Indiana Christian Missionary Association,
        December 4, 1896 to December 4, 1946. N.p., 1946?

258. Histories of the Christian Churches of Hamilton County
        [Indiana] 1834-1944. N.p., 1944?

259. History of the Christian Churches of Hendricks County,
        Indiana. Compiled by Roscoe R. Leak, Leslie
        Zimmerman, and Errett P. Rivers. Lizton? Ind.,
        1959.

260. The History of the First One Hundred Years of the
        Vanderburgh Christian Home. Evansville, Ind.:
        Vanderburgh Christian Home, 1971.

261. Hoge, Dean R. and John E. Dyble. "Changes in
        Theological Beliefs of Protestant Ministers, 1928
        to 1978." American Sociological Association, 1979.

262. "Hold World Meet." Christian Century 52 (September
        11, 1935):1158.

263. Holland, Harold E. "Religious Periodicals in the
        Development of Nashville, Tennessee as a Regional
        Publishing Center, 1830 to 1880." Ph.D. diss.,
        Columbia University, 1976.

264. Holman, C. T. "Northern Baptists Rebuff Disciples."
        Christian Century 47 (June 11, 1930):764-5.

265. Holstead, Roland Edward. "The Differential Responses
        of Protestant Church Polities to Racial Change in
        an Urban Area." Ph.D. diss., University of
        Connecticut, 1982.

266. Holstrom, Eric C. "The Northern Baptist-Disciple
     Quest for Union: A Lesson for Today?" American
     Baptist Quarterly 4 (December 1985):397-407.

267. Hoover, Guy Israel. "The Disciples of Christ and
     Their Educational Work in Indiana." Butler College
     Bulletin 5 (September 1916).

268. Howland, William C. "Do We Belong to the Church: A
     Sermon [On the Visit of Disciples-Roman Catholic
     Dialogue Team to National City Christian Church,
     September 9, 1979]." Mid-Stream 20 (July
     1981):263-6.

269. Hubbard, Helen Kathryn. "A Survey of the Use of
     Theological Terminology with Reference to Jesus
     Christ in Selected Church School Curricula for
     Adults." 1966. (ERIC Document 023045).

270. Hughes, R. "The Role of Theology in the 19th Century
     Division of Disciples of Christ." In American
     Religion: 1974 Proceedings. Preprinted Papers for
     the Group on American Religion, American Academy of
     Religion, 1974, pp. 56-78. Tallahassee, Florida:
     AAR, 1974.

271. Hughes, Richard T. "Civil Religion, the Theology of
     the Republic, and the Free Church Tradition."
     Journal of Church and State 22(1980):75-87.

272. Hughes, Richard T. "Twenty-Five Years of Restoration
     Scholarship: The Churches of Christ [Including
     Division with Disciples]." Restoration Quarterly
     25, no. 4 (1982):233-56; 26, no. 1 (1983): 39-62.

273. Humbert, Royal. "After Utopia - What?" Encounter
     (CTS) 20, no. 3(1959):297-306.

274. Hutchinson, P. "Disciples Through Methodist Eyes."
     Christian Century 41 (October 30, 1924):1398-1401.

275. "Incredible Episode; Linwood Christian Church, Kansas
     City, Mo." Christian Century 47 (February 19,
     1930):233-5.

276. Indianapolis. Central Christian Church. 125
     Significant Years: The Story of Central Christian
     Church (Disciples of Christ) Indianapolis, Indiana,
     1833-1958. Indianapolis, 1958.

277. "International Convention, 1925, Oklahoma City."
     Christian Century 42 (October 22, 1925):1314-15.

278. "James Harvey Garrison." Christian Century 48
        (January 28, 1931): 128-9.

279. Jeansonne, Glen. "Partisan Parson: An Oral History
        Account of the Louisiana Years of Gerald L. K.
        Smith." Louisiana History 23, no. 2 (1982):149-58.

280. Jessopp, A. [Restoration of Churches and Church
        Ownership.] Littell's Living Age 187 (1890):657+.

281. Jeter, Joseph R., Jr. "Kadesh-Barnea, CA [Address,
        Disciples Ministerial Assoc., Pacific Southwest
        Region, Christian Church (Disciples of Christ),
        1984]." Impact (Claremont) 13 (1984): 17-21.

282. Jeter, Joseph R. "Stones and Stories [Sermon,
        Dedication of Central Christian Church, Glendale,
        Calif.; Deut. 27:1-8, Joshua 4:19-22, Luke 19:37-
        40]." Impact (Claremont) 11(1983):55-60.

283. "Jones and the Disciples." Christian Century 95
        (December 6, 1978): 1176.

284. Jones, Edgar D. "Pulpit Princes of the Disciples of
        Christ." Shane Quarterly 12 (October 1951):172-9.

285. Jones, Joe R. "A Theological Analysis of the Design
        [for the Christian Church (Disciples of Christ)]."
        Mid-Stream 19(July 1980):309-21.

286. Jordan, Orvis F. "Religion in Chicagoland." Scroll
        46, no. 4 (1955):24-8.

287. Kane, Charles P. "The Christian Church of
        Springfield, Illinois. Something of Its Beginning
        and Growth, during the First Sixty Years of Its
        History, 1833-1893." Illinois State Historical
        Library. Publications 12 (1907 or 8):298-314.

288. Keene, Laurence C. "Heirs of Stone and Campbell on
        the Pacific Slope: A Sociological Approach."
        Impact (Claremont) 12(1984): 5-91.

289. Kershner, F. D. "Restoration Plea of the Disciples of
        Christ." Constructive Quarterly (London) 1
        (September 1913):449-66.

290. Kinnamon, Michael K. "Authority in the Church: An
        Ecumenical Perspective." Mid-Stream 21 (April
        1982):195-212.

291. Kinnamon, Michael K. "Growing Together towards the
      Unity of the Church." Mid-Stream 23, no. 2
      (1984):189-200.

292. Kinnamon. Michael. "Theological Colloquium on Church
      Union [United Church of Christ and Christian Church
      (Disciples of Christ), Chicago, November 1978]."
      Mid-Stream 18 (April 1979): 188-90.

293. Kucharsky, D. E. "Disciples Turn Corner, Lose 1,124
      Churches." Christianity Today 12 (August 30,
      1968):40.

294. Legge, Russel D. "The Church as Sign the World God
      Wills [Reply, M. O'Gara]." Mid-Stream 23 (October
      1984):381-95.

295. Leggett, Marshall J. "John W. McGarvey: Man of the
      Book, Church and Movement." Lexington Theological
      Quarterly 16, no. 1 (1981):13-17.

296. Lemmon, C. E. "Step Toward Organic Union; Disciples
      View of Church Federal Union." Christian Century
      60 (June 9, 1943):689-90.

297. Lexington, Ky. College of the Bible. That There May
      Be More Ministers: A Report of the Centennial
      Development Convocation Held by the College of the
      Bible...1956. Including the Installation Addresses
      of Professors William R. Baird, Jr., Charles C.
      Manker, Jr. and William L. Reed. Lexington, Ky.,
      1957.

298. Lexington, Ky. College of the Bible. To Do and To
      Teach: Essays in Honor of Charles Lynn Pyatt.
      Lexington, 1953.

299. Leyden, S. G. "An Appeal for Federal Union - An
      American Model of Church Union with Ecumenical
      Horizons." Journal of Ecumenical Studies 20, no. 2
      (1983):276-80.

300. Liggett, Thomas J. "A Profile of the Disciples of
      Christ [1977]." Mid-Stream 18 (October 1979):358-
      66.

301. Liggett, Thomas. "Why the Disciples Chose Unity."
      Lexington Theological Quarterly 15, no. 1
      (1980):25-31.

302. Linberg, Edwin C. "What We Yet May Be: A Sermon on
      the 40th Anniversary of Temple City Christian

Church, California, January 10, 1982 [Phil. 3:7-14]." Impact (Claremont) 8(1982): 31-5.

303.   "Local Churches Will Have A Say in the Proposed Merger of the United Church of Christ and Christian Church (Disciples of Christ)." Christianity Today 24 (November 7, 1980):91.

304.   "Los Gatos Christian Church (California; Photos; Church Profile)." Fundamentalist Journal 2 (June 983):50-1.

305.   Lottick, Kenneth V. "Indigenous Religions in the United States. V. The Disciples of Christ [since 1804]." Social Studies 51 (January 1960):20-6.

306.   Lunger, H. L. "Disciples of Christ Hold Their Largest International Convention in Portland." Christian Century 70(July 29, 1953): 871+.

307.   Lyles, Jean Caffey. "An Activist/Pietist Ice Cream Social [General Assembly, 1979]." Christian Century 96 (November 21, 1979): 1147-8.

308.   Lyles, J. C. "Disciples: Serenity in San Antonio." Christian Century 100 (October 12, 1983):895-7.

309.   Lynch, John E. "Ordination of Women: Protestant Experience in Ecumenical Perspective." Journal of Ecumenical Studies 12 (Spring 1975):173-97.

310.   Lyon, T. Edgar. "Religious Activities and Development in Utah, 1847-1910." Utah Historical Quarterly 35, no. 4 (1967):292-306.

311.   McAllister, Lester G. "Disciples and Evangelism: Yesterday Leads into Today, Today Leads into Tomorrow." Lexington Theological Quarterly 14 (January 1979):1-5.

312.   McAllister, Lester G. "J. W. McGarvey in Perspective." Lexington Theological Quarterly 16, no. 1 (1981):5-12.

313.   McAllister, Lester G. "Reflections on the 2d. Vatican Council." Impact (Claremont) 17 (1986):14-21.

314.   McAllister, Lester G. "Ronald E. Osborn - Churchman." Impact (Claremont) 9 (Fall 1982):7-17.

315.   McAllister, Lester G. "Thomas Campbell: His Significance to the Ecumenical Movement." Encounter (CTS) 24, no. 4 (1963):458-76.

316. McCauley, Lynn. "Robert Clifton Cave: An Atypical
      Disciple." Restoration Quarterly 20, no. 3
      (1977):180-9.

317. McLean, A. "Jubilee Missionary Conventions."
      Missionary Review of the World 23 (February
      1900):121-3.

318. McNab, J. "Disciples Church Acts on Union; Reply."
      Christian Century 74 (March 13, 1957):330.

319. McNamara, Kevin, Bp. "Faith and Tradition: Third
      Annual Meeting of the International Roman
      Catholic/Disciples of Christ Commission for
      Dialogue, Washington, 7-14 September 1979." Furrow
      32 (February 1981):67-78.

320. McWhirter, David I. "Resources for Disciple History."
      Lexington Theological Quarterly 14, no. 3
      (1979):46-53.

321. Mead, Frank Spencer. "Disciples of Christ." In See
      These Banners Go: The Story of the Protestant
      Churches in America, pp. 253-73. Bobbs-Merrill,
      1936.

322. Mead, Frank S. See These Banners Go: The Story of
      the Protestant Churches in America. Indianapolis
      and New York: Bobbs-Merrill, 1936.

323. Meeking, Basil. "Review of the Dynamics and Issues in
      the Previous Five-Year Dialogue." Mid-Stream 23,
      no. 4 (1984):335-45.

324. "Meeting, 1942, Grand Rapids." Christian Century 59
      (August 12, 1942):985+.

325. "Membership." Independent (New York) 52 (March 22,
      1900):737.

326. "Membership Drop." Christian Century 118 (August 26,
      1981):825+.

327. Miller, Phillip V. "No Creed But Christ and Doctrinal
      Preaching among Disciples." Encounter (CTS)
      (Summer 1977):288-95.

328. Miller, Robert Henry. The Miller and Sommer Debate.
      Reported by James Abbott. Mount Morris, Ill.:
      Brethren Publishing House, 1898.

329. Miller, Timothy. "Whither Unity? A Case Study."
      Christian Century 87, no. 29 (1970):891-3.

330.   Moffett, R.   [Position of Campbellites.]   Christian
        Quarterly Review   5 (1886):192+.

331.   Moomaw, Donn D.   "Invocation Given at the Inauguration
        of President Ronald Reagan and Vice-President
        George Bush."   Journal of Presbyterian History 59
        (Spring 1981):1-2.

332.   Moore, W. T.   [Union of Disciples and Baptists.]
        Christian Quarterly 3 (1871):335+.

333.   Morgan, Philip.   "The Risk of Oneness [Address, August
        5, 1981, Anaheim, General Assembly, Christian
        Church (Disciples of Christ)]."   Mid-Stream 21
        (January 1982):54-61.

334.   Morrill, M. T.   "The Christians."   Vermonter 8
        (February 1902 or 3): 228-31.

335.   Morris, Philip D.   "Disciples of Christ - Roman
        Catholic Dialogue."   New Catholic World 220 (July-
        August 1977):196+.

336.   Morrison, C. C.   "Disciples International Convention
        Stresses Note of Catholicity."   Christian Century
        55 (November 2, 1938):1342-4.

337.   Morrison, C. C.   "Disciples Meet at Kansas City."
        Christian Century 53 (October 28, 1936):1428+.

338.   Morrison, John L.   "Alexander Campbell: Moral Educator
        of the Middle Frontier."   West Virginia History 36,
        no. 3 (1975):187-201.

339.   Mort, F. L.   [The Christian Disciple and the Christian
        Examiner.]   New England Quarterly 1 (1928):197+.

340.   Moseley, J. Edward.   "The Christian Church (Disciples
        of Christ) and Overseas Ministries."   In The
        Christian Church (Disciples of Christ, pp. 237-52.
        Edited by G. Beazley. 1973.

341.   Munnell, T.   [Fifty Years of Christian Denomination.]
        Christian Quarterly 8 (1876):289+.

342.   Murphy, Cullen.   "Protestantism and the Evangelicals."
        Wilson Quarterly 5 (Autumn 1981):105-19.

343.   Murphy, Lawrence R.   "William F. M. Arny, Secretary of
        New Mexico Territory, 1862-1867."   Arizona and the
        West 8, no. 4 (1966): 323-38.

344. Mutchmor, J. R. "Disciples Attend Assembly of World Convention of Churches of Christ." *Christian Century* 72 (September 7, 1955): 1030+.

345. "Nelle Reagan." *Saturday Evening Post* (May/June 1985):36-7.

346. Nelson, J. Robert. "Concord at Lexington; Consultation on Church Union." *Christian Century* 82 (May 5, 1965):575-6.

347. "News of the Christian World." *Christian Century* 66 (November 9-16, 1949):1331, 1374.

348. "No Immersionist Bloc." *Christian Century* 53 (July 22, 1936):1006-8.

349. Northeastern Association of Christian Churches. *Preliminary Research*. Schenectady, 1962.

350. Norton, Herman Albert. "Philip Slater Fall [1798-1890]: The Father of Sourthern Disciples." *Harbinger and Discipliana* 14(January 1954):6.

351. "Notable Movement toward Protestant Unity: University of Chicago Divinity School, Chicago Theological Seminary, Meadville Theological School, and Disciples of Divinity House Combine Their Faculties." *School and Society* 58 (July 10, 1943):22.

352. Olbricht, Thomas H., ed. "Perspectives on Division." *Restoration Quarterly* 27, no. 1 (1984):1-64.

353. Olbricht, Thomas H. "Religious Scholarship and the Restoration Movement." *Restoration Quarterly* 25, no. 4 (1982):193-204.

354. Ollila, John Lyle. "The Soul-Politic in Antebellum America: The Political Implications of Alexander Campbell's New Testament Christianity." Ph.D. diss., University of California, Berkeley, 1982.

355. "100 Years of 'The Christian Century.'" *Christian Century* (January 1, 1984):43+.

356. "Opening and Resolutions: International Convention of Christian Churches." *Christian Century* 79 (October 31, 1962):1335-6+.

357. Osborn, Ronald E. "Current Isues in Faith and Order." *Shane Quarterly* 14 (July 1953):111-21.

358.   Osborn, Ronald E.   "Disciples of Christ and Union
       among Denominations."   Shane Quarterly 16 (April
       1955):108-19.

359.   Osborn, Ronald E.   "Disciples Serving Our Day."   Shane
       Quarterly 13(April 1952):58-68.

360.   Osborn, Ronald E.   "The Eldership Among Disciples of
       Christ: A Historical Case-Study in a 'Tent-Making
       Ministry.'"   Mid-Stream 6(Winter 1967):74-112.

361.   Osborn, Ronald E.   "Experiment in Liberty: The Ideal
       of Freedom in the Experience of the Disciples of
       Christ."   Church History 48(December 1979):465.

362.   Osborn, R. E.   "Formula in Flux: Reformation for the
       Disciples of Christ?"   Christian Century 80
       (September 25, 1963):1163-6.

363.   Osborn, Ronald E.   "Mission on the Pacific Slope: A
       Challenge to the Disciples of Christ."   Impact
       (Claremont) 1 (1978):3-49.

364.   Osborn, R. E.   "Ordination for Homosexuals? A Negative
       Answer Qualified by Some Reflections."   Encounter
       (CTS) 40 (Summer 1979):245-63.

365.   Osborn, Ronald E.   "Portrait of a Churchman [Kershner,
       Frederick D.]"   Encounter (CTS) 20 (Spring
       1959):132-67.

366.   Osborn, Ronald E.   "Portrait of a Churchman: The
       Ministry of O. L. Shelton."   Encounter (CTS) 20
       (Spring 1959):132-67.

367.   Osborn, Ronald E.   "Problems of Disciple Participation
       in the Ecumenical Movement."   Shane Quarterly 15
       (1954):13-23.

368.   Osborn, Ronald E.   "The Sacraments in the Thought and
       Practice Disciples of Christ."   Impact (Claremont)
       3 (1979):3-10.

369.   Osborn, Ronald E.   "Seminar: Thinking Through the
       Story [Edited Transcription]."   Impact (Claremont)
       6 (1981):2-16.

370.   Osborn, Ronald E.   "Theological Issues in the
       Restructure of the Christian Church (Disciples of
       Christ): A Not Unbiased Memoir."   Mid-Stream 19
       (July 1980):272-308.

371. Osborn, Ronald E. "Twelve Signs to New Life for the
      Church [or 'The Parting of the Ways']." Impact
      (Claremont) 10 (1983):32-7.

372. Paddock, W. "Stormy Weather or Showers of Blessing?
      National Missionary Convention." Christianity
      Today 18 (December 21, 1973):37.

373. Panel of Scholars. The Renewal of Church: The Panel
      Reports. Edited by William Blakemore. St. Louis:
      Bethany Pr., 1963.

374. A Panorama of the Christian Churches of Greater
      Indianapolis. Prepared for the Observation Tour of
      Churches, Conducted May 11th, 1928. By the Building
      and Grounds Committee of the Indianapolis Christian
      Church Union, Homer Dale, Chairman... [N.p., 1928?]

375. Parker, J. M. "Pilgrim Disciple." Outlook 96
      (November 19, 1910): 642-4.

376. "A Pastor's Group Calls for a Stop to UCC-Disciples
      Merger Talks." Christianity Today 28 (May 18,
      1984):74-5.

377. Paulsell, W. O. [Disciples of Christ and the
      Depression, 1929-1936.] Church History 35
      (1966):354+.

378. Pearson, Samuel C. "An American Apologetic: Disciple
      Articulation of the Christian Faith." Encounter
      (CTS) 46 (Summer 1985): 255-73.

379. Pearson, S. C., Jr. "Association of Disciples for
      Theological Discussion: A Brief Historical
      Appraisal." Encounter (CTS) (Summer 1976):259-83.

380. Pearson, S. C. "Cave Affair: Protestant Thought in
      the Gilded Age." Encounter (CTS) 41 (Spring
      1980):179-203.

381. Pearson, Samuel C., Jr. "Rationalist in an Age of
      Enthusiasm: The Anomalous Career of Robert Cave."
      Missouri Historical Society. Bulletin 35. no. 2
      (1979):99-108.

382. Peskin, Allan. "A Century of Garfield." Hayes
      Historical Journal 3, no. 4 (1981):9-20.

383. Pierce, Lee C. "Making the Ecumenical Movement a
      Reality at Home." Shane Quarterly 16 (April
      1955):101-7.

384. Pierson, R. M. "The Literature of the Disciples of
      Christ and Closely Related Groups." Religion In
      Life 26 (Spring 1957): 274-88.

385. Plowman. E. E. "Disciples Heed Minority-Group Needs."
      Christianity Today 13 (September 12, 1969):56.

386. Pope, R. M. "College of the Bible." College of the
      Bible Quarterly (Lexington) 38 (April 1961):4-27.

387. Pope, Richard M. "Edward Scribner Ames and the
      American Democratic Faith." Encounter (CTS) 39
      (Autumn 1978):395-404.

388. Pope, Richard M. "Persons, Places amd Books That Have
      Influenced My Life." Lexington Theological
      Quarterly 13 (January 1978): 19-26.

389. Pope, Richard Martin. "The Seminary as a Learning
      Community." Lexington Theological Quarterly 5
      (April 1970):33-41.

390. "Portrait of an Ecumenical Dialogue." Origins 10
      (February 12, 1981):555-60.

391. Pyatt, C. L. "Experimental Course in Anti-Semitism
      [College of the Bible, Lexington, Ky.]" Christian
      Education 21 (December 1937):98-9.

392. Quinn, Bernard and Douglas Johnson, eds. Atlas of the
      Church in Appalachia. Administrative Units and
      Boundaries. Washington, D.C.: Commission on
      Religion in Appalachia, 1971.

393. Ragan, Stephen C. "Origin of the Christian Church at
      Westport." Missouri Historical Review 2 (October
      1907):47-54.

394. Reeves, F. W. "Colleges of the Disciples of Christ."
      Christian Education 12 (April 1929):433-8.

395. Reid, Mark K. "Independent Christians and the
      Disciples of Christ: An Ecumenical Dilemma
      [Oregon]." Mid-Stream 24 (January 1985): 77-83.

396. Reisinger, Donald D. "Foreword [To First Issue of
      Impact, A Journal of Thought of Disciples of Christ
      on the Pacific Slope]." Impact (Claremont) 1
      (1978):1-2.

397. Reisinger, Donald D. and Mary A. Parrott, eds.
      "Forrest R. Reed Lectures, 9th Series - Heirs of
      Stone and Campbell on the Pacific Slope: A

Sociological Approach." Impact (Claremont) 12
(1984):4-131.

398. Reisinger, Donald D. and Ronald E. Osborn, eds.   "20th
      Anniversary Celebration Edition [Disciples Seminary
      Foundation, Claremont, California]." Impact
      (Claremont) 5 (1980):1-37.

399. Reister, W. F. Terry. "Foundations of Worship." Mid-
      Stream 22 (January 1983):94-108.

400. "Report and Recommendation, Steering Committee
      Covenant between United Church of Christ and
      Christian Church (Disciples of Christ)." Mid-
      Stream 24 (April 1985):198-21

401. "Report on the International Commission for Dialogue
      Between Disciples of Christ and the Roman Catholic
      Church (1977-1981)." One in Christ 18, no. 4
      (1982):385-97.

402. "Resolutions Adopted by the General Assembly Meeting
      in Anaheim, California, July 31-August 5, 1981."
      In Nuclear Disarmament, pp. 247-52. Edited by R.
      Heyer. 1982.

403. "Response of the Christian Church (Disciples of
      Christ) to 'In Quest of a Church of Christ Uniting'
      [Consultation on Church Union]." Mid-Stream 21
      (April 1982):227-43.

404. Richmond Disciples' Centennial, February 28th to March
      2nd, 1932. Richmond, Va., 1932.

405. Roberts, R. L. "Benjamin Franklin Hall, 1803-1873."
      Restoration Quarterly 20, no. 3 (1977):156-68.

406. Robinson, John L. "David Lipscomb in Texas."
      Restoration Quarterly 21, no. 1 (1978):26-32.

407. Rodgers, E. C. [The Christian Church and Music,
      Missouri.] Missouri Historical Society Bulletin 24
      (1968):255+.

408. Rogers, Cornish R. "Forging New Links for Peace
      [Convention at Anaheim, California]." Christian
      Century 98 (September 16, 1981):893-4.

409. Rogers, Cornish. "Women's Rights, Amnesty Win at
      Disciples Assembly." Christian Century 90
      (November 14, 1973):1117-19.

410. Rossman, P. "How Can Christians Who Disagree Be
      United?" _Christian Century_ 96 (December 5,
      1979):1225-6

411. Rowell, J. Cy. "The Skills, Knowledge and Tasks of
      the Professional Church Educator." _Lexington
      Theological Quarterly_ 16 (April 1981):68-75.

412. Royle, Marjorie H. "Women Pastors: What Happens After
      Placement." _Review of Religious Research_ 24
      (December 1982):116-26.

413. Rushford, Jerry. "James A. Garfield: The Early
      Years." _Restoration Quarterly_ 20, no. 3
      (1977):131-40.

414. _S. S. Bartlett and the Christian Ministry._ Warren,
      Ohio, 1879.

415. Salisbury, Thayer. "Restoration Dangers."
      Restoration Quarterly 26, no. 2 (1983):103-4.

416. Sanders, David W. _Church Creeds and Party Platforms.
      A Comparison of Catholic Preachers. Campbellite
      Priests. and Ministers of Other "Christian"
      Churches..._ Indianapolis: Manual Publishing Co.,
      1907.

417. Savage, Dennis. "Our Church and Our Culture." _Impact_
      (Claremont) 1(1978):50-7.

418. Seaman, John. "Dilemma: The Mythology of Right and
      Left." _Journal of Human Relations_ 17, no. 1
      (1969):43-57.

419. Sears, L. C. "James Harding and the Restoration
      Movement." _Restoration Quarterly_ 20, no. 3
      (1977):169-79.

420. Shelton, Gentry A. "Alonzo W. Fortune: Pastor,
      Teacher, Friend." _Lexington Theological Quarterly_
      15 (April 1980):46-52.

421. Shelton, Orman L. "Disciples' World Brotherhood
      Studies Its Beliefs." _Shane Quarterly_ 16 (October
      1955):173-6.

422. Shepherd, James Walton. _The Church, the Falling Away,
      and the Restoration._ Cincinnati: F. L. Rowe, 1929.

423. Sherlock, Wallace E. "A Church That Refused To Die
      [Lancaster, Iowa]." _Annals of Iowa: A Magazine of
      History_ 32 (July 1953 or 4):376-9.

424. Short, Howard E.; Ronald E. Osborn; and George G.
      Beazley, Jr. "Garrison at Lund." Mid-Stream 3
      (June 1964):200-4.

425. Sinclair, F. S. [Old Christian Church.] Daughters of
      the American Revolution Magazine 76 (1942):629+.

426. Sly, Virgil A. "Christian Unity and World Missions."
      Shane Quarterly 16 (January 1955):40-60.

427. Smith, Harlie L. "The Shifting Role of Church-Related
      Higher Education." Lexington Theological Quarterly
      4, no. 2 (1969):54-61.

428. Smith, William Martin. "Overcoming the Trepidity Trap
      [The Future of Ministry]." Impact (Claremont) 10
      (1983):38-44.

429. Sorich, Carol J. and Roberta Siebert. "Toward
      Humanizing Adoption." Child Welfare 61 (April
      1982):207-16.

430. Special Study of Theological Education: Report of the
      Faculty, January 16, 1959. Indianapolis, 1959.

431. Spence, H. "Disciples of Christ." Look 23 (October
      27, 1959): 106-8+.

432. Stevenson, D. E. "College of the Bible Idea."
      College of the Bible Quarterly [Lexington] 40
      (January 1963):5-9.

433. Stevenson, Dwight E. "J. W. McGarvey: A Disciple
      Original." Lexington Theological Quarterly 16, no.
      1 (1981):40-52.

434. Stevenson, Dwight E. "Models of Governance."
      Theological Education 12 (Autumn 1975):29-35.

435. Stevenson, Evan. Campbellism Unmasked. The
      Tergiversations of Elder D. R. Lucas Exposed. The
      Reformer, Reformed - and the Crusher, Crushed. A
      Lecture upon the Origin, Spirit and Success of
      Methodism. Lafayette, Ind.: Rosser Spring, 1870.

436. Stokes, Kenneth I. "Major Trends in
      Interdenominational Adult Education, 1936-1964."
      1966. (ERIC Document 010080)

437. Stover, Urban C. "Scraps of Early Indiana Church
      History." In Indiana Worker, 1921-2.

438. Straton, Hillyer H. "Alexander Campbell's Influence
     on the Baptists." Encounter (CTS) 30, no. 4
     (1969):355-65.

439. Taylor, A. W. "Linwood Boulevard Christian Church,
     Kansas City, Mo." Homiletic Review 92 (September
     1926):179-82.

440. Teegarden, Kenneth L. "State of the Church [Address,
     Christian Church (Disciples of Christ), Anaheim,
     August 1, 1981]." Mid-Stream 21 (January 1982):11-
     20.

441. "Testimony and Test." Christian Century 78 (August 9,
     1961):947-8.

442. "Theological Seminary Receives Large Gift [Christian
     Theological Seminary]." Christian Century 80
     (December 18, 1963):1569.

443. Thomas, John Hardin. "The Academies of Indiana."
     Indiana Magazine of History 11 (March 1914):8-39.

444. Thompson, David M. "Unity as Gift and Call: The
     Hidden Reality of the Church." Mid-Stream 20 (July
     1981):296-315.

445. Thompson, James W. "New Testament Studies and the
     Restoration Movement." Restoration Quarterly 25,
     no. 4 (1982):223-32.

446. Thomson, E. Roberts. Baptists and Disciples of
     Christ. Attic Pr., 1948.

447. Tobias, Robert. "Conference Findings, Toward a
     Brotherhood Program Disciples of Christ Study
     Conference on Ecumenical Issues, Chicago, August
     1954." Shane Quarterly 16 (April 1955):120-7.

448. Tobias, Robert. "Disciples of Christ Study Conference
     on Ecumenical Issues, Chicago, 1954." Shane
     Quarterly 16 (January 1955):5.

449. "Training Religious Leaders in the Disciples
     Churches." Religious Education 10 (April
     1915):133-58.

450. Trusty, H. C. "The Christian Church in Indiana."
     Indiana Quarterly Magazine of History 6 (March
     1910):17-32.

451. Trusty, H. Clay. "Formation of the Christian Church
         in Indiana." _Indiana Magazine of History_ 6 (March
         1910):17-32.

452. Turner, George. "Profiles in Pietism: Prophets of the
         Restoration Movement." In _Kerygma and Praxis_ pp.
         155-65. Edited by W. Vanderhoof and D. Basinger.
         1984.

453. "Twenty-fifth Congress, 1925, Chicago." _Christian
         Century_ 42 (May 7, 1925):610-11.

454. Tye, Norman B. "Future Mission of Disciples." _Shane
         Quarterly_ 16(April 1955):79-90.

455. Tyler, B. B. "Principal Events of 1899." _Independent_
         (New York) 52(January 4, 1900):26-8.

456. "University Church. Disciples of Christ. Chicago,
         Ill." _Homiletic Review_ 90 (July 1925):6-10.

457. United Christian Missionary Society. Division of
         Church Life and Work. _State and Area Organization
         Briefs. 1961. Christian Churches (Disciples of
         Christ)._ Prepared for the National Church Program
         Co-ordinating Council. 1962.

458. Van Gelder, Craig E. "Growth Patterns of Mainline
         Denominations and Their Churches: A Case Study of
         Jackson, Mississippi, 1900-1980." Belhaven
         College, Jackson, Mississippi: Mid-South
         Sociological Association, 1985.

459. Vedder, H. C. [Origin of Campbellites.] _Christian
         Quarterly Review_ 7 (1888):574+.

460. Vedder, H. C. [Whitsett on Campbellites.] _Baptist
         Review_ 10 (1888): 332+.

461. Wagers, Charles Herndon. "Tradition and Christian
         Unity: Specific Involvements of Discples of
         Christ." _Encounter_ (CTS) 20 (Summer 1959):307-18.

462. Wake, Orville W. "Toward Faith in Man." _Shane
         Quarterly_ 11 (1950): 177-82.

463. Ward, Roy B. "'The Restoration Principle': A Critical
         Analysis." _Restoration Quarterly_ 8, no. 4
         (1965):197-210.

464. Ware, Charles Crossfield. "First Carolina
         Convention." _Discipliana_ 11 (July 1951):19.

465. Wasson, Woodrow W. James A[bram] Garfield. His
      Religion and Education: A Study in the Religious
      and Educational Thought and Activity of an American
      Statesman. Nashville: Tennessee Book Co., 1952.

466. Watkins, B. U. [The Name Christian.] Christian
      Quarterly Review 1(1882):47+.

467. Watkins, Keith. "The American Eucharist, Ambiguous
      Sign of Unity." Impact (Claremont) 9 (Fall
      1982):39-49.

468. Watkins, Keith. "Children in Worship: A Problem for
      the Christian Church (Disciples of Christ)."
      Encounter (CTS) 44 (Summer 1983): 263-76.

469. Watkins, Keith. "Ministers and Elders as Leaders of
      Worship in the Christian Church (Disciples of
      Christ)." Encounter (CTS) 39(Summer 1978):305-20.

470. Watkins, Keith. "Worship in the Christian Church
      (Disciples of Christ)." Worship 51 (November
      1977):486-96.

471. Webb, Henry E. "The Christian Church ('Independent')
      Where From Here: Looking to the Future." Lexington
      Theological Quarterly 16 (January 1981):26-32.

472. Webb, Henry E. "The Union of Christians and Disciples
      - Lexington, Ky., January 1, 1832." Lexington
      Theological Quarterly 17 (July 1982):31-6.

473. Wells, Carl Douglas. The Changing City Church. Los
      Angeles: University of Southern California Pr.,
      1934.

474. Welsh, Robert K. "Reflections on the First Five
      Years: A Disciple of Christ Perspective [Dialogue
      with Catholic Church]." Mid-Stream 23 (October
      1984):346-50.

475. Welsh, W. A. and Ralph G. Wilburn. "The Seminary and
      Restructure." Lexington Theological Quarterly 3,
      no. 2 (1968):33-42.

476. Wentz, Richard E. "Disciples and Catholicity."
      Christian Century 81 (March 25, 1964):400-1.

477. West, Earl Irvin. Elder Ben Franklin: Eye of the
      Storm. Indianapolis: Religious Book Service, 1983.

478. West, Earl. Life and Times of David Lipscomb.
      Henderson, Tenn.: Religious Book Service, 1954.

479. West, Earl I. Search for the Ancient Order. 3 vols.
      1, Nashville: Gospel Advocate, 1949; 2-3,
      Indianapolis Religious Book Service, 1950-1979.

480. West, William Garrett. "A Brief Survey of the Origin,
      Nature, and Mission of the Disciples of Christ
      [1792-1954]." Shane Quarterly 16 (January
      1955):19-39.

481. Whalen, W. "The Disciples of Christ." U. S. Catholic
      40 (May 1964):16-18. "Replies." (August 1964).

482. "What Is Disturbing the Disciples?" Christian Century
      43 (June 3, 1926):701-3.

483. White, Richard C. "Dwight E. Stevenson, Teacher of
      Preachers." Lexington Theological Quarterly 10
      (April 1975):1-6.

484. Whitley, Oliver Read. "The Sect-To Denomination
      Process in an American Religious Movement the
      Disciples of Christ." Social Science Quarterly 36,
      no. 3 (1955):275-81.

485. Wilburn, Ralph G. "A Critique of the Restoration
      Principle." Encounter (UK) 20, no. 3 (1959):333-
      61.

486. Wilburn, Ralph Glenn. "Widening Horizons in
      Theological Education." College of the Bible
      Quarterly (Lexington) 38 (July 1961): 1-10.

487. Willett, H. L. "Disciples Meet, Resolve, Adjourn,"
      Christian Century 48 (October 28, 1931):1351-2.

488. Williams, Albert Ross. "Samuel K. Hoshour: A Pioneer
      Educator." Indiana Magazine of History 27
      (December 1931):288-90.

489. Williams, D. Newell. "Disciples Piety: A Historical
      Review with Implications for Spiritual Formation."
      Encounter (CTS) 47 (Winter 1986):1-25.

490. Williams, D. Newell. "Historical Development of
      Ministry among Disciples [of Christ]." Mid-Stream
      24 (July 1985):293-315.

491. Williams, Oscar W. "Reminiscences of the 1870's: An
      Early College Year in the Hills." West Virginia
      History 28, no.3 (1967):212-27.

492. Williamson, Clark M., ed. "Consultation on Union:
      Talks between the Christian Church (Disciples of

Christ) and the United Church of Christ."
Encounter (CTS) 41 (Winter 1980):1-102.

493. Williamson, Clark M., ed. "Disciple Theology."
      Encounter (CTS) 43(Winter 1982):1-116.

494. Williamson, Clark M., ed. "Disciple Theology:
      Ordination and Homosexuality." _Encounter_ (CTS) 40
      (Summer 1979):197-272.

495. Williamson, Clark M., ed. "Disciple Theology
      [Thematic Issue]." _Encounter_ 47 (Winter 1986):1-
      83.

496. Williamson, Clark M. "Good Stewards of God's Varied
      Grace: Theological Reflections on Stewardship in
      the Disciples of Christ." _Encounter_ (CTS) 47, no.
      1 (1986):61-83.

497. Williamson, Clark M., ed. "Judaic-Christian
      Relations: Disciple Perspectives." _Encounter_
      (CTS) (Summer 1978):215-30.

498. Williamson, C. M. "Theology and Forms of Confession
      in the Disciples of Christ." _Encounter_ (CTS) 41
      (Winter 1980):53-71.

499. Willis, John D. and Charles H. Arnold. "The Golden
      Oracle: 'No Creed but Christ' - The Discples of
      Christ and the Christ of the Disciples." _Encounter_
      (CTS) 46 (Winter 1985):1-14.

500. Willis, S. T. "Disciples of Christ and Their Good
      Works." _Woman's Home Companion_ 31 (April 1904):14-
      15.

501. Wills, Garry. "Nelle's Boy: Ronald Reagan and the
      Disciples of Christ." _Christian Century_ 103
      (November 12, 1986):1002-6.

502. Woodrow, Woody. "The Silence of Scripture and the
      Restoration Movement." _Restoration Quarterly_ 28
      (1985-1986):27-39.

503. "Worried Disciples." _Time_ 82 (October 25, 1963):86.

504. _Year Book of the Christian Church (Disciples of_
      Christ). Indianapolis: Christian Church (Disciples
      of Christ). Annual.

505. Youngblood, Thomas J.   "Created To Be One [Sermon,
         Opening Session, Christian Church (Disciples of
         Christ) General Assembly, Anaheim, Calif., July 31,
         1981]." Mid-Stream 21 (January 1982):1-10.

506. Zabala, Artemio M. "Towards a Living Communication
         and the Open Mind in Theological Formation: The
         Style of F. D. Maurice (1805-1872)." East Asia
         Journal of Theology 2, no. 2 (1984):2949-307.

507. Zens, Jon. "Desiring Unity - Finding Division:
         Historical and Hermeneutical Reflections on the
         19th Century Restoration Movement." Search
         Together 15 (Fall-Winter 1986):1-32.

508. Zimmerman, Leslie and Errett P. Rivers. History of
         the Christian Churches of Hendricks County,
         Indiana. N.p., 1959.

II. NAMES OF PERSONS RELATED TO THE DISCIPLES OF CHRIST AND
     THEIR WORKS

AGRICULTURE/FORESTRY
     Includes Agronomy, Agricultural Engineering and
     Horticulture

*Aldrich, Richard John, 1925-.
     Agronomist.
     509. Chickweed Control in Alfalfa. U. S. Govt. Print.
              Off., 1957.
     510. Weed-Crop Ecology: Principles in Weed Management.
              Breton Publishers, 1984.

Boyd, Wade M. F.
     Professor of forestry.
     511. Long Span Skyline Logging in Intermountain Forests.
              Pullman, Wash.:1976?

Crenshaw, David B.
     Professor of agriculture.
     512. "Cytogenetic Effects of Cyclophosphamide on Ovine
              Chromosomes in Vitro and in Vivo." Ph.D. diss.,
              Univ. of Missouri, 1972.

Curl, Samuel E.
     Professor of agriculture.
     513. Food and Fiber for a Changing World. 2d ed.
              Interstate Printers & Publishers, 1982. (co-author).
     514. Progress and Change in the Agricultural Industry.
              Kendall/Hunt Publishing Co., 1973. (co-author).

Garner, George Bernard.
     See under SCIENCES.

Hagee, Gale Lee, 1949-.
    Professor of agricultural education.
    515.   "Transfer among Psychomotor Tasks in Agricultural
            Power." Ph.D. diss., Univ. of Missouri, 1977.

Huffman, Donald C.
    Professor of agriculture.
    516.   Proceedings of the Southwestern Conference on the
            World Population Explosion and Its Implications for
            Agriculture and the South, Baton Rouge, La., 1966.
            Louisiana State Univ., 1966. (editor).
    517.   Structure and Control of Southern Agriculture.
            Southern Farm Management Research Comm., 1973. (co-
            editor).

King, Larry Dean.
    Professor of agronomy.
    518.   "The Effect of Land Disposal of Liquid Sewage Sludge
            on Growth and Chemical Composition of Coastal
            Bermudagrass and Rye and on Soil Properties." Ph.D.
            diss, Univ. of Georgia, 1971.

Kirtley, Carrol Lake.
    See under BUSINESS.

Law, George Robert John.
    Professor of agricultural science.
    519.   "Blood Groups of Turkeys." Ph.D. diss., Univ. of
            California, Davis, 1961.

Lindstrom, Richard Stadden.
    Professor of horticulture.
    520.   "Greenhouse Plant Production; A Guide for Teachers
            of Vocational Agriculture." Michigan State Univ.,
            1967.

Long, Robert Alexander, 1850-1934.
    Businessman.
    521.   "Forest Conservation." In Governors' Conference,
            pp. 83-95. Washington, 1909.

Meldau, Elizabeth Uzzle.
    Professor of agriculture.
    522.   "The Role of the District Extension Chairman in the
            North Carolina Agricultural Extension Service."
            Ph.D. diss., North Carolina State Univ., 1981.

Niehaus, Merle H., 1933-.
    Professor of agronomy.
    523.   "Combining Ability for Grain Yield and Its Primary
            and Secondary Components in Sorghum Vulgare Pers."
            Ph.D. diss., Purdue Univ., 1964.

Parady, William Harold, 1919-.
  Professor of agricultural engineering.
  524.   "Evaluating Media and Multi-Media Instructional
         Materials Available to Vocational Agriculture
         Teachers of Agricultural Mechanics at the Secondary
         Level." Ph.D. diss, Univ. of Georgia, 1977.
  525.   Tractor Maintenance. 4th ed. American Assoc. for
         Vocational Instructional Materials, 1975.
  526.   Understanding and Measuring Horsepower. Athens,
         Ga., 1969. (co-author).

Pendergrass, Webster.
  College administrator.
  527.   "Research, Education, and Related Activities in
         Grassland Farming." Ph.D. diss., Harvard Univ.,
         1954.

Schmehl, Willard Reed, 1918-.
  Professor of agronomy.
  528.   Agronomy 350: Soil Fertility Management: Laboratory
         Manual. Colorado State Univ., 1978.
  529.   "The Nature of Crop Responses to Liming and the
         Influence of Rate and Method of Application on the
         Yield and Chemical Composition of Plants." Ph.D.
         diss., Cornell Univ., 1948.

Scoville, Orlin James, 1911-.
  Professor of agriculture and economics.
  530.   Agricultural Development in Thailand. Bangkok,
         1964.
  531.   "Influence of Size of Farm on the Combination of
         Resources." Ph.D. diss., Harvard Univ., 1949.
  532.   Irrigated Farms in a Subhumid Cotton Area. U. S.
         Govt. Print. Off., 1951.
  533.   Part-Time Farming. U. S. Govt. Print. Off., 1953.
         (co-author).
  534.   Relationship Between Size of Farm and Utilization of
         Machinery, Equipment and Labor on Nebraska Corn-
         Livestock Farms. U. S. Govt. Print. Off., 1951.
  535.   Summary of Prospects for Reducing the Need for
         Migratory Farm Work. Washington, 1956?
  536.   The Twelve States of Nigeria. Michigan State Univ.,
         1968.
  537.   Vertical Integration in Agriculture. Washington,
         1957.

Stoltenberg, Carl H.
  Professor of forestry.
  538.   Planning Research for Resource Decisions. Iowa
         State Univ. Pr., 1970.

539. The Timber Resources of New Jersey. U. S.
      Northeastern Forest Experiment Station, 1958. (co-
      author).

Vandeveer, Lonnie R.
    See under BUSINESS.

Wiggins, Edward R.
    See under BUSINESS.

Wills, Walter J.
    See under BUSINESS.

ARCHITECTURE
    See FINE ARTS.

BUSINESS/ECONOMICS/MANAGEMENT

Alley, William Edward, 1903-.
    Professor of economics.
    540. The Nationalization of Central Banks, with
          Particular Reference to Developments in Canada,
          England, France and the United States. Urbana,
          Ill., 1941.

Bean, Virginia Livingston, 1932-.
    Professor of business.
    541. Accounting: Concepts and Uses. Allyn & Bacon, 1969.
          (co-author).
    542. Financial Accounting. Allyn & Bacon, 1974 (co-
          author).
    543. "The Implementation of Replacement Cost as a Basis
          for the Valuation of Inventories." Ph.D. diss.,
          Univ. of Texas, 1965.
    544. Managerial Accounting. Allyn & Bacon, 1974. (co-
          author).
    545. Women's Employment: A Survey of Trends and
          Attitudes. Univ. of Colorado?, 1972. (co-author).

Beasley, Theodore Prentis, 1900-.
    Life insurance executive.
    546. Republic National Life Insurance Company: The Story
          of the Company.... Newcomen Soc. in North America,
          1964.

*Becht, J. Edwin, 1918-.
    Professor of geography and transportation; college
    administrator.
    547. Commodity Origins, Traffic, and Markets Accessible
          to Chicago via the Illinois Waterway. Illinois
          River Carriers' Association, 1952.
    548. Mantrap: Management Training Program. 2 vols.
          Houston, 1963.

Berry, Dale Allen, 1931-.
    Professor of economics.
    549.   "Member Bank Borrowing, 1956-1961." Ph.D. diss.,
           Indiana Univ., 1966.

Bomeli, Edwin C.
    Professor of business.
    550.   "The Audit of Management Performance." Ph.D. diss.,
           Univ. of Michigan, 1963.
    551.   Business Financial Management. Houghton Mifflin,
           1967. (co-author).

Brown, Homer A.
    Professor of accounting.
    552.   Accounting and Financial Data for Retail Stores.
           Oklahoma Univ., 1964.
    553.   "Financial Statements for External Analysts."
           D.B.A. diss., Indiana Univ., 1968.

*Buttram, Frank, 1886-1966.
    Oil company executive; philanthropist.
    554.   The Cushing Oil and Gas Field. Norman, 1914.
    555.   The Glass Sands of Oklahoma. Norman, 1913.
    556.   Volcanic Dust in Oklahoma. Norman, 1914.

Campbell, Thomas Corwith.
    Professor of economics.
    557.   The Bituminous Coal Freight-Rate Structure, an
           Economic Appraisal. West Virginia Univ., 1954.
    558.   Freight Rates of West Virgina Wood Products. West
           Virginia Univ., 1965.
    559.   Transportation in Randolph and Upshur Counties, West
           Virginia. West Virginia, 1974.

Dickerson, Earl Samuel, 1901-.
    Professor of business.
    560.   "The Construction of a Standardized Test in Business
           Law." Ed.D. diss., New York Univ., 1941.

Downing, Glenn Dale, 1928-.
    Professor of accounting.
    561.   "A Proposal for a First College Course in
           Management." Ph.D. diss., Univ. of Texas, 1966.

Hartley, Ronald Vernon, 1938-.
    Professor of accounting.
    562.   Cost and Managerial Accounting. Allyn & Bacon,
           1983.
    563.   Operations Research: A Managerial Emphasis.
           Goodyear, 1974.
    564.   "The Role of the Accountant in Operations Research."
           Ph.D. diss., Univ. of Illinois, 1967.

Henry, Donald L.
    Banker.
    565.   <u>Banker's Complete Letter Book.</u> Prentice-Hall, 1978.
            (co-compiler).
    566.   <u>Henry on Credit and Collections.</u> Prentice-Hall,
            1977.
    567.   <u>Secrets of the Million-Dollar Sales Year in Real</u>
            <u>Estate.</u> Prentice-Hall, 1981.

Hoffman, William Michael, 1943-.
    Professor of philosophy.
    568.   <u>Business Ethics.</u> McGraw, 1983. (co-author).
    569   <u>Ethics and the Management of Computer Technology.</u>
            Oelgeschlager, 1982.
    570.   <u>Kant's Theory of Freedom.</u> Univ. Pr. of America,
            1978.
    571.   <u>Power and Responsibility in the American Business</u>
            <u>System.</u> Univ. Pr. of America, 1979.
    572.   <u>Proceedings of the First National Conference on</u>
            <u>Business Ethics.</u> Bentley College, 1977. (editor).
    573.   <u>The Work Ethic in Business.</u> Oelgeschlager, 1981.
            (co-editor).

Housley, Carl Blair, 1939-.
    Professor of economics.
    574.   "An Economic Analysis of Federal and Florida Water
            Quality Legislation." Ph.D. diss., Florida State
            Univ., 1969.

Hulse, Laura.
    Professor of business education.
    575.   <u>Random Rhymes.</u> Foundation Pr., 1978.

*Irwin, William Glanton, 1866-1943.
    Businessman; philanthropist.
    576.   <u>Historical Ligonier Valley: A Souvenir.</u> P. F. Smith
            Printers, 1898.

Jennings, Walter Wilson.
    See under HISTORY.

Keaton, Marjorie.
    Professor of business administration.
    577.   <u>Study Guide for the Professional Legal Secretary</u>
            <u>Examination.</u> Ft. Worth?, 1964.

Kemp, Robert A.
    Professor of business administration.
    578.   "Procedures Used by Firms in Six Manufacturing
            Industries to Select Foreign Vendors." D.B.A.
            diss., Arizona State Univ., 1979.

Kenderdine, James Marshall, 1941-.
    Professor of business administration.
    579.   "Consumer Intentions to Purchase Durable Goods."
           D.B.A. diss., Indiana Univ., 1971.
    580.   Simulations, Games, and Experimental Learning
           Techniques... Proceedings.... Univ. Of Oklahoma,
           1974. (co-editor).

Kirtley, Carrol Lake.
    Professor of agricultural economics.
    581.   "An Investigation into the External Economies or
           Diseconomies Associated with the Density of a Type
           of Farm." Ph.D. diss., Univ. of Missouri, 1966.

Lee, Sang Man.
    Professor of management.
    582.   "The Controllability of Money Supply in a Developing
           Country: The Korea Case." Ph.D. diss., Claremont
           Graduate School, 1985.

McAdoo, Joseph Patrick, 1933-.
    College administrator.
    583.   Energy in America. Mid-America Research, 1978.
           (editor).

McGinty, John J.
    Businessman.
    584.   A Definitionary of Business Terms. Eugene, Or.,
           1962. (co-author).

McKemey, Dale R.
    Professor of management.
    585.   "An Expectancy Theory Approach to the Study of
           Reenlistment Behavior in the Military." D.B.A.
           diss., Indiana Univ., 1979.

Meenen, Henry John, 1919-.
    College administrator; researcher.
    586.   "The Impact of a Flood Control Project upon the
           Economic and Social Structure of the Area." Ph.D.
           diss., Univ. of Missouri, 1959.

Menges, Paul F.
    Professor of business.
    587.   "Analysis of Learning Objectives in Field Experience
           in Relation to Student Achievement." Ph.D. diss.,
           Univ. of Northern Colorado, 1975.

Messmer, Victor C.
    Professor of accounting.
    588.   "An Empirical Investigation of the Effect of State
           Rate Regulation on Price Increases in Acute, Short-

Term, General Hospitals." D.B.A. diss., Univ. of
Kentucky, 1981.

Milano, Duane R.
    Professor of accounting.
    589.   "Independence and the Certified Public Accountant."
            Ph.D. diss., Michigan State Univ., 1979.

Miller, Joseph Irwin, 1909-.
    Businessman; philanthropist.
    590.   "The World of Business and the Church." New York,
            1962?

Orr, John A.
    Professor of economics.
    591.   Economics in American Society. Wadsworth, 1970.
            (co-author).
    592.   "The Impact of the Product Market upon Labor
            Relations in the American Basic Steel Industry."
            Ph.D. diss., Univ. of Wisconsin, 1968.
    593.   Principles of Microeconomics. Kendall/Hunt, 1984.
            (co-author).

Pettengill, Frederick B., 1909-.
    College administrator.
    594.   Perceptive Management and Supervision. 2d. ed.
            Prentice-Hall, 1971. (co-author).

Phillips, Marion Carl, 1920-.
    Professor of business.
    595.   "Methods of Estimating Professional Income of
            Counties of Oklahoma." Ph.D. diss., Univ. of
            Oklahoma, 1959.
    596.   The Credit Practices of Oklahoma Retailers. Univ.
            of Oklahoma, 1963.

Pugh, Charles Ray.
    Professor of economics.
    597.   Cost of Producing Farm Products in North Carolina.
            North Carolina State College, 1956. (co-author).
    598.   An Economic Base Study of the Northern Piedmont Area
            of North Carolina. North Carolina Agricultural
            Extension Service, 1964. (co-author).
    599.   The Structure of the Southern Farms of the Future.
            North
            Carolina State Univ., 1968. (editor).

Redford, Emmette Shelburn.
    See under POLITICAL SCIENCE.

Ryder, Harl Edgar.
    Professor of economics.

600.   "Optimal Accumulation and Trade in an Open Economy."
        Ph.D. diss., Stanford Univ., 1967.

Saenz, Michael.
    See under THEOLOGY.

Sanders, Harland.
    Businessman.
    601.   The Incredible Colonel. Creation House, 1974.
    602.   Life As I Have Known It Has Been Finger Lickin'
            Good. Creation House, 1974.

Scott, Blair Thaw.
    Businessman; grandson of Walter Scott.
    603.   "Faith of Our Fathers: An Address." Baltimore,
            1928.
    604.   God and Man: A Treatise. Fleet-McGinley, 1929.

Sims, Edwin C., 1930-.
    Professor of marketing and finance.
    605.   "Capital Market and Portfolio Theory for
            Institutional Fund Managers and Trustees: A
            Suggested Strategy." Western Illinois Univ., 1976.
    606.   "Student Characteristics Associated with Selected
            Attitudes toward the Free Enterprise System."
            Western Illinois Univ., 1977.
    607.   "A Survey of Student Attitudes toward the Free
            Enterprise System." Western Illinois Univ., 1977.
            (co-author).

Squires, Jan R.
    Professor of business administration.
    608.   "The Bank Holding Company Acquisition Decision."
            D.B.A. diss., Univ. of Virginia, 1984.

Thompson, James Howard, 1919-.
    Professor of economics.
    609.   The Economic Impact of State and Local Taxes in West
            Virginia. West Virginia Univ., 1958. (co-author).
    610.   Methods of Plant Site Selection Available to Small
            Manufacturing Firms. West Virginia Univ., 1961.
    611.   Significant Trends in the West Virginia Coal
            Industry, 1900-1957. West Virginia Univ., 1958.
    612.   West Virginia Statistical Handbook. West Virginia
            Univ., 1955-. (editor).

Vandeveer, Lonnie R.
    Professor of agricultural economics.
    613.   Economic Analysis of Supplemental Irrigation
            Practices for Selected Crops in Louisiana.
            Louisiana State Univ., 1982.

614. "An Economic Analysis of the Western Oklahoma
      Agricultural Land Market." Ph.D. diss., Oklahoma
      State Univ., 1979.
615. <u>Projected Cash Flows for Representative Louisiana
      Farms, 1982.</u> Louisiana State Univ., 1982.
616. <u>Projected Cash Flows for Representative Louisiana
      Farms, 1983.</u> Louisiana State Univ., 1983.
617. <u>Projected Cash Flows for Representative Louisiana
      Farms, 1984.</u> Louisiana State Univ., 1984.

Wardrep, Bruce N., 1945-.
   Professor of finance.
   618. <u>Toward an Economic Theory of Urban Housing Density
         at a Location.</u> 1974.

Ware, Ray M.
   Professor of economics.
   619. <u>The Balance of Payments, History, Methodology,
         Theory.</u> Simmons-Boardman, 1965. (co-author).
   620. <u>Modern International Economics.</u> Schenkman, 1970.
         (co-author).

Warne, Clinton Lee, 1921-.
   Professor of economics.
   621. <u>Cement.</u> Univ. of Kansas, 1955.
   622. <u>The Consumer Looks at Deceptive Packaging.</u> Colorado
         State College, 1961.
   623. <u>The Development of the American Economy.</u> Scott,
         Foresman, 1963. (co-author).
   624. "Some Considerations of the Impact of the Passenger
         Automobile on the Nebraska Economy." Ph.D. diss.,
         Univ. of Nebraska, 1953.

Watkins, Don O.
   College administrator.
   625. <u>A Study of Employment Patterns in the General
         Merchandise Group Retail Stores in New York City.</u>
         City of New York Commission on Human Rights, 1966.
         (co-author).
   626. <u>Toward a Balance Sheet of Puerto Rican Migration.</u>
         1966. (co-author).

Webb, Harold Quentin, 1922-.
   Professor of office administration management.
   627. "The Prognostic Potential of Selected Factors for
         Predicting Achievement in the Study of High School
         Bookkeeping and Accounting." Ph.D. diss., Ohio
         State Univ., 1971.

Wiggins, Edward R.
   Professor of agricultural economics.
   628. <u>Missouri Dairy Farm Costs and Returns.</u> Univ. of
         Missouri, 1971.

Wills, Walter Joe, 1915-.
    Professor of agricultural economics.
    629.   An Introduction to Agri-Business Management.
           Interstate Printers & Publishers, 1973.
    630.   Introduction to Agricultural Sales. Reston, 1983.
    631.   An Introduction to Grain Marketing. Interstate
           Printers & Publishers, 1972.
    632.   "Livestock Marketing Problems in Southern Illinois."
           Ph.D. diss., Univ. of Illinois, 1952.

Zickefoose, Paul Wesley, 1918-.
    Professor of economics.
    633.   Basic Studies, Analyses and Projections for a
           Comprehensive Plan, Ruidoso, Ruidoso Downs, New
           Mexico. Albuquerque, N.M., 1961.
    634.   "Changes in Kansas Income since 1900." Ph.D. diss.,
           Univ. of Kansas, 1954.
    635.   "Economic Survey, the 'Before' Portion of a Highway
           Relocation Impact Study." 5 vols. Santa Fe, 1959-
           60.
    636.   Kansas Income Payments, 1900-1953. Univ. of Kansas,
           1955.
    637.   Population and the Labor Force. Univ. of Kansas,
           1953.
    638.   A Socioeconomic Analysis of the Impact of New
           Highway Constructionat Santa Fe, New Mexico: Final
           Report. New Mexico State Univ., 1973.
    639.   A Socioeconomic Analysis of the Impact of New
           Highway Construction in the Shiprock Growth Center
           Area: Final Report. New Mexico State Univ., 1974.

Zink, Lee B.
    Economist.
    640.   Data Development for Evaluation of Energy Research
           and Development Programs. New Mexico Energy
           Research and Development Institute, 1983.
    641.   Economic Growth and the Banking System. Univ. of
           New Mexico, 1970. (co-author).
    642.   "The Farm Proprietor Income Component of Personal
           Income Estimates." Ph.D. diss., Oklahoma State
           Univ., 1967.
    643.   Hard Choices: Report on the Increasing Gap between
           America's Infrastructure Needs and Our Ability to
           Pay for Them: A Case Study. U.S. Govt. Print.
           Off., 1984.
    644.   Human and Material Resources of Atoka County.
           Southeastern State College, 1965-. (co-author).
    645.   The New Mexico Economy: Change in the 1970's.
           Governor's Council of Economic Advisors, State of
           New Mexico, 1978. (co-author).
    646.   Public Infrastructure Needs, 1982-2000: New Mexico
           Case Study. Univ. of New Mexico, 1983.

647.   <u>Technology Utilization in a Non-Urban Region.</u>
       Southeastern State College, 1968.

COMMUNICATIONS
    See EDUCATION.

COMPUTER SCIENCE

Chapin, David A.
    Computer scientist.
    648.   "Project IMPRESS: An Interactive Social Science
           Software Package." Dartmouth College, 1972.

Losh, Charles Lawrence, 1939-.
    Computer scientist.
    649.   "The Relationship of Student Hemisphericity to
           Performance in a Computer Programming Course."
           Ph.D. diss., Georgia State Univ., 1983.

Margot, Louis III.
    College administrator.
    650.   <u>GOTO/CE: A User's Manual for the Cagle Editor, the</u>
           <u>East Texas State University Text Editing System.</u>
           East Texas State Univ., 1982.

Rickman, Jon T.
    Professor of computer science.
    651.   "Automatic Storage and Retrieval Techniques for
           Large On-Line Abstract Collections." Ph.D. diss.,
           Washington State Univ., 1972.

Sheppard, Sallie.
    Professor of computer science.
    652.   "1984 Winter Simulation Conference Proceedings:
           November 28-30, 1984, Sheraton Dallas Hotel, Dallas,
           Texas." Society for Computer Simulation, 1984. (co-
           editor).

Smith, Noel T.
    Professor of data processing.
    653.   <u>Broadcast Announcer's License Manual: A Guide to</u>
           <u>FCC 3rd Class Exam.</u> Hayden, 1976. (co-author).
    654.   <u>CBer's Factbook.</u> Hayden, 1977.
    655.   <u>An Introduction to Microprocessors: Experiments in</u>
           <u>Digital Technology.</u> Hayden, 1981.

Walstrom, John.
    Professor of quantitative and informational sciences.
    656.   <u>Advanced Topics in Structured COBOL.</u> Western
           Illinois Univ., 1984.

657.   "An Investigation of Outcome Information in
        Management Information Systems for Higher
        Education." Ph.D. diss., Univ. of Nebraska, 1976.

COUNSELING
    See PSYCHOLOGY.

ECONOMICS
    See BUSINESS.

EDUCATION
    See also Christian Education; Education, Higher;
    Theological Education and names of the following
    institutions (in the Subject Index):
            Atlantic Christian College
            Bethany College
            Butler University
            Christian Theological Seminary
            Claremont Graduate School of Theology
            Drake University
            Hiram University
            Lexington Theological Seminary
            Lynchburg College
            Phillips University
            Texas Christian University
            Transylvania University
            University of Chicago
            Yale Divinity School

Adams, Dale T.
    College administrator.
    658.   "An Evaluation of a Summer Business Orientation
            Program for Selected Black Business Majors." Ph.D.
            diss., Univ. of Cincinnati, 1972.

Adams, Donald Van, 1935-.
    College administrator.
    659.   "An Analysis of Student Subcultures at Michigan
            State University." Ph.D. diss., Michigan State
            Univ., 1965.

Alexander, Nelle (Grant).
    See under THEOLOGY.

Allen, Monte R.
    Professor of elementary education.
    660.   Readings in Educational Measurement and Evaluation
            for the Elementary School Teacher. Selected
            Academic Readings, 1968. (co-editor).

Applegate, Jimmie Ray, 1934-.
     Professor of education; college administrator.
     661.   "A Description and Analysis of Role Playing as a
            Student Activity in an Elementary Classroom." Ph.D.
            diss., Washington Univ., 1971.

Athearn, Walter Scott, 1872-1934.
     Educator; college president; editor of <u>Midland Schools</u>
     (1902-7).
     662.   <u>An Adventure in Religious Education.</u> Century, 1930.
     663.   <u>A Brief History of Keokuk County.</u> The News
            (Sigourney, Iowa), 1897.
     664.   <u>Character Building in Democracy.</u> Macmillan, 1924.
     665.   <u>The Church School.</u> Pilgrim Pr., 1914.
     666.   <u>The City Institute for Religious Teachers.</u> Univ. of
            Chicago Pr., 1915.
     667.   <u>The Correlation of Church Schools and Public
            Schools.</u> Malden School of Religious Education,
            1917.
     668.   <u>Dual Control of an Urban University.</u> 1935.
     669.   <u>The Intermediate Department of the Church School.</u>
            1913.
     670.   <u>International Standards for Community Training
            Schools of Religious Education. Presenting Ideals
            and Standards for Community Training Schools of
            Religious Education. A Community System of Religious
            Education and Suggested Courses of Instruction.</u>
            International Sunday School Assoc., 1918.
     671.   <u>An Introduction to the Study of the Mind.</u>
            Westminster, 1921.
     672.   <u>Making Democracy Safe for the World.</u> International
            Sunday School Assoc., 1918.
     673.   <u>The Malden Survey: A Report on the Church Plants of
            a Typical City. Showing the Use of the Interchurch
            World Movement Score Card and Standards for Rating
            City Church Plants.</u> Interchurch World Movement of
            North America, 1920.
     674.   <u>The Master Library.</u> 7 vols. Foundation Pr., 1923.
     675.   <u>Measurements and Standards in Religious Education.</u>
            1924.
     676.   <u>The Minister and the Teacher: An Interpretation of
            Current Trends in Christian Education.</u> Century,
            1932.
     677.   <u>A National System of Education.</u> Doran, 1920.
     678.   <u>The Organization and Administration of the Church
            School.</u> 1917.
     679.   <u>A Reference Library for Community Training Schools.</u>
            International Sunday School Assoc., 1918. (co-
            author).
     680.   <u>Religious Education and American Democracy.</u> 1917.
     681.   <u>Religious Education of Protestants in an American
            Commonwealth.</u> 1923. (editor and co-author).
     682.   <u>Religious Education Survey Schedules.</u> 1924.

683.   <u>Teaching the Teacher: A First Book in Teacher</u>
       <u>Training Section I, The Development of the Church in</u>
       <u>Old Testament Times.</u> Westminster, 1921.
       (contributor).

Bachler, Michael Ray.
    Professor of education.
    684.   "Updating and Revising the Drafting Program at
           Middle Tennessee State University." Ph.D. diss.,
           Univ. of Minnesota, 1976.

Baker, Curtis Cedric, 1920-.
    College administrator.
    685.   "A Study of Some Guiding Principles to Be Used in
           Developing a Handbook for Administrators." Univ. of
           Arkansas, 1957.

Baker, Noel Custer, 1938-.
    College administrator.
    686.   "Description of a Private Liberal Arts College:
           1961-1970." Ed.D. diss., Indiana Univ., 1973.

Barnes, Bill L.
    Seminary administrator.
    687.   <u>Preliminary Report on Exploration of Appropriate and</u>
           <u>Meaningful Ways to Relate Concerns of Theological</u>
           <u>Education to the Washington, D.C. Scene.</u> B.L.
           Barnes, 1974.

*Barraga, Natalie Carter, 1915-.
    Professor of special education.
    688.   <u>Increased Visual Behavior in Low Vision Children.</u>
           American Foundation for the Blind, 1964.
    689.   <u>Visual Handicaps and Learning: A Developmental</u>
           <u>Approach.</u> Wadsworth, 1976.

Beans, Stanley Smith, 1921-.
    Professor of philosophy of education.
    690.   "A Historical and Comparative Study of the American-
           Sponsored School in Sao Paulo, Brazil." Ph.D.
           diss., Univ. of Arkansas, 1968.

Blue, Marion Eugene.
    College administrator.
    691.   "Attitude and Performance Differences Between
           Student Teachers Trained in Team Teaching Stations
           and Student Teachers Trained in Self-Contained
           Stations." Ph.D. diss., Univ. of Akron, 1972.

Boone, Richard Marshall.
    College administrator.

692.   "Electronic Data Processing Equipment as an Aid to
       Administrative Decision Making in Student Teaching
       Programs." Ph.D. diss., Arizona State Univ., 1971.

Bortz, Walter Raymond, 1932-.
    College administrator.
    693.   "The Relationship of Selected High School Courses to
           Success in College." Ph.D. diss., Ohio State Univ.,
           1971.

Bowman, Alden Elbert, 1919-.
    Professor of education.
    694.   "A Longitudinal Study of Individuals Who Entered
           Kansas State Teachers College of Emporia as Non-
           Transfer Freshmen in the Fall of 1960." Ph.D.
           diss., 1965.

*Briggs, Eugene Stephen, 1890-.
    College president; educator.
    695.   A Finding and Broadening Course in Public Speaking.
           Christopher Publishing House, 1933. (co-author).
    696.   The Preparation of Secondary Teachers in Teachers
           Colleges for Guiding and Directing Extra-Class
           Activities. Missouri State Dept. of Education,
           1935.

Broce, Thomas E., 1935-.
    College administrator.
    697.   Directory of Oklahoma Foundations. Univ. of
           Oklahoma Pr., 1974. (co-compiler).
    698.   Fund Raising: The Guide to Raising Money from
           Private Sources. Univ. of Oklahoma, 1979.

Brown, Hilton Ultimus, 1859-1958.
    Journalist; college administrator.
    699.   A Book of Memories. Butler Univ., 1951.
    700.   Hilton U. Brown, Jr., One of Three Brothers in
           Artillery [Letters and Verses by His Son]. 1920.
           (editor).

*Burgess, Otis A., 1829-1882.
    Educator; pastor.
    701.   The Indiana Schools and the Men Who Have Worked in
           Them. Wilson, Hinkle & Co., 1876. (contributor).

Burnette, Horace Jimmie, 1934-.
    College administrator.
    702.   "An Analysis of the Internal Organizational
           Structures of Selected Public Junior Colleges in
           Florida." Ed.D. diss., Univ. of Florida, 1966.

Bush, William Jack.
    Professor of education.

703. "An Analysis of the Outcomes of Functional
      Mathematics as Measured by Certain Tests after
      Completion by the Students of Two Years of Study."
      Ed.D. diss., Univ. of Arkansas, 1959.

Butler, Annie Louise, 1920-.
   Professor of early childhood education.
   704. All Children Want To Learn. Grolier, 1965. (co-
         author).
   705. The Child's Right To Quality Day Care. Assoc. for
         the Childhood Education International, 1970.
   706. Current Concerns in Early Childhood Education.
         Indiana Univ., 1975.
   707. Current Research in Early Childhood Education.
         American Assoc. of Elementary-Kindergarten-Nursery
         Educators, 1970.
   708. Early Childhood Education in Perspective. Indiana
         Univ., 1979.
   709. Early Childhood Education: Planning and
         Administering Programs. Van Nostrand, 1974.
   710. Early Childhood Programs: Developmental Objectives
         and Their Use. Merrill, 1975.
   711. Literature Search and Development. Indiana Univ.,
         1971.
   712. Play as Development. Merrill, 1978. (co-author).
   713. Recent Research in Early Childhood Education. Univ.
         of Illinois, 1971.

Butler, Joseph, 1932-.
   Professor of elementary education.
   714. "Comparisons of Listening Abilities, Categorized as
         Good and Poor, of Inner-City Children in the Sixth
         Grade." Ed.D. diss., Indiana Univ., 1970.

Caldwell, Howard Clay.
   715. "Butler College Years, 1911-1915." In Irvington
         Historical Society. Papers. pp. 28-41.
         Indianapolis, 1965.

Chamberlin, Gary D.
   State education official.
   716. A Study of Higher Education Faculty and
         Administrative Salaries in Arkansas and Contiguous
         States. Commission on Coordination of Higher
         Educational Finance, 1970. (co-author).

Clark, Randolph, 1844-1935.
   Co-founder of AddRan College (now Texas Christian
   University).
   717. Reminiscences Biographical and Historical. L.
         Clark, 1919.

Coffland, Jack Arthur, 1940-.
    Professor of education.
    718.   "Normative Expectations for the Elementary School
            Principal Acting in His Role as Teacher-Evaluator."
            Ph.d. Diss., Univ. of Oregon, 1969.

Costello, Lawrence F., d.1964.
    Media specialist.
    719.   <u>Teach with Television: A Guide to Instructional TV.</u>
            Hastings House, 1961.

Cotten, Carroll C., 1936-.
    College administrator.
    720.   <u>The Imperative Is Leadership.</u> Bethany, 1973.

Cox, Blanche, 1921-.
    College administrator.
    721.   "Recommendations Relative to the Student Personnel
            Program of Date County Junior College." Ed.D.
            diss., Univ. of Miami, 1963.

Crowder, William Waldrop, 1923-.
    Professor of social studies.
    722.   <u>Persistent-Problems Approach to Elementary Social
            Studies.</u> Peacock, 1973.
    723.   "A Study of the Out-of-School Experiences of
            Selected Second Grade Children with Implications for
            Revision of the Social Studies Course of Study."
            Ph.D. diss., Indiana Univ., 1958.

Deselms, Harold.
    College administrator.
    724.   "A Descriptive Study of Practices and Policies for
            Selected Schools and Communities with Programs of
            Shared Facilities." Ph.D. diss., Univ. of Nebraska,
            Lincoln, 1978.

Dobbs, Ralph Cecil, 1922-.
    Professor of education.
    725.   <u>Adult Education in America.</u> Litho Printers, 1970.
    726.   "Self-Perceived Educational Needs of Adults in a
            Declining Community and Non-Declining Community."
            Ed.D. diss., Indiana Univ., 1965.

Epler, Stephen Edward
    See under THEOLOGY.

Epperson, Kenneth Boyd, 1924-.
    College administrator.
    727.   "A Study of Academic Achievement of Graduates and
            Nongraduates at Western Illinois University." Ed.D.
            diss., Indiana Univ., 1970.

Evans, Leslie Paul, 1911-.
  Professor of education.
  728.   "A Survey of Certain Aspects of Teacher Education in
         Some Church-Related Colleges and Universities in
         Texas." Ph.D. diss., Univ. of Texas, 1948.

Fisher, Virginia Lee Slusher.
  Professor of child and family development.
  729.   Child Development Curriculum Materials. Lucas
         Brothers, 1961-.
  730.   "Role Conceptions of Head Start Teachers." Ph.D.
         diss., Univ. of Missouri, 1967.

Geisler, Keith Kane, 1935-.
  College administrator; counselor.
  731.   "Learning Efforts of Adults Undertaken for
         Matriculating into a Community College." Ph.D.
         diss., Texas A & M Univ., 1984.

Gibson, Charles Hugh, 1927-.
  College administrator.
  732.   "The Development of a Model for Utilizing the
         Techniques of Cost-Benefit Analysis in the
         Evaluation of Vocational Programs." Ph.D. diss.,
         Univ of Kentucky, 1969.

Gibson, John Curlee, 1922-.
  Professor of business education.
  733.   "The Relation of Business Education to Other Subject
         Fields in the High Schools of Mississippi." Ed.D.
         diss., Indiana Univ., 1967.

Goodrich, Howard Bruce, 1927-.
  Pastor; college administrator.
  734.   "An Investigation of the Differential Effects of
         Four Different Media on Information Acquisition and
         Perception." Ph.D. diss., Univ. of Maryland, 1970.

Gordon, George Newton, 1926-.
  Professor of communications.
  735.   Classroom Television. Hastings House, 1970.
  736.   Communications and Media: Constructing a Cross-
         Discipline. Hastings House, 1975.
  737.   The Communications Revolution: A History of Mass
         Media in the United States. Hastings House, 1977.
  738.   Educational Television. Center for Applied Research
         in Education, 1965.
  739.   Erotic Communications: Studies in Sex, Sin, and
         Censorship. Hastings House, 1980.
  740.   The Idea Invaders. Hastings House, 1963. (co-
         author).
  741.   The Languages of Communication. Hastings House,
         1969.

742. The Magical Mind. Hastings House, 1967. (co-
      author).
743. Man in Focus: New Approaches to Commercial
      Communications. Hastings House, 1980.
744. On-the-Spot Reporting: Radio Records History.
      Messner, 1967. (co-author).
745. Persuasion. Hastings House, 1971.
746. TV Covers the Action. Messner, 1968. (co-author).
747. Teach with Television. Hastings House, 1961. (co-
      author).
748. "Theatrical Movements in the Theatre Arts Magazine
      from 1916 to 1948." Ph.D. diss., New York Univ.,
      1957.
749. Videocassette Technology in American Education.
      Educational Technology Publications, 1972. (co-
      author).
750. The War of Ideas: America's International Identity
      Crisis. Hastings House, 1973. (co-author).
751. Your Career in Film Making. Messner, 1969.
752. Your Career in TV and Radio. Messner, 1966.

Green, Edith.
   U.S. Congresswoman.
   753. "The Address of the Honorable Edith Green, Given as
         the Clark Lecture, April 13, 1966." Scripps
         College, 1966?
   754. Education and the Public Good: The Federal Role in
         Education. Harvard Univ. Pr., 1964.
   755. The Federal Government and Education. U.S. Govt.
         Print. Off., 1963.

Hassmiller, Robert John.
   College administrator.
   756. "A Study of the Impact of Intra-Self and Self-
         Environment Congruence on Student Persisters and
         Dropouts in Open Learning Courses at a Community
         College." Ph.D. diss., Florida State Univ., 1979.

Hastings, Gregory A., 1936-.
   Professor of education.
   757. "A Study To Assess the Relevance of Activities and
         Programs of the Asian Institute for Teacher
         Educators to the Development of Teacher Education in
         Asia." Ph.D. diss., Michigan State Univ., 1972.

Hawley, Harold Patrick.
   Professor of education.
   758. "The Classroom Communion: A Study of Teacher
         Student Personal Relationships in Education with
         Emphasis on Secondary Education." Ph.D. diss.,
         Indiana Univ., 1978.

Helsabeck, Fred, Sr., 1908-.
  College president.
    759.   "A Study of the Initial Phases of a Curriculum
            Counseling Program." Ph.D. diss., Ohio State Univ.,
            1942.

Helsabeck, Robert E.
  College administrator.
    760.   The Compound System, a Conceptual Framework for
            Effective Decision-Making in Colleges. Univ. of
            California, 1973.

Henschke, John Arthur, 1932-.
  Professor of education.
    761.   "Malcolm S. Knowles: His Contributions to the
            Theory and Practice of Adult Education." Ph.D.
            diss., Boston Univ., 1973.

Hibler, Richard W.
  Professor of education.
    762.   Happiness Through Tranquillity: The School of
            Epicures. Univ. Pr. of America, 1984.
    763.   "The Life, Educational Work and School of Epicures."
            Ed.D. diss., Univ. of Wyoming, 1974.

Hilgedick, Lorraine.
  Professor of education.
    764.   "Proofguides as Instructional Aids in Beginning
            Typewriting." Ph.D. diss., Univ. of Missouri, 1976.

Hinsdale, Burke Aaron, 1837-1900.
  Educator; pastor; professor of history and English.
    765.   "Addresses by Superintendent Hinsdale." Leader
            Printing Co., 1885.
    766.   The American Government, National and State.
            Register Publishing Co., 1891.
    767.   "Arabella Mason Rudolph." Savage, 1879.
    768.   The Art of Study. American Book Co., 1900.
    769.   "The Business Side of City School Systems." Werner
            School Book Co., 1896.
    770.   The Certification of College and University
            Graduates as Teachers of the Common Schools. Univ.
            of Chicago Pr., 1899.
    771.   "Christ and the Common People. A Sermon...."
            Detroit, 1868.
    772.   "Christian Ministers and Education One Duty of the
            Preacher." Cincinnati, 1877?
    773.   Chronicles of the Hinsdale Family. Savage, 1883.
            (compiler).
    774.   "Cleveland Public Schools." N.d.
    775.   "The Culture Value of the History of Education."
            1889.

776. "The Discovery of America. A Commemoration
      Address...." Univ. of Michigan, 1892.
777. Ecclesiastical Tradition: Its Origin and Early
      Growth: Its Place in the Churches, and Its Value.
      Standard Publishing Co., 1879.
778. "The Eclectic Institute: An Address...." Inland
      Pr., 1900.
779. Education in the State Constitutions. 1889?
780. "Eliza Ballon Garfield, Mother of President James A.
      Garfield. Addresses...." Leader Printing Co.,
      1888.
781. The Establishment of the First Southern Boundary of
      the United States. Govt. Print. Off., 1894.
782. "Foreign Influence upon Education in the United
      States." Govt. Print. Off., 1899.
783. Garfield - Hinsdale Letters. Univ. of Michigan Pr.,
      1893.
784. "A General Introduction to the Courses in the
      Science and the Art of Teaching." Univ. of
      Michigan, 1893.
785. The Genuineness and Authenticity of the Gospels.
      Bosworth, Chase & Hall, 1872.
786. "The Government of the United States." In History
      and Civil Government of Louisiana, pp. 283-379. By
      John Rose Ficklen. Chicago, 1901.
787. "Health in the Public Schools; A Paper...."
      Cleveland? 187-.
788. "Hiram College." Cleveland? 1876.
789. "Hiram College and Her Pupils. An Address...."
      Hiram? Ohio, 1877.
790. The History of a Great Mind: A Survey of the
      Education and Opinions of John Stuart Mill.
      Bosworth, Chase & Hall, 1874.
791. "The History of Popular Education on the Western
      Reserve. An Address...." 1896?
792. A History of the Disciples in Hiram, Partage County,
      Ohio. Robison, Savage & Co., 1876.
793. History of the University of Michigan. Univ. of
      Michigan, 1906.
794. Horace Mann and the Common School Revival in the
      United States. Scribner's, 1898.
795. How To Study and Teach History. Appleton, 1894.
796. "In Memoriam: John Wesley Lanphear; His Life and
      Character." Cleveland Printing & Publishing, 1888.
797. "In Memoriam. Mrs. R. N. Woods." Ann Arbor, 1892.
798. Jesus as a Teacher and the Making of the New
      Testament. Christian Publishing Co., 1895.
799. The Jewish-Christian Church. Standard Publishing
      Co., 1878.
800. "The Life and Character of James A. Garfield." New
      York? 1880.
801. "The Life, Character and Public Services of Gen.
      James A. Garfield. An Address...." Cleveland, 1880?

802. Memoir of Louisa Hinsdale: A Brother's Tribute."
      Robison, Savage & Co., 1877.
803. "Memorial Address: The Life, Work and Character of
      Robert R. Sloan, Delivered to the Ohio Christian
      Missionary Society...1878."
804. "Objects To Be Sought in Teaching English Grammar."
      Ann Arbor? 18--.
805. Occasional Addresses and Papers. Savage, 1878.
806. The Old Northwest: With a View of the Thirteen
      Colonies as Constituted by the Royal Charters.
      MacCoun, 1888.
807. "The Ordinance of 1787." Educational Monthly
      Printers, 1887.
808. Our Common-School Education. Robison, Savage & Co.,
      1877.
809. Our Common Schools: A Fuller Statement. Cobb,
      Andrews & Co., 1878.
810. "Pedagogical Chairs in Colleges and Universities."
      Ann Arbor, 1889.
811. President Garfield and Education. Osgood, 1882.
812. "President Hayes' Southern Policy. An Address...."
      1877?
813. "President James Abram Garfield." 1881?
814. The Republican Textbook for the Campaign of 1880.
      Appleton, 1880.
815. Schools and Studies. Osgood, 1884.
816. "The Science and the Art of Teaching." 1896?
817. "The Science of Education...Paper Read before the
      Cleveland Pedagogical Society, February 16, 1886."
      N.d.
818. "Some Sociological Factors in Rural Education in the
      United States." 1896.
819. Studies in Education: Science. Art. History.
      Werner School Book Co., 1896.
820. "Teachers Professional Book List." An Arbor, 1894.
821. Teaching the Language-Arts: Speech. Reading.
      Composition. Appleton, 1896.
822. "The Theoretical and Critical and the Practical
      Courses in Teaching Given in the University of
      Michigan." Register Publishing Co., n.d.
823. Topics in the Educational History of the United
      States. Inland Pr., 18--. (compiler).
824. Training for Citizenship: Suggestions on Teaching
      Civics. Werner School Book Co., 1897.
825. The Training of Teachers. Lyon, 1899.
826. The Works of James Abram Garfield. Osgood, 1882-83.
      (editor).
827. "The Western Literary Institute and College of
      Professional Teachers." Govt. Print. Off., 1900.
828. "Zeb and Arabella Rudolph, a Memorial." N.d.

Hohman, John Terrill.
    College administrator.

829.   "A Comparison of Activists and Four Other Types of
        Undergraduate Campus Group Leaders." Ed.D. diss.,
        George Washington Univ., 1976.

Hopwood, Josephus, 1843-1935.
    Pastor; college president; editor of <u>Pilot</u>.
    830.   <u>A Journey through the Years.</u> Bethany, 1932. (co-
            author).

Hoyle, John R.
    Professor of educational administration.
    831.   "Problem Attack Behavior and Its Relationship to the
            Sex, Prior Teaching Experience, and College
            Preparation of Selected Elementary School
            Principals." Ph.D. diss., Texas A & M Univ., 1967.

Hunter, Jairy Cornelius, 1942-.
    College administrator.
    832.   "A Comparison of the Academic Achievement of
            Sophomores Living in University Residence Halls with
            That of Sophomores Living Off-Campus in Selected
            State Universities in North Carolina." Ph.D. diss.,
            Duke Univ., 1977.

Hust, Mildred Hudgins, 1927-.
    College administrator.
    833.   "The Positions, Roles and Perceptions of Black
            Elected Public School Board Members in Mississippi."
            Ph.D. diss., North Texas State Univ., 1977.

James, Jo Ann, 1918-.
    Professor of education.
    834.   "The National Sorority: Its Administrative
            Relationships and the Scope of Its Activities on the
            Contemporary College and University Campus." Ph.D.
            diss., Syracuse Univ., 1959.

James, William Dale, 1939-.
    Professor of education and psychology.
    835.   "The Influence of Parental Involvement in Classroom
            Activities on the Questioning Behavior of the
            Parent." Ed.D. diss., Oklahoma State Univ., 1976.

Jerry, Robert Howard, 1923-.
    Professor of education.
    836.   "The Duties of a Superintendent and the Allocation
            of Professional Time by Public School
            Superintendents in Indiana." Ed.D. diss., Indiana
            Univ., 1963.
    837.   <u>Legal Rights and Responsibilities of Indiana
            Teachers.</u> 4th ed. Interstate Printers & Publishers,
            1980. (co-author).

Jones, Richard Bruce, 1941-.
  College administrator.
    838.   "Higher Learning for America: A Comparison of
            Abraham Flexner and Robert Maynard Hutchins and
            Their Views on Higher Education." Ph.D. diss.,
            Saint Louis Univ., 1978.

Kellogg, Donald Homer, 1936-.
  Professor of education.
    839.   Critters and Concepts: A Teaching Guide to Oklahoma
            Wildlife for Grades 4-7. Oklahoma Dept. of Wildlife
            Conservation, 1979?
    840.   Environmental and Conservation Instructional
            Activities. Oklahoma Dept. of Education, 1977. (co-
            author).
    841.   "An Investigation of the Effect of the Science
            Curriculum Improvement Study's First Year Unit,
            Material Objects, on Gains in Reading Readiness."
            Ph.D. diss., Univ. of Oklahoma, 1971.

Kelly, William W.
  College president.
    842.   "Transylvania University, Pioneering a Third
            Century." Newcomen Soc. in North America, 1981.

Kimball, Jack Earle, 1932-.
  College administrator.
    843.   "A Proposed Graduate Program of Studies for Foreign
            Student Advisers." Ph.D. diss., Florida State
            Univ., 1964.

Kinoshita, Waunita.
  Missionary nurse; teacher.
    844.   Tanoshii Gakushu - Learning with Enjoyment:
            Activities about Japan for Elementary Students.
            Center for Asian Studies, 1978. (co-author).

Kirkpatrick, Forrest Hunter, 1906-.
  College administrator.
    845.   "The Church College of the Future." Bethany? W.Va.,
            1935?
    846.   Helping Students Find Employment. American Council
            on Education, 1949.
    847.   Progress in Personnel Research. American Management
            Assoc., 1944. (co-author).

Koelling, Charles Houston, 1926-.
  Professor of education.
    848.   Pilot Training Project for Personnel Participating
            in Pilot State Dissemination Programs. Univ. of
            Missouri, 1972.

849.   "The Role of Secretaries to Superintendents in
        Selected Missouri Schools." Ph.D. diss., Univ. of
        Missouri, 1959.

Krubeck, Floyd Earl, 1917-.
    College administrator.
    850.   "Relation of Units Taken and Marks Earned in High
            School Subjects to Achievement in the Engineering
            College." Ph.D. diss., Univ. of Missouri, 1954.

Lafferty, Harry Montgomery, 1911-.
    Professor of educational administration; college
    administrator.
    851.   Sense and Nonsense in Education. Macmillan, 1947.

Lagrone, Herbert F.
    Professor of education.
    852.   "The Availability for Teaching of Noncertified
            College Graduates." Ed.D. diss., Univ. of Texas,
            1959.
    853.   A Proposal for the Revision of the Pre-Service
            Professional Component of a Program of Teacher
            Education. American Assoc. of Colleges for Teacher
            Education, 1964.

Lair, George Scott, 1937-.
    Professor of education.
    854.   "A Study of the Situational Dynamics Influencing
            Client-Centered Counseling in a High School." Ph.D.
            diss., Univ. of Wisconsin, 1963.

Lambert, Joanne Adam, 1934-.
    College administrator.
    855.   "Forecasting Trends of the Adult Learner in Higher
            Education." Ph.D. diss., Univ. of Oklahoma, 1983.

Langston, Ira W.
    College president.
    856.   A Study of Special Support Programs at the Chicago
            Circle Campus of the University of Illinois. Univ.
            of Illinois, 1977.

Lawrence, Sue C.
    Professor of physics.
    857.   "Forecasting Enrollments in a Virginia Community
            College." Ph.D. diss., College of William and Mary,
            1980.

Lewis, Elmer Clifford.
    858.   "A History of Secondary and Higher Education in
            Negro Schools Related to the Disciples of Christ."
            Ph.D. diss., Univ. of Pittsburgh, 1957.

Long, John Cornelius.
    859.   "The Disciples of Christ and Negro Education."
            Ed.D. diss., Univ. of Southern California, 1960.

Luy, Jack Andrew.
    College administrator.
    860.   "Backgrounds, Occupational Aspirations and Attitudes
            of Unemployed Youth in a MDTA Program in St. Louis,
            Missouri." Ed.D. diss., Univ. of Missouri, 1964.
    861.   Wood and Wood Products. Merrill, 1975. (co-author).

McCord, Ivalee Hedge.
    Professor of family and child development.
    862.   "Interparent Similarity in Patterns of Childrearing
            and Its Relation to Some Dimensions of Family
            Structure." Ph.D. diss., Purdue Univ., 1964.

McGee, Howell Walton.
    Professor of education.
    863.   "Guidance Needs of the Adult Extension Student of
            the University of Oklahoma." Ed.D. diss., Univ. of
            Oklahoma, 1960.

McGehee, Larry Thomas.
    Professor of religion; college administrator.
    864.   "Changing Conceptions of American Higher Education,
            1800-1860: Ideas of Five Frontier Presidents on
            Transplanting and Transforming Collegiate
            Education." Ph.D. diss., Yale Univ., 1969.
    865.   The Work of the University in the United States.
            Christian Faith and Higher Education Institute,
            1964. (co-editor).

McGough, Charles Wayne, 1942-.
    Professor of art.
    866.   "Perceptions of Roles and Responsibilities of
            Selected Teachers, Administrators, and Law
            Enforcement Officers Collaborating To Reduce Student
            Absenteeism in Selected Schools of Dallas County,
            Texas." Ed.D. diss., East Texas State Univ., 1982.

McKenney, William Andrew, 1923-.
    Professor of education.
    867.   "The Certification of High School Teachers of the
            Academic Subjects." Ph.D. diss., Florida State
            Univ., 1960.

McLain, Raymond Francis, 1905-.
    Professor of history.
    868.   What Is a Christian College? Assoc. of American
            Colleges, 1952?

Malehorn, Harold Arthur, 1930- .
    Professor of early childhood education.
    869.   Complete Book of Illustrated Learning Aids, Games &
           Activities for the Early Childhood Teacher. Parker,
           1982.
    870.   Elementary Teacher's Classroom Management Handbook.
           Parker, 1984.
    871.   Encyclopedia of Activities for Teaching Grades K-3.
           Parker, 1975.
    872.   K-3 Teacher's Classroom Almanac: Treasury of
           Learning Activities and Games. Parker, 1981.
    873.   Open To Change: Options for Teaching Self-Directed
           Learners. Goodyear, 1978.
    874.   Over 200 Ways to Improve Your Sunday School.
           Concordia, 1982.
    875.   "Some Effects of Specific Visual Training on the
           Perceptual Development of Kindergarten Children."
           Ph.D. diss., Northwestern Univ., 1970.

Markus, Franklin William, 1935- .
    Professor of education.
    876.   "Construction and Utilization of a Model to Identify
           and Predict High-School Drop-Outs." Ph.D. diss.,
           Northwestern Univ., 1964.

Martin, Randel Odell, 1927- .
    Missionary to Congo.
    877.   "The Relationship between Library Resources and
           Indicators of Institutional Quality." Ed.D. diss.,
           Univ. of Kentucky, 1981.

Martin, Warren Bryan.
    College president.
    878.   Alternative Forms of Higher Education. California
           Legislature, 1972.
    879.   A College of Character. American Council on
           Education, 1982.
    880.   Conformity: Standards and Change in Higher
           Education. Jossey-Bass, 1969.
    881.   Inventory of Current Research on Higher Education,
           1968. McGraw-Hill, 1968. (co-author).
    882.   New Perspectives on Teaching and Learning. Jossey-
           Bass, 1981. (editor).
    883.   Redefining Service, Research, and Teaching. Jossey-
           Bass, 1977. (editor).

Mees, John Paul, 1940- .
    College administrator.
    884.   "An Appraisal of Selected Aspects of the Master's
           Degree in Secondary Education in the School of
           Education, Indiana University." Ed.D. diss.,
           Indiana Univ., 1968.

Miller, James Blair, 1916-.
    Professor of education.
    885.   <u>Our Church's Story: Teachers Edition.</u> Christian
           Bd. of Publication, 1961.
    886.   "Patterns of Disagreement Concerning Religion in
           Relation to Public Education in the United States."
           Ed.D. diss., Indiana Univ., 1955.
    887.   <u>Teacher's Book: Year Six, Fall.</u> Judson, 1952.

Miller, Merl Eldon, 1936-.
    Animal scientist.
    888.   "Effectiveness of the 4-H Life Skills Approach to
           Leadership Development." Ed.D. diss., Oklahoma
           State Univ., 1981.

Miller, William Lee.
    Church official; educator.
    889.   <u>The American Round Table: The Common Good.</u>
           Advertising Council, 1962. (editor).
    890.   <u>Education and Some American Temptations.</u> Woodrow
           Wilson Foundation, 1959.
    891.   <u>The Fifteenth Ward and the Great Society: An</u>
           <u>Encounter with a Modern City.</u> Houghton, 1966.
    892.   <u>Lincoln's Second Inaugural: A Study in Political</u>
           <u>Ethics.</u> Poynter Center, Indiana Univ., 1980.
    893.   <u>Of Thee, Nevertheless, I Sing: An Essay on American</u>
           <u>Political Values.</u> Harcourt, 1975.
    894.   <u>Piety along the Potomac: Notes on Politics and</u>
           <u>Morals in the Fifties.</u> Houghton, 1964.
    895.   <u>The Protestant and Politics.</u> Westminster, 1958.
    896.   <u>Religion and the Free Society.</u> Fund for the
           Republic, 1958.
    897.   <u>Welfare and Values in America: A Review of Attitudes</u>
           <u>toward Welfare and Welfare Policies in the Light of</u>
           <u>American History and Culture.</u> Duke Univ., 1977.
    898.   <u>Yankee from Georgia: The Emergence of Jimmy Carter.</u>
           Times Books, 1978.

Mix, Clarence Rex.
    Professor of communications.
    899.   "Interpersonal Communication Patterns, Personal
           Values, and Predictive Accuracy." Ph.D. diss.,
           Univ. of Denver, 1972.
    900.   <u>Life and Death Issues: A Report of a Four-Year</u>
           <u>Exploration into the Value of Human Life.</u> Univ. of
           Texas, 1977.
    901.   <u>Toward Effective Teaching: Youth.</u> Warner, 1970.
           (co-author).

Morton, Raymond Clark, 1917-.
    Professor of education.
    902.   "Turnover and Training of Missouri Superintendents
           of Schools." Ph.D. diss., Univ. of Missouri, 1955.

Moudy, James M.
     College president.
     903.   "Education Without Magic." Texas Christian Univ.,
             1965.
     904.   _A Hope of Wisdom: Two Essays on Education._ Texas
             Christian Univ. Pr., 1973.

Mungello, David E., 1943-.
     Educator.
     905.   "China Mission Studies (1550-1800): Directory."
             Mungello, 1978. (editor).
     906.   _Leibniz and Confucianism, the Search for Accord._
             Univ. Pr. of Hawaii, 1977.

Murfin, Mark.
     Professor of education.
     907.   _Cross-Number Puzzles: Whole Numbers._ Science
             Research Assocs. (Canada), 1976.

Newby, Maybelle Reid, 1924-.
     Educator; missionary to Switzerland.
     908.   "Piaget's Theory of the Development of Concrete
             Logical Thinking." Ed.D. diss., Univ. of Tulsa,
             1972.

Nixon, Evelyn.
     College administrator.
     909.   "Employees on the Four-Day Workweek and Their Adult
             Education Participation." Ph.D. diss., Univ. of
             Michigan, 1977.

Paulin, Philip Edwin, 1924-.
     Professor of journalism.
     910.   "The Viability of Cable Television as a Community
             Education Delivery System in a Selected Market,
             Tulsa, Oklahoma." Ed.D. diss., Oklahoma State
             Univ., 1979.

Payne, Ronald Glenn, 1944-.
     Professor of communication.
     911.   "Effects of Rate-Controlled Speech, Methods of
             Testing, Sex and Time on Listening Comprehension."
             Ed.D. diss., Oklahoma State Univ., 1984.

Pebworth, Thomas Formalt.
     Professor of education.
     912.   "Perceptions of Recent Graduates about the
             Educational Program in a Selected Alabama School
             System." Ph.D. diss., Univ. of Alabama, 1973.

Peters, George Llewellyn.
     913.   _Dreams Come True._ Culver-Stockton College, 1941.

Petty, John Edward, 1931-.
    Professor of education; college administrator.
    914.   "Some Next Steps in the Development of a Statewide
            System of Kindergarten in Virginia." Ed.D. diss.,
            Univ. of Virginia, 1966.

Pierce, Linda Lou.
    Professor of communications; college administrator.
    915.   Sex Differences in Persuasion. Ohio State Univ.,
            1977.

Powell, William Ray, 1932-.
    Professor of education.
    916.   "A Comparative Evaluation of the Joplin Plan."
            Ed.D. diss., Indiana Univ., 1962.
    917.   Elementary Reading Instruction. Allyn & Bacon,
            1969. (co-editor).
    918.   "The Nature of Individual Differences." In
            Organizing for Individual Differences.
            International Reading Assoc., 1967.

Powers, Wanda C.
    Professor of education.
    919.   "Developmental Sentence Scoring as a Measure of
            Readability for First Grade Reading Textbooks."
            Ph.D. diss., Univ. of North Carolina at Greensboro,
            1975.

Preusz, Gerald Clyde, 1938-.
    College administrator.
    920.   "A Comparative Study of College-Bound and Non-
            College Bound Negroes." Ed.D. diss., Indiana Univ.,
            1970.

Price, Sharon.
    Professor of education.
    921.   "Effects of Selected Early Childhood Programs in
            Missouri on Certain Cognitive Kindergarten
            Achievement Outcomes." Ph.D. diss., Univ. of
            Missouri-Columbia, 1977.

Reeves, Floyd Wesley.
    922.   College Organization and Administration: A Report
            Based upon a Series of Surveys of Church Colleges.
            Bd. of Education, Disciples of Christ, 1929. (co-
            author).

Reisert, John E.
    College administrator.
    923.   The Principalship in Perspective. Indiana Univ.,
            1968. (editor).

924.   "A Study of Selected Teacher Characteristics of
        Elementary Teachers with Different Preparation
        Backgrounds." Ed.D. diss., Indiana Univ., 1965.

Reuling, Walter Swanson, 1933-.
    College administrator.
    925.   "Cultural Spoor as a Focus for Inquiry in the Social
            Studies." Ed.D. diss., Univ. of Massachusetts,
            1970.

Richardson, Robert Clayton.
    College administrator.
    926.   "An Analysis of Teacher Perceptions of the Role of
            District Curriculum Director in Two Selected
            Secondary Schools." Ph.D. diss., Univ. of Colorado,
            1966.

Riley, Nancy, 1947-.
    Professor of education.
    927.   "Attainment of Piagetian Cognitive Tasks as Related
            to Reading and Mathematics Achievement among Fourth
            and Fifth Grade Learning Disabled and Non-Learning
            Disabled Pupils." Ph.D. diss., Univ. of Missouri-
            Columbia, 1983.

Ritchey, Charles.
    928.   _Drake University, Through Seventy-Five Years, 1881-_
            _1956._ Drake Univ., 1956.

Ritter, Donald Earl, 1933-.
    Educator.
    929.   "The Effectiveness of Selected Multi-Media Workshops
            on Teacher Instructional Practices." Ed.D. diss.,
            Indiana Univ., 1971.

Rouse, Sue Thompson.
    Professor of education.
    930.   "Effects of a Training Program on the Productive
            Thinking of Educable Mental Retardates." Ed.D.
            diss., George Peabody College for Teachers, 1963.

Satterthwaite, Lester Lee, 1929-.
    Professor of communication.
    931.   _Graphics: Skills, Media, and Materials._
            Kendall/Hunt Publishing Co., 1972.
    932.   "An Investigation of Selected Cues for Implying
            Motion in Non-Motion Media." Ed.D. diss., Indiana
            Univ., 1965.

Savage, Dennis Ben, 1919-.
    College administrator.
    933.   _One Life To Spend._ Bethany, 1962.

Sherman, Charles.
  Professor of education.
  934.   "Differences in the Personal and Interpersonal
          Values of Negro and White College Freshmen." Ph.D.
          diss., Northern Illinois Univ.,1969.

Shirley, James Clifford, 1892-.
  College administrator.
  935.   The Redwoods of Coast and Sierra. Univ. of
          California Pr., 1936.

Shorrock, Hallam Carey, Jr., 1923-.
  Professor of education.
  936.   Is the Emergency Over? Korea Church World Service,
          1960.

Short, Edmund C.
  Professor of education.
  937.   Competence: Inquiries into Its Meaning and
          Acquisition in Educational Settings. Univ. Pr. of
          America, 1984. (editor).
  938.   Contemporary Thought on Public School Curriculum.
          Brown, 1968. (co-editor).
  939.   Papers of the Society for the Study of Curriculum
          History. Pennsylvania State Univ., 1981. (editor).
  940.   A Search for Valid Content for Curriculum Courses.
          Univ. of Toledo, 1970. (editor).

Shuster, Albert Henry.
  Professor of education.
  941.   The Emerging Elementary Curriculum. Merrill, 1963.
          (co-author).
  942.   Leadership in Elementary School Administration and
          Supervision. Houghton Mifflin, 1958.
  943.   The Principal and the Autonomous Elementary School.
          Merrill, 1973. (co-author).
  944.   "A Study of the Advantages and Disadvantages of the
          Collegiate Certificate in Virginia." Ed.D. diss.,
          Univ. of Virginia, 1955.
  945.   Social Science Education in the Elementary School.
          Merrill, 1971. (co-author).
  946.   The Young Citizen Observes the Law. Univ. Classics,
          1983. (co-author).

Smith, Wendell L.
  College administrator.
  947.   Collaboration in Lifelong Learning. American Assoc.
          for Adult and Continuing Education, 1983. (editor).

Snipes, Paul David, 1928-.
  Professor of mass communications.

948.   "Communication Behavior and Personal Adjustment
        among American and Foreign Students at Indiana
        University." Ed.D. diss., Indiana Univ., 1969.

Sosebee, Allen Louie, 1921-.
    College administrator.
    949.   "Four Year Follow-Up of Students in the Indiana
            University Reading Program, 1958." Ed.D. diss.,
            Indiana Univ., 1963.

Sotrines, Frank Anthony.
    College administrator.
    950.   "An Approach to Assessing Business Continuing
            Education Needs of Small Business Owner/Managers."
            Ph.D. diss., Kansas State Univ., 1984.

Spear, George E.
    Professor of education.
    951.   Adult Education Staff Development: Selected Issues,
            Alternatives, and Implications. Univ. of Missouri-
            Kansas City, 1976. (editor).
    952.   Lifelong Learning: Formal, Nonformal, Informal, and
            Self-Directed. Ohio State Univ., 1982. (co-author).
            (ERIC Doc.).
    953.   Urban Education: A Guide to Information Sources.
            Gale, 1978. (co-author).

Spence, John Allen, 1919-.
    Professor of education.
    954.   Conference Handbook. Univ. of Tennessee, 1958.
    955.   Opportunities for Professional Training in Adult
            Education Offered by Colleges and Universities in
            1952-1953. Ohio State Univ., n.d.
    956.   "A Study of the Need for the Extension and
            Improvement of the Adult Education Services of the
            Ohio State University." Ph.D. diss., Ohio State
            Univ., 1956.

Spencer, Thomas Morris, 1916-.
    College president.
    957.   The Legislative Process, Texas-Style. San Jacinto
            College Pr., 1981.
    958.   "Population Characteristics in the Elections To
            Establish San Jacinto College." Ph.D. diss., Univ.
            of Texas, 1964.

Spice, Byron L., 1925-.
    Missionary to Mexico.
    959.   Discipulos Americanos (Spanish American Disciples)
            Sixty-Five Years of Christian Churches Ministry to
            Spanish-Speaking Persons. United Christian
            Missionary Soc., 1964.

960.   Highlights of the NEA Retirement Issues Forum, 1979.
        National Education Assoc., 1980.
961.   Potential Termination of Social Security: Guidelines
        for Education Associations. National Education
        Assoc., 1979.

Stahr, Elvis J., 1916-.
    College president.
    962.   "Inaugural Address of Elvis J. Stahr, Jr., President
            of Indiana University." Bloomington, 1965?

Strickland, Benny Ray.
    Professor of education.
    963.   "Selected Tenets of Soren Kierkegaard's
            Philosophico-Religious View of Man Relative to
            Counseling Theory." Ed.D. diss., North Texas State
            Univ., 1964.

Stromberg, Frances Ireland, 1922-.
    Professor of education.
    964.   "Young Children's Responses to Difficulty." Ph.D.
            diss., Florida State Univ., 1963.

Swank, Theron Edwin, 1928-.
    Professor of audio-visual education.
    965.   "An Analysis of the Social Diffusion of an Audio-
            Visual Message through a Church Congregation."
            Ed.D. diss., Indiana Univ., 1961.

Tiller, Thomas Columbus, 1934-.
    College administrator.
    966.   "A Study at Lynchburg College of the Relationship
            Between Congruence and Non-Congruence of Student
            Needs with College Environmental Press and Selected
            Attitudes and Behaviors." Ph.D. diss., Florida
            State Univ., 1968.

Turner, Dean Edson, 1927-.
    Pastor; professor of philosophy of education.
    967.   The Autonomous Man: An Essay in Personal Identity
            and Integrity. Bethany, 1970.
    968.   Commitment to Care: An Integrated Philosophy of
            Science, Education and Religion. Devin-Adair, 1977.
    969.   The Einstein Myth. Devin-Adair, 1977.
    970.   The Ives Papers. Devin-Adair, 1977.
    971.   Krinkle Nose: A Prayer of Thanks. Devin-Adair,
            1977.
    972.   Lonely God, Lonely Man: A Study in the Relation of
            Loneliness to Personal Development. Philosophical
            Lib., 1960.

Turner, Geraldine Alice, 1929-.
    Professor of education.
    973.   "The Attitudes of White and Black Fifth-Grade Low
             and Middle Class Children toward Selected Individual
             Rights in the United States." Ed.D. diss., Ball
             State Univ., 1973.

Tyer, Harold Latham, 1914-.
    Professor of education.
    974.   "The Legal Status of Pupil Placement in the Public
             Schools of the United States." Ed.D. diss., Duke
             Univ., 1965.

Tyndall, Jesse Parker, 1925-.
    Professor of biology.
    975.   "The Teaching of Science in Elementary Schools by
             Recent Graduates of Atlantic Christian College as
             Related to Their Science Preparation." Ed.D. diss.,
             Univ. of Florida, 1956.

Wake, Orville Wentworth.
    College president.
    976.   "A History of Lynchburg College, 1903-1953." Ph.D.
             diss., Univ. of Virginia, 1957.

Wall, Sandy A.
    Professor of education.
    977.   <u>Information Manual for Theses and Dissertations.</u>
             Texas Christian Univ., 1967.
    978.   <u>Study One: Beliefs about Public Education.</u> Texas
             Christian Univ., 1962.

Walter, James Ellsworth, 1938-.
    Professor of education.
    979.   <u>Continuation of the Dissemination/Implementation of</u>
             <u>Individually Guided Education, 1974-1975.</u> Univ. of
             Wisconsin, 1976. (editor).
    980.   <u>Manual for Starting and Maintaining State IGE</u>
             <u>Networks.</u> Univ. of Wisconsin, 1984. (co-author).
    981.   <u>Models for Cooperative Relationships and Activities</u>
             <u>for Implementing IGE.</u> Univ. of Wisconsin, 1973.
             (co-editor).
    982.   <u>Principal Vacancies in St. Louis City and County--</u>
             <u>1983 to 1993.</u> Univ. of Missouri-St. Louis, 1983.
    983.   <u>The Relationship of Organizational Structure to</u>
             <u>Organizational Adaptiveness in Elementary Schools.</u>
             Univ. of Wisconsin, 1973.
    984.   <u>A Status Report on the Implementation of IGE, 1971-</u>
             <u>1974.</u> 2 vols. Univ. of Wisconsin, 1975. (co-author).

Warford, Malcolm L.
    See under THEOLOGY.

Weaver, Ben H.
    Professor of education.
    985.   The Student Exploiters. Phillips Univ. Pr., 1970.

Wetzler, Wilson F.
    College administrator.
    986.   Leadership in Elementary School Administration and
         Supervision. Houghton Mifflin, 1958. (co-author).

White, Ralph, 1921-.
    Professor of special education.
    987.   "Effects of Teacher Accurate Empathy, Non-Possessive
         Warmth, and Genuineness on Achievement of Mentally
         Retarded Students." Ed.D. diss., George Peabody
         College for Teachers, 1968.

Whitlock, Charles Douglas, 1943-.
    College administrator.
    988.   "An Analysis of Opinion about Public Higher
         Education in Kentucky." Ed.D. diss., Univ. of
         Kentucky, 1981.

Whitmer, Jean Elizabeth Abel.
    Professor of education.
    989.   "A Psycholinguistic Description of the Total Miscue
         Responses of Third Grade Linguistically Different
         Spanish Surnamed and Anglo Children." Ph.D. diss.,
         Univ. of Colorado at Boulder, 1978.

Whittier, Charles Taylor, 1912-.
    Professor of education.
    990.   The Conduct of Business Overseas: An Oklahoma
         Perspective. Univ. of Oklahoma, 1974. (co-editor).
    991.   "The Reorganization of Six Governmental Services in
         Lake County, Indiana." Ph.D. diss., Univ. of
         Chicago, 1948.
    992.   Teachers, Administrators and Collective Bargaining.
         Crowell, 1968. (co-author).

Williamson, Rick Paul, 1947-.
    Professor of communication.
    993.   "The Adoption of Satellite Program Delivery by
         Television Broadcasters." Ph.D. diss., West
         Virginia Univ., 1982.

Womack, Jan George, 1944-.
    College administrator.
    994.   "A Study of Motivator and Hygiene Factors of Adult
         Women Students in Nursing Programs." Ph.D. diss.,
         Univ. of Oklahoma, 1976.

Wood, Darrell Elroy, 1934-.
    Professor of education.

995.   "A Paradigm for the Study and Performance of
        Integrales and Hyperprism, Two Instrumental Works by
        Edgard Varese." D.A. diss., Ball State Univ., 1974.

Woolery, William Kirk.
  996.   The Story of Old Bethany from Her Founding Years
        through a Century of Trial and Triumph. Standard
        Publishing Co., 1941.

Zion, Carol Lee, 1930-.
  997.   "The Desegregation of a Public Junior College: A
        Case Study of Its Negro Faculty." Ph.D. diss.,
        Florida State Univ., 1964.

ENGINEERING/INDUSTRIAL ARTS/TECHNOLOGY

Akers, David J., Jr.
    Professor of engineering science.
  998.   Dewatering of Mine Drainage Sludge, Phase II. U.S.
        Govt. Print. Off., 1973.
  999.   Gob Pile Stabilization, Reclamation, and
        Utilization. Office of Coal Research, 1973. (co-
        author).
 1000.   The Rapid Analysis of Acid Mine Drainage. West
        Virginia Univ., 1976. (co-author).

Bagley, Ronald E., 1936-.
    Professor of practical arts.
 1001.   "A Study To Determine the Contributions of
        Industrial Arts to the Leisure Time Activities of
        the Graduates of Northeast Missouri State Teachers
        College." Ed.D. diss., Colorado State College,
        1965.

Bailey, Gerald Duane.
    Professor of industrial arts.
 1002.   "Foundry Technology: A Technological Research and
        Curriculum Analysis, with Implications for Junior
        High School Industrial Arts." Ed.D. diss., Univ. of
        Missouri, 1964.

Baker, William Ernest, 1929-.
    Professor of mechanical engineering.
 1003.   "Strain-Rate Effects on the Propagation of Torsional
        Plastic Waves in Thin-Walled Cylinders." Ph.D.
        diss., Univ. of Texas, 1966.

Blank, Leland T.
    Professor of industrial engineering.
 1004.   Engineering Economy. 2d. ed. McGraw, 1983. (co-
        author).

1005. Statistical Procedures for Engineering. Management. and Science. McGraw, 1980.

Blomgren, Roger Dean, 1921-.
    Professor of industrial arts.
    1006. "An Experimental Study To Determine the Relative Growth of a Selected Group of Industrial Arts Education Majors toward Gaining an Understanding of American Industry." Ph.D. diss., Univ. of Illinois, 1962.

Cliett, Charles B.
    Professor of aerospace engineering.
    1007. Aerodynamics of Rotors and Propellers. State College, 1972.

Cook, Billy Cy.
    Professor of engineering.
    1008. The Effects of Recreation Pool Size on Irrigation and Power Generation at Elephant Butte Reservoir. Texas Tech. Univ., 1974. (co-author).
    1009. Project Completion Report: Variation of Urban Runoff with Duration and Intensity of Storms. Texas Tech. Univ., 1971. (co-author).

Craft, Clyde O'Brien, 1936-.
    Professor of industrial education.
    1010. "Creativity in Engineering Graphics." Ph.D. diss., Texas A & M Univ., 1967.

Crist, Leroy, 1930-.
    Professor of industrial arts.
    1011. "Personality Variables of Industrial Arts Majors." Ph.D. diss., Colorado State College, 1961.

Ehlers, Glenn Leroy, 1943-.
    Professor of industrial arts.
    1012. "Professional Growth Activities and Needs of Practicing Ohio Industrial Arts Teachers." Ph.D. diss., Ohio State Univ., 1973.

Evans, Norman Allan.
    Professor of engineering.
    1013. Hydraulics of Flow in Small. Rough Channels. Colorado State Univ., 1961.
    1014. Inventory of Current Research at Colorado State University. Colorado State Univ., 1973.
    1015. "Osmotic Flow." Ph.D. diss., Colorado State Univ., 1963.
    1016. Water and Western Destiny. Colorado State Univ., 1969.
    1017. Water Measurement with U.S. Steel Irrigation Gates. Colorado State Univ., 1969.

1018. <u>Water Requirements of Crops.</u> American Soc. of Agricultural Engineers, 1962.

Garrison, George Walker, 1939-.
Professor of mechanical engineering.
1019. "Stability Analysis of a Linear Hall Current Ion Accelerator." Ph.D. diss., North Carolina State Univ. at Raleigh, 1966.

Harbaugh, James Forrest.
Professor of industrial education.
1020. "A Comparison of Career Maturity Attitudes of Industrial Arts Curriculum Project Students, Conventionally-Taught Industrial Arts Students and Non-Industrial Arts Students." Ed.D. diss., Texas A & M Univ., 1974.

Jones, Millard Lawrence, Jr., 1933-.
Professor of clinical engineering.
1021. "Thermodynamic Properties of Methane and Nitrogen at Low Temperatures and High Pressures." Ph.D. diss., Univ. of Michigan, 1961.

Keefer, Gary Bruce, 1952-.
Professor of civil engineering.
1022. "Utilization and Recycle of Acid Mine Drainage Neutralization Sludge." Ph.D. diss., West Virginia Univ., 1979.

Labadie, John W.
Professor of civil engineering.
1023. <u>Cost-Effective Design and Operation of Urban Stormwater Control Systems.</u> Colorado State Univ., 1984.
1024. <u>Metropolitan Water Intelligence Systems.</u> Colorado State Univ., 1974. (co-author).
1025. <u>A River Basin Network Model for Conjunctive Use of Surface and Groundwater.</u> Colorado State Univ., 1983. (co-author).
1026. <u>Synthesis and Calibration of a River Basin Water Management Mode.</u> Colorado Water Resources Research Institute., 197-.
1027. <u>Urban Stormwater Control Package for Automated Real-Time Systems.</u> Colorado State Univ., 1978.
1028. <u>Water Management Model for Front Range River Basins.</u> Colorado State Univ., 1979. (co-author).

Lutes, Loren Daniel.
Professor of civil engineering.
1029. "Stationary Random Response of Bilinear Hysteretic Systems." Ph.D. diss., California Institute of Technology, 1967.

Manchester, Harland Frank, 1898-.
    1030. <u>New World of Machines.</u> Armed Services, 1945.
    1031. <u>Trail Blazers of Technology: The Story of Nine
          Inventors.</u> Scribner, 1962.

Nedderman, Wendell Herman, 1921-.
    Professor of engineering; college president.
    1032. <u>Secondary Buckling in Hollow Rectangular Column
          Sections of Steel Plates.</u> Ames, Iowa, 1951. (co-
          author).

Oberlender, Garold D.
    College professor.
    1033. <u>Laboratory Manual for Construction Planning and
          Scheduling.</u> Oklahoma State Univ., 1981. (co-author).

Reed, Howard Odin, 1906-.
    Professor of education.
    1034. "Evaluation of Industrial Arts in Secondary Schools
          of Illinois." Ph.D. diss., Univ. of Illinois, 1948.
    1035. <u>General Shop Metal Work.</u> Bloomington, Ill., 1947.
          (co-author).

Schriever, Errol G.
    Professor of English and drafting.
    1036. <u>Electrical Drafting.</u> Prentice-Hall, 1984.

Talkington, Joe Ed, 1931-.
    Professor of industrial technology.
    1037. "An Analysis of Industrial Arts Objectives as
          Determined by Q-Techniques." Ph.D. diss., Colorado
          State College, 1962.

ENGLISH LANGUAGE AND LITERATURE
    Includes Journalism and Speech

Allen, James Lane, 1849-1925.
    Writer; professor of Latin and English.
    1038. <u>Aftermath.</u> Harper, 1895,
    1039. <u>The Alabaster Box.</u> Harper, 1893.
    1040. <u>The Blue-Grass Region of Kentucky.</u> Harper, 1892.
    1041. <u>The Bride of the Mistletoe.</u> Macmillan, 1909.
    1042. <u>A Cathedral Singer.</u> Century, 1916.
    1043. <u>Chimney Corner Graduates.</u> Home Correspondence
          School, 1900.
    1044. <u>The Choir Invisible.</u> Macmillan, 1897.
    1045. <u>Crypts of the Heart.</u> Macmillan, 1903.
    1046. <u>The Doctor's Christmas Eve.</u> Macmillan, 1910.
    1047. <u>The Emblems of Fidelity.</u> Doubleday, 1919.
    1048. <u>Flute and Violin.</u> Harper, 1891.
    1049. <u>The Heroine in Bronze.</u> Macmillan, 1912.
    1050. <u>Homesteads of the Blue-grass.</u> 1907.

    1051. <u>The Increasing Purpose.</u> Macmillan, 1900.
    1052. <u>John Gray.</u> Lippincott, 1893.
    1053. <u>A Kentucky Cardinal.</u> Harper, 1895.
    1054. <u>The Kentucky Warbler.</u> Doubleday, 1918.
    1055. <u>The Landmark.</u> Macmillan, 1925.
    1056. <u>The Last Christmas Tree.</u> Mosher, 1914.
    1057. <u>The Mettle of the Pasture.</u> Macmillan, 1903.
    1058. <u>The Reign of Law.</u> Macmillan, 1900.
    1059. <u>Sister Dolorosa and Posthumous Fame.</u> 1892.
    1060. <u>Summer in Arcady.</u> Macmillan, 1896.
    1061. <u>The Sword of Youth.</u> Century, 1915.
    1062. <u>Two Gentlemen of Kentucky.</u> Harper, 1899.

Aylesworth, Barton O., 1860-1933.
    Pastor; college president.
    1063. <u>"Thirteen."</u> Christian Publishing Co., 1892.
    1064. <u>Short Stories and Twelve Others from the Adirondacks</u>
           <u>and Elsewhere.</u> 1895.
    1065. <u>Song and Fable.</u> Kenyon, 1897.

Bailey, Dennis Lee, 1941-.
    Professor of communication arts.
    1066. "Rhetorical Genres in Early American Public Address,
           1652-1700." Ph.D. diss., Univ. of Oklahoma, 1971.

Bailey, Mabel Driscoll, 1904-.
    Professor of English and humanities.
    1067. "Maxwell Anderson: The Playwright as Prophet."
           Ph.D. diss., State Univ. of Iowa, 1955. Also pub. by
           Abelard Schuman, 1957.

Baird, John Edward, 1922-.
    Professor of speech.
    1068. <u>Communication for Business and the Professions.</u>
           Brown, 1980. (co-author).
    1069. <u>Communication: The Essence of Group Synergy.</u>
           Brown, 1977.
    1070. <u>Corinthians: Study Guide.</u> New Life Books, 1975.
    1071. <u>The Dynamics of Organizational Communication.</u>
           Harper, 1977.
    1072. <u>Effective Employment Interviewing.</u> Scott, Foresman,
           1982. (co-author).
    1073. "The Effects of Speech Summaries upon Audience
           Comprehension of Expository Speeches of Varying
           Quality and Complexity." Ph.D. diss., Indiana
           Univ., 1972.
    1074. <u>Funeral Meditations.</u> Abingdon, 1966. (co-author).
    1075. <u>Group Communication.</u> Brown, 1981. (co-author).
    1076. <u>A Guide to Conducting Meetings.</u> Abingdon, 1965.
    1077. <u>Matthew: Study Guide.</u> New Life Books, 1975.
    1078. <u>Preparing for Platform and Pulpit.</u> Abingdon, 1968.
    1079. <u>Quality Circles Facilitor's Manual.</u> Waveland, 1983.
           (co-author).

1080. <u>Quality Circles Leader's Manual.</u> Waveland, 1982.
1081. <u>Speaking for Results.</u> Harper, 1981.

Bartholomew, Barbara, 1941-.
  Professor of arts and humanities.
  1082. <u>The Cereal Box Adventures.</u> Chariot Books, 1981.
  1083. <u>Flight into the Unknown.</u> Chariot Books, 1982.
  1084. <u>The Great Gradepoint Mystery.</u> Macmillan, 1983.
  1085. <u>The Journal of Thomas Moore.</u> 4 vols. Associated
         Univ. Pr., 1983-1987. (co-editor).
  1086. <u>Something Special.</u> G. K. Hall, 1984.

Bedford, William Charles, 1910-.
  Professor of English.
  1087. "Elizabeth Sprague Coolidge. The Education of a
         Patron of Chamber Music: The Early Years." Ph.D.
         diss, Univ. of Missouri, 1964.

Bond, Reece Alexander.
  Professor of English.
  1088. "Whitman's Visual Imagination." Ph.D. diss., Univ.
         of Minnesota, 1971.

*Bro, Margueritte (Harmon), 1894-1977.
  Writer; editor; missionary.
  1089. <u>Al's Technique.</u> Eldridge Entertainment House, 1931.
  1090. <u>The Animal Friends of Peng-U.</u> Doubleday, 1965.
  1091. <u>Every Day a Prayer.</u> Willett, Clark & Co., 1943.
  1092. <u>How the Mouse Deer Became King.</u> Doubleday, 1966.
  1093. <u>In the One Spirit: The Autobiography of Harrie
         Vernette Rhodes as Told to Margueritte Harmon Bro.</u>
         Harper, 1951.
  1094. <u>Indonesia: Land of Challenge.</u> Harper, 1954.
  1095. <u>Invitation to the Theater.</u> Harper, 1951. (co-
         author).
  1096. <u>Let's Talk about You.</u> Doubleday, Doran & Co., 1945.
  1097. <u>More Than We Are.</u> Harper, 1948, 1965.
  1098. <u>Nothing So Strange: The Autobiography of Arthur
         Ford, in Collaboration with Margueritte Harmon Bro.</u>
         Psychic P., 1966.
  1099. <u>Sarah.</u> Doubleday, 1949.
  1100. <u>Stub, a College Romance.</u> Doubleday, 1952.
  1101. <u>Su-mei's Golden Year.</u> Doubleday, 1950.
  1102. <u>Three, and Domingo.</u> Doubleday, 1953.
  1103. <u>Thursday at Ten.</u> Willett, Clark & Co., 1942.
  1104. <u>Urban Scene.</u> Friendship Pr., 1938.
  1105. <u>Wheat Magic, a Course for Junior Boys and Girls on
         Rural Life around the World.</u> Friendship Pr., 1931.
         (co-author).
  1106. <u>When Children Ask.</u> Willett, Clark & Co., 1940.

Brothers, Barbara.
  Professor of English.

1107.   "Henry Green's Comic Vision: A Study of Green's
        Novels." Ph.D. diss., Kent State Univ., 1973.

Brown, Ella Lees, 1926-.
    Professor of English.
    1108.   "The Uses of the Landscape: A Study in Eighteenth
            Century Poetry." Ph.D. diss., Washington Univ.,
            1972.

Carty, James W., Jr.
    Professor of communications.
    1109.   Advertising the Local Church. Augsburg, 1965.
    1110.   Communicating with God. Upper Room, 1964.
    1111.   Cuban Communications. Bethany College, 1978.
    1112.   An Educator's Guide for Preparing Articles for
            Periodicals. Bethany, W.Va., 1962.
    1113.   The Gresham Years. Bethany, W. Va., 1970.
    1114.   Nashville as a World Religious Center. Cullom &
            Ghertner Co., 1958.
    1115.   Religious Journalism on the African Continent.
            African Studies Assoc., 1975.
    1116.   Working with the Latin American Press. Algonquin,
            1966.

Cecil, Levi Moffitt.
    Professor of English.
    1117.   "Our Japanese Romance: The Myth of Japan in
            American, 1853-1905." Ph.D. diss., Vanderbilt
            Univ., 1952.

Challen, James.
    See under THEOLOGY.

Clark, Thomas Curtis, 1877-1954.
    Editor of Twentieth Century Quarterly; publisher; poet;
    composer.
    1118.   Abraham Lincoln: Thirty Poems. Flavel, 1934.
    1119.   A Child's Thought of God. Minton, Balch & Co.,
            1927. (co-compiler.)
    1120.   Christ in Poetry. Association Pr., 1952.
    1121.   Enduring Poems for Daily Needs. Sun Dial Pr., 1952.
            (editor).
    1122.   Friendly Town. 1915.
    1123.   God's Dreams. Willett, Clark & Co., 1943.
    1124.   The Golden Book of Immortality: A Treasury of
            Testimony. Association Pr., 1954. (co-compiler).
    1125.   The Golden Book of Religious Verse: The Golden Book
            of Faith. Garden City Publishing Co., 1937.
            (compiler).
    1126.   Home Roads and Far Horizons, Songs and Sonnets.
            Willett, Clark & Co., 1935.
    1127.   It Shall Not Be Again. R. R. Smith, 1931.
    1128.   Lincoln, and Others. Doran, 1923.

1129. Lincoln: Fifty Poems. Trovillion Private Pr., 1943.

1130. Love Off to the War, and Other Poems. J. T. White & Co., 1918.

1131. The Master of Men. Quotable Poems about Jesus. R. R. Smith, 1930. (compiler).

1132. The New Patriotism; Poems of World Brotherhood. Bobbs-Merrill, 1927. (compiler).

1133. One Hundred Poems of Immortality; An Anthology. Willett, Clark & Co., 1935. (compiler).

1134. One Hundred Poems of Peace; An Anthology. Willett, Clark & Co., 1934. (co-compiler).

1135. 1000 Quotable Poems; An Anthology of Modern Verse. Willett, Clark & Co., 1937. (co-compiler).

1136. Poems and Songs. 1909.

1137. Poems for Daily Needs; An Anthology. Round Table Pr., 1936. (editor).

1138. Poems for Life; Quotable Verse from the Seers and Singers of Yesterday and Today. Willett, Clark & Co., 1941. (compiler).

1139. Poems for Special Days and Occasions. R. R. Smith, 1930. (compiler).

1140. Poems for the Great Days. Abingdon-Cokesbury Pr., 1948. (co-compiler).

1141. Poems of Justice. Willett, Clark & Colby, 1929. (compiler).

1142. 300 Favorite Poems. Willett, Clark & Co., 1945. (compiler).

1143. Quotable Poems; An Anthology of Modern Religious Verse. 2 vols. Willett, Clark & Colby, 1928-1931. (compiler).

Cochran, Louis, 1899-.
Attorney; writer.

1144. Black Earth: A Novel. B. Humphries, 1937.

1145. Boss Man. Caxton Printers, 1939.

1146. Captives of the Word. Doubleday, 1969. (co-author).

1147. FBI Man: A Personal History. Duell, Sloan & Pearce, 1966.

1148. Flood Tides: A Novel. B. Humphries, 1931.

1149. The Fool of God: A Novel. Duell, Sloan & Pearce, 1958.

1150. Hallelujah, Mississippi. Duell, Sloan & Pearce, 1955.

1151. Raccoon John Smith: A Novel Based on the Life of the Famous Pioneer Kentucky Preacher. Duell, Slaon & Pearce, 1963.

1152. Row's End. Duell, Sloan & Pearce, 1954.

1153. Son of Haman. Caxton Printers, 1937.

1154. The Story of the Lowly Gnome: When the King's Daughter Came out of the Sea; How the Red Rose Came To Be Red. Dorrance, 1929.

Coombs, James Vincent, 1849-1920.
    College president; professor of literature and history.
    1155. <u>Campaigning for Christ.</u> 1897.
    1156. <u>The Christ of the Church. Sermons. Lectures and
          Illustrations.</u> Standard Publishing Co., 1916.
    1157. <u>Christian Evangelism.</u> Standard Publishing Co.,
          1908.
    1158. <u>English Pronunciation.</u> J. E. Sherrill, 1886.
    1159. <u>Religious Delusions: A Psychic Study.</u> Standard
          Publishing Co., 1904.
    1160. <u>School Management and Methods of Instruction.</u>
          Indianapolis, 1886.
    1161. <u>A Ten Week's Course in Elocution.</u> Hinds & Noble,
          1899. (co-author).

Cooper, Guy LeRoy, 1911-.
    Professor of English.
    1162. "Paul Hogan: American Synthesis." Ph.D. diss.,
          Univ. of Arkansas, 1971.

Croft, Blanton, 1933-.
    Professor of speech communication and theatre.
    1163. "Birch Bayh on Direct Election: A Rhetorical
          Analysis of Persuasive Speaking, 1966-70." Ph.D.
          diss., Purdue Univ., 1971.

Donley, Carol Cram, 1937-.
    Professor of English.
    1164. <u>Einstein as Myth and Muse.</u> Cambridge Univ. Pr.,
          1985. (co-author).
    1165. "Einstein's Influence on Modern Poetry." in <u>After
          Einstein</u>. Memphis State Univ. Pr., 1981.

Duns, Donald Frederick, 1936-.
    Professor of communications.
    1166. "A Study of the Relationship Between Dogmatism and
          Speech Behavior." Ph.D. diss., Northwestern Univ.,
          1961.
    1167. <u>A Guidebook to Public Speaking.</u> Allyn & Bacon,
          1964. (co-author).

Ellis, John William, 1839-1910.
    Attorney; pastor; college president; writer.
    1168. <u>Antigone of Sophocles.</u> 1879. (translator).
    1169. <u>The Life Mission.</u> C. E. Ware & Co., 1876.
    1170. <u>Song of Songs.</u> 1897.

Erisman, Fred Raymond, 1937-.
    Professor of English.
    1171. <u>Fifty Western Writers: A Bio-bibliographical
          Sourcebook.</u> Greenwood Pr., 1982 (co-editor).
    1172. <u>Frederick Remington.</u> Boise State Univ., 1975.

1173.   "There Was a Child Went Forth: A Study of St.
        Nicholas Magazine and Selected Children's Authors,
        1890-1915." Ph.D. diss., Univ. of Minnesota, 1966.

Flanagan, James M.
    Professor of English, speech and drama.
    1174.   What We Believe. Bethany, 1960. (editor).

Fowler, Elizabeth Thomas.
    1175.   "Annotated Edition of the Letters of Vachel Lindsay
            to Nellie Vieira." Ph.D. diss., Univ. of Tennessee,
            1968.

Fujii, Gertrude Sugioka.
    Professor of English.
    1176.   "The Veritism of Hamlin Garland." Ph.D. diss.,
            Univ. of Southern California, 1970.

Goff, Lewin A.
    Professor of drama.
    1177.   "The Popular Priced Melodrama in America, 1890 to
            1910 with Its Origins and Development to 1890."
            Ph.D. diss., Western Reserve Univ., 1948.

Goodwin, Donald Francis.
    Professor of English.
    1178.   "The Fiction of C. P. Snow." Ph.D. diss., Univ. of
            Iowa, 1966.

Goodwin, Marcia Melissa Bassett.
    Editor of Christian Monitor. Missionary Tidings.
    1179.   Autumn Leaves. Christian Publishing Co., 1880.
    1180.   Mary Holmes: Or. Pride and Repentance. Carroll,
            1870.
    1181.   Pride and Repentance. Carroll, 1871.
    1182.   Sammy Stone's Red Apples and Other Stories.
            Carroll, 1876.
    1183.   Willie Welch. and Other Temperance Tales. Carroll,
            1870.

Gorsuch, Arthur Bennette.
    Professor of English.
    1184.   "Individualized Reading in the High-School
            Literature Program." Ohio State Univ., 1937.

Graham, Lorenz B.
    Writer.
    1185.   Carolina Cracker. Houghton Mifflin, 1972.
    1186.   David He No Fear. Crowell, 1971.
    1187.   Detention Center. Houghton Mifflin, 1972.
    1188.   Directions. Houghton Mifflin, 1972.
    1189.   Every Man Heart Lay Down. Crowell, 1970.
    1190.   Firebird Books. Scholastic Book Services, 1970.

1191. <u>God Wash the World and Start Again.</u> Crowell, 1971.
1192. <u>Hongry Catch the Foolish Boy.</u> Crowell, 1973.
1193. <u>I. Momolu.</u> Crowell, 1966.
1194. <u>John Brown. A Cry for Freedom.</u> Crowell, 1980.
1195. <u>John Brown's Raid: A Picture History of the Attack on Harpers Ferry. Virginia.</u> Scholastic Book Services, 1972.
1196. <u>North Town.</u> Crowell, 1965.
1197. <u>Return to South Town.</u> Crowell, 1976.
1198. <u>A Road Down in the Sea.</u> Crowell, 1970.
1199. <u>Runaway.</u> Houghton Mifflin, 1972.
1200. <u>Song of the Boat.</u> Crowell, 1975.
1201. <u>South Town.</u> Follett Publishing Co., 1958.
1202. <u>Stadt im Su"den.</u> Union Verlag, 1962.
1203. <u>The Ten Commandments.</u> Gilbertson, 1956.
1204. <u>Whose Town?</u> Crowell, 1969.

Griggs, Harry Hubert, 1927-.
    Professor of journalism.
    1205. "Coverage of National Economic Conditions by Five Mass Circulation Daily Newspapers During Three Critical Months of the 1957-58 Recession." Ph.D. diss., Univ. of Iowa, 1962.

Grimes, Larry Edward, 1942-.
    Professor of English.
    1206. <u>The Religious Design of Hemingway's Early Fiction.</u> UMI Research Pr., 1985.

Hammack, Henry Edgar.
    Professor of theatre.
    1207. "A History of the Dallas Little Theatre, 1920-1943." Ph.D. diss., Tulane Univ., 1967.

Hane, Norman R., 1939-.
    Professor of English.
    1208. "Nature's Moralist in Wilderness and Society: A Study of James Fenimore Cooper's Fiction." Ph.D. diss., Univ. of Chicago, 1968.

Harris, Lester Lee.
    Professor of speech pathology.
    1209. "A Clinical Study of Nine Stuttering Children in Group Psychotherapy." Ph.D. diss., Univ. of Southern California, 1950.

Hawkes, Terence.
    Professor of English.
    1210. <u>Coleridge on Shakespeare.</u> Penguin, 1969. (editor).
    1211. <u>Linguistics and English Prosody.</u> Univ. of Buffalo, 1959. (co-author).
    1212. <u>Metaphor.</u> Methuen, 1972.
    1213. <u>Shakespeare's Talking Animals: Language and Drama</u>

in Society. Edward Arnold, 1973.
1214. Structuralism & Semiotics. Univ. of California Pr.,
       1977.
1215. That Shakespearian Rag: Essays on a Critical
       Process. Methuen, 1986.
1216. Twentieth Century Interpretations of Macbeth: A
       Collection of Critical Essays. Prentice-Hall, 1977.
       (editor).
1217. Writings on Shakespeare. Penguin, 1969. (editor).

Hayden, Donald E.
    Professor of English.
    1218. After Conflict, Quiet: A Study of Wordsworth's
           Poetry in Relation to His Life and Letters.
           Exposition, 1951.
    1219. Classics in Composition. Philosophical Library,
           1969. (compiler).
    1220. Classics in Linguistics. Philosophical Library,
           1967. (co-editor).
    1221. Classics in Semantics. Philosophical Library, 1965.
           (co-editor).
    1222. His Firm Estate. Univ. of Tulsa, 1967. (editor).
    1223. Introspection: The Artist Looks at Himself. Univ.
           of Tulsa, 1971.
    1224. Literary Studies: The Poetic Process. Univ. of
           Tulsa, 1978.
    1225. Wordsworth's Walking Tour of 1790. Univ. of Tulsa,
           1983.

Hazelrigg, Charles Tabb.
    Professor of English.
    1226. American Literary Pioneer: A Biographical Study of
           James A. Hillhouse. Bookman, 1953. (Ph.D. diss.,
           Yale Univ.)

Hedges, Thayne Alden, 1921-.
    Professor of communications.
    1227. "The Relationship between Speech Understandability
           and the Diadocho-Kinetic Rates of Certain Speech
           Musculatures among Individuals with Cerebral Palsy."
           Ph.D. diss., Ohio State Univ., 1955.

Heffernan, Miriam M.
    1228. "The Ideas and Methods of Vachel Lindsay." Ph.D.
           diss., New York Univ., 1949.

Hemby, James B., 1934-.
    College president.
    1229. "A Study of Irony in Paradise Lost." Ph.D. diss.,
           Texas Christian Univ., 1965.

Hensley, Carl Wayne, 1936-.
    Professor of communications.

1230.   "The Rhetorical Vision of the Disciples of Christ:
         A Rhetoric of American Millennialism." Ph.D. diss.,
         Univ. of Minnesota, 1972.

Hewitt, Ray Storla, 1912-.
    Professor of English.
    1231.   "Foreshadowing in Elizabethan Tragedy." Ph.D.
             diss., Univ. of California, 1951.
    1232.   1890-1965: A History of the First Christian Church
             of Corvallis (Oregon). Corvallis, 1965. (editor).

Highlander, James Lee, 1928-.
    Professor of theatre.
    1233.   "Daniel Frohman and the Lyceum Theatre." Ph.D.
             diss., Univ. of Illinois, 1960.

Hogan, Bernice Harris, 1929-.
    Writer.
    1234.   Abingdon Party Parade. Abingdon, 1954.
    1235.   Abingdon Shower Parade. Abingdon, 1957.
    1236.   The Church Is a Who. Bethany, 1979.
    1237.   Deborah. Abingdon, 1964.
    1238.   Fun Party Games. Revell, 1969.
    1239.   Grains of Sand. Abingdon, 1961.
    1240.   Listen for a Rainbow! Revell, 1965.
    1241.   More from Your Class Meetings. Abingdon, 1959.
    1242.   Now I Lay Me Down To Wonder. Abingdon, 1961.
    1243.   Party Planner. Revell, 1967.
    1244.   Pre-School Party Parade. Abindon, 1958.
    1245.   A Small Green Tree and a Square Brick Church.
             Abingdon, 1967.

Houser, David John, 1942-.
    Professor of English literature.
    1246.   "The Tradition of Honesty in Elizabethan and
             Jacobean Drama." Ph.D. diss., Univ. of Wisconsin,
             1970.

Howard, Guy, 1891-.
    Pastor; writer.
    1247.   Give Me Thy Vineyard: A Novel of the Ozarks.
             Zondervan , 1949.
    1248.   Walkin' Preacher of the Ozarks. Harper, 1944.
    1249.   Wings of Dawn. Zondervan, 1953.

Jones, Alexander Elvin, 1920-.
    Professor of English.
    1250.   Butler University: A Hoosier Tradition in
             Excellence. Newcomen Soc. in North America, 1968.
    1251.   Creative Exposition. Holt, 1957.
    1252.   Writing Good Prose: A Structural Approach to
             Writing Paragraphs and Themes. Scribner, 1961. (co-
             author).

Kelly, Emma Chenault, 1905-.
    Professor of English.
    1253. "Coordinating Symbolic Logic with Grammatical
          Discourse." Ed.D. diss., New York Univ., 1953.

Lanier, Dorothy Copeland, 1922-.
    Professor of humanities.
    1254. "Black Dialect: Selected Studies since 1865."
          Ed.D. diss., East Texas State Univ., 1974.

*Lindsay, Vachel, 1879-1931.
    Writer; poet.
    1255. <u>Adventures, Rhymes & Designs, With an Essay by</u>
          <u>Robert F. Sayre.</u> Eakins Pr., 1968.
    1256. <u>Adventures While Preaching the Gospel of Beauty.</u>
          Macmillan, 1916, c1914.
    1257. <u>The Art of the Moving Picture...Being the 1922</u>
          <u>Revision of the Book First Issued in 1915.</u>
          Liveright, 1970, c1922.
    1258. <u>Collected Poems.</u> Macmillan, 1925.
    1259. <u>The Congo Jive.</u> Boosey & Hawkes Music Pub., 1974.
    1260. <u>Letters of Vachel Lindsay.</u> B. Franklin, 1978.
    1261. <u>Poezje Wybrane. [Selected Works].</u> Ludowa
          Spoldzielnia Wydawnicza, 1977.
    1262. <u>Selected Poems.</u> Macmillan, 1963.
    1263. <u>Springfield Town is Butterfly Town, and Other Poems</u>
          <u>for Children.</u> Kent State Univ. Pr., 1969.

For works about him written by Disciple authors, see
    Fowler, Elizabeth Thomas,
    Hefferman, Miriam M.,
    Taylor, Marjorie Anne,
    Wolfe, Glenn Joseph, and
    Yarrou, Michael under ENGLISH section; and
    Gilliland, Marshall Allan under HISTORY section.

Lindsey, Victor Ewart.
    Professor of English.
    1264. "Satire in the Poetry of Percy Bysshe Shelley."
          Ph.D. diss., Univ. of Arkansas, 1982.

Livingston, James Thomas, 1931-.
    Professor of English.
    1265. <u>Caribbean Rhythms: The Emerging English Literature</u>
          <u>of the West Indies.</u> Washington Square Pr., 1974.
    1266. "The Problem of Affirmation in the Modern Short
          Novel." Ph.D. diss., Univ. of Chicago Divinity
          School, 1963.

McCormick, Judith Kay.
    Professor of writing.

1267. "Biography and the Pattern of Regeneration in the
        Late Romances of William Morris." Ph.D. diss.,
        Kansas City Univ., 1980.

MacDoniels, Joseph W.
    Professor of communications.
    1268. "Factors Related to the Level of Open Expression in
            Small Group Laboratory Learning Experiences." Ph.D.
            diss., Univ. of Kansas, 1972.

McGavran, Grace Winifred, 1896-.
    Writer for children.
    1269. <u>All through the Year: A Devotional Reader for Boys
            and Girls.</u> Bethany, 1958.
    1270. <u>And When You Pray. A Guide of Prayer for Children.</u>
            Pilgrim, 1941.
    1271. <u>Boy of the Congo Forest.</u> Bethany, 1961.
    1272. <u>Creating Friendly Attitudes through the Home.</u>
            Friendship, 1941.
    1273. <u>Far Round the World.</u> Friendship, 1939.
    1274. <u>Fig Tree Village.</u> Friendship, 1946.
    1275. <u>The Garden of Friends.</u> Friendship, 1938.
    1276. <u>The Golden Coin.</u> Friendship, 1963.
    1277. <u>I Learn of Jesus. A Manual for Teachers of Junior
            Highs in Vacation Church School....</u> Westminster,
            1955.
    1278. <u>I Use My Bible: A Manual for Teachers of Junior
            Highs in Vacation Church School....</u> Westminster,
            1953.
    1279. <u>Jewels the Giant Dropped: A Course on the
            Philippine Islands for Junior Boys and Girls.</u>
            Friendship, 1929.
    1280. <u>Joy and Gladness Bringing: A Play for Christmas.</u>
            Meigs, 1942.
    1281. <u>A Junior Teacher's Guide to Accompany Far Round the
            World.</u> Friendship, n.d.
    1282. <u>A Junior Teacher's Guide on Churches for New Times.</u>
            Friendship, 1961. (co-author).
    1283. <u>Learning How Children Worship.</u> Bethany, 1964.
    1284. <u>Lifting Today above Its Past: A Unit of Work for
            Intermediate Groups Studying the Church in Rural
            America.</u> Council of Women for Home Missions and
            Missionary Education Movement, 1937.
    1285. <u>Men Who Dared in Bible Times. Teacher's Book. A Co-
            operative Vacation School Text for Use with Junior
            Boys and Girls.</u> Bethany, 1961.
    1286. <u>Mpenge of the Congo.</u> Friendship, 1945.
    1287. <u>Ricardo's Search.</u> Friendship, 1956.
    1288. <u>The Shepherd Who Stayed Behind.</u> Baker, 1927.
    1289. <u>Star Child: A Play of India for Intermediate Girls.</u>
            Friendship, 1938.
    1290. <u>Stories of the Book of Books.</u> Friendship, 1947.

1291. Teacher's Book: Year Five, Summer. Judson, 1952.
(co-author).
1292. Telling the Good News. A Vacation Church School Text
(10 Sessions). Judson, 1956.
1293. They Live in Bible Lands. Friendship, 1950.
1294. The Thunder Egg. Friendship, 1961.
1295. We Gather Together. Friendship, 1941.
1296. Where the Carp Banners Fly. Friendship, 1949.
1297. Yakima Boy. Friendship, 1952.

MacKenzie, Christine Beckwith (Butchart).
Writer.
1298. Out at Home. Bethany, 1967.
1299. A Year Is Forever. Bethany, 1964.

Mann, Russell A.
Journalist.
1300. "Investigative Journalism in the Gilded Age." Ph.D.
diss., Southern Illinois Univ., 1977.

*Markham, Edwin, 1852-1940.
Educator; poet.
1301. Anthology of the World's Best Poems. Wise, 1948.
(compiler).
1302. Archibald Henderson: An Appreciation of the Man.
University Pr. (Sewanee, Tenn.), 1918.
1303. The Ballad of the Gallows Bird. Antioch Pr., 1967.
1304. The Book of American Poetry. Wise, 1934.
(compiler).
1305. The Book of Modern English Poetry, 1830-1934. Wise,
1934. (editor).
1306. The Book of Poetry. Wise, 1926. (compiler).
1307. The Burt-Markham Primer. Ginn & Co., 1907. (co-
author).
1308. California the Wonderful. Hearst's International
Library Co., 1914.
1309. Campbell Mecker. Vinal, 1925.
1310. Children in Bondage. Hearst's International Library
Co., 1914. (co-author).
1311. Concerning James Whitcomb Riley. Mayfield, 1949.
1312. Edwin Markham's The Man with the Hoe. Aurand Pr.,
1934.
1313. Foundation Stones of Success. 10 vols. Howard-
Severance Co., 1917. (editor).
1314. Lincoln and Other Poems. McClure, 1908, c1901.
1315. Lincoln: The Man of the People. 1906.
1316. The Man with the Hoe. Doxey's, 1899.
1317. The Man with the Hoe and Other Poems. Doubleday &
McClure Co., 1899.
1318. The Man With the Hoe: Written after Seeing Millet's
World-Famous Painting. Book Club of California,
1916.
1319. The Marvellous Year. Huebsch, 1909.

1320.   <u>New Poems: Eighty Songs at Eighty: The Fifth Book
         of Verse.</u> Doubleday, Doran, 1933, c1932.

Marshall, David Franklin, 1938-.
    Professor of English.
    1321. <u>Creative Ministries.</u> Pilgrim, 1968.
    1322. "Current Problems in the Generation of English
           Restrictive Relative Clauses." Ph.D. diss., New
           York Univ., 1975.
    1323. <u>Quadrant: Notes on Analytical Psychology.</u> C. G.
           Jury Foundation for Analytical Psychology, n.d.

Martin, Henry G.
    College administrator.
    1324. <u>Pickin' up the Porters.</u> The Author, 1983.
    1325. <u>Webb.</u> 2d. ed. The Author, 1978.

Miculka, Jean H.
    Professor of speech communication.
    1326. <u>Improving Oral English: For the Bi-lingual Spanish-
           Speaking Student.</u> Kendall/Hunt, 1973. (co-author).

Moore, Jerome Aaron, 1903-.
    College administrator.
    1327. "The Romancero in the Chronicle-Legend Plays of Lope
           de Vega." Ph.D. diss., Univ. of Pennsylvania, 1937.
    1328. <u>Texas Christian University: A Hundred Years of
           History.</u> Texas Christian Univ. Pr., 1974.

Muir, Kenneth Arthur.
    Professor of English literature.
    1329. <u>The Comedy of Manners.</u> Hutchinson, 1970.
    1330. <u>Elizabethan and Jacobean Prose. 1550-1620.</u> Penguin,
           1956.
    1331. <u>Elizabethan Lyrics: A Critical Anthology.</u> Harrap,
           1952. (editor).
    1332. <u>English Poetry. A Student's Anthology.</u> Oxford Univ.
           Pr., 1938. (compiler).
    1333. <u>Introduction to Elizabethan Literature.</u> Random
           House, 1967.
    1334. <u>John Keats. A Reassessment.</u> Liverpool Univ. Pr.,
           1958.
    1335. <u>John Milton.</u> Longmans, Green, 1955.
    1336. <u>Last Periods of Shakespeare. Racine. Ibsen.</u> Wayne
           State Univ. Pr., 1961.
    1337. <u>Life and Letters of Sir Thomas Wyatt.</u> Liverpool
           Univ. Pr., 1963.
    1338. <u>Liverpool English Texts and Studies.</u> Liverpool,
           1948-. (editor).
    1339. <u>The Nettle and the Flower and Other Poems.</u> Oxford
           Univ. Pr., 1933.
    1340. <u>A New Companion to Shakespeare Studies.</u> Cambridge
           Univ. Pr., 1971. (co-author).

1341. <u>Shakespeare as Collaborator.</u> Methuen, 1960.
1342. <u>Shakespeare: Hamlet.</u> Arnold, 1963.
1343. <u>Shakespeare Survey.</u> Cambridge Univ. Pr., 1970.
1344. <u>Shakespeare: The Comedies: A Collection of Critical Essays.</u> Prentice-Hall, 1965.
1345. <u>Shakespeare's Sources.</u> Methuen, 1957-.
1346. <u>Sir Philip Sidney.</u> Longmans, Green, 1960.
1347. <u>Sir Thomas Wyatt and His Circle.</u> Liverpool Univ. Pr., 1961. (editor).
1348. <u>Unpublished Poems [by] Thomas Wyatt and His Circle.</u> Liverpool Univ. Pr. (editor).
1349. <u>The Voyage to Illyria: A New Study of Shakespeare.</u> Methuen, 1937.
1350. <u>William Shakespeare: The Great Tragedies.</u> Longmans, Green, 1961.

Naff, Monza Lea, 1947-.
    Professor of English.
    1351. "The Woman as Object, Partner and Persona: Renaissance Conventions of Love in English Poetry of the Sixteenth and Seventeenth Centuries." Ph.D. diss., Univ. of Oregon, 1978.

Odom, Keith Conrad, 1931-.
    Professor of English.
    1352. "The Brontes and Romantic Views of Personality." Ph.D. diss., Univ. of Wisconsin, 1961.
    1353. <u>Henry Green.</u> Twayne, 1978.

Oldsey, Bernard Stanley, 1923-.
    Professor of English.
    1354. <u>The Art of William Golding.</u> Indiana Univ. Pr., 1968, c1965.
    1355. "Aspects of Combat in the Novel, 1900-1950." Ph.D. diss., Pennsylvania State Univ., 1955.
    1356. <u>British Novelists, 1930-1959.</u> 2 vols. Gale Research, 1983. (editor).
    1357. <u>Ernest Hemingway, The Papers of a Writer.</u> Garland, 1981. (editor).
    1358. <u>From Fact to Judgment.</u> Macmillan, 1957. (co-author).
    1359. <u>Hemingway's Hidden Craft: The Writing of A Farewell to Arms.</u> Pennsylvania State Univ. Pr., 1979.
    1360. <u>The Spanish Season.</u> Harcourt, 1970.
    1361. <u>Visions and Revisions in Modern American Literary Criticism.</u> Dutton, 1962. (co-editor).

Olumo (James Cunningham), 1936-.
    Poet.
    1362. <u>The Blue Narrator.</u> Third World Pr., 1974.
    1363. <u>Blues for Dreamers.</u> Free Black Pr., 1968.

1364. Brooks, _Jump Bad_; Brown, Lee and Ward, _To Gwen with Love._ [Anthology].
1365. Chapman, _New Black Voices._ [Anthology].

Overton, Patrick Miles.
    Writer.
    1366. _The Leaning Tree [Poems]._ Bethany, 1975.

Pendleton, Winston K.
    Writer; speaker.
    1367. _Aw, Stop Worryin'._ Bethany, 1966.
    1368. _Complete Speaker's Galaxy of Funny Stories, Jokes and Anecdotes._ Parker, 1979.
    1369. _505 Jokes You Can Tell._ Bethany, 1978.
    1370. _Handbook of Inspirational and Motivational Stories, Anecdotes, and Humor._ Parker, 1982.
    1371. _How To Make Money Speaking._ Pelican, 1977.
    1372. _How To Stop Worrying--Forever._ Pelican, 1975.
    1373. _How To Win Your Audience with Humor._ Essandess Special Edition, 1969.
    1374. _Pursuit of Happiness: A Study of the Beatitudes._ Bethany, 1963.
    1375. _Speaker's Handbook of Successful Openers and Closers._ Prentice-Hall, 1984.
    1376. _2121 Funny Stories and How To Tell Them._ Bethany, 1964.

Phillips, William Louis, 1921-.
    Professor of English.
    1377. _How Sherwood Anderson Wrote "Winesburg, Ohio."_ American Lit., 1951.
    1378. _The Imagery of Dreiser's Novels._ PMLA, 1963.
    1379. "Sherwood Anderson's 'Winesburg, Ohio.'" Ph.D. diss., Univ. of Chicago, 1949.

Pippin, Frank Johnson, 1906-.
    Pastor; poet.
    1380. _The Christmas Light and the Easter Hope. [Devotions]._ Crowell, 1959.
    1381. _In the Night His Song. [Devotions]._ Christopher, 1956.
    1382. _Only This Throne, and Other Poems._ Burton, 1949.
    1383. _The Roads We Travel._ Bethany, 1966.
    1384. _Thoughts in the Night._ Christopher, 1953.

Pruitt, Elaine.
    Professor of general studies.
    1385. _Herman Melville's Moby Dick._ Monarch, 1984.

Rall, Eilene M.
    Professor of English.
    1386. _Structures in Composition._ Scott, Foresman, 1970. (co-compiler).

Rice, Ward A.
    Professor of speech and homiletics..
    1387. "How To Read the Bible in Public." Eugene, Ore.,
        1962?

Ross, Elizabeth (Williams), 1852-1926.
    Poet.
    1388. Altar Songs. Powell & White, 1925.
    1389. The Golden Room: Some Characteristic Letters and
        Quotations of Elizabeth W. Ross. Powell & White,
        1927.
    1390. A Road of Remembrance. Powell & White, 1921.

Rouse, Margery T.
    Professor of English.
    1391. The Story of the Pewter Basin and Other Occasional
        Writings Collected in Southern Ohio and Northern
        Kentucky. T.I.S. Publishers, 1981. (co-editor).

Sajdak, Bruce Thomas, 1945-.
    Librarian.
    1392. "Silence on the Shakespearean Stage." University
        Microfilms, 1981.

Sessions, Will A. Jr.
    Writer.
    1393. Casual History of the First Christian Church,
        Owensboro, Kentucky. 1967?
    1394. Greater Men and Women of the Bible. Bethany, 1958.
    1395. Saints and Sinners from the Time of Christ till Now.
        Independence Boulevard Christian Church, 1949.
    1396. Week of the Cross. Bethany, 1960.

Slaughter, Eugene Edward, 1909-.
    Professor of English.
    1397. "Love and the Virtues and Vices in Chaucer." Ph.D.
        diss., Vanderbilt Univ., 1946.
    1398. Virtue According to Love - in Chaucer. Bookman,
        1972.

Smith, Rose Marie.
    Professor of communications and theatre.
    1399. "A Critical Study of the Literature of N. Scott
        Momaday as Intercultural Communication." Ph.D.
        diss., Univ. of Southern California, 1975.

Snyder, Karl E.
    Professor of English.
    1400. A Critical Edition of the Faire Maide of the
        Exchange, by Thomas Heywood. Garland, 1980.
        (editor).

Solt, Marilyn J., 1921-.
    Professor of English.
    1401. "The Newbery Award: A Survey of Fifty Years of
           Newbery Winners and Honor Books." Ph.D. diss.,
           Bowling Green State Univ., 1973.

Spear, Henry C.
    Poet.
    1402. "Biographical Sonnets on 'New Testament Women.'"
           Beaver Dam? Wisc., 195?
    1403. "Biographical Sonnets on the Twelve Disciples."
           Beaver Dam? Wisc., 196?
    1404. "Columbus." An Historical Comedy in Four Acts.
           Written by the English Classes of the Junior High
           School, Rosendale, Wisc. Supervised by Henry C.
           Spear. Rosendale, Wisc., 1920.
    1405. Sonnets for Living: Life-Time Devotions in Poetry.
           Badger Poetry House, 1966?
    1406. "Spear Points" [Humorous Couplets]. Beaver Dam?
           Wisc., 195?
    1407. "Ten Christmas Sonnets." Beaver Dam? Wisc., 195?
    1408. Wisconsin High School Poetry. Badger Poetry House,
           1961-.
    1409. Wisconsin History in Poetry. Badger Poetry House,
           1975. (editor).

Stewart, James Tate, 1923-.
    Professor of English.
    1410. "Elizabethan Psychology and the Poetry of Edmund
           Spenser." Ph.D. diss., Vanderbilt Univ., 1954.

Stewart, Paul Robert, 1922-.
    College administrator.
    1411. Keys to English Mastery. Econ. Co., 1970.
    1412. Keys to Good English. 3 vols. Econ. Co., 1970. (co-
           author).
    1413. The Prairie Schooner Story. Univ. of Nebraska,
           1955.

Taylor, Marjorie Anne.
    1414. "The Folk Imagination of Vachel Lindsay." Ph.D.
           diss., Wayne State Univ., 1976.

Thomason, Tommy G., 1949-.
    Professor of journalism.
    1415. "Freedom of the Student Press at Southern Baptist
           Colleges and Universities." Ed.D. diss., East Texas
           State Univ., 1974.

Turpin, Thomas Jerry.
    Professor of drama.
    1416. "The Cheyenne World View as Reflected in the Stories
           of Their Culture Heroes, Erect Horns and Sweet

Medicine." Ph.D. diss., Univ. of Southern
California, 1975.

Vincent, Mary Louise, 1916-.
    Professor of English.
    1417. "Lafcadio Hearn and Late Romanticism." 2 vols.
            Ph.D. diss., Univ. of Minnesota, 1967.

Walwik, Theodore Joseph, 1937-.
    College administrator.
    1418. A Research Manual for the Performance Course in
            Speech. Harper, 1967. (co-author).
    1419. "Speaking of American Socialists in Opposition to
            World War I." Ph.D. diss., Ohio State Univ., 1967.

Watson, Roy Alvin, 1938-.
    Professor of English.
    1420. "The Archetype of the Family in the Drama of
            Tennessee Williams." Ph.D. diss., Univ. of Tulsa,
            1973.

Weaver, Gustine Nancy (Courson), 1873-1942.
    1421. The Boydstun Family. Powell & White, 1927.
    1422. Canticles of a Minister's Wife from My House of Life
            - the Manse. Bethany, 1930.
    1423. The Cotton Doll Farm. Inc.: An Operetta. Powell &
            White, 1932.
    1424. The Gustine Compendium. Powell & White, 1929.
    1425. Hop-Run and Six Other Pageants. Powell & White,
            1927.
    1426. The House That a Jap Built. Reilly & Britton, 1909.
    1427. The Howard Lineage. Powell & White, 1929.
    1428. The Minister's Wife. Powell & White, 1928.
    1429. Our Guest. Bethany, 1928.
    1430. Santa's Cotton Doll Farm. Bethany, 1930.
    1431. "Towed In." A Compilation of Stories about Certain
            Guests in Our Homes for the Aged. Christian Bd. of
            Publication, 1930.
    1432. Welch and Allied Families. Powell & White, 1932.

Welshimer, Helen, 1901-.
    Writer; poet.
    1433. Candlelight. and Other Selected Poems. NEA Service,
            1934.
    1434. Girlhood Today. Standard, 1938.
    1435. Love without Music. Arcadia, 1940.
    1436. The Questions Girls Ask. Dutton, 1939.
    1437. Shining Rain. Dutton, 1943.
    1438. Singing Drums. Dutton, 1937.
    1439. Society Editor. Gramercy, 1938.
    1440. Souvenirs and Other Selected Poems. NEA Service,
            1933.

1441. <u>Twins: A Farce in One Act.</u> French, 1935.
1442. <u>Wings of Youth.</u> Arcadia, 1941.

Winsor, Jerry Lee.
    Professor of speech communication.
    1443. "A Rhetorical Analysis of George S. McGovern's
           Campaign for Reelection in 1974." Ph.D. diss.,
           Univ. of Nebraska-Lincoln, 1975.

Wolfe, Glenn Joseph.
    1444. "Vachel Lindsay: The Poet as Film Theorist." Ph.D.
           diss., Univ. of Iowa, 1964.

Wright, Harold Bell, 1872-1944.
    Pastor; writer.
    1445. <u>The Calling of Dan Mathews.</u> Burt, 1909.
    1446. <u>The Devil's Highway.</u> Appleton, 1932. (co-author).
    1447. <u>Exit.</u> Appleton, 1930.
    1448. <u>The Eyes of the World: A Novel.</u> Book Supply Co.,
           1914.
    1449. <u>God and the Groceryman.</u> Appleton, 1927.
    1450. <u>Helen of the Old House.</u> Appleton, 1921.
    1451. <u>Long Ago Told (Huh-kewah-kah) Legends of the Papago
           Indians.</u> Appleton, 1929.
    1452. <u>Ma Cinderella.</u> Harper, 1932.
    1453. <u>The Man Who Went Away.</u> Harper, 1942.
    1454. <u>The Mine with the Iron Door: A Romance.</u> Appleton,
           1923.
    1455. <u>The Re-creation of Brian Kent. A Novel.</u> Book Supply
           Co., 1919.
    1456. <u>The Shepherd of the Hills. A Novel.</u> Burt, 1907.
    1457. <u>A Son of His Father.</u> Appleton, 1925.
    1458. <u>The Printer of Udell's. A Story of the Middle West.</u>
           Burt, 1911.
    1459. <u>Their Yesterdays.</u> Burt, 1918.
    1460. <u>To My Sons.</u> Harper, 1934.
    1461. <u>The Uncrowned King.</u> Book Supply Co., 1910.
    1462. <u>When a Man's a Man. A Novel.</u> Book Supply Co., 1916.
    1463. <u>The Winning of Barbara Worth.</u> Book Supply Co.,
           1911.

Yatron, Michael.
    1464. "The Influences of Populism on Edgar Lee Masters,
           Vachel Lindsay and Carl Sandburg." Ph.D. diss.,
           Temple Univ., 1957.

Ziemer, Penny Benson.
    Professor of English.
    1465. "Humor and Faith in the Works of Thomas More."
           Ph.D. diss., Emory Univ., 1984.

FINE ARTS
    Includes Architecture, Art and Music

Bond, Leroy.
    Professor of art.
    1466.   "The Influence of Modern Abstract Painting on
            Advertising Art, 1930-1950." Oklahoma Baptist
            Univ., 1954.

Bryden, John Rennie, 1913-.
    Professor of music.
    1467.   Chant Index. Wayne State Univ., 1962.
    1468.   An Index of Gregorian Chant. Harvard Univ. Pr.,
            1969. (co-compiler).
    1469.   List of String Duos. Detroit, 1957.
    1470.   "The Motets of Orazio Benevoli." Ph.D. diss., Univ.
            of Michigan, 1951.

Castle, Conan Jennings, 1927-.
    Professor of music.
    1471.   "The Grand Motets of Andree Campra." 2 vols. Ph.D.
            diss., Univ. of Michigan, 1962.

Clark, Stephen Lee.
    Professor of music.
    1472.   "Death Perspectives: Fear of Death, Guilt and Hope,
            as Functions of Christian Faith." Ph.D. diss.,
            Rosemead Graduate School, 1978.

Ernst, F. Gene.
    Professor of architecture.
    1473.   Housing Facilities for Rural Elderly. Kansas State
            Univ., 1974. (co-author).

Evans, Benjamin H.
    Professor of architecture.
    1474.   "AIA Research Survey." American Institute of
            Architects, 1965.
    1475.   Architectural Programming. American Institute of
            Architects, 1969. (co-author).
    1476.   Daylight in Architecture. McGraw, 1982.
    1477.   Daylighting in Architecture. Architectural Record
            Books, 1981.
    1478.   "Lift-Shape Construction." A & M College of Texas,
            1962. (co-author).
    1479.   "Proceedings [Architect-Researcher's Conference]."
            American Institute of Architects, 1964.

Feierabend, John M.
    Professor of music.
    1480.   Music for Very Little People. Boosey & Hawkes,
            1986.

Fisher, Hoover Page, 1928-.
    Professor of music.

1481. "Music Teacher Preparation at Oklahoma State University." Ed.D. diss., Univ. of Oklahoma, 1969.

Fountain, Marcia Taylor.
Professor of music.
1482. "A Comprehensive Performance Project in Cello Literature with an Essay on Materials for Teaching Twentieth Century Styles to Young Cellists...." D.M.A. diss., Univ. of Iowa, 1971.

Garcia, William Burres.
Professor of music.
1483. "The Life and Choral Music of John Wesley Work (1901-1967)." Ph.D. diss., Univ. of Iowa, 1973.

Gatwood, Dwight D., Jr.
Professor of music.
1484. Techniques for Including Musical Examples in Theses and Dissertations. Nashville Research Publications, 1970.
1485. "Wallingcord Riegger: A Biography and Analysis of Selected Works." Ph.D. diss., George Peabody College for Teachers, 1970.

George, Zelma Watson, 1903-.
Sociologist.
1486. "A Guide to Negro Music. An Annotated Bibliography." Ed.D. diss., New York Univ., 1954.

Gibson, David Allen, 1928-.
Professor of music.
1487. "Peter Philips' Keyboard Music." Ph.D. diss., Boston Univ., 1972.

Hackleman, William Edward Michael, 1868-1927.
Musician; printer.
1488. American Church and Church School Hymnal. Hope, 1927. (editor).
1489. Brotherhood Hymns. Hackleman Music Co., 1911.
1490. Excell's Male Quartets and Choruses. Excell, 1925. (co-compiler).
1491. The Gospel Call: Revised and Enlarged. Part II. Christian Publishing Co., 1897.
1492. Hackleman's "Clover Leaf" Male Quartets. Standard, 1910.
1493. Hackleman's Male Quartets. Hackleman Music Co., 1901.
1494. Sing His Praise. Hackleman Music Co., n.d. (co-editor).

Hartenberger, Aurelia Winifred.
Professor of music.

1495. "Selected Aspects for the Historical, Psychological
       and Philosophical Principles of Instrumental Music
       Education in American Secondary Schools." Ed.D.
       diss., Washington Univ., 1981.

Hicks, John Martin.
    Professor of art.
    1496. "Personal Contact with Thirteen Aspects of
           Information Dissemination by Selected High School
           Art Teachers." Ed.D. diss., Indiana Univ., 1972.

Hoagland, Bruce D.
    Professor of music.
    1497. "A Study of Selected Motets of Stephano Felis."
           Ph.D. diss., Univ. of Missouri at Kansas City, 1967.

Jorgenson, Dale Alfred, 1926-.
    Professor of fine arts.
    1498. "A History of Theories of the Minor Triad." Ph.D.
           diss., Indiana Univ., 1957.
    1499. Christianity and Humanism . College Pr., 1983.

Kershner, Frederick Doyle.
    See under THEOLOGY.

McCoy, Wesley Lawrence, 1935-.
    Professor of music.
    1500. "A Comparison of Select Psychomotor Abilities of a
           Sample of Undergraduate Instrumental Music Majors
           and a Sample of Undergraduate Non-Music Majors."
           Ph.D. diss., Louisiana State Univ., 1970.

Maus, Cynthia Pearl.
    See under THEOLOGY.

Osterberg, Myron Levi, 1926-.
    Professor of music.
    1501. "Teaching Problems in High School Choral Directors
           in North and South Dakota." Ph.D. diss., Colorado
           State College, 1964.

Owen, George Earle.
    See under THEOLOGY.

Peterson, Larry.
    Professor of music.
    1502. "Messiaen and Rhythm: Theory and Practice." Ph.D.
           diss., Univ. of North Carolina, 1973.

Philips, Mary Kathryn, 1925-.
    Professor of music.

1503. "Recitative-Arioso: A Survey, with Emphasis on
       Contemporary Opera." Ph.D. diss., Univ. of
       California at Los Angeles, 1965.

Rhoads, William E.
    Professor of music.
    1504. Advanced Studies from the Works of Julius
           Weissenborn. Southern Music Co., 1973.
    1505. El Aguanieve = The Sleet: A Mexican Dance for
           Concert Band. Elkan-Vogel, 1976.
    1506. Baermann for the Alto and Bass Clarinet. Southern
           Music Co., 1963. (co-author).
    1507. Grand Dialogue: For Winds. T. Presser, 1974.
    1508. Latin Elegy for Symphonic Band. Southern Music Co.,
           1973.
    1509. March "Academe": A Processional. IRN Music Pub.,
           1984.
    1510. A Pleasantry for Woodwinds: From an Organ Work by
           Louis Verne: Setting for Woodwind Choir. Shawnee,
           1981.
    1511. Scherzo / C. M. Widor. [Arranged for Brass Quintet.]
           Southern Music Co., 1978.

Roller, Dale Alvin, 1930-.
    Professor of music.
    1512. "The Secular Choral Music of Jean Berger." Ph.D.
           diss., Univ. of Illinois at Urbana-Champaign, 1974.

Ross, Allan Anderson, 1939-.
    Professor of music.
    1513. "A Study of Hieremiae Prophetae Lamentationes of
           Orlando Di Lasso." D. Mus. diss., Indiana Univ.,
           1967.
    1514. Techniques for Beginning Conductors. Wadsworth,
           1976.

Selleck, John Hugh.
    Professor of music.
    1515. "Achieving a Structural Unity: A Discussion of the
           Formal Techniques Used in the Composition of
           Divisions, a Work for Large Chamber Orchestra."
           Ph.D. diss., Columbia Univ., 1976.

Staplin, Carl Bayard, 1934-.
    Professor of music.
    1516. Let Us Break Bread Together. A Folk Communion
           Service. Bethany, 1971.
    1517. "Stylistic Changes in the Chorale Preludes of J. S.
           Bach." Ph.D. diss., Washington Univ., 1966.

Stegall, R. Carroll.
    Professor of music.

1518. "The Tours Easter Play: A Critical Performing
       Edition." Ph.D. diss., Univ. of Iowa, 1974.

Taff, Merle E., 1919-.
    Professor of music.
    1519. "A Study of Vowel Modification and Register
           Transition in the Male Singing Voice." D. Mus.
           diss., Indiana Univ., 1964.

Thibodeaux, Carole.
    Professor of music.
    1520. "Performance Analysis: A System for Increasing in
           Piano Students an Awareness of Stylistic
           Interpretation as Applied to Selected Twentieth
           Century Piano Music." Ph.D. diss., Univ. of
           Oklahoma, 1976.

Tromblee, Maxell Ray, 1935-.
    Professor of music.
    1521. "An Investigation of the Effectiveness of Programmed
           Drill Training in Teaching Intonation Discrimination
           Skills." Ph.D. diss., Univ. of Illinois, 1973.

Uerkvitz, Thomas David, 1930-.
    Professor of music.
    1522. "The Development of a Course of Study for Beginning
           Students of Piano in Latin America." Ph.D. diss.,
           Univ. of Oklahoma, 1966.

Webster, Jesse A.
    Professor of music.
    1523. "The Discovery of Enrico Leboffe Immigrant American-
           Italian Composer." Ph.D. diss., Univ. of Oklahoma,
           1978.

Welch, Rosa Page.
    Singer; missionary to Nigeria.
    1524. "Rosa Page Welch Sings of God's World and 'His
           Wondrous Love.'" [Sound disc]. Major Recording
           Co., 1970?
    1525. "Rosa Page Welch Sings to the Glory of God." [Sound
           recording]. Rosa Page Welch, 1983

For works about her by Disciple authors, see
    Myers, Oma Lou under HISTORY section.

FORESTRY
    See AGRICULTURE.

HISTORY
    Includes Disciple History
    See also under Disciples - History in Subject Index.

Arnold, Charles Harvey, 1920- .
    Professor of religion and history; librarian.
    1526. God before You and behind You: The Hyde Park Union
           Church through a Century, 1874-1974. Hyde Park
           Union Church, 1974.
    1527. Near the Edge of Battle: A Short History of the
           Divinity School and the Chicago School of Theology,
           1866-1966. Univ. of Chicago, 1966.

Arps, Louisa W.
    1528. Faith on the Frontier: Religion in Colorado before
           August 1876. Colorado Council of Churches, 1976.
           (editor).

Atwood, Dee James.
    1529. "The Impact of World War I on the Agencies of the
           Disciples of Christ." Ph.D. diss., Vanderbilt
           Univ., 1978.

Ayer, Hugh M., 1924- .
    Professor of history.
    1530. "Hoosier Labor in the Second World War." Ph.D.
           diss., Indiana Univ., 1958.

Bailey, Fred Arthur.
    1531. "The Status of Women in the Disciples of Christ
           Movement, 1865-1900." Ph.D. diss., Univ. of
           Tennessee, 1979.

Barber, James Frederick.
    1532. "The Basis for a Theological Dialogue between the
           Contemporary Disciples of Christ and the Reformation
           Thinker John Calvin on the Subject of the Lord's
           Supper." D.Div. diss., Vanderbilt Divinity School,
           1971.

Baxter, William, 1820-1880.
    See under THEOLOGY.

Bennett, Rollo James.
    1533. "History of the Founding of Educational Institutions
           by the Disciples of Christ in Virginia and West
           Virginia." Ph.D. diss., Univ. of Pittsburgh, 1932.

Bennett, Thomas J., 1893-1970?
    1534. History of First Christian Church: 1876-1961. 1961.

Bennett, Weldon Bailey.
    1535. "The Concept of the Ministry in the Thought of
           Representative Men of the Disciples of Christ (1804-
           1906)." Ph.D. diss., Univ. of Southern California,
           1971.

*Bernard, Richard Marion, 1948-.
   Professor of history.
   1536. The Melting Pot and the Altar: Marital Assimilation
          in Early Twentieth Century Wisconsin. Univ. of
          Minnesota Pr., 1980.
   1537. The Poles in Oklahoma. Univ. of Oklahoma Pr., 1980.
   1538. Sunbelt Cities: Politics and Growth since World War
          II. Univ. of Texas Pr., 1983.

Billington, Monroe Lee, 1928-.
   Professor of history.
   1539. American Democracy on Trial. McCutchan, 1968. (co-
          compiler).
   1540. The American South: A Brief History. Scribner,
          1971.
   1541. Forging of a Nation. McCutchan, 1968. (co-editor).
   1542. The South: A Central Theme. Holt, 1969. (editor).
   1543. Southern Politics Since the Civil War. Krieger,
          1984.
   1544. "Thomas P. Gore: Oklahoma's Blind Senator." Ph.D.
          diss., Univ. of Kentucky, 1955. (Also pub. by Univ.
          of Kansas Pr., 1967).

Blair, Leon Borden, 1917-.
   Professor of history.
   1545. Essays on Radicalism in Contemporary America. Univ.
          of Texas Pr., 1972.
   1546. Western Window in the Arab World. Univ. of Texas
          Pr., 1970.

Boren, Carter E.
   1547. Religion on the Texas Frontier. Naylor, 1968.

Boyd, Maurice, 1921-.
   Professor of history.
   1548. American Civilization: An Introduction to the
          Social Sciences. Allyn & Bacon, 1964.
   1549. Cardinal Quiroga. Inquisitor General of Spain.
          Brown, 1954.
   1550. Contemporary America. Allyn & Bacon, 1968. (co-
          author).
   1551. "Don Gaspar de Quiroga: A Study of His
          Ecclesiastical and Inquisitorial Policies in Spain,
          1572-1574." Ph.D. diss.,
          Univ. of Michigan, 1951.
   1552. Eight Tarascan Legends. Gainesville, 1958.
   1553. Kiowa Voices. 2 vols. Texas Christian Univ. Pr.,
          1981-83.
   1554. "The Story of a Poetic Legacy." In The Lonely
          Hearth...Poems. by William Knox. Sage, 1966.
   1555. Tarascan Myths and Legends. Texas Christian Univ.
          Pr., 1969.

Braden, Gayle Anderson.
    1556. A History of the Christian Church, Maysville,
           Kentucky [1828-1948]. Official Board of the
           Maysville Christian Church, 1948. (co-author).

Breen, Quirinus, 1896-1975.
    Professor of history.
    1557. Christianity vs. Humanism. Eerdmans, 1968.
    1558. De Veris Principiis Philosophia. Fratelli Bocca,
           1956. (editor).
    1559. John Calvin: A Study in French Humanism. Eerdmans,
           1931.

Brewer, Thomas Bowman, 1932-.
    Professor of history.
    1560. "The Formative Period of 140 American Manufacturing
           Companies, 1789-1929." Ph.D. diss., Univ. of
           Pennsylvania, 1962.
    1561. "A History of the Department of History of the
           University of Texas, 1883-1951." M.A. thesis, Univ.
           of Texas, 1957.
    1562. The Robber Barons: Saints or Sinners? Holt, 1970.
           (editor).

Brown, Phyllis G.
    1563. A Century with Christian Women in Virginia.
           Christian Women's Fellowship, Christian Church
           (Disciples of Christ) in Virginia, 1975.

Brumback, Robert H.
    1564. History of the Church through the Ages, from the
           Apostolic Age, through the Apostasies, the Dark
           Ages, the Reformation and the Restoration. Mission
           Messenger, 1957.

Burlingame, Merrill Gildea, 1901-.
    Professor of history.
    1565. Big Sky Disciples: A History of the Christian
           Church (Disciples of Christ) in Montana. Christian
           Church in Montana, 1984. (co-author).
    1566. Gallatin Century of Progress. Artcraft Printers,
           1964?
    1567. A History: Montana State University, Bozeman,
           Montana. Montana State Univ., 1968.
    1568. A History of Montana. Lewis Historical Publishing
           Co., 1957.
    1569. John M. Bozeman, Montana Trailmaker. Gallatin
           County Herald, 1971.
    1570. The Military-Indian Frontier in Montana, 1860-1890.
           Iowa City, 1938.
    1571. The Montana Frontier. State Publishing Co., 1942.
    1572. Report Concerning Lands Ceded to the U. S. Garland,
           1974.

Cannon, John H., Jr.
1573. Where There Is Vision: A History of the Lamar
Avenue Church of Christ, 1869-1980. Lamar Avenue
Church of Christ, 1981.

Carpenter, Leewell Hunter.
1574. The Tall Sycamore of the Wabash: A Historical Novel
Based on the Life of Dr. L. L. Carpenter. Wabash,
Ind., 1971.

Cartwright, George Washington.
1575. "The Rhetorical Practice and Theory of Edgar DeWitt
Jones [Born 1876]. Ph.D. diss., Univ. of Illinois,
1951.

Castleberry, Ottis L.
1576. He Looked for a City [Lewis, John Thomas]. Cogdill,
1980.
1577. They Heard Him Gladly: A Critical Study of Benjamin
Franklin's Preaching. Old Paths, 1963.
1578. "A Study of the Nature and Sources of the
Effectiveness of the Preaching of Benjamin Franklin
[1812-78] in the Restoration Movement in America,
1840-1878." Ph.D. diss., Pennsylvania State Univ.,
1957.

Cauble, Commodore Wesley, 1874-1935.
Pastor; church official.
1579. Disciples of Christ in Indiana: Achievements of a
Century. Meigs Publishing Co., 1930.

Charles, Searle Franklin, 1923-.
College administrator.
1580. Balancing State and Local Control. Jossey-Bass,
1978.
1581. "Harry L. Hopkins: New Deal Administrator, 1933-
1938." Ph.D. diss., Univ. of Illinois, 1953.
1582. Minister of Relief: Harry Hopkins and the
Depression. Syracuse Univ. Pr., 1963.

Chrisman, James Riley, 1949-.
Professor of history.
1583. "The Rhetoric of the Presidential Campaign of 1948:
A Content Analysis of Selected Addresses of Harry S.
Truman and Thomas E. Dewey." Ph.D. diss., Oklahoma
State Univ., 1974.

Church, Samuel Harden, 1858-1943.
Historian.
1584. The American Verdict on the War: A Reply to the
Appeal to the Civilized World of 93 German
Professors. Norman, Remington Co., 1915.
1585. Beowulf: A Poem. Frederick A. Stokes Co., 1901.

1586. <u>The Danger of Peace Discussion.</u> 1916.
1587. <u>The Farmers and the Railroads.</u> Carnegie Institute Pr., 1923.
1588. <u>Flames of Faith.</u> Boni & Liveright, 1924.
1589. <u>Horatio Plodgers: A Story of To-Day.</u> W. B. Smith & Co., 1882.
1590. <u>Is There a Conspiracy Against Organized Labor?</u> New York, 1922.
1591. <u>John Marmaduke, A Romance of the English Invasion of Ireland in 1649.</u> G. P. Putnam's Sons, 1897.
1592. <u>The Liberal Party in America, Its Principles and Its Platform.</u> G. P. Putnam's Sons, 1931.
1593. <u>Oliver Cromwell, A History.</u> G. P. Putnam's Sons, 1894.
1594. <u>Penruddock of the White Lambs: A Tale of Holland, England and America.</u> F. A. Stokes Co., 1902.
1595. <u>Russian Persecution of the Jews.</u> Alliance Israelite Universelle,1903.
1596. <u>A Short History of Pittsburgh, 1758-1908.</u> DeVinne Pr., 1908.

Cochran, Bess (White).
1597. <u>Captives of the Word.</u> Doubleday, 1969. (co-author).
1598. <u>The First One Hundred Years: Being a More or Less Lighthearted Look at the History of the Nashville YMCA, 1875-1975.</u> Metropolitan Board of the YMCA, 1975.
1599. <u>Without Halos.</u> Bethany, 1947.

Collins, Johnnie Andrew.
1600. "Pacifism in the Churches of Christ, 1866-1945." Ph.D. diss., Middle Tennessee State Univ., 1984.

Cramblet, Wilbur Haverfield, 1892-1975.
Professor of mathematics; college president; publisher.
1601. <u>The Christian Church [Disciples of Christ] in West Virginia: A History of Its Cooperative Work.</u> Bethany, 1971.

Crandall, Joseph Raymond.
Pastor.
1602. "The Early History of the Disciples of Christ in Indiana." M. A. thesis, Univ. of Chicago, 1925.

*Cummins, D. Duane, 1935-.
Professor of history; church official.
1603. <u>The American Frontier.</u> Benziger, 1968. (co-author).
1604. <u>The American Revolution.</u> Benziger, 1968. (co-author).
1605. <u>Combat and Consensus: The 1940's and 1950's.</u> Glencoe Publishing Co., 1980. (co-author).
1606. <u>Contrasting Decades, the 1920's and 1930's.</u> Benziger, 1972. (co-author).

1607. The Disciples Colleges: A History. CBP Pr., 1987.
1608. An Enlisted Soldier's View of the Civil War: The
       Wartime Papers of Joseph Richardson Ward, Jr. Belle
       Publications, 1981. (co-editor).
1609. A Handbook for Today's Disciples in the Christian
       Church [Disciples of Christ]. Bethany, 1981.
1610. The Origins of the Civil War. Benziger, 1973,
       c1972. (co-author).
1611. The Search for Identity: Disciples of Christ--The
       Restructure Years (1960-1985). CBP Pr., 1987. (co-
       author).
1612. William Robinson Leigh, Western Artist. Univ. of
       Oklahoma Pr., 1980.

Dare, Philip Ned, 1938-.
     Historian; librarian.
     1613. "John A Bingham and Treaty Revision with Japan:
            1873-1885." Ph.D. diss., Univ. of Kentucky, 1975.

Darst, Henry Jackson.
     1614. Ante-Bellum Virginia Disciples: An Account of the
            Emergence and Early Development of the Disciples of
            Christ in Virginia [1825-70]. Christian Missionary
            Soc., 1959.

Davis, Donald Edward, 1936-.
     Professor of history.
     1615. "Levin's Theory of War." Ph.D. diss., Indiana
            Univ., 1969.

DeGroot, Alfred Thomas, 1903-.
     Professor of church history; pastor; college administrator.
     1616. Check List, Faith and Order Commission: Official,
            Numbered Publications, Series I, 1910-1948, Series
            II, 1948 to Date (1962). Geneva, 1963.
     1617. The Churches of Christ in Owen County, Indiana.
            1935.
     1618. Disciple Thought: A History. Texas Christian
            Univ., 1965.
     1619. The Disciples of Christ. Christian Bd. of
            Publication, 1948. (co-author).
     1620. Eighty Years in Iowa, by Benjamin H. Gavitt.
            Chicago, 1939. (editor).
     1621. The Grounds of Divisions Among the Disciples of
            Christ. Chicago, 1939.
     1622. An Index to the Doctrines, Persons, Events, etc., of
            the Faith and Order Commission, World Council of
            Churches, Given in the English Language Editions,
            Official, Numbered Publications, 1910-1948, and
            Check List, Faith and Order Commission, Official,
            Numbered Publications, Series I, 1910-1948, Series
            II, 1948-1970. World Council of Churches, 1970.

1623. The Literature of the Disciples of Christ. Hustler,
       1933. (co-compiler).
1624. The Nature of the Church. 1961.
1625. New Possibilities for Disciples and Independents.
       With a History of the Independents. Church of Christ
       Number Two. Bethany, 1963.
1626. The Restoration Principle. Bethany, 1960.

Dobkins, Betty Eakle.
    Professor of history.
    1627. The Spanish Element in Texas Water Law. Univ. of
           Texas Pr., 1959.

Doolen, Richard M.
    Historian; librarian.
    1628. "The Greenback Party in the Great Lakes Middlewest."
           Ph.D. diss., Univ. of Michigan, 1969.
    1629. Michigan's Polar Bears: The American Expedition to
           North Russia. 1918-1919. Univ. of Michigan, 1965.

Douglas, Crerar, 1944-.
    Professor of religion.
    1630. Autobiography of Augustus Hopkins Strong. Judson,
           1981. (editor).
    1631. "The Coherence of Andreas Bodenstein von Karlstadt's
           Early Evangelical Doctrine of the Lord's Supper,
           1521-1525." Ph.D. diss., Hartford Seminary
           Foundation, 1973.

Duke, James Oliver, 1946-.
    Professor of church history.
    1632. Horace Bushnell: On the Vitality of Biblical
           Language. Scholars Pr., 1984.
    1633. "The Prospectus for Theological Hermeneutics: Hegel
           versus Schleiermacher?" Ph.D. diss., Vanderbilt
           Univ., 1975.

Edmunds, Russell David, 1939-.
    Professor of history.
    1634. American Indian Leaders. Univ. of Nebraska Pr.,
           1980. (editor).
    1635. "A History of the Potawatomi Indians, 1615-1795."
           Ph.D. diss., Univ. of Oklahoma, 1972.
    1636. The Otoe-Missouria People. Indian Tribal Series,
           1976.
    1637. The Potawatomis. Keepers of the Fire. Univ. of
           Oklahoma Pr., 1978.

Erlewine, Walter William, 1892-1965.
    1638. History of the First Christian Church. Marion.
           Indiana. 1876-1964. Bainbridge Print., 1964 or 5.

*Evans, Madison, 1834-1866.
    College professor.
    1639. <u>Biographical Sketches of the Pioneer Preachers of</u>
          <u>Indiana.</u> J. Challen, 1862.

Evans, Mary Louis.
    1640. <u>Historical Sketch of the North Middletown Christian</u>
          <u>Church [Disciples of Christ]. North Middletown,</u>
          <u>Kentucky. 1833-1983: A Proud Heritage. A Promised</u>
          <u>Hope.</u> 1983.

Everman, Henry Esli, 1941-.
    Professor of history.
    1641. <u>Governor James Garrard.</u> Cooper's Run Pr., 1981.
    1642. "Herbert Hoover and the New Deal, 1933-1940." Ph.D.
          diss., Louisiana State Univ., 1971.
    1643. <u>The History of Bourbon County, 1785-1865.</u> Bourbon
          Pr., 1977.

Filbeck, David.
    1644. <u>The First Fifty Years: A Brief History of the</u>
          <u>Direct-Support Missionary Movement.</u> College Pr.,
          1980.

Fletcher, John.
    1645. <u>The History of the Christian Church of East Prairie,</u>
          <u>Missouri... 1883-1950.</u> 1950.

Forster, Ada L.
    1646. <u>A History of the Christian Church and Church of</u>
          <u>Christ in Minnesota.</u> Christian Bd. of Publication,
          1953.

Foster, Dow B.
    1647. <u>History of Richland Church.</u> Monroe County
          Historical Soc. [Bloomington, Ind.], 1908.

Frey, Robert Lovell, 1938-.
    Professor of history; college administrator.
    1648. "A Technological History of the Locomotives of the
          Northern Pacific Railway Company." 2 vols. Ph.D.
          diss., Univ. of Minnesota, 1970.

Gandy, Essie M.
    Pastor.
    1649. <u>No Woman Is an Island: A History of Organized</u>
          <u>Women's Work. Oklahoma Christian Churches [Disciples</u>
          <u>of Christ] 1894-1974.</u> 1975?

Gearhart, Edgar W.
    Pastor.
    1650. "A History of the Christian Churches of Wabash
          County, Indiana." B.D. thesis, Butler Univ., 1956.

Gilliland, Marshall Allan.
 1651. "Vachel Lindsay: Poet and Newspaper Columnist in
     Spokane, 1924- 1929." Ph.D. diss., Washington State
     Univ., 1968.

Goodpasture, Albert Virgil, 1885-1942.
 Historian.
 1652. <u>Andrew Jackson, Tennessee and the Union.</u> Brandon
     Printing Co., 1895.
 1653. <u>History of Tennessee, Its People and Its</u>
     <u>Institutions.</u> Brandon Printing Co., 1900. (co-
     author).
 1654. <u>Life of Jefferson Dillard Goodpasture.</u> Cumberland
     Presbyterian Publishing House, 1897. (co-author).

Haley, Thomas Preston.
 1655. <u>Historical and Biographical Sketches of the Early</u>
     <u>Churches and Pioneer Preachers of the Christian</u>
     <u>Church Missouri.</u> Christian Publishing Co., 1888.

Hall, Colby Dixon, 1875-1963.
 Pastor; professor of church history.
 1656. "The Fellowship Road of the Nineteenth Century
     Reformation Movement." Texas Convention of
     Christian Churches, 1951.
 1657. <u>Gay Nineties.</u> Naylor, 1961.
 1658. <u>History of Texas Christian University, a College of</u>
     <u>the Cattle Frontier.</u> Texas Christian Univ. Pr.,
     1947.
 1659. <u>The "New Light Christians:" Initiators of the</u>
     <u>Nineteenth-Century Reformation.</u> Colby D. Hall,
     1959.
 1660. <u>Rice Haggard, the American Frontier Evangelist Who</u>
     <u>Revived the Name Christian.</u> University Christian
     Church (Fort Worth, Tex.),1957.
 1661. <u>Texas Disciples.</u> Texas Christian Univ. Pr., 1953.

Hamlin, Charles Hunter, 1890-.
 Professor of history.
 1662. <u>Conflicting Forces in North Carolina Education.</u>
     George Peabody College for Teachers, 1941.
 1663. <u>Educators Present Arms: The Use of Schools and</u>
     <u>Colleges as Agents of War Propaganda, 1914-1918.</u>
     Record, 1939.
 1664. <u>Lobbyists and Lobbying in the North Carolina</u>
     <u>Legislature.</u> Raleigh, N.C., 1933.
 1665. <u>Ninety Bits of North Carolina Biography.</u> Dunn,
     1946.
 1666. <u>A Pilgrimage in Ideas.</u> Atlantic Christian College,
     1970.
 1667. <u>Propaganda and Myth in Time of War.</u> Garland, 1973.
 1668. <u>A Scrap Book of Reflections.</u> Wilson, 1957.

1669. The War Myth in United States History. Vanguard,
       1927.

Hardcastle, David Paul, 1937-.
     Professor of history.
     1670. "The Defense of Canada under Louis XIV, 1643-1701."
            Ph.D. diss., Ohio State Univ., 1970.

Harmon, Marion F.
     1671. A History of the Christian Churches in Mississippi.
            Aberdeen, MS, 1929.

Harris, Ted C.
     Professor of history.
     1672. "Jeannette Rankin: Suffragist, First Woman Elected
            to Congress, and Pacifist." Ph.D. diss., Univ. of
            Georgia, 1972.

Harrison, Ida (Withers), 1851-1927.
     Laywoman.
     1673. Beyond the Battle's Rim: A Story of the Confederate
            Refugees. Neale, 1918.
     1674. Four Little Bridges. Alden, 1890.
     1675. Forty Years of Service: A History of the Christian
            Woman's Board of Missions, 1874-1914. 2d. ed. 19--.
     1676. Gardens All the Year. Stratford, 1927.
     1677. History of the Christian Woman's Board of Missions
            [1874-1919]. 1920.
     1678. Memoirs of William Temple Withers. Christopher,
            1924.

Harrison, Richard Leigh, Jr., 1946-.
     Professor of religious studies and philosophy.
     1679. The Life and Times of John Rogers, 1800-1867, of
            Carlisle, Kentucky. Lexington Theol. Sem., 1984.
     1680. "The Reformation of the Theological Faculty of the
            University of Tubingen, 1534-1555." Ph.D. diss.,
            Vanderbilt Univ., 1975.
     1681. "Westward - Why? The Stone-Campbell Churches on the
            Pacific Slope." In Heirs of Stone and Campbell on
            the Pacific Slope, edited by Lawrence C. Keene.
            Disciples Seminary Foundation, 1984.

Hartling, Harvey C.
     1682. Big Sky Disciples: A History of the Christian
            Church (Disciples of Christ) in Montana. Christian
            Church in Montana (Disciples of Christ), 1984. (co-
            author).

Haynes, Nathaniel Smith.
     1683. History of the Disciples of Christ in Illinois,
            1819-1914. Standard, 1915.

Hefley, John Theodore.
    1684. "'The Christian Century' in American Culture, 1920-
           1941." Ph.D. diss., Univ. of Minnesota, 1953.

Hendricks, Kenneth C.
    Pastor; missionary.
    1685. History of Student Religious Activities at the
           University of Oregon, 1876 to 1915. 1920.

Hinsdale, Burke Aaron.
    See under EDUCATION.

Hockman, Daniel Mack, 1937-.
    Professor of history.
    1686. "The Dawson Brothers and the Virginia Commissariat,
           1743-1760." Ph.D. diss., Univ. of Illinois, 1975.

Hodge, Frederick Arthur.
    1687. The Plea and the Pioneers in Virginia. Waddey,
           1905, c1895.

Hoffman, Wilson Jesse, Jr., 1933-.
    Professor of history.
    1688. "Mr. Secretary Thurice: His Role in the Domestic
           Affairs of Oliver Cromwell's Protectorate." Ph.D.
           diss., Western Reserve Univ., 1963.

Hooper, Robert E.
    1689. A Call To Remember: Chapters in Nashville
           Restoration History. Gospel Advocate, 1977.
    1690. Crying in the Wilderness: A Biography of David
           Lipscomb. David Lipscomb College, 1979.
    1691. "The Political and Educational Ideas of David
           Lipscomb." Ph.D. diss., George Peabody College for
           Teachers, 1965.

Hopson, Ella (Lord).
    1692. Memoirs of Dr. Winthrop Hartly Hopson. Standard,
           1887. (editor).

House, Charles T.
    Journalist.
    1693. History of Oklahoma. First National Bank and Trust
           Co. of Oklahoma City, 1957. (co-author).

Howenstine, Lydia (Kimmel).
    1694. From the Cradle to the Grave: Life of Elder Solon
           A. Howenshine [1856-1893]. D. W. Underwood,
           Printer, 1894.

Hughes, Richard T.
    1695. Called To Serve: A Biography of the South National

Church of Christ, Springfield, Missouri. Gospel
Publishing House, 1967.

Humble, B. J.
    1696. The Story of the Restoration. Firm Publishing
          House, 1969.

Humphrey, Inez Faith.
    Historian; naturalist.
    1697. From the Prairies to the Mountains: Memories.
          Especially of Illinois and Eastern Kentucky.
          Exposition Pr., 1968.

Huston, James Alvin, 1918-.
    Professor of history.
    1698. Across the Face of France: Liberation and Recovery.
          1944-63. Purdue Univ. Studies, 1963.
    1699. "Biography of a Battalion." Ph.D. diss., New York
          Univ., 1947.
    1700. Combat History of World War II. Army & Navy
          Publishing Co., 1946?
    1701. One For All: NATO Strategy and Logistics through
          the Formative Period (1949-1969). Univ. of Delaware
          Pr., 1984.
    1702. Out of the Blue: U. S. Army Airborne Operations in
          World War II. Purdue Univ. Studies, 1972.
    1703. The Sinews of War: Army Logistics. 1775-1953. U.S.
          Govt. Print. Off., 1966.

Ide, Fumiko Fukuyama, 1920-.
    Publisher.
    1704. Jiyu Sore Wa Watakushi Jishin. [Anarchy in Japan].
          Chikuma Shobo, 1979.
    1705. Mitsukuri Genpachi. Taio "Fukubai Nikki."
          [Mitsukuri's Journeys in Europe]. Tokyo Daigaku
          Shuppankai, 1984.
    1706. Seito No Oninatachi. [Women in Japan]. Kaien Shobo,
          1975.

Jackson, Willis G.
    Professor of history.
    1707. "We Would Like To Have a Round of Cokes": Civil
          Rights Demonstrations in Talladega. 1961-1963.
          Alabama Center for Higher Education, 1979.

Jennings, Walter Wilson, 1887-.
    Professor of history.
    1708. The American Embargo. 1807-1809. Univ. of Iowa,
          1921.
    1709. A Dozen Captains of American Industry. Vantage,
          1954.
    1710. A History of Economic Progress in the United States.
          Crowell, 1926.

1711. <u>A History of the Economic and Social Progress of</u>
       <u>European Peoples.</u> Univ. of Kentucky, 1936.
1712. <u>A History of the Economic and Social Progress of the</u>
       <u>American People.</u> Southwestern, 1937.
1713. <u>Introduction to American Economic History.</u> Crowell,
       1928.
1714. <u>Introduction to the Economic History of the European</u>
       <u>Peoples.</u> Brown, 1951.
1715. <u>Introduction to the Economic History of the American</u>
       <u>People.</u> Brown, 1951.
1716. "Origin and Early History of the Disciples of
       Christ...between 1809 and 1835." Ph.D. diss., Univ.
       of Illinois, 1918.
1717. <u>A Short History of the Disciples of Christ.</u>
       Bethany, 1929.
1718. <u>Some Religious Talks by a University Professor.</u>
       Christopher, 1933.
1719. <u>Transylvania. Pioneer University of the West.</u>
       Pageant, 1955.
1720. <u>20 Giants of American Business.</u> Expositional Pr.,
       1953.

Johnson, Daniel Thomas.
   Professor of history.
   1721. <u>History of Mercer County. Illinois. 1882-1976.</u>
          Mercer County Bicentennial Comm., 1977.
   1722. "Puritan Power in Illinois Higher Education Prior To
          1870." Ph.D. diss., Univ. of Wisconsin, 1975.

Jones, Charles Thomas, Jr.
   Professor of history.
   1723. "George Champlin Sibley: The Prairie Puritan (1782-
          1863)." Ph.D. diss., Univ. of Missouri, 1969.
   1724. <u>Missouri. the Heart of the Nation.</u> Forum, 1980.
          (co-author).

Jones, Willis Rumble, 1908-.
   Historian.
   1725. "Archival Gleanings - NBA Style." Disciples of
          Christ Historical Soc., 1968.
   1726. "Iowa's Heritage of Splendor." Disciples of Christ
          Historical Soc., 1967 or 8.
   1727. "Restructure Study. Church School - Vine Street
          Christian Church." Disciples of Christ Historical
          Soc., 1967.

Kelley, Delores Goodwin.
   Professor of American studies.
   1728. "A Rhetorical Analysis of an 1884-1888 Controversy
          in American Religious Thought: Response within the
          Presbyterian Church in the United States to
          Evolutionism." Ph.D. diss., Univ. of Maryland,
          1977.

Layton, Roland Vanderbilt, 1930-.
    Professor of history.
    1729. "The Voelkischer Beobachter, 1925-1933, A Study of
           the Nazi Party Newspaper in the Kampfzeit." Ph.D.
           diss., Univ. of Virginia, 1965.

Leach, Douglas Edward, 1920-.
    Professor of history.
    1730. Arms for Empire: A Military History of the British
           Colonies in North America, 1607-1763. Macmillan,
           1973.
    1731. "The Causes and Effects of King Philip's War."
           Ph.D. diss., Harvard Univ., 1950.
    1732. Flintlock and Tomahawk: New England in King
           Philip's War. Macmillan, 1958.
    1733. The Northern Colonial Frontier, 1607-1763. Holt,
           1966.
    1734. A Rhode Islander Reports on King Philip's War.
           Rhode Island Historical Soc., 1963. (co-author).

Lee, George R.
    Professor of history, political science and sociology.
    1735. The Beaubiens of Chicago. Canton? Mo., 1973.
    1736. Carl Johann: Builder of Christian Higher Education.
           Culver-Stockton College, 1975.
    1737. Culver-Stockton College: The First 130 Years.
           Culver-Stockton College, 1984.

Lessner, Richard Edward.
    1738. "The Imagined Enemy: American Nativism and the
           Disciples of Christ, 1830-1925." Ph.D. diss.,
           Baylor Univ., 1981.

Lewis, John Thomas.
    1739. The Voice of the Pioneers on Instrumental Music and
           Societies. Gospel Advocate Co., 1932.

Lobdell, George Henry, 1922-.
    Professor of history.
    1740. "A Biography of Frank Knox." Ph.D. diss., Univ. of
           Illinois, 1954.

Lollis, Lorraine.
    1741. The Shape of Adam's Rib: A Lively History of
           Women's Work in the Christian Church. Bethany, 1970.

Loos, Charles Louis, 1823-1912.
    College president; professor of ancient languages.
    1742. "Introductory Period [of the Disciples of Christ]."
           In The Reformation of the Nineteenth Century, pp.
           16-123, by James Harvey Garrison. St. Louis, 1901.
    1743. Our First General Convention: Held at Cincinnati,
           Ohio, October 22 to 27, 1849. Guide, 1891.

Lucas, Daniel R.
    See under THEOLOGY.

Lyda, Hap.
    Professor of religion and philosophy.
    1744. "A History of Black Christian Churches (Disciples of
           Christ) in the United States through 1899." Ph.D.
           diss., Vanderbilt Univ., 1972.

McAllister, Lester Grover, 1919-.
    Professor of church history.
    1745. <u>An Alexander Campbell Reader.</u> CBP Pr., 1988.
    1746. <u>God Speaks to the Church: Hoosier Women in Mission</u>
           <u>across a Century.</u> Christian Women's Fellowship,
           Christian Church (Disciples of Christ) in Indiana,
           1973.
    1747. <u>Journey in Faith: A History of the Christian Church</u>
           <u>(Disciples of Christ).</u> Bethany, 1975. (co-author).
    1748. "Let's Think about Our History." United Christian
           Missionary Soc., 1967.
    1749. <u>Z. T. Sweeney: Preacher and Peacemaker.</u> Christian
           Bd. of Publication, 1968.

McElroy, Charles Foster, 1876-.
    1750. <u>Ministers of First Christian Church (Disciples of</u>
           <u>Christ) Springfield, Illinois, 1833-1962.</u> Bethany,
           1962.

McGuire, Edna.
    Historian; educator.
    1751. <u>Adventuring in Youth America.</u> Macmillan, 1929. (co-
           author).
    1752. <u>America Then and Now.</u> Macmillan, 1940.
    1753. <u>Backgrounds of American Freedom.</u> Macmillan, 1953.
    1754. <u>A Brave Young Land.</u> Macmillan, 1937.
    1755. <u>Building Our Country.</u> Macmillan, 1929. (co-author).
    1756. <u>Daniel Boone.</u> Wheeler, 1945.
    1757. <u>A Full-Grown Nation.</u> Macmillan, 1937.
    1758. <u>Glimpses into the Long Ago.</u> Macmillan, 1937.
    1759. <u>The Growth of Democracy.</u> Macmillan, 1941.
    1760. <u>The Maoris of New Zealand.</u> Macmillan, 1968.
    1761. <u>Our Free Nation.</u> Macmillan, 1954. (co-author).
    1762. <u>The Past Lives Again.</u> Macmillan, 1949.
    1763. <u>The Peace Corps. Kindlers of the Spark.</u> Macmillan,
           1966.
    1764. <u>Puerto Rico. Bridge to Freedom.</u> Macmillan, 1963.
    1765. <u>The Rise of Our Free Nation.</u> Macmillan, 1942. (co-
           author).
    1766. <u>The Story of American Freedom.</u> Macmillan, 1952.
    1767. <u>Teacher's Manual for Our Free Nation.</u> Macmillan,
           1962. (co-author).
    1768. <u>They Made America Great: A First Book in American</u>
           <u>History.</u> Macmillan, 1950.

1769. <u>With Liberty and Justice for All.</u> U. S. Off. of Education, 1948.

McPherson, Chalmers.
    1770. <u>Disciples of Christ in Texas.</u> Standard, 1920.

McWhiney, Grady.
    Professor of history.
    1771. <u>Attack and Die: Civil War Military Tactics and the Southern Heritage.</u> Univ. of Alabama Pr., 1982. (co-author).
    1772. <u>Braxton Bragg and Confederate Defeat.</u> Columbia Univ. Pr., 1969-.
    1773. <u>Grant, Lee, Lincoln and the Radicals: Essays on Civil War Leadership.</u> Northwestern Univ. Pr., 1964. (editor).
    1774. <u>Historical Vistas: Readings in United States History.</u> 2 vols. Allyn & Bacon, 1963-4. (co-editor).
    1775. "The Ordeal of Command: Bragg Before Chickamauga." Ph.D. diss., Columbia Univ., 1960.
    1776. <u>Reconstruction and the Freedmen.</u> Rand McNally, 1963. (editor).
    1777. <u>Southerners and Other Americans.</u> Basic Bks., 1973.
    1778. <u>To Mexico with Taylor and Scott: 1845-1847.</u> Blaisdell, 1969. (co-editor).

Major, James Brooks.
    1779. "The Role of Periodicals in the Development of the Disciples of Christ, 1850-1910." Ph.D. diss., Vanderbilt Univ., 1966.

Minniear, Deloris Jeanne.
    1780. "The High School Young People's Conferences of Indiana, 1921-1954." M.R.E. thesis, College of the Bible, Lexington, 1955.

Moorhouse, William Mervin.
    1781. "The Restoration Movement: The Rhetoric of Jacksonian Restorationism in a Frontier Religion." Ph.D. diss., Indiana Univ., 1968.

Morison, William James, 1943-.
    Professor of history.
    1782. "George Frederick Wright in Defense of Darwinism and Fundamentalism, 1838-1921." Ph.D. diss., Vanderbilt Univ., 1971.
    1783. <u>Historical Evidence of Ohio River Bank Erosion.</u> U. S. Army Engineer District, 1983.

Morrill, Milo True.
    1784. <u>A History of the Christian Denomination in America, 1794-1911 A.D.</u> Christian Publishing Assoc., 1912.

Morrison, Matthew C.
    1785. <u>Like a Lion: Daniel Sommer's Seventy Years of</u>
           <u>Preaching.</u> Dehoff Publications, 1975.

Murphy, Frederick Ira, 1933-.
    Professor of history.
    1786. "The American Christian Press and Pre-War Hitler's
           Germany, 1933-1939." Ph.D. diss., Univ. of Florida,
           1970.

Myers, Oma Lou.
    1787. <u>Rosa's Song: The Life and Ministry of Rosa Page</u>
           <u>Welch.</u> CBP Pr., 1984.
    1788. <u>This One Thing I Do: A Biography of Frank Hamilton</u>
           <u>Marshall [Born 1868], Pioneer Christian Educator.</u>
           Portland? 1953.

North, James Brownlee.
    1789. "The Fundamentalist Controversy among the Disciples
           of Christ, 1890-1930." Ph.D. diss., Univ. of
           Illinois, 1973.

Nunnelly, Donald A.
    1790. "The Disciples of Christ in Alabama, 1860-1910."
           M.A. thesis, College of the Bible (Lexington), 1954.

*Payne, John Barton, 1931-.
    Pastor; professor of church history.
    1791. <u>Erasmus: His Theology of the Sacraments.</u> John Knox
           Pr., 1970.

Pearson, Samuel Campbell, 1931-.
    Professor of history.
    1792. <u>The Great Awakening and Its Impact on American</u>
           <u>History.</u> Forum Pr., 1978.
    1793. "The Growth of Denominational Self-Consciousness
           among American Congregationalists 1801-1852." Ph.D.
           diss., Univ. of Chicago, 1964.

Peoples, Robert Hayes, 1903-1983.
    Pastor; church official.
    1794. "The History of the Administration of Negro Work."
           The Christian Plea, 1943?

Peters, George L.
    1795. <u>The Disciples of Christ in Missouri, Celebrating One</u>
           <u>Hundred Years of Co-operative Work.</u> Centennial
           Commission, 1937.

Peterson, Oscar William.
    Pastor.
    1796. <u>History of the Christian Church in Boscawen.</u>

Canterbury and Concord. Organized 1826... Penacook,
N.H., 1923.

Phelps, Mrs. John U.
   1797. A History of the Christian Churches of Jackson
         County, Indiana. 1950.

*Pinkerton, Lewis Letig, 1812-1875.
   Physician; pastor; editor; college professor.
   1798. A Discourse Concerning Some Effects of the Late
         Civil War. Cincinnati, 1866.

For works about him written by Disciple authors, see
Shackleford, John under THEOLOGY section.

Plummer, Mark A., 1929-.
   Professor of history.
   1799. Frontier Governor: Samuel J. Crawford of Kansas.
         Univ. Pr. of Kansas, 1971.
   1800. "Governor Crawford." Ph.D. diss., Kansas Univ.,
         1960.
   1801. The Kansas Centennial Politics and Business 100
         Years Ago. Univ. of Kansas, 1960. (co-author).
   1802. Robert G. Ingersoll: Peoria's Pagan Politician.
         Western Illinois Univ., 1984.
   1803. A Short History of Japan. Kansas Univ., 1958?

Potter, Marguerite, 1907-.
   Professor of history.
   1804. "British Policy During the Italo-Ethiopian Crisis."
         2 vols. Ph.D. diss., Univ. of Texas, 1956.
   1805. Grass Roots Diplomat. Neville G. Penrose. Texas
         Christian Univ., 1961.
   1806. Missouri. Its History, Geography and Government.
         Laidlaw, 1941. (co-author).
   1807. Personalities and Policies: Essays on English and
         European History Presented in Honor of Dr.
         Marguerite Potter. Edited by E. Deanne Malpass.
         Texas Christian Univ. Pr., 1977.
   1808. Snide Lights on Texas History. Naylor, 1959.
   1809. Workbook in Missouri History. Harlow, 1940. (co-
         author).

Proctor, Ben Hamill.
   Professor of history.
   1810. "John H. Reagan." Ph.D. diss., Harvard Univ., 1961.
   1811. The Texas Heritage. Forum Pr., 1980. (co-editor).
   1812. Texas: The Land and Its People. Hendrick-Long
         Publishing Co., 1972. (co-author).
   1813. Texas under a Cloud. Jenkins Publishing Co., 1972.
         (co-author).

Ramsey, Bobby Gene.
     Professor of history.
     1814.   "Scientific Exploration and Discovery in the Great
              Basin from 1831-1891." Ph.D. diss., Brigham Young
              Univ., 1972.

Randall, Max Ward.
     1815.   The Great Awakenings and the Restoration Movement.
              College Pr., 1983.

Ray, C. N.
     1816.   The Campbellite Church. 1889.

Reagan, John S.
     1817.   Historic Sketches of Christian Churches in Hendricks
              County, Indiana. Plainfield, Ind., 1962.

Redford, Ramon N.
     1818.   The Saga of Christian Churches (Disciples of Christ)
              in District V [Lynchburg and Adjacent Area] 1830-
              1974. Redford, 197?.

Reed, Forrest F.
     1819.   "Background of Division - Disciples of Christ and
              Churches of Christ." Disciples of Christ Historical
              Soc., 1968.

For works about him written by Disciple authors, see
     Craddock, Fred B. in GENERAL section.

Reinhardt, Wayne, 1927-.
     Professor of history.
     1820.   "Ferdinand Christian Baur: On the Writing of Church
              History." In A Library of Christian Thought.
              Oxford Univ. Pr., 1968.
     1821.   Social and Psychological Factors in Brotherhood
              Problems. United Christian Missionary Soc., 1962.

Rice, Bradley Robert, 1948-.
     Professor of history.
     1822.   Progressive Cities: The Commission Government
              Movement in America, 1901-1920. Univ. of Texas Pr.,
              1977.
     1823.   "The Rise and Fall of the Galveston - Des Moines
              Plan: Commission Government in American Cities,
              1901-1920." Ph.D. diss., Univ. of Texas at Austin,
              1976.
     1824.   Sunbelt Cities: Politics and Growth since World War
              II. Univ. of Texas Pr., 1983 (co-editor).

Robinson, John L.
     1825.   David Lipscomb: Journalist in Texas, 1872. Norton,
              1973.

Rushford, Jerry Bryant.
    1826. "Political Disciple: The Relationship between James
           A. Garfield and the Disciples of Christ." Ph.D.
           diss., Univ. of California, Santa Barbara, 1977.

Schnell, Kempes Yoder, 1919-.
    Professor of history.
    1827. "Court Cases Involving Slavery." Ph.D. diss., Univ.
           of Michigan,1955.

Schuster, Monroe.
    1828. A Brief History of the Madison County [Indiana]
           Christian Churches. Presented at the County
           Convention at Chesterfield, March 27, 1966.

Scott, Barbara Kerr, 1942-.
    Professor of history and humanities.
    1829. "An Analysis of Critical and Aesthetic Ideas in
           Eighteenth-Century Britain." Ph.D. diss., Univ. of
           Oklahoma, 1978.

Sechler, Earl Truman.
    1830. Brief History of Christian Churches (Disciples of
           Christ) in Cedar County and St. Clair County.
           Missouri. 1852-1952. The Index (Hermitage, Mo.),
           1953.
    1831. Four Women Pastors of Missouri Christian Churches.
           Appleton, Mo., 1957?
    1832. History of Dade County. Missouri. Christian
           Churches. 1839-1958. Springfield, Mo.: The Author,
           1960.
    1833. History of Hickory County. Missouri. Christian
           Churches (Disciples of Christ) [1843-1950]. With
           Memberships as Listed in October 1950. The Index
           (Hermitage, Mo.), 1950.
    1834. Our Religious Heritage: Church History of the
           Ozarks. 1806-1906. Westport, 1961.
    1835. Sadie McCoy Crank (1863-1948). Pioneer Woman
           Preacher in the Christian Church (Disciples).
           Springfield? Mo., 1950.

Sharp, Paul Frederick, 1918-.
    College president; historian.
    1836. The Agrarian Revolt in Western Canada. Univ. of
           Minnesota, 1948.
    1837. Old Orchard Farm: Story of an Iowa Boyhood. Iowa
           State College, 1952.
    1838. "Three Frontiers: Some Comparative Studies of
           Canadian, American and Australian Settlement." In
           The West of the American People, 1970.
    1839. Whoop-Up Country: The Canadian-American West. 1865-
           1885. Univ. of Minnesota Pr., 1955.

Sharratt, William Bert.
    1840.   "The Theory of Religious Education of Alexander
           Campbell and Its Influence upon the Educational
           Attitude of the Disciples of Christ." Ph.D. diss.,
           New York Univ., 1930.

Shaw, Chandler.
    Professor of history and politics.
    1841.   <u>Etruscan Perugia.</u> Johns Hopkins Pr., 1939.
    1842.   <u>Hellenistic and Roman Civilization.</u> Morgantown? W.
           Va., 1961.
    1843.   <u>History of Ancient Culture. From Demosthenes to</u>
           <u>Diocletian.</u> Univ. Lithoprinters (Ypsilanti, Mich.),
           1941.
    1844.   <u>Nebuchadnezzar to Christ.</u> Morgantown? W. Va., 1957.
    1845.   <u>Seven Centuries That Rocked the World: A</u>
           <u>Biographical History of Ancient Culture from the</u>
           <u>Decline of the Greek City-State to the Triumph of</u>
           <u>Christianity.</u> Bethany? W. Va., 1950.
    1846.   "A Study of Perugia in Prehistoric and Etruscan
           Times." Ph.D. diss., Univ. of North Carolina, 1935.

Shaw, Henry King, 1904- .
    Librarian; professor of Disciple literature.
    1847.   <u>Buckeye Disciples: A History of the Disciples of</u>
           <u>Christ in Ohio.</u> Christian Bd. of Publication, 1952.
    1848.   "Elyria Disciples: The Story of the Disciples of
           Christ in Elyria, Ohio." Elyria, 1956.
    1849.   "Having Fun with Periodicals, An Address..."
           Disciples of Christ Historical Soc., 1960.
    1850.   <u>Hoosier Disciples: A Comprehensive History of the</u>
           <u>Christian Churches (Disciples of Christ) in Indiana.</u>
           Bethany, 1966.
    1851.   <u>Saga of a Village Church. 1877-1937: The Story of</u>
           <u>Religion in Medina and the Founding and</u>
           <u>Accomplishments of the Church of Christ. Medina.</u>
           <u>Ohio...</u> Medina, 1937.
    1852.   "Writing the History of Your Church." Disciples of
           Christ Historical Soc., 1958.

Shelton, William A.
    Professor of history.
    1853.   <u>The Young Jefferson Davis. 1808-1846.</u> Arno Pr.,
           1982 (Ph.D. diss., 1977).

*Sherwood, Henry Noble, 1882-1956.
    Professor of history and political science; college
    president.
    1854.   <u>Citizenship.</u> Bobbs-Merrill, 1936.
    1855.   <u>Civics and Citizenship.</u> Bobbs-Merrill, 1929.
    1856.   <u>Journal of Miss Susan Walker. March 3d to June 6th.</u>
           <u>1862.</u> Jennings & Graham, 1912.
    1857.   <u>Makers of the New World.</u> Bobbs-Merrill, 1929.

1858.   Manual of Character Education. Auxiliary
        Educational League, 1927. (co-editor).
1859.   Movement in Ohio to Deport the Negro. Jennings &
        Graham, 1912.
1860.   Our Country's Beginnings. Bobbs-Merrill, 1924.

Small, James.
    1861.   The Old Days, the Old Ways and the Old Friends.
            Being a History and Souvenir of the Christian
            Churches of Bartholomew County, Indiana, and the
            Church at Nashville, Brown County. Bartholomew
            Christian Missionary Assoc., 1928.

Smith, Agnes Monroe.
    Professor of history.
    1862.   Bourgeois, Sans-Culottes and Other Frenchman:
            Essays on the French Revolution in Honor of John
            Hall Stewart. Wilfred Laurier Univ. Pr., 1981. (co-
            editor).
    1863.   "The First Historians of the French Revolution."
            Ph.D. diss., Western Reserve Univ., 19?

Smith, Clyde Curry, 1929-.
    1864.   "The Impact of Assyriology upon Old Testament Study
            with Special Reference to the Publications of
            Leonard William King." Ph.D. diss., Univ. of
            Chicago, 1968.
    1865.   Who Was Who in Assyriology: A Provisional Bio-
            Bibliographical Index. Univ. of Wisconsin, 1978.
            (co-author).

Smith, James Frantz.
    Professor of history.
    1866.   "John A'Lasco and the Strangers' Churches." Ph.D.
            diss., Vanderbilt Univ., 1964.

Smith, Jerry Coleman.
    Pastor.
    1867.   "The Disciples of Christ and the Expansionist
            Movement, 1898-1899." D.Div. diss., Vanderbilt
            Univ., 1970.

Spelman, Dorothy Cerny.
    1868.   The Church on the Hill: A History of the Christian
            Church (Disciples of Christ) of North Royalton,
            Ohio, 1829-1979. The Church (North Royalton, Ohio),
            1979.

Spencer, Justina K.
    1869.   A Synoptic History (One Half Century) of the
            Christian Church. Roanoke Tribune, 1959. (editor).

Spillman, W. B.
    1870. <u>The Hastening Time. Vol. 1. A History of the</u>
           <u>Restoration Movement.</u> Herald House, 1987.

Stanger, Allen B.
    1871. <u>The Virginia Christian Missionary Society: One</u>
           <u>Hundred Years. 1875-1975.</u> Christian Church in
           Virginia, 1975.

Strassburger, John Robert, 1942-.
    Professor of history.
    1872. "The Origins and Establishment of the Morris Family
           in the Society and Politics of New York and New
           Jersey 1630-1746." Ph.D. diss., Princeton Univ.,
           1976.

Svanoe, Harold C.
    1873. "The Preaching and Speaking of Burris [Atkins]
           Jenkins [1869-1945]." Ph.D. diss., Northwestern
           Univ., 1954.

Talbert, Charles Gano, 1912-.
    Professor of history.
    1874. <u>Benjamin Logan. Kentucky Frontiersman.</u> Univ. of
           Kentucky Pr., 1962.
    1875. "The Life and Times of Benjamin Logan." Ph.D.
           diss., Univ. of Kentucky, 1960.
    1876. <u>The University of Kentucky: The Maturing Years.</u>
           Univ. of Kentucky Pr., 1965.

Taylor, Rhea Alec, 1902-.
    Professor of history.
    1877. "Conflicts in Kentucky as Shown by the
           Constitutional Convention of 1890-1891." Ph.D.
           diss., Univ. of Chicago, 1948.

Thompson, Rhodes.
    Missionary to Japan; professor of religion.
    1878. <u>Cane Ridge Meeting-House: A Temple of Christian</u>
           <u>Unity.</u> Christian Bd. of Publication, 1959.
    1879. <u>Voices from Cane Ridge.</u> Bethany, 1954. (editor).

*Toulouse, Mark G., 1952-.
    Professor of church history.
    1880. <u>The Transformation of John Foster Dulles: From</u>
           <u>Prophet of Realism to Priest of Nationalism.</u> Mercer
           Univ. Pr., 1985.

Tracy, Lena (Harvey).
    1881. <u>How My Heart Sang: The Story of Pioneer Industrial</u>
           <u>Welfare Work.</u> R. R. Smith, 1950.

Trickel, John Andrew.
      Professor of history.
      1882.   The American Story. Beginnings to 1877. 2d. ed.
              Addison-Wesley, 1981. (co-author).
      1883.   "Two Strategies for Improving the Retention Rate of
              the High-Risk Students in an Instructional
              Television History Course." Ed.D. diss., North
              Texas State Univ., 1980.

Trimble, John Clifton.
      1884.   "The Rhetorical Theory and Practice of John W.
              McGarvey." Ph.D. diss., Northwestern Univ., 1966.

Tucker, William E., 1932-.
      Administrator; professor of church history.
      1885.   J. H. Garrison and Disciples of Christ. Bethany,
              1964.
      1886.   Journey in Faith: A History of the Christian Church
              (Disciples of Christ). Bethany, 1975. (co-author).

Tuttle, Dwight William.
      Professor of history.
      1887.   Alaska's Kodiak Island-Shelikof Strait Region: A
              History. Bureau of Land Management, 1982.
      1888.   Harry L. Hopkins and Anglo-American-Soviet
              Relations. 1941-1945. Garland, 1983.

Underwood, Maude Jones.
      1889.   C[harles] R[eady] Nichol [Born 1876]: A Preacher of
              Righteousness. Nichol, 1952.

Updegraff, John C.
      1890.   The Christian Church (Disciples of Christ) in
              Florida: Its History & Development. Anna
              Publishers, 1981.

Van Kirk, Hiram.
      1891.   A History of the Theology of the Disciples of
              Christ. Christian Publishing Co., 1907.
      1892.   The Rise of the Current Reformation: Or, A Study in
              the History of Theology of the Disciples of Christ.
              Christian Publishing Co., 1907.

Vaughter, John B., 1838-1897.
      Pastor; soldier.
      1893.   Prison Life in Dixie. Giving a Short History of the
              Inhuman and Barbarous Treatment of Our Soldiers by
              Rebel Authorities...To Which Is Added a Speech of
              Gen. J. A. Garfield. Central Book Concern, 1880.

Visser t'Hooft, W. A.
      1894.   The Background of the Social Gospel in America.
              Bethany, 1928.

Wachs, William Ronald, 1938-.
   Professor of history.
   1895.   "Samuel Wait." In Dictionary of North Carolina
           Biography.

Wake, Orville Wentworth.
   College president; church official; publisher.
   1896.   "A History of Leesburg College, 1903-1953." Ph.D.
           diss., Univ. of Virginia, 1957.

Walker, Dean Everest.
   See under THEOLOGY.

Wallace, William E.
   1897.   Daniel Sommer, 1850-1940, A Biography. 1969.

Ware, Charles Crossfield, 1886-.
   Historian.
   1898.   Albermarle Annals [North Carolina]. Owen Dunn,
           1961.
   1899.   Barton Warren Stone, Pathfinder of Christian Union.
           Bethany, 1932.
   1900.   Bibliography Available to C. C. Ware, Wilson, N.C.
           to Jan. 28, 1926, in Historical Research. North
           Carolina Disciples of Christ, 1926.
   1901.   "A Carolina Landmark, 1762-1962; Bi-Centennial,
           Southwest Church, Lenoir County, North Carolina,
           October 21, 1962." Wilson, N.C.,1962.
   1902.   The Church Bell: A History of the First Christian
           Church, Wilson, N.C. First Christian Church
           (Wilson), 1963.
   1903.   Coastal Plain Christians. Wilson, N.C., 1964.
   1904.   A History of Atlantic Christian College: Culture in
           Coastal Carolina. Atlantic Christian College, 1956.
   1905.   Hookerton History. New Bern? N.C., 1960.
   1906.   Kentucky's Fox Creek: Vignettes of the Village
           Church and of the R. H. Crossfield Heritage.
           Wilson, N.C., 1957.
   1907.   Mill Creek Story. Wilson, N.C., 1959.
   1908.   Miscellaneous Memoranda in the Life of David
           Purivance. 1926.
   1909.   North Carolina Disciples of Christ. Christian Bd.
           of Publication, 1927.
   1910.   "Onslow's Oldest Church." Carolina Discipliana
           Library, 1956.
   1911.   Pamlico Profile. New Bern? N.C., 1961.
   1912.   Rountree Chronicles, 1827-1840: Documentary Primer
           of a Tar Heel Faith. North Carolina Christian
           Missionary Convention, 1947.
   1913.   South Carolina Disciples of Christ: A History.
           Christian Churches of South Carolina, 1967.

1914. Star in Wachovia: Centennial History of the
       Christian Church Disciples of Christ. Pfafftown.
       N.C. Wilson, N.C., 1965.
1915. Tar Heel Disciples. 1841-1852: Proceedings of the
       North Carolina Convention...during Its First Twelve
       Years. Dunn, 1942.

Warren, Louis Austin, 1885-.
   Historian.
   1916. Abraham Lincoln. A Concise Biography. Lincoln
          National Life Insurance Co., 1934.
   1917. Abraham Lincoln Interprets the Constitution.
          Lincoln National Life Insurance Co., 1940.
          (compiler).
   1918. Abraham Lincoln's Gettysburg Address: An
          Evaluation. Merrill, 1946?
   1919. From White House to Log Cabin. Herald News Co.,
          1921. (compiler).
   1920. Lincoln's Gettysburg Declaration: "A New Birth of
          Freedom." Lincoln National Life Foundation, 1964.
   1921. Lincoln's Parentage and Childhood. Century, 1926.
   1922. Lincoln's Youth: Indiana Years. Seven to Twenty-One.
          1816-1830. Indiana Historical Soc., 1959.
   1923. Louisville Lincoln Loop: A Day's Tour in "Old
          Kentucky." Standard, 1922.
   1924. Pilgrimage Conducted June 20-30. 1937...on the 300th
          Anniversary of Lincoln's Landing in America.
          Morton, 1937.
   1925. The Slavery Atmosphere of Lincoln's Youth.
          Lincolniana Publishers, 1933.
   1926. Souvenir of Abraham Lincoln's Birthplace.
          Hodgenville. Kentucky. Munford, 1927.
   1927. Souvenir of Lincoln National Park. Hodgenville.
          Kentucky. Herald, 1920.

Wasson, Woodrow Wilson, 1919-.
   College administrator.
   1928. "James A. Garfield and Religion: A Study in the
          Religious Thought and Activity of an American
          Statesman." Ph.D. diss., Univ. of Chicago, 1947.
   1929. James A. Garfield: His Religion and Education.
          Tennessee Book Co., 1952.
   1930. Alva Wilmot Taylor: A Register of His Papers in the
          Disciples of Christ Historical Society. Nashville,
          1964.
   1931. "Factors Creating Controversies among the Disciples
          of Christ." Disciples of Christ Historical Soc.,
          1963.

Watson, George H.
   1932. History of the Christian Churches in the Alabama
          Area. Bethany, 1965. (co-author),

Webb, Henry E.
    1933.   "Sectional Conflict and Schism within the Disciples
            of Christ Following the Civil War." In Essays on
            New Testament Christianity pp. 115-27. Edited by C.
            R. Wetzel. Standard, 1978.

Webber, Percy R., d. 1972.
    1934.   "Primrose Christian Church [S. Africa]: A History."
            1954.

West, Donald F.
    Educator; missionary to Indonesia.
    1935.   History of the First Christian Church of Pomona.
            California. 1883-1943. Pomona, 1943. (co-author).

Whitaker, David B.
    Professor of journalism.
    1936.   Beargrass Christian Church. A History. One Hundred
            Twenty-Fifth Anniversary. 1842-1967. Beargrass
            Christian Church, 1968.

White, Benton R.
    Professor of history.
    1937.   "The Last Cattle King: The Story of F. G. Oxsheer."
            Ph.D. diss., Texas Christian Univ., 1984.

White, Bob.
    Professor of history.
    1938.   The Child of an Eagle: Mississippi Steamboating.
            Southeast Missouri State Univ., 1980.

Whitten, Woodrow Carlton, 1915-.
    Professor of history.
    1939.   "Criminal Syndicalism and the Law in California:
            1919-1927." Ph.D. diss., Univ. of California, 1946.
            (Also American Philosophical Soc., 1969.)
    1940.   Out of the South: An Autobiography. 1979.

Wilburn, James R.
    1941.   The Hazard of the Die: Tolbert Fanning and the
            Restoration Movement. 1969.

Wilcox, Alanson, 1832-1924.
    Historian; state politician.
    1942.   An Autobiography. Judson Printing Co., 1912.
    1943.   A History of the Disciples of Christ in Ohio.
            Standard, 1918.

Williams, David Newell, 1950-.
    Professor of church history.
    1944.   "Barton Warren Stone, Evangelist." Vanderbilt
            Univ., 1973.

1945. "The Theology of the Great Revival in the West as
       Seen through the Life and Thought of Barton Warren
       Stone." Ph.D. diss., Vanderbilt Univ., 1979.

Williams, Ernest Russ, 1934-.
    Professor of history.
    1946. "The Florida Parish Ellises and Louisiana Politics,
           1820-1918." Ph.D. diss., Univ. of Southern
           Mississippi, 1969.
    1947. Kinsmen All. Genealogy of the Family of Wettenhall
           Warner of South Carolina and Louisiana. 1964.

Williams, John Augustus.
    1948. Life of Elder John Smith. With Some Account of the
           Rise and Progress of the Current Reformation.
           Carroll, 1870.

Willis, Cecil.
    1949. W. W. Otey: Contender for the Faith. A History of
           Controversies in the Church of Christ from 1860-
           1960. The Author [Akron, Ohio], 1964.
    1950. "W. W. Otey, Controversialist." M.A. thesis, Butler
           Univ., 1962.
    1951. The Willis-Jenkins Debate. Codgill Foundation,
           1976.

Wineman, Walter Ray.
    Professor of social sciences.
    1952. "Calendar of the Landon Carter Papers in the Sabine
           Hall Collection and a Biographic Sketch of Colonel
           Landon Carter." Ph.D. diss., Univ. of Pittsburgh,
           1957.

Wood, Lester Aaron.
    1953. Rev. George F. Wood: A Pictorial History of "a Man
           and His Families." L. A. Wood (Richardson, Texas?),
           1985.

Wrather, Eva Jean.
    1954. Creative Freedom in Action: Alexander Campbell on
           the Structure of the Church. Bethany, 1968.

Wynn, Malcolm Morgan, 1926-.
    Professor of history.
    1955. "Agrippa d' Aubigne': Huguenot Historian." Ph.D.
           diss., Ohio State Univ., 1958.

Young, Charles Alexander.
    1956. Historical Documents Advocating Christian Union.
           Chicago: Christian Century Co., 1904. (editor).

Young, William L., 1922-.
    Professor of history and political science.

        1957. "The John F. Kennedy Library Oral History Project:
               The West Virginia Democratic Presidential Primary,
               1960." Ph.D. diss., Ohio State Univ., 1982.

HOME ECONOMICS

Channels, Vera G.
        Professor of home economics, psychology and education.
        1958. Career Education in Home Economics. Interstate
               Printers & Publishers, 1973. (co-author).
        1959. Experiences in Interpersonal Relationships.
               Interstate Printers & Publishers, 1975.
        1960. Freedom Is an Inside Job. John Knox Pr., 1978. (co-
               author).
        1961. Home Economics Careers. Interstate Printers &
               Publishers, 1974. (co-author).
        1962. The Layman Builds a Christian Home. Bethany, 1959.

Griffin, Jean.
        Professor of home economics.
        1963. Clothing Selection. 3d. ed. Lucas, 1978.

Harlan, Jennie, d. 1913.
        1964. The Sunnyside Cook Book and Home Receipt Guide.
               Ogilvie, 1890.

Harris, Phoebe Todd, 1918-.
        Professor of home economics.
        1965. "An Experimental Investigation of Joint Decision-
               Making by Husbands and Wives in Relation to Four
               Interest-Values." Ph.D. diss., Pennsylvania State
               Univ., 1963.

Morgan, Sarah.
        Secretary; writer.
        1966. Bread. Being a Thorough Compendium of More Than 100
               Recipes & Directions for Mixing. Kneading. Covering.
               Letting Rise & Baking the Staff of Life... Encino
               Pr., 1975.
        1967. The Church Supper: New Trends in Cooking for Crowds.
               Bethany, 1976.
        1968. Cooking for Crowds. Bethany, 1973.
        1969. Dining with the Cattle Barons: Yesterday and Today.
               Texian Pr.,1981.
        1970. The Saga of Texas Cookery: An Historical Guide of
               More Than One Hundred Twenty Recipes Illustrating
               the French Influence on Texas Cuisine. the Spanish
               Influence & the Mexican Influence. Encino Pr.,
               1973.

Owens, Barbara L., 1936-.
        Professor of home economics.
        1971. "Organizational Climate and Perceived Performances

of Vocational Administrators." Ph.D. diss.,
Southern Illinois Univ., 1980.

Schmalhausen, Myrtle Ruth, 1899-.
    Professor of home economics.
    1972. "An Investigation of the Opportunities for
           Employment of Girls Graduating from the High Schools
           of Illinois..." Ph.D. diss., Pennsylvania State
           College, 1944?

INDUSTRIAL ARTS
    See ENGINEERING.

INTERNATIONAL RELATIONS
    See POLITICS.

JOURNALISM
    See ENGLISH LANGUAGE AND LITERATURE.

LAW

Barclay, Julian Magarey, 1916-.
    Attorney.
    1973. Our America and Our Party: An Identification of Our
           Nation and Our Culture with the Essence of God's
           Teachings. William Frederick Pr., 1952.

*Black, Jeremiah Sullivan, 1810-1883.
    U. S. Attorney General; U. S. Secretary of State; judge.
    1974. An Appeal to the Senate, to Modify Its Policy, and
           Save from Africanization and Military Despotism the
           States of the South. Democratic Executive
           Committee, 1868. (co-author).
    1975. A Contribution to History. Cole, Morwitz & Co.,
           1871. (co-author.)
    1976. The Doctrines of the Democratic and Abolition
           Parties Contrasted. "Age," 1864.
    1977. Essays and Speeches of Jeremiah S. Black. Appleton,
           1885.
    1978. Federal Jurisdiction in the Territories. Deseret
           News Co., 1883.
    1979. Index to Judicial Opinions of Jeremiah Sullivan
           Black, Chief Justice of the Supreme Court of
           Pennsylvania. Greensburg, Pa, 1935.
    1980. Memoirs of John Bannister Gibson, Late Chief Justice
           of Pennsylvania. J. Eichbaum & Co., 1890. (co-
           author).
    1981. The Milligan Case. Knopf, 1929. (contributor).
    1982. Opinions and Award of Arbitrators on the Maryland
           and Virginia Boundary Line. McGill & Witherow
           Printers, 1877. (contributor).

1983. Railroad Monopoly, Argument of J. S. Black, to the
       Judiciary Committee of the Senate of Pennsylvania,
       Thursday, May 24, 1883. 1883.

Blackmar, Charles B., 1922-.
    Professor of law.
    1984. Federal Jury Practice and Instructions. 2d. ed.
           West, 1970. (co-author).

Campbell, Alexander Morton, 1907-1968.
    Attorney; politician; Asst. U. S. Attorney General.
    1985. Building Our Defenses.
    1986. The Choice Before Civilization.
    1987. The Christian Evangelist.
    1988. World Order Through Law.

*Henry, Frederick Augustus, 1867-1949.
    Attorney; judge; professor of law.
    1989. Captain Henry of Geauga. Gates, 1942.

Jouett, Edward Stockton, 1863-.
    Attorney; judge.
    1990. Digest of Decisions Relating to the Validity of
           State Statutes Regulating the Operation of Motor
           Vehicles. Louisville, 1933.
    1991. Jack Jouett's Ride. 1950.
    1992. The Unfair Competition between the Railroads and
           Motor Carriers for Hire. Louisville, 1931.

*Schroeder, Oliver Charles, Jr., 1916-.
    Professor of law.
    1993. The Back: A Law-Medicine Problem. 2d. ed.
           Anderson, 1965. (editor).
    1994. Criminal Investigation and Interrogation. Anderson,
           1962. (co-editor).
    1995. Criminal Investigation and Interrogation (1972
           Appendix of Supplementary Material). Anderson,
           1972. (co-editor).
    1996. De Facto Segregation and Civil Rights: Struggle for
           Legal and Social Equality. Hein, 1965. (co-editor).
    1997. Dental Jurisprudence: A Handbook of Practical Law.
           PSG Publishing Co., 1980.
    1998. The Dynamics of Technology: From Medicine and Law to
           Health and Justice. Law-Medicine Center
           (Cleveland), 1972.
    1999. The Extremities: A Law-Medicine Problem. Anderson,
           1961. (editor).
    2000. Handbook of Dental Jurisprudence and Risk
           Management. PSG Publishing Co., 1987.
    2001. Homicide in an Urban Community. Thomas, 1960. (co-
           author).
    2002. International Crime and the U. S. Constitution.
           Press of Western Reserve Univ., 1950.

2003. Lawyer Discipline: The Ohio Story. Cleveland, 1967.
2004. A Legal Study Concerning the Forensic Sciences
       Personnel. U. S. Govt. Print. Off., 1977.
2005. Medical Facts for Lawyers. Multi-stat Copy Co.,
       1957. (editor).
2006. Medical Facts for Legal Truth. Anderson, 1961.
       (editor).
2007. The Mind: A Law-Medicine Problem. Anderson, 1962.
       (editor).
2008. Schroeder-Katz Ohio Criminal Law and Practice: A
       Guide to Ohio's New Criminal Law and Criminal
       Procedure under the Rules. 2 vols. Banks-Baldwin,
       1974. (co-author).

Vestal, Allan D.
    Professor of law.
    2009. County Zoning in Iowa: History and Practice. Univ.
           of Iowa, 1983. (co-author).
    2010. Federal Courts: Cases, Materials, and Problems.
           Bender, 1972- .
    2011. Iowa Land Use and Zoning Law. Univ. of Iowa, 1979.
    2012. Iowa Practice. Callaghan, 1974- . (co-author).
    2013. Moore's Manual: Federal Practice and Procedure.
           Bender, 1962- . (co-author).
    2014. Res Judicata/Preclusion. Bender, 1969.

LIBRARY SCIENCE

Burns, Robert Whitehall, Jr., 1928- .
    Librarian.
    2015. The Design and Testing of a Computerized Method of
           Handling Library Periodicals. U. S. Dept. of H. E.
           W., 1970.
    2016. The Elements of Access to Agricultural Sciences
           Information within Colorado, Montana, New Mexico,
           and Wyoming. Colorado State Univ. Libraries, 1974.
           (co-author).
    2017. Evaluation of the Holdings in Science/Technology in
           the University of Idaho Library. Moscow, 1968.
    2018. Guide to the Literature of Metallurgy. Univ. of
           Idaho, 1960.
    2019. Library Performance Measures as Seen in the
           Descriptive Statistics Generated by a Computer
           Managed Circulation System. Colorado State Univ.
           Libraries, 1975.
    2020. Science and Technology Literature: A Selected
           Bibliography of Sources. Univ. of Idaho, 1964.
    2021. Serial Holdings in Forestry in the University of
           Idaho Library. Moscow, 1966.
    2022. A Survey of User Attitudes toward Selected Services
           Offered by the Colorado State University Libraries.
           Colorado State Univ. Libraries, 1973. (co-author).

Cook, Joseph Lee.
    Librarian.
    2023. The Alcoholic Employee. Vance Bibliographies, 1979.
           Ambulance Services: A Selected Bibliography.
           Council of Planning Librarians, 1978.
    2024. Arson, for Insurance and Protest: A Bibliography,
           1965-1977. Council of Planning Librarians, 1975.
           (co-author).
    2025. A Bibliogrpahy on Eminent Domain, 1960-1975.
           Council of Planning Librarians, 1975. (co-author).
    2026. Coal Gasification as an Energy Alternative. Vance
           Bibliographies, 1980.
    2027. Coal Slurry Lines: A Bibliography, 1967-1977.
           Council of Planning Librarians, 1978. (co-author).
    2028. The Development of Superports since 1960. Vance
           Bibliographies, 1979. (co-author).
    2029. Employee Stock Option Plans and Trusts. Vance
           Bibliographies, 1980. (co-author).
    2030. Employment-at-Will. Vance Bibliographies, 1985.
           (co-author). Gasohol. Vance Bibliographies, 1979.
    2031. Gun Control and the Second Amendment. Vance
           Bibliographies, 1980. (co-author).
    2032. Health Maintenance Organizations and Prepaid Group
           Practices: A Bibliography. Vance Bibliographies,
           1979. (co-author).
    2033. Industrial Spying and Espionage. Vance
           Bibliographies, 1985. (co-author).
    2034. Oil Shale as a Possible Fossil Fuel Resource. Vance
           Bibliographies, 1980. (co-author).
    2035. Sexual Harassment on the Job. Vance Bibliographies,
           1980. (co-author).
    2036. Shore Erosion: A Survey of Literature since 1969.
           Vance Bibliographies, 1980.
    2037. The Transportation of Hazardous Materials. Vance
           Bibliographies, 1980.

Galbraith, Leslie R.
    Librarian.
    2038. The Mind of a Faculty: Essays Presented to Beauford
           A. Norris. Christian Theol. Sem., 1973. (co-
           editor).

Galegar, Jean.
    Librarian.
    2039. Annotated Literature References on Land Treatment of
           Hazardous Waste. Oklahoma State Univ., 1984.

Grosse, Fay Wiseman.
    2040. "Christian Church (Disciples of Christ) Libraries."
           In Church and Synagogue Libraries. pp. 192-202.
           Edited by J.F. Harvey. Scarecrow Pr., 1980.

Gwinn, Mary Jane.
    Librarian.
    2041. Bibliography and Index of Missouri Geology, 1969-
          1976. Washington Univ., 1977.

Hamburger, Roberta.
    Librarian.
    2042. An Illustrated Guide to the Anglo-American
          Cataloging Rules. Seminary Pr., 1971. (co-
          compiler).
    2043. An Illustrated Guide to the International Standard
          Bibliographic Description for Monographs. Seminary
          Pr., 1975. (co-compiler).
    2044. An Index of Festschriften in Religion in the
          Graduate Seminary Library of Phillips University.
          Haymaker Pr., 1970. (co-author).
    2045. Theological Bibliography and Research. Phillips
          Univ., 1973. (co-author).
    2046. Tools for Theological Research. 3d. rev. ed.
          Seminary Pr., 1975. (co-editor).
    2047. Tools for Theological Study. Phillips Univ., 1977.
          (co-author).

Hanson, Kenneth C.
    Librarian.
    2048. "Alphabetic Acrostics: A Form of Critical Study."
          Ph.D. diss., Claremont Grad. School, 1984.

Judah, J. Stillson, 1911-.
    Librarian; historian.
    2049. Hare Krishna and the Counter Culture. Wiley, 1974.
    2050. The History and Philosophy of the Metaphysical
          Movements in America. Westminster, 1967.
    2051. Index to Religious Periodical Literature. Chicago,
          1949-. (editor).
    2052. "A List of Periodicals and Other Serial Publications
          Which Have Been Indexed in Current Indexes or
          Bibliographies, Pertinent to Theological or
          Philosophical Research." Pacific School of
          Religion, 1956.
    2053. A Union List of Periodicals Currently Received by
          California Theological Libraries. Pacific School of
          Religion, 1953. (compiler).

Kuykendall, William Henry Frazer.
    See under THEOLOGY.

Lanier, Gene Daniel, 1934-.
    Librarian.
    2054. "The Transformation of School Libraries into
          Instructional Materials Centers." Ph.D. diss.,
          Univ. of North Carolina, 1968.

McWhirter, David Ian.
    Pastor; librarian.
    2055. <u>The Doctrine of the Christian Church (Disciples of</u>
          <u>Christ: A Bibliography</u>). Tonawanda, N.Y., 1959.
    2056. <u>An Index to the Evangelist and the Christian.</u>
          College Pr., 1983.
    2057. <u>An Index to the Millennial Harbinger.</u> College Pr.,
          1981.

Martin, Randel Odell.
    See under EDUCATION.

Pierson, Roscoe Mitchell.
    Librarian.
    2058. <u>The Disciples of Christ in Kentucky: A Finding List</u>
          <u>of the Histories of Local Congregations of Christian</u>
          <u>Churches.</u> College of the Bible [Lexington] Library,
          1962.
    2059. <u>The Frolic: The Courtship of Raccoon John Smith.</u>
          College of the Bible [Lexington], 1964.
    2060. <u>Hand List of the Histories of Local Congregations of</u>
          <u>Disciples of Christ in Kentucky...</u> College of the
          Bible [Lexington], 1956. (co-compiler).
    2061. <u>John Allen Gano, 1805-1887.</u> Lexington Theol. Sem.,
          1982. (compiler and editor).
    2062. <u>The Life and Times of John Rogers, 1800-1867, of</u>
          <u>Carlisle, Kentucky.</u> Lexington Theol. Sem., 1984.
          (co-author).
    2063. "A Listing of Theses Presented for Degrees from the
          College of the Bible, 1916-1952." Lexington, 1953.
    2064. "Planning for the Church's Birthday." Disciples of
          Christ Historical Soc., 1958.
    2065. <u>A Preliminary Checklist of Lexington, Ky., Imprints,</u>
          <u>1821-1850.</u> Bibliographical Soc. of the Univ. of
          Virginia, 1953.
    2066. <u>Puerto Rican Sabbatical.</u> College of the Bible
          [Lexington], 1959.
    2067. <u>To Do and To Teach, Essays in Honor of Charles Lynn</u>
          <u>Pyatt.</u> Lexington, 1953. (editor).
    2068. <u>A Union List of Periodicals Currently Received by</u>
          <u>Protestant Theological Libraries....</u> College of the
          Bible [Lexington], 1957.
    2069. "West Indian Church History; A Finding List of
          Printed Materials Relating to the History of the
          Church in the English Speaking Caribbean Area."
          Lexington Theol. Sem. Library, 1967. (compiler).

Sayre, John Leslie, 1924-.
    Pastor; librarian.
    2070. <u>Basic Books for the Minister's Library.</u> Seminary
          Pr., 1978. (editor).

2071. Basic Reference Materials. Phillips Univ., 1972.
       Catalogue of Theses. 1913-1965. Phillips Univ.,
       1966. (editor).
2072. "The History of Disciples Student Work." Yale
       Divinity School,1948.
2073. "A History of Disciples Student Work." United
       Christian Missionary Soc., 1951.
2074. An Illustrated Guide to the Anglo-American
       Cataloging Rules. Seminary Pr., 1971. (co-
       compiler.)
2075. An Illustrated Guide to the International Standard
       Bibliographic Description for Monographs. Seminary
       Pr., 1975. (co-author).
2076. An Index of Festschriften in Religion in the
       Graduate Seminary Library of Phillips University.
       Haymaker Pr., 1970. (co-compiler).
2077. A Manual of Bibliographical and Footnote Forms: For
       Use by Theological Students. Seminary Pr., 1974.
       (editor).
2078. A Manual of Forms for Research Papers and D. Min.
       Field Project Reports. Seminary Pr., 1981.
2079. A Manual of Forms for Term Papers and Theses.
       Seminary Pr., 1973.
2080. The Personalized System of Instruction in Higher
       Education: Readings in PSI--the Keller Plan.
       Seminary Pr., 1972. (co-compiler).
2081. A Practical Guide to Typing High School Term Papers.
       Seminary Pr., 1979.
2082. Recommended Reference Books and Commentaries for a
       Minister's Library. Seminary Pr., 1978. (editor).
2083. Theological Bibliography and Research. Phillips
       Univ., 1973. (co-author).
2084. Tools for Theological Research. Seminary Pr., 1975.
       (co-editor).
2085. "Utilization of Individualized Instruction [Non-
       Computerized] in Accredited Graduate Library Schools
       in the United States and Canada." Ph.D. diss.,
       Univ. of Texas at Austin, 1973.

Scheer, Gladys Elizabeth, 1914-.
    Librarian.
2086. The Church Library: Tips and Tools. Bethany, 1973.
2087. "A Manual for Writers of Theses and Term Papers at
       the College of the Bible." College of the Bible
       [Lexington], 1957.

Shaw, Henry King.
    See under THEOLOGY.

Spencer, Claude Elbert
    See under THEOLOGY.

Stillings, Craig T.
   Librarian.
   2088. <u>North Alabama Union List of Serials. Phase II.</u>
       Alabama Lib. Exchange, 1984.

Wezeman, Frederick, 1915-1981.
   Librarian.
   2089. <u>Billings Public Library. Billings. Montana.</u>
       Billings Public Lib., 1964.
   2090. <u>Building Survey and Proposals for a New Central</u>
       <u>Library.</u> Public Lib. (Manitowoc, Wisc.), 1959.
   2091. <u>The Cedar Rapids. Iowa. Public Library.</u> Cedar
       Rapids, 1958. <u>Cedar Rapids Public Library. Cedar</u>
       <u>Rapids. Iowa.</u> Cedar Rapids, 1966.
   2092. <u>Combination School and Public Libraries in</u>
       <u>Pennsylvania.</u> Pennsylvania State Lib., 1965.
   2093. <u>Duluth Public Library. Duluth. Minnesota.</u> Duluth
       Public Lib., 1966.
   2094. <u>Extension of Library Service in the Birmingham-</u>
       <u>Bloomfield Area of Michigan.</u> Baldwin Public Lib.,
       1962.
   2095. <u>The Fond du Lac Public Library. Fond du Lac.</u>
       <u>Wisconsin.</u> Minneapolis, 1957.
   2096. <u>The Great Falls Public Library. Great Falls.</u>
       <u>Montana.</u> Great Falls Public Lib., 1957.
   2097. <u>The Helena Public Library. Helena. Montana.</u>
       Minneapolis, 1957.
   2098. <u>Neighborhood Library Service: A Survey of the</u>
       <u>Extension Services of the Public Library of Des</u>
       <u>Moines.</u> Public Lib. of Des Moines, 1959.
   2099. <u>The Public Libraries of Minneapolis and Hennepin</u>
       <u>County.</u> Minneapolis Public Lib., 1956.
   2100. <u>Public Library Service. Anoka County. Minnesota.</u>
       Minneapolis, 1957.
   2101. <u>Public Library Service. Ramsey County. Minnesota.</u>
       Ramsey County Public Lib., 1958.
   2102. <u>Reference/Information Services in Iowa Libraries.</u>
       Iowa City, 1969.
   2103. <u>Sheldon Public Library. Sheldon. Iowa.</u> Sheldon,
       1966.
   2104. <u>Sioux Public Library. Sioux City. Iowa.</u> Sioux City
       Public Lib., 1963.
   2105. <u>Spencer Public Library. Spencer. Iowa.</u> Spencer
       Public Lib., 1964.
   2106. <u>A Study of Branch Libraries: Lincoln City</u>
       <u>Libraries. Lincoln. Nebraska.</u> Iowa City, 1967.
   2107. <u>The Tulsa Public Library. Tulsa. Oklahoma.</u> Tulsa
       Public Lib.,1958.
   2108. <u>The Whitefish Bay. Wisconsin. Public Library. A</u>
       <u>Survey.</u> Minneapolis, 1955.
   2109. <u>Would a Combined College and Public Library Building</u>
       <u>Be a Good Thing for Billings. Montana.</u> 1963.

Williams, Marvin Dale, 1935-.
   Librarian.
   2110. "Hints for the Beginning 'Church Paper' Journalist."
          Central Christian Church (Indianapolis), 1954.
   2111. "Processing the Hampton Adams Papers: A Practical
          Examination of Decision-Making [an Address]."
          Disciples of Christ Historical Soc., 1969.
   2112. "A Survey of the Carolina Discipliana Library at
          Atlantic Christian College, Wilson, North Carolina."
          Disciples of Christ Historical Soc., 1968.

Zink, James Keith,
   Librarian.
   2113. "The Use of the Old Testament in the Apocrypha."
          Ph.D. diss., Duke Univ., 1964.

MATHEMATICS/STATISTICS

Boyer, John Elvin, 1947-.
   Professor of statistics.
   2114. "Some Admissibility Considerations in the Finite
          State Component Compound and Empirical Boxes
          Decision Problems." Ph.D. diss., Michigan State
          Univ., 1976.

Brown, Francis Robert, 1914-.
   Professor of mathematics.
   2115. "The Effect of an Experimental Course in Geometry on
          Ability to visualize in Three Dimensions." Ph.D.
          diss., Univ. of Illinois, 1955.
   2116. Handbook for Elementary Mathematics Workshops.
          Illinois Dept. of Public Instruction, 1966?
   2117. Intergovernmental Cooperation. Illinois State
          Univ., 1967.

Burney, Gilbert M.
   Professor of mathematics.
   2118. "The Construction and Validation of an Objective
          Formal Reasoning Instrument." Ph.D. diss., Univ. of
          Northern Colorado, 1974.

Chen, Kuo-Tsai, 1923-.
   Professor of mathematics.
   2119. An Application of Coordinates Straining Method.
          1977.
   2120. TINA Ch'uan ts'ao Niu-meng - Hsi-ma shih po hsing
          fen hsi fa t'an t'ao chi yen chiu. 1978.

Cleaver, Charles, 1938-.
   Professor of mathematics.
   2121. Banach Spaces of Analytic Functions. Springer-
          Verlag, 1977.

Colquitt, Landon Augustus, 1919-.
    Professor of mathematics.
    2122. "On Paths of Minimum Flight Time." Ph.D. diss.,
           Ohio State Univ., 1948.

Coltharp, Forrest Lee, 1933-.
    Professor of mathematics.
    2123. "A Comparison of the Effectiveness of an Abstract
           and a Concrete Approach in Teaching of Integers to
           Sixth Grade Students." Ed.D. diss., Oklahoma State
           Univ., 1968.

Gosnell, Jack Leslie, 1944-.
    Professor of mathematics.
    2124. "Conformational Studies on Selected Six-Member
           Rings." Ph.D. diss., Northwestern Univ., 1971.

Gulick, Dennis.
    Professor of mathematics.
    2125. <u>Calculus with Analytic Geometry.</u> Harcourt, 1978.
           (co-author).
    2126. <u>Calculus with Analytic Geometry: Solutions Manual
           for Chapters 1-10.</u> Harcourt, 1978. (co-author).

Gulick, Frances.
    Professor of mathematics.
    2127. <u>Abstract Algebra: An Active Learning Approach.</u>
           Houghton, 1976. (co-author).

Hayden, Robert W., 1944-.
    2128. "A History of the 'New Math' Movement in the United
           States." Ph.D. diss., Iowa State Univ., 1981.

Helsabeck, Fred, Jr., 1936-.
    Professor of mathematics.
    2129. "An Analysis of Difficulties in Abstract Syllogistic
           Reasoning." Ph.D. diss., Michigan State Univ.,
           1973.

Helsabeck, Henry Carter.
    Professor of mathematics.
    2130. "The Minimal Conjugate Point of a Family of
           Differential Equations." Ph.D. diss., Univ. of
           Missouri, 1975.

Hornaback, Joseph Hope, 1910-.
    Professor of mathematics.
    2131. "Integral Equations Related to the Representation of
           Functions by Potentials." Ph.D. diss., Univ. of
           Illinois, 1952.

Hubbard, Bertie Earl, 1928-.
    Professor of mathematics.

2132. <u>Symposium on the Numerical Solution of Partial</u>
       <u>Differential Equations.</u> Academic Pr., 1965-. (co-
       editor).

Huffman, Louie Clarence, 1926-.
    Professor of mathematics.
    2133. "Generalized Functions of Two Discrete Variables."
           Ph.D. diss., Univ. of Texas at Austin, 1969.

Johnson, Wendell Gilbert, 1922-.
    Professor of mathematics.
    2134. <u>Modern Analytic Geometry.</u> 3d. ed. Intext
           Educational Publishers, 1972. (co-author).
    2135. <u>Modern Introductory Mathematics.</u> McGraw, 1966. (co-
           author).
    2136. "A Relation between High-School and College
           Mathematics Grades." Ph.D. diss., Syracuse Univ.,
           1956.

Johnston, Glenn Eric, 1950-.
    Professor of mathematics.
    2137. "Model Green's Functions and the Axioms of Quantum
           Field Theory." Ph.D. diss., Univ. of Maryland, 1978.

McGaughey, A. Wayne.
    Professor of mathematics.
    2138. "Lacunary Double Fourier Series..." Ph.D. diss.,
           Univ. of Cincinnati, 1940.

Maness, Dale Dwayne, 1942-.
    Professor of mathematics.
    2139. "Solvolysis of Aryl Substituted Vinyl Sulfonates by
           a Heterolytic Mechanism." Ph.D. diss., Univ. of
           Florida, 1969.

Megginson, Robert Eugene, 1948-.
    Professor of mathematics.
    2140. "The Semi-Kadec-Klee Condition and Nearest-Point
           Properties of Sets in Normed Linear Spaces." Ph.D.
           diss., Univ. of Illinois, 1984.

Moyer, Robert E.
    Professor of mathematics.
    2141. "Effects of a Unit in Probability on Ninth Grade
           General Mathematics Students' Arithmetic Computation
           Skills, Reasoning, and Attitude." Ph.D. diss.,
           Univ. of Illinois, 1974.

Oxley, Theron D., Jr., 1931-.
    Professor of mathematics.
    2142. "A Study of a Generalized Factorial Series." Ph.D.
           diss., Purdue Univ., 1956.

Peck, Lawrence Keith.
     Professor of mathematics.
     2143. "The Effects of Two Geometrical Instructional
            Paradigms in Grades Four, Six, and Eight." Ed.D.
            diss., Univ. of Missouri, 1970.

Porter, Jack R., 1938-.
     Professor of mathematics.
     2144. "A Note on Common Fixpoints for Commuting
            Functions." Univ. of Oklahoma, 1966?
     2145. <u>On Noncompact, H-Closed Spaces amd Semiregular
            Spaces.</u> Univ. of Oklahoma, 1966.

Rice, Earl Clifton.
     Professor of mathematics.
     2146. "The Transfer of Generalizing Ability from
            Mathematics to Other High-School Subjects." Ph.D.
            diss., George Peabody College for Teachers, 1958.

Turnidge, Darrell Ray, 1941-.
     Professor of mathematics and computer science.
     2147. "Tortion Theories and Rings of Quotients." Ph.D.
            diss., Univ. of Oregon, 1968.

MEDICAL SCIENCES

*Brown, Ryland Thomas, 1807-1890.
     Physician; state geologist; professor of natural science
     and physiology.
     2148. <u>Autobiography of Samuel K. Hoshour.</u> John Burns,
            1884. (co-editor).
     2149. <u>Elements of Physiology and Hygiene.</u> American Book
            Co., 1872, 1900.
     2150. <u>Indiana and Her Resources.</u> Douglass & Conner, 1868.
            (compiler).

For works about him written by Disciple authors, see
     Denny, Robert under THEOLOGY section.
     Brown, Caroline in GENERAL section.

Denton, James Harold.
     Professor of veterinary medicine.
     2151. "The Effect of Further Processing System on Selected
            Microbiological, Physical and Chemical Attributes of
            Turkey Meat Products." Ph.D. diss., Texas A & M
            Univ., 1978.

Fox, Hazel M., 1921-.
     Professor of nutrition.
     2152. "A Survey of Research on Human Nutrition...." U. S.
            Dept. of Agriculture, 1971." (co-compiler).

Haldiman, Jerrold T.
    Professor of veterinary medicine.
    2153. <u>Studies on the Morphology of the Skin, Baleen,</u>
           <u>Respiratory System, Urinary System, Vascular System,</u>
           <u>Brain and Eye of the Bowhead Whale, Balaena</u>
           <u>Mysticetus.</u> Louisiana State Univ., 1982.

Hassinger, Edward Wesley.
    See under SOCIOLOGY.

Henthorn, Barbara Searle.
    Professor of nursing.
    2154. "Disengagement and Reinforcement in the Elderly: An
           Explanatory Survey." D.P.H. diss., Univ. of
           Oklahoma, 1975.

Hinton, Maxine Armstrong, 1919-.
    Professor of nutrition.
    2155. "Factors Related to the Eating Behavior and Dietary
           Adequacy of Girls 12 to 14 Years of Age." Ph.D.
           diss., Iowa State Univ., 1962.

Nash, David Allen, 1942-.
    Professor of dentistry.
    2156. "Profile of Organizational Characteristics of
           Colleges of Dentistry." Ed.D. diss., West Virginia
           Univ., 1984.

Nichols, Andrew Wilkinson.
    Professor of medicine.
    2157. <u>Community Health Resources Handbook.</u> Univ. of
           Arizona, 1981.
    2158. <u>Public Health and Community Medicine.</u> Williams &
           Wilkins, 1980. (co-author).
    2159. <u>Rural Health and Air Mobility.</u> Univ. of Arizona
           College of Medicine? 1972? (co-editor).

Overman. Ralph Theodore, 1919-.
    Professor of nuclear medicine.
    2160. <u>Basic Concepts of Nuclear Chemistry.</u> Reinhold,
           1963.
    2161. "The Kinetics and Mechanism of the Alkaline Fading
           of Iodo Phenol Blue." Ph.D. diss., Louisiana State
           Univ., 1943.
    2162. <u>Radioisotope Techniques.</u> McGraw-Hill, 1960. (co-
           author).
    2163. <u>Who Am I? The Faith of a Scientist.</u> Word, 1971.

Presler, Elizabeth Pettit, 1944-.
    Professor of nursing.
    2164. "The Meaning of Competence in the Education of the
           Helping Professions." Ed.D. diss., Univ. of
           Kentucky, 1984.

Schmal, Philipp, J.R.
>   2165. A Course in Normal Histology, by Rudolf Krause.
>   Rebman, 1913. (translator).
>   2166. The Logic of Faith: An Invitation To Pause and
>   Reflect. Philosophical Lib., 1965.

Spohn, Eric E., 1941-.
>   College administrator; dentist.
>   2167. Operative Dentistry Procedures for Dental
>   Auxiliaries. Mosby, 1981. (co-author).

Stober, Buena Rose.
>   Missionary nurse to Zaire.
>   2168. Mbatela Bana Ba Tosisi [Child Hygiene]. Disciples
>   of Christ Congo Mission, 1936.

MODERN LANGUAGES

Adams, Charles Lindsey, 1923-.
>   Professor of Spanish.
>   2169. "Traditional and Novelesque Elements in the
>   Development of Plot in the Dated Plays of Lope de
>   Vega." Ph.D. diss., Stanford Univ., 1954.

Anderson, Edwin Graham, 1923-.
>   Professor of French.
>   2170. L'Influence Française dans l'Oeuvre de Herman
>   Melville. Univ. of Toulouse (France), 1951.
>   2171. Le Jansenisme dans l'Oeuvre de François Mauriac.
>   Univ. of Kentucky, 1949.

Barb, Arthur Lee (Barb-Mingo, Arturo), 1944-.
>   Professor of foreign languages.
>   2172. Composing Black. 1976.
>   2173. Of the Hue. 1973.
>   2174. Poesías. Pioneer Pr., 1972, 1977.

Bettler, Alan Raymond, 1940-.
>   Professor of foreign languages.
>   2175. "A Chronicle of the Beginning of French
>   Existentialism." Ph.D. diss., Indiana Univ., 1970.

Booker, James Arthur.
>   Professor of foreign languages.
>   2176. "The Major Hermannsschlacht Dramas." Ph.D. diss.,
>   Univ. of Nebraska, 1975.

Cardwell, Walter Douglas, Jr.
>   Professor of modern languages.
>   2177. "The Dramaturgy of Eugene Scribe." Ph.D. diss.,
>   Yale Univ., 1971.

Fitch, C. Bruce.
    Professor of Spanish.
    2178. "El Cavallero del Cisne." Ph.D. diss., Univ. of
          Kentucky, 1974.

Fountain, Anne Owen, 1946-.
    Professor of Spanish.
    2179. "Jose Marti and North American Authors." Ph.D.
          diss., Columbia Univ., 1973.

Mills, Dorothy Hurst.
    Professor of Spanish.
    2180. "A Descriptive Analysis of the Diminutives ito,
          illo, ico, uelo, and of Their Increments...As Used
          in Spanish America." Ph.D. diss., Univ. of Southern
          California, 1955.

Reedy, Daniel R.
    Professor of languages.
    2181. <u>Narraciones Ejemplares de Hispano-America.</u>
          Prentice-Hall, 1967. (co-editor).
    2182. <u>Obra Completa.</u> by Juan del Valle y Caviedes.
          Biblioteca Ayacucho, 1984. (editor).
    2183. "The Poetic Art of Juan del Valle Caviedes." Ph.D.
          diss., Univ. of Illinois, 1962. (Univ. of North
          Carolina Pr., 1964).

Reynolds, Bonnie Hildebrand.
    Professor of foreign languages.
    2184. "Tragedy and Contemporary Spanish American Theatre."
          Ph.D. diss., Univ. of Kansas, 1979.

*Smith, Harlie Lawrence, Jr., 1927-.
    Professor of French and Arabic.
    2185. <u>Modern Written Arabic.</u> U. S. Govt. Print. Off.,
          1969. (editor).

Woods, Jean M.
    Professor of German.
    2186. "Imagery in the Secular Poetry of Georg Rudolf
          Weckherlin." Ph.D. diss., Univ. of Oregon, 1968.
    2187. <u>Schriftstellerinnen. Ku"nstlerinnen und Gelehrte</u>
          <u>Frauen des Deutschen Barock: Ein Lexikon.</u> Metzler,
          1984. (co-author).

NURSING
    See MEDICAL SCIENCES.

NUTRITION
    See MEDICAL SCIENCES.

PHYSICAL EDUCATION/RECREATION

*Bellamy, George Albert, 1872-1960.
    Social settlement director; member of Church of Christ
    2188. Play and Recreation: Four Papers Read at the
           Indiana State Conference on Play and Recreation Held
           in the Claypool Hotel, Indianapolis, May 25, 26, 27,
           1916. Indiana Univ., 1916. (co-author).

Burton, Sid, 1931-.
    Professor of physical education.
    2189. "The Effect of Participation or Non-Participation in
           Student Activities Programs on the Attitudes of
           Sophomore Students toward School in the Midwest
           City-Del City Schools." Ph.D. diss., Univ. of
           Oklahoma, 1977.

Fox, James Crawford.
    Professor of physical education.
    2190. "Establishing Physical Fitness Norms for Fifteen-
           Year-Old Boys and Girls in Virginia Schools." Ed.D.
           diss., Univ. of Virginia, 1961.

Goodloe, Nancy Ruth, 1946-.
    Professor of health and physical education.
    2191. "A Study of the Perceived Qualifications of Women
           Athletic Directors." Ed.D. diss., Univ. of Oregon,
           1978.

Green, Jerry.
    Professor of physical education.
    2192. Detroit Lions. Macmillan, 1973.

Harris, Ed.
    Athletic director.
    2193. Golden Memories of Ed Harris: 50 Years in Big
           Orange Country. 1972?

Hulett, Florence M.
    Professor of physical education.
    2194. "A Quantitative and Qualitative Study of Facilities
           for School Camping and Outdoor Education on State
           Owned Lands in Illinois." Ed.D. diss., Univ. of
           Oregon, 1960.

McBride, Jack E., 1933-.
    Professor of education, psychology and physical education.
    2195. "The History and Development of Faculty Controls of
           Intercollegiate Athletics at Oklahoma University."
           Ph.D. diss., Univ. of Oklahoma, 1965.

Parrish, Margaret Ware.
    Professor of physical education.

2196. <u>Outstanding Kentucky Women in Sports.</u> Midway, Ky.?,
       1968?

Regnier, Earl Hubert.
    Professor of rural recreation.
    2197. <u>Fun with the Family.</u> Stipes, 1958? (co-author).
    2198. <u>A New Approach to Student Welfare and Training for</u>
           <u>Agricultural [and other] Universities in India.</u>
           Uttar Pradesh Agricultural Univ., 1966? (co-author).

Rohde, Dale W.
    Professor of physical education.
    2199. "The Effect of Isometric and Isotonic Exercises on
           the Development of Muscular Strength." Ph.D. diss.,
           Southern Illinois Univ., 1967.

Southard, Danny Lee.
    Professor of physical education.
    2200. "Relationships between Important Competencies and
           Curriculums in Physical Education in Iowa High
           Schools." Ph.D. diss., Univ. of Iowa, 1980.

Standifer, James William, 1913-.
    Professor of physical education.
    2201. "A Study of the Permanence of Recreational Interests
           of College Graduates in Selected Professions."
           Ph.D. diss., Univ. of Michigan, 1958.

Toms, Jack Marshall, 1946-.
    Professor of physical education.
    2202. "An Investigation to Analyze Differences in
           Leadership Characteristics of Directors of Athletics
           in the Three Divisions of the National Collegiate
           Athletic Association and the National Association of
           Intercollegiate Athletics." Ph.D. diss., West
           Virginia Univ., 1978.

Toth, Floyd Delano, 1935-.
    Professor of physical education.
    2203. "Attitudes of Educators toward Collective
           Negotiations." Ph.D. diss., Univ. of Missouri,
           1974.

Vanderpool, Kenneth Gene.
    2204. "The Attitudes of Selected Nineteenth-Century
           Disciples of Christ Leaders Regarding Physical
           Activity." Ph.D. diss., Temple Univ., 1973.

POLITICS/INTERNATIONAL RELATIONS/PUBLIC ADMINISTRATION

Bennett, Marion Tinsley, 1914-.
   U. S. Congressman.
   2205. <u>American Immigration Policies</u>. Public Affairs Pr.,
         1963.
   2206. "The Judges, 1855-1976." In <u>The United States Court</u>
         <u>of Claims</u>, pt. 1, Comm. on the Bicentennial of
         Independence and the Constitution of the Judicial
         Conference of the United States, 1976.

Blowers, Russell Franklin, 1924-.
   2207. <u>This is Communism: A Brief Study for Concerned</u>
         <u>Christians</u>. Starken Publishing Co., 1962.

Bowdler, Georoe A., 1920-.
   Professor of political science.
   2208. <u>A Comparison and Evaluation of Current World Peace</u>
         <u>Force Models</u>. College & University Pr., 1975.
   2209. "Political Participation in El Salvador." Ph.D.
         diss., University of South Carolina, 1974.
   2210. <u>Voter Participation in Central America, 1954-1981.</u>
         Univ. Pr. of America, 1982. (co-author).

Brenneman, Lyle Eugene, 1934-.
   College administrator.
   2211. "Conflict and Change in the Republic of Zaire."
         Ph.D. diss., American Univ., 1976.

Brewer, Marion Carey, 1927-.
   U. S. government official; college president.
   2212. <u>Civil Defense in the United States: Federal, State</u>
         <u>and Local.</u> Washington, 1951.
   2213. <u>Implications of a National Service Program in the</u>
         <u>United States....</u> Washington, 1951.

Bullard, Todd Hupp.
   College president.
   2214. <u>Labor and Legislature: The West Virginia Labor</u>
         <u>Federation and the West Virginia Legislature, 1957-</u>
         <u>1961.</u> West Virginia Univ., 1965.
   2215. <u>Manual of West Virginia Municipal Government.</u> West
         Virginia Univ., 1957. (co-author).

*Chase, Ira Joy, 1834-1895.
   Pastor; governor of Indiana.
   2216. <u>The Jewish Tabernacle.</u> 1883.

*Clark, Champ, 1850-1921.
   Attorney; college president; editor; congressman.
   2217. <u>My Quarter Century of American Politics.</u> 2 vols.
         Harper, 1920.

Clay, Comer, 1910-.
    Professor of government.
    2218. Issues and Attitudes on the Texas Water Plan. Univ.
           of Texas, 1971.
    2219. Legends and Stories of West Texas. Abilene High
           School, 1933.
    2220. "The Lower Colorado River Authority." Ph.D. diss.,
           Univ. of Texas, 1948.
    2221. Your Texas Government. Benson, 1952. (co-author).

Cooper, Myers Young, 1873-1958.
    Businessman; governor of Ohio.
    2222. "Organization To Promote Employment in the State of
           Ohio, 1929 and 1930." U. S. Govt. Print. Off.,
           1930.

Fulbright, James William, 1905-.
    U. S. senator; ambassador to United Nations; college
    president; attorney.
    2223. Amending the Arms Control And Disarmament Act.
           Washington, 1963.
    2224. Claims against Communist China. Washington, 1966.
    2225. The Crippled Giant: American Foreign Policy and Its
           Domestic Consequences. Random House, 1972.
    2226. The Elite and the Electorate. Center for the Study
           of Democratic Institutions, 1963.
    2227. Financial Control of Government Corporations. U. S.
           Govt. Print. Off., 1945.
    2228. Fulbright of Arkansas: The Public Positions of a
           Private Thinker. Luce, 1963.
    2229. Militarism: Impact of the Military upon American
           Democracy. Denison Univ., 1969.
    2230. The New World Looks at the Old World. Univ. of
           Toronto, 1947.
    2231. Old Myths and New Realities. Random House, 1964.
    2232. The Pentagon Propaganda Machine. Liveright, 1970.
    2233. Prospects for the West. Harvard Univ. Pr., 1963.
    2234. The Role of Congress in Foreign Policy. American
           Enterprise Institute for Public Policy Research,
           1971. (co-author).
    2235. Toward a Permanent Peace. A Compilation of Addresses
           and Comments. Nobel Center, 1945.
    2236. The Tripartite Conference at Moscow, October 19-30,
           1943. Carnegie Endowment for International Peace,
           1943.
    2237. The Two Americas. Univ. of Connecticut, 1966.

Gammon, Gary Eldon.
    College administrator.
    2238. "The Role of the United States Senate: Its
           Conception and Its Performance." Ph.D. diss.,
           Claremont Grad. School, 1978.

*Garfield, James Abram, 1831-1881.
   President of the United States; teacher; college president;
      soldier.
    2239. The Diary of James A. Garfield. 4 vols. Michigan
          State Univ., 1967-1981.
    2240. Garfield's Words. Houghton, Mifflin, 1881.
    2241. Gems of the Campaign of 1880. Lincoln Assoc., 1881.
    2242. The Great Speeches of James Abram Garfield! J.
          Burns, 1881.
    2243. Investigation into the Causes of the Gold Panic. U.
          S. Govt. Print. Off., 1870.
    2244. James A. Garfield, 1831-1881: Chester A. Arthur,
          1830-1886: Chronology, Documents, Bibliographical
          Aids. Edited by Howard B. Furer. Oceana
          Publications, 1970.
    2245. James A. Garfield, His Speeches at Home, 1880. C.
          S. Carpenter, 1880.
    2246. The Milligan Case. A. A. Knopf, 1929. (co-author).
    2247. Oration on the Life and Character of Gen. George H.
          Thomas, Delivered before the Society of the Army of
          the Cumberland. R. Clarke & Co., 1871.
    2248. Politics and Patronage in the Gilded Age: The
          Correspondence of James A. Garfield and Charles E.
          Henry. State Historical Soc. of Wisconsin, 1970.
    2249. Speeches of Hon. James A. Garfield, of Ohio, in the
          House of Representatives at the Extra Session. U.
          S. Govt. Print. Off., 1879.
    2250. The Wild Life of the Army: Civil War Letters of
          James A. Garfield. Michigan State Univ. Pr., 1964.
    2251. The Works of James A. Garfield. 2 vols. J.R.
          Osgood, 1882.

For works about him written by Disciple authors, see

                Hinsdale, Burke Aaron, under EDUCATION section;
                Green, Francis Marion,
                Moore, William Thomas,
                Short, Howard Elmo,
                Vaughter, John B. under THEOLOGY section;
                Peskin, Allan in GENERAL section;
                Wasson, Woodrow Wilson in THEOLOGY and GENERAL
                section and
                Rushford, Terry in HISTORY and GENERAL section.

Gibson, Lorenzo Tucker, Jr., 1941-.
   Professor of political science.
    2252. "The Role of the Governor in the Legislative
          Process: A Comparative Study of the Governor of
          Maryland and the Governor of Virginia." Ph.D.
          diss., Univ. of Virginia, 1968.

Green, Edith.
   See under EDUCATION.

Griffin, Charles Hudson, 1926-.
  U. S. Congressman.
  2253. Mississippi Legislature: 1982 Handbook. Jackson,
         Miss., 1981.
  2254. Mississippi Legislature: 1984 Handbook. Jackson,
         Miss., 1984.
  2255. An Oral History with Hon. Charles H. Griffin.
         Jackson, Miss., 1980.

Hargis, Billy James.
  See under THEOLOGY.

Heinlein, David L.
  Professor of political science.
  2256. "The Truman Doctrine: A Chief Executive in Search
         of the Presidency." Ph.D. diss., Johns Hopkins
         Univ., 1974.

Hine, William C.
  College administrator.
  2257. "Frustration, Factionalism and Failure: Black
         Political Leadership and the Republic Party in
         Reconstruction Charleston, 1865-1877." Ph.D. diss.,
         Kent State Univ., 1979.

Hinsdale, Burke Aaron, 1837-1900.
  See under EDUCATION.

Hopper, Rex D.
  See under SOCIOLOGY.

Inman, Samuel Guy, 1877-1965.
  Pastor; missionary; specialist in Latin American affairs.
  2258. America Revolucionaria: Conferencias y Ensayos. J.
         Morata, 1933.
  2259. America's Debt to the West Indies. N.d.
  2260. Andre Bello, a South American Humanist. 1949.
  2261. Bibliography of Writings of Samuel Guy Inman. New
         York?, 1934.
  2262. Building an Inter-American Neighborhood. National
         Peace Conference, 1937.
  2263. Christian Cooperation in Latin America. Committee
         on Cooperation in Latin America, 1917.
  2264. Conferencias Dadas en la Universidad Nacional de
         Mexico. Talleres Graficos de la Nacion, 1929.
  2265. Cultural Relations with Latin America. 1940.
  2266. Democracy and the Americas. Philadelphia, 1939.
         (co-editor).
  2267. Democracy versus the Totalitarian State in Latin
         America. American Academy of Political and Social
         Science, 1938.
  2268. Economics and World Peace. World Alliance for
         International Friendship through the Churches, 1925?

2269.   <u>Evangelicals at Havana.</u> Committee on Cooperation in
        Latin America, 1929.
2270.   <u>The Ever-Nearer Near East.</u> Worldover Pr., 1955.
2271.   <u>A Gentleman and a Scholar.</u> [Biography of Charles
        Thomas Paul.]
2272.   <u>Hacia la Solidaridad Americana.</u> D. Jorro, 1924.
2273.   <u>A History of Latin America for Schools.</u> Macmillan
        Co., 1944. (co-author).
2274.   <u>An Inside View of the Inter-American Conference.</u>
        <u>Mexico City. February 21 - March 9. 1945.</u> Southern
        Council on International Relations, 1954.
2275.   <u>Inter-American Conference for the Maintenance of</u>
        <u>Peace.</u> Friend's Peace Committee, 1936.
2276.   <u>Inter-American Conferences. 1826-1954: History and</u>
        <u>Problems.</u> Washington Univ. Pr., 1965.
2277.   <u>The Inter-American Defense Treaty. An Appraisal.</u>
        Commission on the World Community, National Peace
        Conference, 1948.
2278.   <u>Intervention in Mexico.</u> Association Pr., 1919.
2279.   <u>Latin America. Its Place in World Life.</u> Willett,
        Clark & Co., 1937.
2280.   <u>A New Day in Guatemala: A Study of the Present</u>
        <u>Social Revolution.</u> Worldover Pr., 1951.
2281.   <u>La Nueva Democracia.</u> Committee on Cooperation in
        Latin America, 1920.
2282.   <u>Pan American Conferences and Their Results.</u> 1924.
2283.   <u>Problems in Pan Americanism.</u> Doran, 1921.
2284.   <u>Social and International Conflicts in Latin America.</u>
        Church Peace Union, 1933.
2285.   <u>South America Today: Social and Religious Movements</u>
        <u>as Observed on A Trip to the Southern Continent in</u>
        <u>1921.</u> Committee on Cooperation in Latin America,
        1921.
2286.   <u>Through Santo Domingo and Haiti. a Cruise with the</u>
        <u>Marines.</u> Committee on Cooperation in Latin America,
        1919.
2287.   <u>Trailing the Conquistadores.</u> Friendship Pr., 1930.
2288.   <u>Ventures in Inter-American Friendship.</u> Missionary
        Education Movement of the United States and Canada,
        1925.
2289.   <u>What the South Americans Think of Us.</u> R. M. McBride
        & Co., 1945.
2290.   <u>Which Way South America?</u> Committee on Cooperation
        in Latin America, 1933.

For works about him by Disciple authors, see
    Castleman, William J. under THEOLOGY section; and
    Woods, Kenneth Flint under POLITICS section.

Johnson, Lyndon Baines, 1908-1973.
    U. S. President.
    2291.   <u>America as a Great Power.</u> U. S. Govt. Print. Off.,
            1964.

2292. The Atlantic Community. U. S. Govt. Print. Off.,
       1965.
2293. The Choices We Face. Bantam Books, 1969.
2294. Dear President Johnson. W. Morrow, 1964.
2295. The Johnson Humor. Simon & Schuster, 1965.
2296. The Johnson Presidential Press Conferences. 2 vols.
       E. M. Coleman Enterprises, 1978.
2297. The Johnson Wit. Citadel Pr., 1965.
2298. Legislative Record. U. S. Govt. Print. Off., 1960.
2299. Letters from the Hill Country: The Correspondence
       of Rebekah and Lyndon Baines Johnson. Thorp Springs
       Pr., 1983.
2300. Lyndon B. Johnson. A Biography. By Harry Provence.
       Fleet Publishing Corp., 1964.
2301. Lyndon B. Johnson, 1908-: Chronology--Documents--
       Bibliographical Aids. Oceana Publications, 1971.
2302. Lyndon B. Johnson on Conservation. 5 vols. U. S.
       Dept. of the Interior, 1965.
2303. My Hope for America. Random House, 1964.
2304. A Nation of Cities: Essays on America's Urban
       Problems: A Message by President Johnson and Essays
       by James Q. Wilson and Others. Rand-McNally, 1968.
       (co-author).
2305. President Johnson's Design for a 'Great Society'
       [Speeches]. Congressional Quarterly, 1965.
2306. The President Speaks. on Prosperity and Poverty.
       Civil Rights. Nuclear War. Communism. Your Future!
       Dell, 1964.
2307. Presidential Rhetoric: The Imperial Age. 1961-1974.
       Kendall/Hunt Publishing Co., 1978.
2308. Public Papers of the Presidents of the United
       States. Lyndon B. Johnson...1963/64-1967. 8 vols.
       U. S. Govt. Print. Off., 1965-68.
2309. The Quotable Lyndon B. Johnson. New York, 1968.
2310. Quotations from Chairman LBJ. Simon & Schuster,
       1968.
2311. This America. Random House, 1966.
2312. A Time for Action: A Selection from the Speeches
       and Writings of Lyndon B. Johnson. 1953-64.
       Atheneum Publishers, 1964.
2313. The Vantage Point: Perspectives of the Presidency.
       1963-1969. Holt, 1971.

For works about him see Bird, John and "Faith of the
President..." under GENERAL Section; Miller, William Lee under
EDUCATION section; and Spain, August O. under POLITICS.

Johnson, Tom Loftin, 1854-1911.
   Politician; businessman.
   2314. Assessment of Taxes in the District of Columbia. U.
          S. Govt. Print. Off., 1892.
   2315. My Story. B. W. Huebsch, 1911.

2316.   Protection or Free Trade? U. S. Govt. Print. Off.,
        1892.

Kullowatz, Vernon F.
    College administrator.
    2317.   Operation Countdown: Character and Citizenship
            Manual. U. S. Civil Air Patrol, 1962.

Martin, Edwin W.
    Professor of diplomacy.
    2318.   Southeast Asia and China: The End of Containment.
            Westview, 1977.

Miller, William Lee.
    See under EDUCATION.

Ossman, Albert John, 1927-.
    Professor of political science.
    2319.   "The Development of Canadian Foreign Policy." Ph.D.
            diss., Syracuse Univ., 1963.

Phillips, Thomas Wharton, Jr., 1874-1956.
    Oil executive; Congressman.
    2320.   "Abraham Lincoln...Extension of Remarks...in the
            House of Representatives." U. S. Govt. Print.
            Off., 1927.
    2321.   "Americanism above Republicanism." Butler, Pa.,
            1937.
    2322.   "Constitutional Innovations...Speech..." U. S.
            Govt. Print. Off., 1927.
    2323.   "The Eighteenth Amendment...Speech..." U. S. Govt.
            Print. Off., 1927.
    2324.   "Unless the Sixteenth Amendment Is Repealed or
            Drastically Modified, Our System of Government as
            Established by the Founding Fathers Will Perish."
            1938.

Price, David Eugene.
    Professor of political science.
    2325.   Bringing Back the Parties. CQ Pr., 1984.
    2326.   The Commerce Committees: A Study of the House and
            Senate Commerce Committees. Grossman Publishers,
            1975.
    2327.   The Ideological Backdrop of American Foreign Policy:
            Domestic Reformers and World War I. Duke Univ.,
            1977.
    2328.   The Impact of Reform: The House Commerce
            Subcommittee on Oversight and Investigations. Duke
            Univ., 1978.
    2329.   Policymaking in Congressional Committees: The
            Impact of "Environmental" Factors. Univ. of Arizona
            Pr., 1979.
    2330.   Who Makes the Laws? Creativity and Power in Senate
            Committees. Schenkman Publishing Co., 1972.

Reagan, Ronald Wilson, 1911-.
   U. S. President; actor.
   2331.   The Creative Society: Some Comments on Problems
          Facing America. Devin-Adair, 1968.
   2332.   I Goofed: The Wise and Curious Sayings of Ronald
          Reagan. Diablo, 1968.
   2333.   "I Hope You're All Republicans." [Quotations by
          Ronald Reagan and Other Commentators.] Catalyst
          Pr., 1981.
   2334.   The Official Ronald Wilson Reagan Quote Book.
          Chain-Pinkham, 1980.
   2335.   The Quotable Ronald Reagan: The Common Sense and
          Straight Talk of Former California Governor, Ronald
          Reagan. JRH & Associates, 1975.
   2336.   Ronald Reagan's Call To Action. Warner, 1976.
   2337.   Sincerely, Ronald Reagan. Green Hill, 1976.
   2338.   Where's the Rest of Me? Duell, 1965.

See also under Moomaw, Don D., "Nelle's Reagan" and
   Wills, Garry in GENERAL section.

Redford, Emmette Shelburn, 1904-.
   Professor of public administration.
   2339.   Administration of National Economic Control.
          Macmillan, 1952.
   2340.   American Government and the Economy. Macmillan,
          1965.
   2341.   Centralized and Decentralized Political Impacts on a
          Developing Economy. American Soc. for Public
          Administration, 1967.
   2342.   Congress Passes the Federal Aviation Act of 1958.
          Univ. of Alabama, 1961. (co-author).
   2343.   Democracy in the Administrative State. Oxford Univ.
          Pr., 1969.
   2344.   Field Administration of Wartime Rationing. Office
          of Price Administration (Washington, D. C.). 1947.
   2345.   The General Passenger Fare Investigation. Univ. of
          Alabama Pr., 1960.
   2346.   Ideal and Practice in Public Administration. Univ.
          of Alabama Pr.,   1958.
   2347.   National Regulatory Commissions. Univ. of Maryland,
          1959.
   2348.   Organizing the Executive Branch. Univ. of Chicago
          Pr., 1981.
   2349.   Political Science in a University. Southern Meth.
          Univ., 1961.
   2350.   Politics and Government in the United States.
          Harcourt, 1965.
   2351.   Potential Public Policies To Deal with Inflation
          Caused by Market Power. U. S. Govt. Print. Off.,
          1959.
   2352.   Public Administration and Policy Formation. Univ.
          of Texas Pr., 1956. (editor).

2353.   The Regulatory Process, with Illustrations from
        Commercial Aviation. Univ. of Texas Pr., 1969.
2354.   The Role of Government in the American Economy.
        Macmillan, 1966.

Reynolds, Harry Wesley, 1924-.
    Professor of public administration.
    2355.   "Gubernatorial Coordination of Administrative Boards
            and Commissions in Pennsylvania." Ph.D. diss.,
            Univ. of Pennsylvania, 1954.
    2356.   Intergovernmental Relations in the United States.
            American Academy of Political and Social Sciences,
            1965. (editor).

Rice, Ross Richard, 1922-.
    Professor of political science.
    2357.   American Issues Forum. Arizona State Univ., 1976.
            (co-author).
    2358.   An Annotated Bibliography of Arizona Politics and
            Government. Arizona State Univ., 1976. (compiler).
    2359.   Extremist Politics: An Arizona Recall Election.
            McGraw, 1964. "The Politics of Missouri Basin
            Development." Ph.D. diss., Univ. of Chicago, 1956.

Richards, Claud Henry, Jr., 1917-.
    Professor of political science.
    2360.   "Jehovah's Witnesses: A Study in Religious
            Freedom." Ph.D. diss., Duke Univ., 1945.

Schwabe, George Blaine, 1886-1942.
    U. S. Congressman.
    2361.   Memorial Services Held in the House of
            Representatives of the United States, Together with
            Remarks Presented in the Eulogy of George Blaine
            Schwabe. U. S. Govt. Print. Off., 1952.

Sherwood, Henry Noble.
    See under HISTORY.

Smith, Gerald Lyman Kenneth, 1898-1976.
    2362.   Besieged Patriot: Autobiographical Episodes Exposing
            Traitorism and Zionism from the Life of Gerald L. K.
            Smith. Christian Nationalist Crusade, 1978.
    2363.   Dangerous Enemies. Committee of 1,000,000, 1939.
    2364.   Handbook for the Courageous. Christian Nationalist
            Crusade, 1956.
    2365.   Matters of Life and Death: A Handbook for Patriots
            Dealing with the Issues on Which America Will Rise
            or Fall. Christian Nationalist Crusade, 1958.
    2366.   Mysterious Facts behind the Death of Senator Joseph
            McCarthy. Christian Nationalist Crusade, 1957.
    2367.   The Plot To Undermine the Republic. Christian
            Nationalist Crusade, 195-.

2368. Speeches and Miscellaneous Material. 3 vols.
       Detroit, 1939-42.
2369. Too Much and Too Many Roosevelts. Christian
       Nationalist Crusade, 1950.
2370. Too Much Roosevelt. Detroit? 1940.
2371. War Mongers and the Threat of War. Committee of
       1,000,000, 1941.

Snell, De Witt Smith, 1898-.
    2372. Let's Save What We Can! Essays, Letters and
           Addresses on the Crisis before America, Resulting
           from Hitler's Conquest of Europe. Gazette, 1942.
    2373. The Lindberghs - An Appreciation. D. S. Snell,
           1941.
    2374. Pamphlets on Neutrality. Schenectady, 1939-41.
    2375. Unheeded Warnings: Or, The History of a Futile
           Effort to Avert National Disaster. Gazette, 1940.

Spain, August O., 1907-.
    Professor of government.
    2376. Legislative Redistricting in Texas. Southern
           Methodist Univ., 1965. (co-author).
    2377. The 1964 Presidential Election in the Southeast.
           Southern Methodist Univ., 1966.

Spainhower, James I.
    Professor of political science.
    2378. Pulpit, Pew and Politics. Bethany, 1979.

Waldrop, W. Earl.
    College administrator.
    2379. How To Combat Communism. Bethany, 1962.
    2380. What Makes America Great? Bethany, 1957.
    2381. You've Got a Problem! Naylor, 1962.

Watson, Gerald Glenn, 1945-.
    Professor of political science.
    2382. "Recruitment and Representation: A Study of the
           Social Backgrounds and Political Career Patterns of
           Members of the West German Bundestag, 1949-1969."
           Ph.D. diss., Univ of Florida, 1971.

Welsh, Matthew Empson, 1912-.
    Governor of Indiana.
    2383. View from the State House: Recollections and
           Reflections, 1961-1965. Indiana Historical Bureau,
           1981.

Woods, Kenneth Flint.
    2384. "Samuel Guy Inman His Role in the Evolution of
           Inter-American Cooperation." Ph.D. diss., American
           Univ., 1962.

PSYCHOLOGY/COUNSELING
   See also under Pastoral Care in the Subject Index.

Alexander, Ralph Jon.
   Professor of psychology.
   2385.   "Some Relationships between Childhood Memories and
           Personality Patterns in Therapy and Nontherapy
           Populations." Ph.D. diss., Univ. of Oklahoma, 1976.

Ball, Wilbert R., 1934-.
   Professor of counseling.
   2386.   "Physical Contact as a Variable in Encounter Group
           Programming of Counselors in Training." Ed.D.
           diss., Indiana Univ., 1971.

Bell, Walter Presley.
   Pastor; psychologist.
   2387.   The Case for Pastoral Clinical Training.
           Christopher Publishing House, 1967.

Bergman, Rita Elizabeth, 1925-.
   Professor of psychology.
   2388.   Children's Behavior. Exposition Pr., 1968.
           (editor).
   2389.   "The Contribution of the Helicopter to Mass
           Transportation." Hs.D. thesis., Indiana Univ.,
           1959.
   2390.   "An Investigation of Adolescent Attitudes toward
           Safety." Ed.D. diss., Indiana Univ., 1959.
   2391.   The Sociopath. Exposition Pr., 1968. (compiler).

Bixler, Lawrence M.
   Professor of psychology and Christian education.
   2392.   How To Teach. Standard, 1964.

Boeyink, David Earl.
   See under THEOLOGY.

Browning, Don S.
   See under THEOLOGY.

Bryant, Marcus David.
   Professor of psychology.
   2393.   The Art of Christian Caring. Bethany, 1979.
   2394.   The Church and Community Resources. Bethany, 1977.
   2395.   Come Alive! American Board of Education and
           Publication, 1971.
   2396.   "Patterns of Religious Thinking of University
           Students as Related to Intelligence." Ph.D. diss.,
           Univ. of Nebraska, 1958.

Buckner, Robert Dale.
   Guidance counselor.

2397. "An Experiment to Study the Effectiveness of School Directed Parental Assistance to Elementary School Pupils with Reading Problems." Ed.D. diss., Univ. of Nebraska, 1972.

Cade, Alex J.
Professor of counseling.
2398. Psychological Responses of Modern Man to Present-Day Society. Nebraska School of Religion, 1971.

Caldwell, Lee Syers, 1921-.
Professor of psychology.
2399. The Effect of an Analgesic Agent on Muscular Work Decrement. Army Medical Research Laboratory (Fort Knox), 1962. (co-author).
2400. How Man Controls and Uses the Factors of His Environment. Benton Review Shop, 1938. (co-author).
2401. How Man Is Influenced by the Factors of His Environment. Benton Review Shop, 1938.
2402. "The Mononuclear Count as an Index of Emotionality of the Rat." Ph.D. diss., Univ. of Kentucky, 1960.

Calhoun, Audrey Albrecht, 1939-.
Professor of psychology; college administrator.
2403. "The Development of a Method for Assessing Priorities among Various Educational Goals and Results." Ph.D. diss., Duke Univ., 1977.

Carlson, Keith Wilbert.
Professor of psychology.
2404. "Reinforcement of Empathy: An Operant Paradigm for the Training of Counselors." Ph.D. diss., Northern Illinois Univ., 1971.

Channels, Vera Grace, 1915-.
Clinical psychologist; professor.
2405. Career Education in Home Economics. Interstate, 1973. (co-author).
2406. Experiences in Interpersonal Relationships. Interstate, 1975.
2407. Freedom Is an Inside Job. John Knox, n.d.
2408. Home Economics Careers. Interstate, 1974. (co-author).
2409. The Layman Builds a Christian Home. Bethany, 1959.
2410. Resources for Teaching about Family Life Education. National Council on Family Relations, 1976. (contributor).

Cheatham, Richard Beauregard, 1916-.
Professor of psychology.
2411. "A Study of the Effects of Group Counseling on Self-Concept and on the Reading Efficiency of Low-

Achieving Readers in a Public-Intermediate School."
Ph.D. diss., American Univ., 1968.

Cole, Steven George, 1938-.
Professor of psychology.
2412.   An Evaluative Investigation of the Initial Clinic
         Session at JPSH and PP. Texas Christian Univ.,
         1972. (co-author).
2413.   A Sourcebook of Vasectomy. Texas Christian Univ.,
         1972. (co-author).
2414.   "A Note on Verbalized Strategies in a Three-Person
         Political Convention Situation." Ph.D. diss.,
         Michigan State Univ., 1967.

Colston, Lowell G.
See under THEOLOGY.

Corwin, Betty Jane, 1920-.
Professor of psychology.
2415.   "An Investigation of Extinction of the Running
         Response under Varying Conditions of Shock
         Punishment." Ph.D. diss., Ohio State Univ., 1951.
2416.   The Macro-Programmed Curriculum. Ohio Univ., 1972?
         (co-author).

Cox, Charles Leonard.
Professor of psychology.
2417.   "Differential Use of Informational Sources between
         Sociopaths and Nonsociopaths within an Attributional
         Framework." Ph.D. diss., Univ. of Texas at Austin,
         1977.

Daniel, Robert Strongman, 1914-.
Professor of psychology.
2418.   Comprehensive Annotated Bibliography on the Teaching
         of Psychology. Anerican Psychological Assoc., 1974.
         (co-author).
2419.   Contemporary Readings in General Psychology.
         Houghton Mifflin, 1959. (editor).
2420.   Human Sexuality Methods and Materials for Education,
         Family Life and Health Professors. Heuristicus
         Publishing Co., 1979.
2421.   Professional Problems in Psychology. Prentice-Hall,
         1953. (co-author).

Demaree, Robert Glenn, 1920-.
Professor of psychology.
2422.   Behavioral Measures and Related Criteria for
         Assessment of Outcomes during Treatment for Drug
         Users in the DARP. Texas Christian Univ., 1973.
2423.   "An Experimental Program for Relating Transfer of
         Training to Pilot Performance and Degree of

Simulation." U. S. Naval Training Device Center, 1965.

2424. Follow-Up Study of the September, 1959, Freshmen Enrollees in the College of Liberal Arts at the University of Illinois. Univ. of Illinois, 1963. (co-author).

2425. "An Investigation of Homogeneity in the Interpretation and Scaling of Test Results." Ph.D. diss., Univ. of Illinois, 1950.

2426. The Law School Admission Test and Pre-Legal Record as Predictors of First Semester Grades. Urbana, 1966? (co-author).

2427. Needed Research on the Genes and Environment in Human Psychological Development. Texas Christian Univ., 1971. (co-editor).

2428. Perceptions of the University by Freshman and Sophomore Enrollees of the College of Liberal Arts and Sciences. Univ. of Illinois, 1963.

2429. Students' Evaluations of Various Aspects of the University. Univ. of Illinois, 1963. (co-author).

2430. A Trial Study in Maintenance of Section Enrollment Data. 2 vols. Univ. of Illinois, 1963. (co-author).

De Young, Quintin R.
    Professor of psychology.
2431. "A Study of Contemporary Christian Existential Theology [Kierkegaard and Tillich] and Modern Dynamic Psychology [Freud and Sullivan] Concerning Guilt Feelings." Ph.D. diss., Univ. of Southern California, 1959.

Ewing, Larry Eugene, 1943-.
    Professor of counseling.
2432. "Career Development of College Athletes: Implications for Counseling Activities." Virginia Polytechnic Institute and State Univ., 1975.

Gorsuch, Richard Lee, 1937-.
    Professor of institutional behavior and research.
2433. "The Classification of Some Superego Factors." Ph.D. diss., Univ. of Illinois, 1965.

2434. Evaluation of Treatment in DARP Cohort 3 Based on Behavioral Outcomes during Treatment. Texas Christian Univ., 1975. (co-author).

2435. Factor Analysis. Saunders, 1974.

2436. The Nature of Man: A Social Psychological Perspective. Thomas, 1976. (co-author.)

2437. The Psychology of Religion: An Empirical Approach. Prentice-Hall, 1985. (co-author).

Hill, Edwin S., 1926-.
    Professor of psychology.
    2438. "An Analysis of the Results of Special Training in
           Listening Compared to Special Training in Reading
           Skills." Ed.D. diss., Indiana Univ., 1961.

Honey, Richard David, 1927-.
    Professor of psychology.
    2439. "The Psychological Margin of Safety." Ph.D. diss.,
           Univ. of Chicago, 1962.

Hull, Debra Beery.
    Professor of psychology.
    2440. "Some Interpersonal Effects of Non-Assertion,
           Assertion and Aggression." Ph.S. diss., Kent State
           Univ., 1977.

Hull, John Howard.
    Professor of psychology.
    2441. "Instrumental Response Topographies in the Rat."
           Kent State Univ., 1975.

Johnson, Frank P., 1935-.
    College professor; counselor.
    2442. _Joining Together: Group Theory and Group Skills._
           Prentice-Hall, 1975. (co-author).

Knight, Walter Rea.
    Professor of psychology and biology.
    2443. "Early Social Experience, Aggressive Behavior, and
           Social Stress in Laboratory Rats." Ph.D. diss.,
           Pennsylvania State Univ., 1961.

Laughrun, James O.
    Professor of psychology.
    2444. "Religious Resources as a Source of Emotional
           Stability and Therapeutic Change." University
           Microfilms, 1968.

Ligon, Ernest Mayfield, 1897-.
    2445. "A Comparative Study of Certain Incentives in the
           Learning of the White Rat." Ph.D. diss., Yale
           Univ., 1927.
    2446. _Dimensions of Character._ Macmillan, 1956.
    2447. _Exploring Christian Potential [Character Research_
           Project]. Schenectady, N.Y., n.d.
    2448. _A Greater Generation._ Macmillan, 1948.
    2449. _The Marriage Climate._ Bethany, 1963. (co-author).
    2450. _Parent Roles._ Union College. 1959.
    2451. _The Psychology of Christian Personality._ Macmillan,
           1935.
    2452. _Their Future Is Now: The Growth and Development of_
           Christian Personality. Macmillan, 1935.

2453.   Union College Studies in Character Research. Union
        College, 1953.

McConahay, John B.
     Professor of psychology.
2454.   Comprehensive Statistical Survey. Durham Urban
        Observatory, 1977.
2455.   A Cross-Cultural Study of Sexual Permissiveness.
        Sex-Role Rigidity and Violence. Duke Univ., 1977.
        (co-author).
2456.   The Effects of School Desegregation upon Student
        Racial Attitudes and Behavior: A Critical Review of
        the Literature and a Prolegomena to Future Research.
        Duke Univ., 1978.
2457.   Has Racism Declined?: It Depends Upon Who's Asking
        and What Is Asked. Duke Univ., 1980. (co-author).
2458.   Is It the Buses or the Blacks?: Self-Interest
        versus Symbolic Racism as Predictors of Opposition
        to Busing in Louisville. Duke Univ., 1981. (co-
        author).
2459.   The Los Angeles Riot Study. Univ. of California,
        1967. (co-author).
2460.   The Politics of Violence: The New Urban Blacks and
        the Watts Riot. Univ. Pr. of America, 1973. (co-
        author).
2461.   Psychology and America's Urban Dilemmas. McGraw-
        Hill, 1975. (co-author).

Miller, Wilbur C., 1923-.
     Professor of psychology; college president.
2462.   Personality, Social Class and Delinquency. Wiley,
        1966. (co-author).

Owen, Dan Kelley.
     Missionary.
2463.   "Early Recollections: Idiographic Assessment and
        Millon Diagnostic Categories." Ph.D. diss., Univ.
        of Texas, 1979.

Parshall, Clyde Joseph.
     Professor of psychology.
2464.   "Expressions of Aggression and Guilt in Hypnotic
        Dreams." Ph.D. diss., Univ. of Missouri, 1967.

Pollard, Lucille Addison, 1917-.
     Professor of psychology.
2465.   "Women on College and University Faculties." Ph.D.
        diss., Univ. of Georgia, 1965.

Ranken, Howard Benedict.
     Professor of psychology.
2466.   "The Effect of Stimulus-Response Order on Mediated
        Association." Ph.D. diss., Columbia Univ., 1956.

Schippers, Louis, 1938-.
    Professor of psychology.
    2467. "Patterns of Identification with Parental Moral
           Values among Late Adolescents and Related Measures
           of Superego Expression." Ph.D. diss., Boston Univ.,
           1970.

Snider, Fred Louis.
    Professor of psychology.
    2468. "Effects of Learning Rate, Presentation Rate and
           Incentives on Acquisition of Paired Associates."
           Ph.D. diss., Univ. of Missouri, 1968.

Strickland, Benny Ray.
    See under EDUCATION.

Walker, James Lynwood.
    Psychologist.
    2469. Body and Soul: Gestalt Therapy and Religious
           Experience. Abingdon, 1971.

Yarbrough, Robert Clyde, 1907-.
    2470. Make Life Count: Suggested Attitudes and Methods
           for Significant Living. Christopher, 1957.
    2471. Triumphant Personality: Suggested Paths to Great
           and Noble Living. Macmillan, 1949.

PUBLIC ADMINISTRATION
    See POLITICS.

SCIENCES

Anderson, Gerald Clifton, 1920-.
    Professor of animal science.
    2472. "Nutritional Requirements of Swine." Ph.D. diss.,
           Univ. of Missouri, 1952.

Azbill, Wilson Kendrick, 1848-1929.
    Pastor; missionary.
    2473. Science and Faith: The Spiritual Law in the
           Physical World. Standard, 1914.

Becker, Lawrence Charles, 1934-.
    Professor of physics.
    2474. "A Study of the N^{14} [N^{14}, N^{13}] N^{15} Reaction at Energies
           below the Coulomb Barrier." Ph.D. diss., Yale
           Univ., 1964.

Bennett, Lloyd Morris, 1928-.
    Professor of marine biology and science education.
    2475. "A Study of the Comparison of Two Instructional

Methods, the Field Method and the Classroom Method,
Involving Science Content in Ecology for the
Seventh Grade." Ph.D. diss., Florida State Univ.,
1963.

2476.   A Study Concerning the Effectiveness of the
Secondary Level Guidance Counselor in Test
Interpretation. Texas Woman's Univ., 1965. (co-
author).

Berlin, Kenneth Darrell, 1933-.
Professor of chemistry.
2477.   "Conjugate Addition of Griguard Reagents with 1-
Naphthyl Triphenylmethyl Ketone." Ph.D. diss.,
Univ. of Illinois, 1959.
2478.   Fundamentals of Organic Chemistry. Ronald Pr. Co.,
1972. (co-author).
2479.   Organophosphorus Stereochemistry. Halsted Pr.,
1975. (co-editor).

Binkley, Stephen Bennett, 1910-.
Professor of mathematics and biochemistry.
2480.   The Antihemorrhagic Factors Isolation and Chemical
Studies of Vitamin K_2. 1939. (co-author).
2481.   Basic Biochemistry. Macmillan, 1965. (co-author).
2482.   "Ortho-Arsenated Phenoxyalkanols and Meta-Arsenated
Phenoxyethanols." Ph.D. diss., Univ. of Nebraska,
1938.

Birkholz, Dick Wayne.
Professor of biology.
2483.   "Variation in Andropogon Gerardi Vitman." Ph.D.
diss., Univ. of Kansas, 1970.

Blankenbecler, Richard.
Professor of physics.
2484.   "Relativistic Effects in the Two-Body Current
Operator." Ph.D. diss., Stanford Univ., 1958.
2485.   Differential Equations of Quantum Field Theory.
Stanford Research Institute, 1956.
2486.   Proceedings of Summer Institute on Particle Physics.
1974.
2487.   Singularities of Scattering Amplitudes on Unphysical
Sheets and Their Interpretation. Centro Brasileiro
de Pesquisas Fisicas, 1961.

Bocksch, Robert Donald, 1931-.
Professor of chemistry.
2488.   "Studies on the Synthesis of a Ring C-D Bicyclic
Intermediate for 17-Carboxy Steroids." Ph.D. diss.,
Univ. of Wisconsin, 1960.

Boleman, Larry Livingston.
     Professor of animal science.
     2489.   "Effect of Source of Nitrogen in Liquid Supplements
             on the Utilization of Roughage by Growing Beef
             Calves." Ph.D. diss., Texas A & M Univ., 1976.

Born, Jerry Lynn.
     Professor of pharmacology.
     2490.   "Synthesis of Certain Substituted Benzo (g)
             Quinolines." Ph.D. diss., Univ. of Iowa, 1970.

Boschke, Friedrich Ludwig, 1920-.
     Nuclear chemist.
     2491.   Analytical Problems. Springer-Verlag, 1981.
             (editor).
     2492.   Bioactive Organo-Silicon Compounds. Springer-
             Verlag, 1979. (editor).
     2493.   Creation Still Goes On. McGraw, 1964.
     2494.   Die Chemische Bindung: Eine Versta"ndliche
             Einfu"hrung. Springer-Verlag, 1975. (co-author).
     2495.   Englisch fu"r Chemiker. Wissenschaftliche
             Verlagsgesellschaft MBH, 1973.
     2496.   Erde von Anderen Sternen. Econ-Verlag, 1965.
     2497.   Die Herkunft des Lebens. Econ-Verlag, 1970.
     2498.   Host Guest Complex Chemistry. No. II. Springer-
             Verlag, 1982.
     2499.   Inorganic and Analytical Chemistry. Springer-
             Verlag, 1972. (editor).
     2500.   Inorganic and Physical Chemistry. Springer-Verlag,
             1978. (editor).
     2501.   Inorganic Chemistry. Springer-Verlag, 1981.
             (editor).
     2502.   Inorganic Ring Systems. Springer-Verlag, 1982.
             (editor).
     2503.   Large Amplitude Motion in Molecules Two. Springer-
             Verlag, 1975. (editor).
     2504.   Medicinal Chemistry. Springer-Verlag, 1977.
             (editor).
     2505.   Micelles. Springer-Verlag, 1980. (editor).
     2506.   Molecular Orbitals. Springer-Verlag, 1971.
             (editor).
     2507.   New Methods in Chemistry. Springer-Verlag, 1972.
             (editor).
     2508.   New Trends in Chemistry. Springer-Verlag, 1982.
             (editor).
     2509.   Nuclear Quadrupole Resonance. Springer-Verlag,
             1972. (co-editor).
     2510.   Organic Chemistry. Springer-Verlag, 1980. (editor).
     2511.   Organotin Compounds. Springer-Verlag, 1982.
             (editor).
     2512.   Silicon Chemistry. Springer-Verlag, 1974. (editor).
     2513.   Stereo and Theoretical Chemistry. Springer-Verlag,
             1972. (editor).

2514. Structure and Transformations of Organic Molecules.
       Springer-Verlag, 1972. (co-editor).
2515. Und 1000 Jahre Sind Wie ein Tag. Bertelsmann, 1979.
2516. Das Unerforschte: Die Unbekannte Welt. Econ-
       Verlag, 1975.

Brenton, Charles L.
    Professor of meteorology.
    2517. "A Resume on the State of the Art for Show
           Forecasting." USAF Environmental Technical
           Applications Center, 1973.

Britton, Joseph C., Jr.
    Professor of biology.
    2518. "The Lucinidae [Mollusca: Bivalvia] of the Western
           Atlantic Ocean." Ph.D. diss., George Washington
           Univ., 1970.
    2519. Proceedings, First International Corbicula
           Symposium. Texas Christian Univ. Research
           Foundation, 1979. (editor).

Brooks, Wayne Maurice.
    Professor of entomology.
    2520. "The Role of the Holotrichous Ciliates, Tetrahymena
           Limacis (Warren) and Tetrahymena Rostrata (Kahl) as
           Parasites of the Gray Field Slug." Univ. of
           California, 1966.

Brown, David Francis, 1935-.
    Microbiologist.
    2521. "Gas Chromatographic Determination of Chances in
           Concentration of Pipecolic Acid and Other Free Amino
           Acids in Hypersensitive Tobacco Plants Induced by
           Tobacco Mosaic Virus and Temperature." Ph.D. diss.,
           Utah State Univ., 1969.

Bryant, Frederick Cordus.
    Professor of environmental science.
    2522. "Botanical and Nutritive Content in Diets of Sheep,
           Angora Goats, Spanish Goats and Deer Grazing a
           Common Pasture." Ph.D. diss., Texas A & M Univ.,
           1977.

Burchill, Brower Rene.
    Professor of biology.
    2523. "Effects of Metabolic Inhibitors and Radiations on
           Regeneration in the Ciliate Stentor Coeruleus."
           Ph.D. diss., Western Reserve Univ., 1966.

Burkhead, Carl E.
    Professor of ecology.

2524. <u>Characteristics and Soil Treatment of Biologically</u>
       <u>Treated Swine Waste.</u> Kansas Water Resources
       Research Institute, 1974.
2525. <u>The Development of Water Quality Criteria for</u>
       <u>Ammonia.</u> Kansas Water Resources Research Institute,
       1979. (co-author).
2526. <u>Inorganic Phosphorus Species and Transfer Mechanisms</u>
       <u>in Soils to Sediments for Two Small Kansas</u>
       <u>Watersheds.</u> Kansas Water Resources Research
       Institute, 1978. (co-author).

Bursewicz, John.
    Professor of biology.
    2527. <u>Environmental Resources Inventory.</u> Culver-Stockton
           College, 1978? (co-author).

Bywaters, James Humphreys, 1907-.
    Professor of chemistry and biology.
    2528. "The Hereditary and Environmental Portions of the
           Variance in Weaning Weights of Poland-China Pigs."
           Ph.D. diss., Iowa State College, 1936.

Carpenter, Kenneth Halsey, 1939-.
    Professor of physics.
    2529. "Phase Transitions in the Spherical Model of a
           Lattice Gas and Related Models." Ph.D. diss., Texas
           Christian Univ., 1966.

Caves, Thomas Courtney, 1940-.
    Professor of chemistry.
    2530. "A Study of Hartree-Fock Perturbation Theory in
           Atoms and Molecules." Ph.D. diss., Columbia Univ.,
           1968.

Collias, Eugene E.
    Oceanographer.
    2531. <u>Atlas of Physical and Chemical Properties of Puget</u>
           <u>Sound and Its Approaches.</u> Univ. of Washington Pr.,
           1974. (co-author).
    2532. <u>Bibliography of Literature: Puget Sound Marine</u>
           <u>Environment.</u> Univ. of Washington, 1971. (co-
           author.)
    2533. <u>Eastern North Pacific and Gulf of Alaska, Offshore</u>
           <u>Physical and Chemical Data, April 1954 - January</u>
           <u>1955.</u> Univ. of Washington, 1956. (co-author).
    2534. <u>Index to Physical and Chemical Oceanographic Data of</u>
           <u>Puget Sound and Its Approaches, 1932-1966.</u> State of
           Washington, Dept. of Natural Resources, 1970.
    2535. <u>Machine Processing of Geological Data.</u> Univ. of
           Washington, 1963.
    2536. <u>A Manual for Oceanographic Observers aboard U.S.</u>
           <u>Fish and Wildlife Service Exploratory Fisheries</u>
           <u>Vessels.</u> Univ. of Washington, 1956.

2537. An Oceanographic Survey of the Bellingham-Samish Bay
       System. Univ. of Washington, 1962.
2538. Physical and Chemical Data for Puget Sound and
       Approaches. January 1964 - December 1965. Univ. of
       Washington, 1966.
2539. A Program for Baseline Studies Related to Marine
       Waters of the State of Washington. State of
       Washington, 1974.
2540. Puget Sound Marine Environment: An Annotated
       Bibliography. Univ. of Washington Pr., 1977.
2541. A Study of the Nutrients in the Main Basin of Puget
       Sound. Metro, 1977. (co-author).

Collier, Robert Eugene, 1926-.
   Biologist; college president.
   2542. "A Study of Sporogenesis in 'Clostridium Roseum.'"
          Ph.D. diss., Univ. of Illinois, 1959.

Cook, Robert Edward, 1927-.
   Professor of poultry science.
   2543. "The Genetic and Environmental Relationships between
          Reproductive Traits and Body Measurements in
          Turkeys." Ph.D. diss., North Carolina State
          College, 1958.

Corbett, Robert G., 1935-.
   Professor of geology.
   2544. Energy Resources, Canton-Cadiz Area. Kent, Ohio,
          1974.

Denham, Joseph Milton, 1930-.
   Professor of chemistry.
   2545. "Substituted Aryl-Phosphonic and Phosphonic Acids
          and Related Compounds as Possible Plant Growth
          Substances." Ph.D. diss., Ohio Univ., 1959.

Doane, Joseph William.
   Professor of physics.
   2546. "Nuclear Spin Pumping in Sodium Bromate." Ph.D.
          diss., Univ. of Missouri, 1965.
   2547. A Review of the Structure and Physical Properties of
          Liquid Crystals. CRC Pr., 1971. (co-author).

Dooley, Donald.
   Professor of physics.
   2548. "The Infrared Spectrum of Methane at Low
          Temperature." Ph.D. diss., Ohio State Univ., 1940.
   2549. Observations on the Deformation of Ice at Los
          Stresses. Ohio State Univ., 1964.

Draper, John Daniel, 1919-.
   Professor of chemistry.

2550. "A Study of Etherification by an Azeotropic Method."
       Ph.D. diss., Univ. of Maryland, 1948.

Dreisbach, Dale Alson.
    Professor of chemistry.
    2551. Liquids and Solutions. Houghton Mifflin, 1966.
    2552. "The Total and Partial Vapor Measurements of Binary
           Liquid Systems by an Improved Method." Ph.D. diss.,
           Western Reserve Univ., 1937.

Fairhurst, Alfred, 1843-1921.
    See under THEOLOGY.

Fields, Noland Embry, 1933-.
    Professor of geology.
    2553. "The Bryozoan Adeonellopsis in the Paleogene of the
           Southeastern United States." Ph.D. diss., Louisiana
           State Univ., 1971.

Forsyth, John Wiley, 1913-.
    Professor of biology.
    2554. "The Histology of Anuran Limb Regeneration." Ph.D.
           diss., Princeton Univ., 1946.

Forte, Leonard R., Jr.
    Professor of pharmacology.
    2555. Hormone Receptors: Proceedings of the Midwest
           Conference on Endocrinology and Metabolism. Plenum
           Pr., 1978. (co-editor).

Frahm, Richard R.
    Professor of animal science.
    2556. "An Evaluation of Limousin Cattle." Oklahoma State
           Univ., 1976. (co-author).

Friesen, Delbert Ray, 1942-.
    Professor of physics.
    2557. "Electron Paramagnetic Resonance Instabilities in
           Ruby." Ph.D. diss., Univ. of Colorado, 1971.

Friesner, Ray Clarence, 1894-1952.
    Professor of botany; college administrator.
    2558. "Daily Rhythms of Elongation and Cell Division in
           Certain Roots." Press of the New Era Printing Co.,
           1920. (Ph.D. diss., Univ. of Michigan, 1920.)

Funk, Emerson Gornflow, 1931-.
    Professor of physics.
    2559. "Gamma Gamma Directional Correlation Measurements in
           Se^{76} and Cd^{110}." Ph.D. diss., Univ. of Michigan,
           1958.

Garner, George Bernard, 1927-.
  Professor of agricultural chemistry.
  2560. "Factors Affecting Cellulose Digestion and Rumen
         Microflora in Vitro and Vivo." Ph.D. diss., Univ.
         of Missouri, 1957.

Garren, Donald Ray, 1932-.
  Professor of life science.
  2561. "Effects on Achievement When Excerpts from Physics
         Are Interjected into Programmed High School
         Biology." Ed.D. diss., Indiana Univ., 1970.

Glawe, Lloyd Neil, 1932-.
  Professor of geology.
  2562. "Pecten Perplanus Stock (Oligocene) of Southeastern
         United States." Ph.D. diss., Louisiana State Univ.,
         1966.
  2563. Laboratory Exercises in Physical Geology.
         Contemporary, 1978.

Granberg, Charles Boyd, 1921-.
  Professor of pharmacology.
  2564. "The Roles of Titanium Dioxide, Bentonite and Sodium
         Carboxymethylcellulose in the Radiography of the
         Gastrointestinal Tract." Ph.D. diss., Univ. of
         Illinois, 1954.
  2565. Remarkable Pharmacists. Rob Lee Hill, 1973. (co-
         editor).

Grigg, Neil Sadler.
  Ecologist.
  2566. Computerized City-Wide Control of Urban Stormwater.
         American Soc. of Civil Engineers, 1976.
  2567. Development of a Drainage and Flood Control
         Management Program for Urbanizing Communities. 2
         vols. Environmental Resources Center, 1978.
  2568. Metropolitan Water Intelligence Systems: Completion
         Report--Phase III. Colorado State Univ., 1974.
  2569. Metropolitan Water Intelligence Systems: Completion
         Report--Phase II. Colorado State Univ., 1973.
  2570. "Motion of Single Particles in Sand Channels."
         Ph.D. diss., 1969.
  2571. Transfer of Water Resources Knowledge: An
         Assessment. Univ. of North Carolina, 1978.
  2572. Urban Drainage and Flood Control Projects:
         Economic, Legal and Financial Aspects. Colorado
         State Univ., 1976.
  2573. Voluntary Basinwide Management: South Platte River
         Basin, Colorado. Colorado State Univ., 1984.
  2574. Water Knowledge Transfer: Proceedings of the Second
         International Conference on Transfer of Water
         Resources Knowledge, June 1977, Fort Collins,
         Colorado, U.S.A. 2 vols. Fort Collins, Col., 1977.

Gugler, Carl Wesley.
    Professor of zoology.
    2575. "A Study of the Myology of the Least Shrew." Ph.D.
           diss., Univ. of Nebraska, 1959.

Guldenzopf, E. Charles.
    Professor of geology and zoology.
    2576. Gravity and Magnetic Investigations of the National
           Petroleum Reserve in Alaska. Energy Management
           Division (Houston), 1982. (co-author).
    2577. Petroleum Exploration of NPRA, 1974-1981: Final
           Report. 3 vols. Energy Management Division
           (Houston), 1982. (co-author).

Hamon, J. Hill, 1931-.
    Professor of biology.
    2578. A Lamp in the Forest: National Philosophy in
           Transylvania University, 1799-1859. Transylvania
           Univ. Pr., 1982. (co-author).
    2579. "Osteology and Paleontology of the Passerin Birds of
           the Reddick Pleistocene." Ph.D. diss., Univ. of
           Florida, 1961.

Hanan, Joe John, 1931-.
    Professor of horticulture.
    2580. Greenhouse Management. Springer-Verlag, 1978.
    2581. Handbook for Student Employees at the W. D. Holley
           Plant University. Colorado State Univ., 1977.
    2582. "The Influence of Soil Moisture and Soil Aeration in
           Four Root Media on the Growth and Flowering of
           Antirrhinum Majus." Ph.D diss., Cornell Univ.,
           1963.
    2583. Ozone and Ethylene Effects on Some Ornamental Plant
           Species. Colorado State Univ., 1978.
    2584. Plant Environmental Measurement. Bookmakers Guild,
           1984.

Hankins, Warren Mason, 1938-.
    Professor of chemistry.
    2585. "Some New Chemistry of Dihydrofurylium Salts, 2,5-
           Dihydrofurans and 2,5-Dihydrofurahols." Ph.D.
           diss., Univ. of Virginia, 1969.

Herbel, Carlton H.
    Range scientist.
    2586. Improved Range Plants: Papers Presented at Annual
           Meeting, Society for Range Management, Tucson,
           Arizona, February 5, 1974. Range Research. U.S.
           Dept. of Agriculture, 1981?

Hewatt, Willis Gilliland, 1904-.
    Professor of biology.

2587.   <u>Notes on the Breeding Seasons of the Rocky Beach
        Fauna of Monterey Bay, California.</u> San Francisco,
        1938.

Houts, Larry Lee, 1942-.
    Professor of biology.
    2588.   "Morphogenetic Properties of the Zone of Polarizing
            Activity of the Chick Wing Bird as Affected by Aging
            in Vitro and as Tested on Leg-Bud Mesoderm Aged in
            Vitro." Ph.D. diss., State Univ. of New York at
            Albany, 1976.

Humphrey, George L.
    Professor of chemistry.
    2589.   "Some Thermodynamic Properties of Silicon Carbide."
            U.S. Bureau of Mines, 1952. (co-author).

Jensen, Harold James, 1921-.
    Professor of biology.
    2590.   <u>Annotated Bibliography of Nematode Pests of Potato.</u>
            International Potato Center? (Lima, Peru), 1979.
            (co-author).
    2591.   <u>Bibliography of Nematode Interactions with Other
            Organisms in Plant Disease Complexes.</u> Oregon State
            Univ., 1976. (co- compiler).
    2592.   "The Biology and Morphology of the Root Lesion
            Nematode Parasite on Walnuts in California." Ph.D.
            diss., Univ. of California, 1950.
    2593.   <u>Indexed Bibliography of Nematode-Resistance in
            Plants.</u> Oregon State Univ., 1978. (co-compiler).
    2594.   <u>Predaceous Nematodes (Mononchidae) of Oregon.</u>
            Oregon State Univ. Pr., 1968. (co-author).

Johnson, Gordon Verle, 1933-.
    Professor of biology.
    2595.   <u>An Analysis of Mercurials in the Elephant Butte
            Ecosystem.</u> New Mexico State Univ., 1974. (co-
            author).
    2596.   <u>Analysis of Nutrient Supplies for Algae in Elephant
            Butte Reservoir.</u> New Mexico State Univ., 1974. (co-
            author).
    2597.   <u>An Investigation of Primary Productivity Using the
            14C Method and an Analysis of Nutrients in Elephant
            Butte Reservoir.</u> New Mexico Water Resources
            Research Institute, 1972. (co-author).

Kloek, Gerrit.
    Professor of biology.
    2598.   "Functional Morphology of the Feeding Apparatus in
            Procellariiform Birds." Ph.D. diss., Southern
            Illinois Univ., 1973.

Labbe, Robert Ferdinand.
    Professor of bio-chemistry.
    2599.   <u>Symposium on Laboratory Assessment of Nutritional
            Status.</u> Saunders, 1981. (editor).
    2600.   "Tracer Studies of Pyruvic Acid Metabolism in
            Yeast." Ph.D. diss., Oregon State College, 1951.

Lambert, David Dillon.
    Professor of geology.
    2601.   "Geochemical Evolution of the Stillwater Complex,
            Montana...." Ph.D. diss., Colorado School of
            Mines, 1982.

Larson, Gary Eugene.
    Professor of biology.
    2602.   <u>The Aquatic and Wetland Vascular Plants of North
            Dakota.</u> North Dakota Water Resources Research
            Institute, 1983. (co-author).
    2603.   "The Bioelectric Potentials Surrounding the Root of
            Zea Mays." Ph.D. diss., Rutgers Univ., 1965.

Lewis, Bert Kenneth, 1911-.
    Professor of science.
    2604.   "The Etherates of Magnesium Halides." Ph.D. diss.,
            Univ. of Oklahoma, 1958.

Lindamood, John Benford, 1929-.
    Professor of nutrition.
    2605.   "Evaluation of External Information Needs of Ohio
            Dairy Farms." Ph.D. diss., Ohio State Univ., 1974.

Lingafelter, Edward Clay, 1914-.
    Professor of chemistry.
    2606.   "Complexes of Mercury and Ammonia." Ph.D. diss.,
            Univ. of California, 1939.

Livesay, Billy Ray, 1933-.
    2607.   <u>Evaluation & Characterization Studies.</u> Georgia
            Institute of Technology, 1982.
    2608.   <u>An Evaluation of Reliability Factors for Electronic
            Components in a Storage Environment.</u> Georgia
            Institute of Technology, 1975-1977.
    2609.   <u>Investigations of Mechanical-Environmental
            Interactions in VLSI Bond Interfaces.</u> Georgia
            Institute of Technology, 1983-1985.
    2610.   <u>Investigations of Relationships between
            Microstructure Magnetic Properties and the Hydriding
            Process in Intermetallic Compounds of Rare Earth and
            Transition Metals.</u> Georgia Institite of Technology,
            1977-1983.
    2611.   <u>Remote Detection of Magnetic Fields.</u> Georgia
            Institute of Technology, 1983-1986.

Long, Norman Oliver, 1909-.
    Professor of chemistry.
    2612.   "The Measurement of the Magnetic Susceptibilities of
           Certain Inorganic Complexes." Ph.D. diss., Univ. of
           Buffalo, 1935.

McMahan, Dorothy G.
    Professor of chemistry.
    2613.   "Synthesis and Reaction Studies of Aziridinones."
           Ph.D. diss., Univ. of Nebraska, 1976.

Mather, Kirtley Fletcher, 1888-.
    Geologist.
    2614.   Adult Education. A Dynamic for Democracy. Appleton-
           Century, 1937. (co-author).
    2615.   Christian Fundamentals in the Light of Modern
           Science. Times Pr., 1924.
    2616.   Crusade for Life. Univ. of North Carolina Pr.,
           1949.
    2617.   Do We Still Need Religion? Three Addresses and
           Discussions. Association Pr., 1942. (co-author).
    2618.   The Earth Beneath Us. Random House, 1964.
    2619.   Enough and to Spare: Mother Earth Can Nourish Every
           Man in Freedom. Harper, 1944.
    2620.   "The Fauna of the Morrow Group of Arkansas and
           Oklahoma." Ph.D. diss., Univ. of Chicago, 1915.
    2621.   The Future of American Science. CIO, 1944.
    2622.   "Is There Purpose in the Universe?" Brookline,
           Mass., 1964.
    2623.   A Laboratory Manual for Geology. Appleton, 1950-.
           (co-author).
    2624.   A Laboratory Manual of Dynamic and Structural
           Geology. Harvard Univ. Pr., 1926.
    2625.   A Laboratory Manual of Historical Geology. Harvard
           Univ. Pr., 1929.
    2626.   A Laboratory Manual of Physical and Historical
           Geology. Appleton, 1934.
    2627.   List of Members of the Society of the Alumni of
           Denison University. 1840-1920. Granville Times
           Printers, 1921. (co-compiler).
    2628.   Oil and Gas Resources of the Northeastern Part of
           Sumner County. Tennessee. Williams, 1920.
    2629.   The Oil Fields of Allen County. Kentucky.... Govt.
           Print. Off., 1919. (co-author).
    2630.   Old Mother Earth [Lectures]. Harvard Univ. Pr.,
           1928.
    2631.   Physiography and Quaternary Geology of the San Juan
           Mountains. Colorado. U.S. Govt. Print. Off., 1932.
           (co-author).
    2632.   Pleistocene Geology of Western Cape Cod.
           Massachusetts. Boston, 1942.
    2633.   A Preliminary Report on the Geology of Western Cape
           Cod. Massachusetts. Boston, 1940. (co-author).

2634. <u>Science in Search of God.</u> Holt, 1928.
2635. <u>Sons of the Earth: The Geologist's View of History.</u>
       Norton, 1930.
2636. <u>A Source Book in Geology.</u> McGraw-Hill, 1939.
       (compiler).

Maxwell, Ross A.
    Research scientist.
    2637. <u>The Big Bend of the Rio Grande.</u> Univ. of Texas,
           1968.
    2638. <u>A Brief History of the Big Bend Museum with List of
           Specimens.</u> Austin, Tex., 1940.
    2639. <u>Correlation of Tertiary Rock Units, West Texas.</u>
           Univ. of Texas, 1970.
    2640. <u>Geologic and Historic Guide to the State Parks of
           Texas.</u> Univ. of Texas, 1970.
    2641. <u>Geology of Big Bend National Park.</u> Univ. of Texas,
           1967.
    2642. <u>Mineral Resources of South Texas.</u> Univ. of Texas,
           1962.

Mell, Galen Palmer, 1934-.
    Professor of chemistry.
    2643. "Sarcosine Dehydrogenase." Ph.D. diss., Univ. of
           Washington, 1961.

Miller, Victor J., 1921-.
    Professor of horticulture.
    2644. "The Relation of Plastid Pigments to Color in Golden
           Delicious Apples." Ph.D. diss., Univ. of Illinois,
           1946.

Moss, David Billy Ross, 1940-.
    Professor of chemistry.
    2645. "Steric and Internal Conjugate Base Effects in
           Chelation Kinetics." Ph.D. diss., Wayne State
           Univ., 1970.

Neff, John S., 1934-.
    Professor of astronomy.
    2646. <u>Activities in Astronomy.</u> Kendall/Hunt, 1978. (co-
           author).
    2647. <u>Astronomy: Activities and Experiments.</u>
           Kendall/Hunt, 1974. (co-author).
    2648. "A Spectrophotometric Study of the Eclipsing Binary
           SZ Camelopardalis." Ph.D. diss., Univ. of
           Wisconsin, 1961.

Norbeck, Edwin, 1930-.
    Professor of physics.
    2649. "New Nuclear Reactions Induced by 2 Mev Lithium
           Ions." Ph.D. diss., Univ. of Chicago, 1956.

Norris, David Otto, 1939-.
    Professor of biology.
    2650.   "Radiothyroidectomy in the Salmonid Fishes Salmo
            Gairdnerii Richardson and Oncorhynchus Tshawytscha
            Walbaum." Ph.D. diss., Univ. of Washington, 1966.
    2651.   Vertebrate Endocrinology. Lea & Febiger, 1980.

Pennington, Sam N.
    Professor of bio-chemistry.
    2652.   "Gas Chromatographic Analyses and a Study of Certain
            Antiradiation Compounds." Ph.D. diss., Kansas State
            Univ., 1967.

Peterson, Raleigh J., Jr.
    See under THEOLOGY.

Pritchard, Mary Hanson, 1924-.
    Professor of life sciences.
    2653.   The Collection and Preservation of Animal Parasites.
            Univ. of Nebraska Pr., 1982. (co-compiler).
    2654.   A Guide to the Parasite Collections of the World.
            American Soc. of Parasitologists, 1982.

Rider, Paul Edward.
    Professor of chemistry.
    2655.   "Spectral and Calorimetric Hydrogen Bonding Studies
            of di-t- butyl Carbinol." Ph.D. diss., Kansas State
            Univ. of Agriculture and Applied Science, 1969.

Rosenburg, Dale Weaver, 1927-.
    Professor of chemistry.
    2656.   "The Preparation of Some Simple Structural Analogs
            of Khellin." Ph.D. diss., Univ. of Missouri, 1958.

Rosser, Edward Barry, 1911-.
    Professor of chemistry.
    2657.   "The Application of Thionyl Chloride as a Parent
            Solvent." Ph.D. diss., Western Reserve Univ., 1952.

Rothenbuhler, Walter C.
    Professor of entomology, zoology and genetics.
    2658.   "Disappearing Disease: A Comparison of Seven
            Different Stocks of the Honey Bee." Ohio State
            Univ., 1984. (co-author).

Sager, Ray Stuart, 1942-.
    Professor of chemistry.
    2659.   "The Crystal Structures and Properties of Copper
            (11) and Zinc (11) Compleses of B-Diketones and
            Aromatic N-Oxides." Ph.D. diss., Texas Christian
            Univ., 1968.

Salzsieder, John C.
  Professor of chemistry.
  2660. "Application of Quasi-Equilibrium Theory to
         Hexafluoroacetylacetone." Ph.D. diss., North Dakota
         State Univ., 1975.

Schmulbach, Charles David, 1929-.
  Professor of chemistry.
  2661. "A Spectroscopic Study of the Formation of Amide-
         Iodine Molecular Addition Compounds." Ph.D. diss.,
         Univ. of Ilinois, 1959.

Sigler, Julius Alfred, 1940-.
  Professor of physics.
  2662. The Fluorescent Lamp. McGraw, 1975. (co-author).
  2663. "An Investigation of Some Properties of Three
         Dimensional Voids in Face Centered Cubic Metals."
         Ph.D. diss., Univ. of Virginia, 1967.

Singleton, Edgar Bryson, 1926-.
  Professor of physics.
  2664. "Effects of Foreign Gases on the Total Absorption of
         Entire Bands in the Infrared." Ph.D. diss., Ohio
         State Univ., 1958.

Sterling, Duane Ray, 1938-.
  College administrator; scientist.
  2665. "Isometric Strength Position Specificity Resulting
         from Isometric and Isotonic Training as a
         Determinant in Performance." Ph.D. diss., Louisiana
         State Univ., 1969.

Teppert, William Allan, 1915-.
  Professor of pharmacology.
  2666. "Determination of Free Amino Acids in the Developing
         Grasshopper Egg of Melanoplus Differentialis."
         Ph.D. diss., State Univ. of Iowa, 1958.
  2667. A Laboratory Manual for Pharmacology. 2d. ed.
         Drake Univ., 1964.

Ward, James Britton, 1931-.
  Professor of poultry science.
  2668. "The Effect of Certain Dietary Ingredients upon the
         Incidence of Bloodspots in Chicken Eggs." Ph.D.
         diss., Michigan State Univ., 1962.

White, Jesse Edmund, 1927-.
  Professor of chemistry.
  2669. "A Modified Forward-Scattering Particle Counter
         Suitable for Aerosol Coagulation Studies." Ph.D.
         diss., Indiana Univ., 1958.

Wilson, Leland L.
    Professor of chemistry.
    2670.   Exploring the Physical Sciences. Prentice-Hall,
          1965. (co-author).

Wiltshire, Charles Thomas, 1941-.
    Professor of biology.
    2671.   "The Developmental Morphology of Cyzicus Morsei from
          Hatching through Adulthood with Comments on Taxonomy
          within the Family Cyzicidae." Ph.D. diss., Univ. of
          Missouri-Columbia, 1973.

Wright, Charles Gerald, 1930-.
    Professor of entomology.
    2672.   "Biology and Control of the Southern Lyctus Beetle."
          Ph.D. diss., North Carolina State College, 1958.
    2673.   A Laboratory Notebook for Introductory Applied
          Entomolgy. North Carolina State Univ., 1966.
    2674.   Laboratory Notebook for Turf, Ornamental and Shade
          Tree Entomology. North Carolina State Univ., 1983.
    2675.   The Lace Bugs of North Carolina and Their Hosts.
          North Carolina Agricultural Experiment Station,
          1979. (co-author).

Wright, E. Ronald.
    Professor of biology.
    2676.   General Microbiology. Times Mirror/Mosby, 1984.

SOCIAL SCIENCES
    Includes Anthropology, Geography and Social Work
    See also POLITICAL SCIENCE, PSYCHOLOGY, SOCIOLOGY.

Akin, Wallace Elmus, 1923-.
    Professor of geography.
    2677.   Earth: The Stuff of Life. 2d. ed. Univ. of
          Oklahoma Pr., 1986. (co-author).
    2678.   The North Central United States. Van Nostrand,
          1968.

Cheek, William Henry, 1942-.
    Professor of geography.
    2679.   Economic and Social Atlas of Missouri. Southwest
          Missouri State Univ., 1975. (co-author).
    2680.   "Mobile Home Parks in Southern Michigan: Factors
          Influencing the Location of an Evolving Residential
          Land Use." Ph.D. diss., Michigan State Univ., 1976.

Johnston, Francis E., 1931-.
    Professor of anthropology.
    2681.   Anthropology, the Biocultural View. Brown, 1978.
          (co-author).

2682. Biosocial Interrelations in Population Adaptation.
       Mouton, 1975. (co-editor).
2683. Genetics, Evolution, and Disease. Liss, 1983. (co-
       editor).
2684. Height and Weight of Children: Socioeconomic
       Status, United States. U.S. Govt. Print. Off.,
       1972. (co-author).
2685. Height and Weight of Youths, 12-17 Years, United
       States. U.S. Govt. Print. Off., 1973. (co-author).
2686. Human Physical Growth and Maturation. Plenum, 1980.
       (co-editor).
2687. "A Longitudinal Study of Skeletal Maturation and Its
       Relationship to Growth in Philadelphia White
       Children." Ph.D. diss., Univ. of Pennsylvania,
       1962.
2688. Microevolution of Human Populations. Prentice-Hall,
       1973.
2689. Physical Anthropology. Brown, 1982.
2690. Skinfold Thickness of Children, 6-11 Years, United
       States. U.S. Govt. Print. Off., 1972.
2691. Skinfold Thickness of Youths, 12-17 Years, United
       States. U.S. Govt. Print. Off., 1974.
2692. Social and Biological Predictors of Nutritional
       Status, Physical Growth, and Neurological
       Development. Academic Pr., 1980. (co-editor).
2693. Symposium on Biosocial Interrelations in Population
       Adaptation. Mouton, 1976.

Kelly, Charles Robert, 1932-.
     Professor of geography.
2694. "The Canadian River Municipal Water Authority
       Project in West Texas: A Geographic Analysis."
       Ph.D. diss., Univ. of Oklahoma, 1971.

Longwell, Alden Richard, 1930-.
     Professor of geography.
2695. "The Cananea Ejidos: From Private Ranch to
       Collective in Sonora." Ph.D. diss., Univ. of
       Nebraska, 1974.
2696. Nebraska Atlas. Nebraska Atlas Publishing Co.,
       1964. (co-author).

Mancil, Ervin, 1926-.
     Professor of social science.
2697. "An Historical Geography of Industrial Cypress
       Lumbering in Louisiana." 2 vols. Ph.D. diss.,
       Louisiana State Univ., 1972.

Munson, Carlton E.
     Professor of social work.
2698. Family of Origin Applications in Clinical
       Supervision. Haworth, 1984. (editor).

2699. <u>An Introduction to Clinical Social Work Supervision.</u>
Haworth, 1983.
2700. <u>Social Work Education and Practice: Historical
Perspectives.</u> JoVon, 1978.
2701. <u>Social Work Papers.</u> Houston, 1978. (editor).
2702. <u>Social Work Supervision: Classic Statements and
Critical Issues.</u> Free Pr., 1979. (editor).
2703. <u>Social Work with Families.</u> Free Pr., 1980.
(editor).
2704. <u>Supervising Student Internships in Human Services.</u>
Haworth Pr., 1984. (editor).
2705. "The Uses of Structural, Authority and Teaching
Models in Social Work Supervision." D.S.W. diss.,
Univ. of Maryland, 1975.

Nelipovich, Michael, 1945-.
Professor of rehabilitation.
2706. "The National Accreditation Council for Agencies
Serving the Blind and Visually Handicapped." Ph.D.
diss., Southern Illinois Univ., 1981.

*Pendleton, William Kimbrough, 1817-1899.
Attorney; college president; editor of <u>Millennial
Harbinger</u>.
2707. <u>A System of Modern Geography.</u> Rev. ed. J. H.
Butler & Co., 1877. (co-author).

For works about him written by Disciple authors, see
Power, Frederick Dunglison under THEOLOGY section.

Taylor, Alva Wilmot, 1871-1957.
Social worker; writer.
2708. <u>Christianity and Industry in America.</u> Friendship
Pr., 1933.
2709. <u>Social Progress and Christian Ideals.</u> Cokesbury,
1931. (co-author).
2710. <u>The Social Work of Christian Missions.</u> Foreign
Christian Missionary Soc., 1911.

For works about her written by Disciple authors, see
Harbison, Stanley Lincoln and
Wasson, Woodrow Wilson under THEOLOGY section.

SOCIOLOGY

*Acuff, Frederick Gene, 1931-.
Professor of sociology.
2711. <u>From Man to Society: Introductory Sociology.</u>
Dryden, 1973. (co-author).

Barger, George William, 1923-.
Professor of sociology.

2712.   "Historical Sociology: Its Nature and Methods."
        Ph.D. diss., Univ. of Missouri, 1965.
2713.   <u>Social Participation and Life Satisfaction of Senior
        Citizens.</u> Univ. of Nebraska, 1968. (co-author).

Becker, Edwin Lewis, 1917-.
    See under THEOLOGY.

Cox, Harold Glenwood, 1935-.
    Professor of sociology.
    2714.   "Bureaucracy, Alienation, and Teachers'
            Organizations." Ph.D. diss., Indiana Univ., 1972.

Else, John F.
    Professor of sociology.
    2715.   <u>Designing Field Education.</u> Thomas, 1983. (co-
            author).
    2716.   <u>Purposive Social Change: A Radical Humanist
            Perspective.</u> Univ. of Iowa, 1977.

Givens, Howard Lytle, 1940-.
    Professor of sociology.
    2717.   "Occupational Entry and Anticipatory Exiting within
            a Limited-Duration Occupation: The Flight
            Attendant." Ph.D. diss., Univ. of Georgia, 1975.

Grupp, Stanley E.
    Professor of sociology and criminology.
    2718.   <u>Community-Based Corrections.</u> Davis, 1976. (co-
            editor).
    2719.   <u>Marihuana.</u> Merrill, 1971. (editor).
    2720.   <u>The Marihuana Muddle.</u> Lexington, 1973.
    2721.   "The Nalline Test and Addict Attitudes." Ph.D.
            diss., Indiana Univ., 1967.
    2722.   <u>Theories of Punishment.</u> Indiana Univ. Pr., 1972,
            c1971. (editor).

Gustafson, Paul Moody, 1919-.
    2723.   "Structural Elements and Organizational Behavior: A
            Study of Ten Protestant Denominations in Minnesota."
            Ph.D. diss., Univ. of Minnesota, 1963.

Haddox, Benjamin Edward, 1923-.
    Professor of sociology.
    2724.   <u>Joint Decision-Making Patterns and Related Factors
            Among Low-Income Rural Families.</u> Mississippi
            Agricultural Experiment Station, 1965.
    2725.   "A Sociological Study of the Institution of Religion
            in Colombia." Ph.D. diss., Univ. of Florida, 1962.

Hall, Robert Burnett, 1949-.
    Professor of sociology.

2726. "The Presentation of the Deceased in Upper East
       Tennessee, 1900-1975." Ph.D. diss., Univ. of
       Tennessee, 1980.

Hankins, Wes.
    Professor of sociology.
    2727. Guide to Undergraduate Education in Urban and
           Regional Planning. Assoc. of Collegiate Schools of
           Planning, 1982. (co-editor).

Hassinger, Edward Wesley.
    Professor of sociology.
    2728. Background and Community Orientation of Rural
           Physicians Compared with Metropolitan Physicians in
           Missouri. Univ. of Missouri, 1963.
    2729. "Factors Associated with Population Changes in
           Agricultural Trade Centers of Southern Minnesota."
           Ph.D. diss., Univ. of Minnesota, 1956.
    2730. A Restudy of Physicians in Twenty Rural Missouri
           Counties. Springfield, Va., 1979.
    2731. The Rural Component of American Society. Interstate
           Printers & Publishers, 1978.
    2732. Rural Health Organization: Social Networks and
           Regionalization. Iowa State Univ. Pr., 1982.
    2733. Rural Health Services: Organization, Delivery, and
           Use. Iowa State Univ. Pr., 1976. (co-editor).

Hesser, Gary W.
    Professor of sociology.
    2734. Continuing Education and Occupational Stress Among
           Protestant Clergy. Soc. for the Advancement of
           Continuing Education for Ministry, 1972. (co-
           author).

Hopper, Rex D., 1898-1966.
    Sociologist.
    2735. Un Siglo de Revolucion. Mexico, 1959. (co-author).

Hunt, Chester L.
    Professor of sociology.
    2736. Cotabato, Melting Pot of the Philippines. UNESCO,
           1954.
    2737. Ethnic Dynamics: Patterns of Intergroup Relations
           in Various Societies. 2d. ed. Learning
           Publications, 1979. (co-author).
    2738. Research Report on Integrated Housing in Kalamazoo.
           Western Michigan Univ., 1959.
    2739. Social Aspects of Economic Development. McGraw,
           1966.
    2740. Social Class Factors in the College Adjustment of
           Married Students. Western Michigan Univ., 1965.
    2741. Social Foundations of Community Development.
           Garcia, 1964.

2742. <u>Society and Culture in Rural Philippines.</u> Rev. ed.
       Alemar, 1978. (editor).
2743. <u>Sociology.</u> McGraw, 1964. (co-author).
2744. <u>Sociology in the Philippine Setting.</u> Alemar, 1954.

*Kaufman, Harold Frederick, 1911-.
    Professor of sociology.
    2745. <u>Community Development Programs in the Southeast</u>.
           Mississippi State College, 1956.
    2746. <u>Community Structure and Leadership</u>. Mississippi
           State Univ., 1967.
    2747. <u>Defining Prestige in a Rural Community</u>. Beacon
           House, 1946.
    2748. <u>Group Identity in the South: Dialogue between the
           Technological and the Humanistic</u>. Mississippi State
           Univ., 1965. (co-author).
    2749. <u>Levels of Community Analysis</u>. Mississippi State
           Univ., 1965. (co-author).
    2750. <u>Mississippi Churches: A Half Century of Change</u>.
           Mississippi State Univ., 1959.
    2751. <u>Mississippi Churches: A Statistical Supplement</u>.
           Mississippi State Univ., 1959.
    2752. <u>Prestige Classes in a New York Rural Community</u>.
           Cornell Univ., 1943.
    2753. <u>Poverty Programs and Social Mobility</u>. Mississippi
           State Univ., 1966.
    2754. "Religious Organization in Kentucky." Univ. of
           Kentucky, 1948.
    2755. "Rural Churches in Kentucky, 1947." Univ. of
           Kentucky, 1949.
    2756. <u>Rural Sociology and Rural Development Programs</u>.
           Mississippi State College, 1956. (co-author).
    2757. "A Social Psychological Study of a New York Rural
           Community." Ph.D. diss., Cornell Univ., 1942.
    2758. <u>Villages Upward Bound: Community Structure and
           Technological Development in Selected Indian
           Villages</u>. Editions Indian (Calcutta), 1975.

Keene, Laurence C.
    Professor of sociology.
    2759. "Abraham-King Elementary School, An Experiment in
           Desegregation and Multi-Cultural Education." Ph.D.
           diss., Univ. of Southern California, 1978.
    2760. <u>Communion, Meditations, and Prayers.</u> Standard,
           1982.
    2761. <u>Heirs of Stone and Campbell on the Pacific Slope: A
           Sociological Approach.</u> School of Theology at
           Claremont, 1984.

Ketch, Clarence Willard, 1921-.
    Professor of sociology.
    2762. <u>Religious Economic Survey of Springfield, Missouri.</u>
           Springfield, Mo., 1966.

2763.   "A Situational Analysis of the Effects of Drouth as
        a Disaster on the Mobility of a Selected Rural-Farm
        Population." Ph.D. diss., Louisiana State Univ.,
        1961.

Layman, Marvin Virgil, 1926-.
    Professor of sociology.
    2764.   "Differential Reaction to Stress: The Social-
            Psychological Effects of Disaster." Ph.D. diss.,
            Univ. of Texas, 1965.

Mitchell, Irvine Eugene, 1912-.
    Professor of sociology and anthropology.
    2765.   "The Maturity of Delinquent and Nondelinquent
            Adolescents as Defined by the Developmental Task
            Concept." Ph.D. diss., Boston Univ., 1957.

Pittman, Riley Herman.
    Professor of sociology.
    2766.   "The Meaning of Salvation in the Thought of George
            Albert Coe." Ph.D. diss., Univ. of Southern
            California, 1946.

Platt, Robert Martin, 1928-.
    Professor of sociology.
    2767.   About Us: An Introduction to Psychology. Boyd &
            Fraser Publishing Co., 1972.
    2768.   Case Studies in Crime Prevention. Criminal Justice
            Pr., 1974. (editor).
    2769.   Case Studies in Education. Criminal Justice Pr.,
            1974. (editor).
    2770.   Case Studies in Minority Programs. Criminal Justice
            Pr., 1974. (compiler).
    2771.   The Concept of Police-Community Relations. Criminal
            Justice Pr., 1973. (editor).
    2772.   Improving the Police Image. Criminal Justice Pr.,
            1974.
    2773.   The I-Opener: An Introduction to Philosophy.
            Prentice Hall, 1976.
    2774.   Programs for Chronic Offenders. Criminal Justice
            Pr., 1974. (editor).

Rector, Franklin E.
    Professor of sociology.
    2775.   Facts About Our Churches and a Changing America.
            United Christian Missionary Soc., 1956. (co-author).

Sayre, Cynthia Woolever.
    Professor of sociology.
    2776.   "Urban Neighborhood Differentiation: A Contextual
            Approach to Social Behavior and Attitudes." Ph.D.
            diss., Indiana Univ., 1983.

Seaman, Thomas Warren, 1942-.
      Professor of sociology.
      2777.   "An Exploration of the Systemic Model as a Basis for
               Planning and Evaluating Crime Control Practices."
               Ph.D. diss., Univ. of Maryland, 1978.

Song, Han Kyu.
      Professor of sociology.
      2778.   "Family Changes in Modernizing Korea." Ph.D. diss.,
               American Univ., 1978.

Talbert, Robert Harris.
      Professor of sociology.
      2779.   Cowtown-Metropolis. Texas Christian Univ., 1956.
      2780.   Crime, Suicide and Social Well-Being in Your State
               and City. Fort Worth, 1948. (co-author).
      2781.   Demographic and Related Socioeconomic
               Characteristics Affecting Public Education in Texas.
               Texas Education Agency, 1962.
      2782.   Fort Worth Area Census Tract and Market Fact Book.
               Fort Worth Chamber of Commerce, 1972.
      2783.   Mid-Century Crime in Our Culture. Fort Worth, 1954.
               (co-author).
      2784.   Spanish-Name People in the Southwest and West.
               Texas Christian Univ., 1955.

Taylor, Lloyd Andrew, 1921-.
      Professor of sociology.
      2785.   "Aphasia in Children." Ph.D. diss., Univ. of
               Nebraska, 1968.
      2786.   From Man to Society: Introductory Sociology.
               Dryden, 1973. (co-author).

Whitley, Oliver Reed.
      See under THEOLOGY.

SPEECH
      See ENGLISH LANGUAGE AND LITERATURE

STATISTICS
      See MATHEMATICS

TECHNOLOGY
      See ENGINEERING

THEOLOGY/PHILOSOPHY/RELIGION
      See also HISTORY for more works on Disciple history.

Abbott, Byrdine Akers, 1866-1936.
      Pastor; editor.
      2787.   At the Master's Table. 1925.
      2788.   The Disciples, An Interpretation. Bethany, 1924.
      2789.   The Life of Chapman S. Lucas. 1897.

2790. Miracles under Fire, A Treatise for Modern Thinkers.
       Bethany, 1930. (editor).

Abel, John Albert, 1912-.
    Pastor; professor of philosophy.
    2791. "Edward Scribner Ames' Conception of Religion."
           Th.D. diss., Iliff School of Theology, 1938.

Abernethy, Arthur Talmage, 1872-.
    Pastor.
    2792. Center-Shots at Sin [Sermons]. Standard, 1918.

Adams, Hampton, 1897-1965.
    Pastor; seminary professor.
    2793. Ambassador in Chains and Other Sermons. Bethany,
           1947.
    2794. Calling Men for the Ministry. Bethany, 1945.
    2795. Christian Answers to War Questions. Revell, 1943.
    2796. The Pastoral Ministry. Cokesbury, 1932.
    2797. A Register of His Papers in the Disciples of Christ
           Historical Society. 1969.
    2798. Vocabulary of Faith. Bethany, 1956.
    2799. Why I Am a Disciple of Christ. 1957.
    2800. The Why of Protestantism. 1949.
    2801. You and Your Minister. Bethany. 1940.
    2802. Your Life Work: The Christian Ministry. United
           Christian Missionary Soc., n.d.

See also under Disciples of Christ Historical Society in
GENERAL section, and Williams, Marvin Dale under LIBRARY
SCIENCE section.

Adams, Harry Baker, 1924-.
    Pastor; professor of pastoral theology; seminary
    administrator.
    2803. Priorities and People. Bethany, 1975.
    2804. What Jesus Asks: Meditations on Questions in the
           Gospels. CBP Pr., 1986.
    2805. "Worship among the Disciples of Christ, 1865-1920."
           United Christian Missionary Soc., 1966.

Ainslie, Peter, 1867-1934.
    Pastor; editor of Christian Union Quarterly; founder of
    Council on Christian Union (COCU).
    2806. Among the Gospels and the Acts: Being Notes and
           Comments Covering the Life of Christ in the Flesh,
           and the First Thirty Years' History of His Church.
           Temple Seminary Pr., 1908.
    2807. A Book of Christian Worship for Voluntary Use among
           Disciples of Christ and other Christians. Seminary
           House Pr., 1923. (co-author).
    2808. Christ or Napoleon--Which? Revell, 1915.
    2809. God and Me. Temple Seminary Pr., 1908.

2810. If Not a United Church--What? Revell, 1920.
2811. Introduction to the Study of the Bible: Being the
       Outline of a Full Course of Bible Study, Including a
       System of Marking the Bible. Temple Seminary Pr.,
       1910.
2812. The Message of the Disciples for the Union of the
       Church, Including Their Origin and History. Revell,
       1913.
2813. My Brother and I. Revell, 1911.
2814. Peter Ainslie Memorial Lecture. Rhodes Univ. (S.
       Africa), n.d.
2815. Plain Talks to Young Men on Vital Issues. Christian
       Publishing Co.,1897.
2816. Recollections and Reflections. Scribner's, 1926.
       (co-author).
2817. Religion in Daily Doings. 1903.
2818. The Scandal of Christianity. Willett, Clark &
       Colby, 1929.
2819. Some Experiments in Living. Association Pr., 1933.
2820. Studies in the Old Testament. 1907.
2821. Towards Christian Unity. Association for the
       Promotion of Christian Unity, 1918.
2822. The Unfinished Task of the Reformation. 1910.
2823. The Way of Prayer. Revell, 1924.
2824. Week-day Sermons in King's Chapel. Macmillan, 1925.
2825. Working with God. Christian Bd. of Publication,
       1917.

For works about him written by Disciple authors, see
   Idleman, Finis Schuyler under THEOLOGY section.

Albert, Frank J., 1918-1965.
   Professor of religion and history.
   2826. "A Study of the Eastern Orthodox Churches in the
          Ecumenical Movement." Ph.D. diss., Harvard Univ.,
          1964.

Alexander, Nelle (Grant).
   Missionary to India.
   2827. Disciples of Christ in India. United Christian
          Missionary Soc., 1946.
   2828. The Improvement of Reading in Secondary Schools.
          Texas Education Agency, 1953. (co-author).

Allen, Basil Louis, 1865-1934.
   Pastor.
   2829. Autobiography of Louis Allen. N.d.

Allen, Ronald James, 1949-.
   Professor of New Testament.
   2830. Contemporary Biblical Interpretation for Preaching.
          Judson, 1984.

2831.   "Feeling and Form in Exegesis and Preaching." Ph.D.
        diss., Drew Univ., 1977.
2832.   Our Eyes Can Be Opened: Preaching the Miracle
        Stories of the Synoptic Gospels Today. Univ. Pr. of
        America, 1982.

Allen, William Burwell.
    Pastor.
    2833.   "The Development of an Episcopal Office in the
            Christian Church (Disciples of Christ)." D. Min.
            thesis, School of Theology at Claremont, 1981.

Ames, Edward Scribner, 1870-1958.
    Pastor; philosopher.
    2834.   Beyond Theology: The Autobiography of Edward
            Scribner Ames. Univ. of Chicago Pr., 1935.
    2835.   The Church at Work in the Modern World. Univ. of
            Chicago Pr., 1935.
    2836.   The Divinity of Christ [Sermons]. New Christian
            Century Co., 1911.
    2837.   Experiments in Personal Religion. The American
            Institute of Sacred Literature, 1930.
    2838.   The Higher Individualism. Houghton Mifflin, 1915.
    2839.   Humanism. Chicago Literary Club, 1931.
    2840.   Letters to God and the Devil [Sermons]. Harper,
            1933.
    2841.   The New Orthodoxy. Univ. of Chicago Pr., 1918.
    2842.   Prayers and Meditations of Edward Scribner Ames.
            Edited by Van Meter Ames. 1970.
    2843.   The Psychology of Religious Experience. Houghton
            Mifflin, 1910.
    2844.   Religion.   Holt, 1929.

For works about him written by Disciple authors, see
    Abel, John Albert and
    Garrison, Winfred under THEOLOGY section,
    Arnold, Charles Harvey and
    Pope, Richard M. in GENERAL section.

Anderson, Leroy Dean, 1876-1961.
    Pastor; professor of homiletics and evangelism; co-editor
    of Christian Courier.
    2845.   The Business of Living. Doran, 1923.
    2846.   Perfected into One. 1926.
    2847.   Stranger and Pilgrims. 1950.
    2848.   What We Believe. 1957.

*Andry, Carl F., 1918-.
    Professor of philosophy.
    2849.   Paul and the Early Christians. Prinit, 1978.
    2850.   Problems in Early Christianity. Prinit, 1978.

Andry, E. Robert, 1907-.
   Professor of biblical history and literature.
   2851. "Paul's Use of 'Pneumatikos' and 'Psychikos.'"
       Ph.D. diss., Southern Baptist Theological Seminary,
       1942.

Arant, Francis M.
   2852. "P. H." - The Welshimer Story. Standard, 1958.

Archer, Cathaline (Alford).
   2853. John Clark Archer [1881-1957]: A Chronicle.
       Hamden? Conn., 1959.

Armstrong, H. C.
   Church official.
   2854. A Book of Christian Worship for Voluntary Use among
       Disciples of Christ and Other Christians. Seminary
       House Pr., 1923. (co-author).

Armstrong, Housen Parr.
   2855. Living in the Currents of God [Sermons]. Bethany,
       1962.
   2856. "Problems in Adjustment Between High School Pupils
       and Their Parents." D.B. thesis, Univ. of Chicago,
       1931.

Ash, Anthony L.
   Pastor.
   2857. "Attitudes Toward the Higher Criticism of the Old
       Testament Among the Disciples of Christ: 1850-1905."
       Ph.D. diss., Univ. of Southern California, 1966.
   2858. The Word of Faith [Sermons]. Biblical Research Pr.,
       1973.

Ashton, Donald George.
   Pastor.
   2859. "History of the Pulaski County Christian Churches."
       B.D. thesis, Butler Univ., 1947.

Atwater, Anna Robison, 1859-1941.
   Laywoman; educator.
   2860. Disciples of Christ in Mexico. Christian Woman's
       Bd. of Missions, 1920.
   2861. Forms of Work Conducted by the Christian Woman's
       Board of Missions. Christian Woman's Bd. of
       Missions, 19?
   2862. Speak - That They Go Forward. United Christian
       Missionary Soc., 1927.

Atwater, John Milton, 1837-1900.
   Pastor.
   2863. Jehovah's War Against False Gods and Other
       Addresses. Christian Publishing Co., 1903.

Austin, Spencer Peter, 1910-.
    Pastor; church official.
    2864. The Bible Speaks on Baptism, the Lord's Supper and
          Stewardship. United Christian Missionary Soc., 19?
          (compiler).
    2865. The Bible Speaks on Becoming a Christian. United
          Christian Missionary Soc., 19? (compiler)
    2866. Evangelism. Church Program Planning Committee
          (Indianapolis), 19?
    2867. "Fifty Fruitful Years." In Irvington Historical
          Society, Collected Papers, 1970-1972. pp. 55-84.
          Indianapolis, 1952.
    2868. If You Are the Sons of God: The 97th Commencement
          Address at the College of the Bible. College of the
          Bible (Lexington), 1962.
    2869. Instructions for Visitors: Home Visitation
          Evangelism. United Christian Missionary Soc., 19?
    2870. Open Letter - Mission Inventory. 1951.
    2871. Visitation Evangelism for Town and Country Churches.
          United Christian Missionary Soc., 19? (co-author).

Bader, Jesse Moren, 1886-1963.
    Pastor; church official.
    2872. Evangelism in a Changing America. Bethany, 1957.
    2873. The Message and Method of the New Evangelism. Round
          Table Pr., 1937. (editor).

Baird, William Robb, Jr., 1924-.
    Professor of New Testament.
    2874. The Corinthian Church - A Biblical Approach to Urban
          Culture. Abingdon, 1960.
    2875. First and Second Corinthians. Knox, 1980.
    2876. Paul's Message and Mission. Abingdon, 1960.
    2877. The Quest of the Christ of Faith - Reflections on
          the Bultmann Era. Word, 1977.

Ballinger, James Lawrence, 1919-.
    Pastor; Christian educator.
    2878. Chi Rho Fellowship Handbook. Christian Bd. of
          Publication, 1950. (co-author).
    2879. Church Conferences for Youth & Adults. Bethany,
          1965.

Banks, Gabriel Conklyn.
    Pastor.
    2880. Echoes from the Altar, Sermons. Exposition Pr.,
          1966.

Barber, William Joseph.
    2881. The Disciple Assemblies of Eastern North Carolina.
          Bethany, 1966.

Barclay, John, 1893- .
   Pastor.
   2882. <u>What Ought To Be Can Be [Sermons]</u>. Bethany, 1966.

Barclay, Julia Ann, 1813-1908.
   2883. <u>Julia Ann Barclay: A Register of Correspondence in the Disciples of Christ Historical Society.</u> 1966.

Barnes, Bill Lloyd, 1926- .
   Pastor; seminary administrator.
   2884. "A Pattern of Worship for Disciples of Christ." B.D. thesis, Butler Univ., 1952.
   2885. "A Study of the Inception and Development of the Affton Christian Church." M.S. thesis, Butler Univ., 1957.

Barr, William Richard, 1934- .
   Professor of theology.
   2886. <u>Dwight E. Stevenson: A Tribute by Some of His Former Students.</u> Lexington Theological Seminary, 1975. (editor).
   2887. "The Enactment of the Person of Christ." Ph.D. diss., Yale Univ., 1969.

Bartchy, Stuart Scott, 1936- .
   Professor of religion.
   2888. "Mallon Chresae: First Century Slavery and the Interpretation of I Corinthians 7:21." Ph.D. diss., Harvard Univ., 1971. Also published by Soc. of Biblical Literature for the Seminar on Paul, 1973.

Basham, Don Wilson, 1926- .
   Pastor; editor of <u>New Wine</u> (1976-).
   2889. <u>Beyond Blessing to Obedience.</u> Christian Growth Ministries, 1976.
   2890. <u>Can a Christian Have a Demon?</u> Whitaker, 1970.
   2891. <u>Deliver Us from Evil.</u> Chosen Bks., 1972.
   2892. <u>Face up with a Miracle.</u> Whitaker, 1967.
   2893. <u>Handbook on Holy Spirit Baptism.</u> Whitaker, 1968.
   2894. <u>Handbook on Tongues, Interpretation and Prophecy.</u> Whitaker, 1970.
   2895. <u>How God Guides Us.</u> Manna, 1975.
   2896. <u>Manual for Spiritual Welfare.</u> Manna, 1974.
   2897. <u>Ministering the Baptism in the Holy Spirit.</u> Whitaker, 1969.
   2898. <u>Miracle of Tongues.</u> Revell, 1973.
   2899. <u>The Most Dangerous Game.</u> Manna, 1974.
   2900. <u>True and False Prophets.</u> Manna, 1973.

Bateman, Georgia B.
   Missionary to Zaire.
   2901. <u>Hygiene pour les Ecoles Africainnes.</u> Disciples of Christ Congo Mission, 1937.

2902. Lisolo la Bonkanda. Disciples of Christ Congo
       Mission, 1934.

Bates, Daniel M., 1849-1899.
    Founder of The Evangelist.
    2903. Christ in Modern Thought. Whittaker, 1889.

Bates, Ernest Sutherland.
    2904. The Bible Designed To Be Read as Living Literature:
           The Old and New Testaments in the King James
           Version. Simon & Schuster, 1972, c.1936. (editor).
    2905. "Creedless Frontier." In American Faith: Its
           Religious, Political and Economic Foundations. pp.
           319-40. Norton, 1940.

*Bates, Miner Searle, 1897-1978.
    Pastor; professor of history; missionary.
    2906. China in Change: An Approach to Understanding.
           Friendship Pr., 1969.
    2907. Half of Humanity: Far Eastern Peoples and Problems.
           Church Peace Union, 1942.
    2908. An Introduction to Oriental Journals in Western
           Languages, With an Annotated Bibliography of
           Representative Articles. Univ. of Nanking, 1933-.
    2909. Missions in Far Eastern Cultural Relations.
           American Council, Institute of Pacific Relations,
           1942.
    2910. The Nanking Population: Employment, Earnings and
           Expenditures; A Survey. Mercury Pr., 1939.
    2911. The Prospects of Christianity Throughout the World.
           Scribner, 1964. (co-editor).
    2912. Religious Liberty. Church World Service, 1947.

Bates, Robert Searle, 1928-.
    Missionary to Sri Lanka.
    2913. "Cultural Unity and Diversity: A Study in Religio-
           Ethnic Relations in Ceylon (Sri Lanka)." Ph.D.
           diss., Univ. of Chicago, 1974.

Battenfield, Ben F.
    2914. The Restoration Message. Incoming Kingdom
           Missionary Unit, n.d.
    2915. Restoring the Kingdom of Heaven. Incoming Kingdom
           Missionary Unit, h.d.

Battenfield, John Adam, 1876-?
    2916. Behold the Bridegroom. Incoming Kingdom Missionary
           Unit, 1919.
    2917. The Gospel of the Kingdom. Incoming Kingdom
           Missionary Unit, 1919.
    2918. The Great Demonstration, a Harmony of All the
           Prophetic Visions of the Holy Bible. Standard,
           1914.

2919. <u>Primary Lessons in the Science of Prophecy.</u>
       Incoming Kingdom Missionary Unit, 1918.

Batzka, David L.
   2920. <u>Coming of Age in the Christian Church (Disciples of</u>
          <u>Christ): Northeast Older Adult Study Report.</u> 1973.
          (co-author).
   2921. <u>Instruction Manual for the Older Adult Church Survey</u>
          <u>Project.</u> National Benevolent Assoc., 1974.

*Baxter, William, 1820-1880.
   Pastor; college president.
   2922. <u>Life of Elder Walter Scott: With Sketches of His</u>
          <u>Fellow Laborers.</u> Chase & Hall, 1874.
   2923. <u>Life of Knowles Shaw, The Singing Evangelist.</u>
          Central Book Concern, 1879.
   2924. <u>Pea Ridge and Prairie Grove.</u> Poe & Hitchcock, 1864.

*Bayer, Charles H., 1927-.
   Pastor.
   2925. <u>A Guide to Liberation Theology for Middle-Class</u>
          <u>Congregations.</u> CBP Pr., 1986.

Beard, Roger Stanton.
   2926. "A Study of Decisions for Church-Related Vocations
          Made in Selected Youth Camps Related to the
          Christian Churches from 1960-1970." D.R.E. diss.,
          Southern Baptist Theological Seminary, 1971.

*Beazley, George Grimes, Jr., 1914-1973.
   Pastor; church official; editor of <u>Mid-Stream</u>.
   2927. <u>The Christian Church (Disciples of Christ): An</u>
          <u>Interpretative Examination in the Cultural Context.</u>
          Bethany, 1973. (editor).

*Beckelhymer, Paul Hunter, 1919-.
   Pastor; seminary professor.
   2928. <u>Dear Connie: Letters to a Co-Ed From Her Christian</u>
          <u>Father.</u> Bethany, 1967.
   2929. <u>Meeting Life on Higher Levels.</u> Abingdon, 1956.
   2930. <u>Questions God Asks [Sermons].</u> Abingdon, 1961.
   2931. <u>The Vital Pulpit of the Christian Church: A Series</u>
          <u>of Sermons by Representative Men among the Disciples</u>
          <u>of Christ.</u> Bethany, 1969. (compiler).
   2932. <u>The Word We Preach: Sermons in Honor of Dean Elmer</u>
          <u>D. Henson by Faculty and Trustees of Brite Divinity</u>
          <u>School, Texas Christian University.</u> Texas Christian
          Univ. Pr., 1970. (editor).

Becker, Edwin Lewis, 1917-.
   Professor of sociology of religion.

2933.   "Christian Church (Disciples of Christ)." In
        Ministry in America/Survey, pp. 307-31. 1980. (co-
        editor).
2934.   Disciples of Christ in Town and Country. United
        Christian Missionary Soc., 1950.
2935.   Four Parts of the Whole: A Bible Study. Christian
        Bd. of Publication, 1973.
2936.   "Religious Field Work as Experience in the Social
        Roles of the Minister." Ph.D. diss., Yale Univ.,
        1956.
2937.   Responding to God's Call. Bethany, 1970.

Beittel, Adam Daniel.
    Pastor; professor of sociology and religion.
    2938.   "The Kingdom of God and the Messianic Conceptions in
            the Book of Enoch, in the Psalms of Solomon, and in
            the Apocalypse of Baruch." 1923?
    2939.   "The Rise of the Virgin-Birth Tradition." Ph.D.
            diss., Univ. of Chicago, 1929.

*Belcastro, Joseph, 1910-.
    Pastor.
    2940.   The Church Challenges the Charismatic-Tongues.
            [Work in progress].
    2941.   The Relationship of Baptism to Church Membership.
            Bethany, 1963.

Bell, Robert Monroe, 1889-1960?
    Pastor; college professor.
    2942.   Reasoning Together. College Pr., 1967.
    2943.   The Unhappy Critic. 1966 or 7.

Bennett, Joseph R.
    College administrator.
    2944.   "A Study of the Life and Contributions of Emily H.
            Tubman." B.D. thesis, Butler Univ. School of
            Religion, 1958.

Berry, Stephen Pressley.
    Pastor.
    2945.   "An Enquiry into the Role of the Holy Spirit in the
            Development and Nurture of Faith, As Understood by
            Robert Richardson." D.Min. thesis, San Francisco
            Theological Seminary, 1984.

Best, Thomas F.
    Professor of religion.
    2946.   Hearing and Speaking the Word: Selections from the
            Works of James Muilenburg. Scholars Pr., 1984.
            (editor).
    2947.   The Sociological Study of the New Testament:
            Promise and Peril of a New Discipline. Scottish
            Academic Pr., 1983.

2948. Survey of Church Union Negotiations 1981-1983.
       World Council of Churches, 1984. (editor).
2949. "Transfiguration and Discipleship in Matthew."
       Ph.D. diss., Graduate Theological Union, 1974.

Bingham, Walter D., 1921-.
    Pastor.
    2950. "Let's Think about the Lord's Supper." Christian
           Bd. of Publication, 1952.

Black, J. F.
    2951. The Bible Way: An Antidote to Campbellism.
           Jennings & Graham, 1906.

Blackman-Sexton, Maribeth.
    2952. "What Do We Call You." In Women as Pastors. pp.
           56-62. Edited by L. Schaller. 1982.

Blakely, Fred Orville, 1910-.
    Pastor.
    2953. The Apostles' Doctrine: A Book of Sermon-Studies in
           the Field of Basic Christian Teaching. Highland,
           Ind., 1957.

Blakemore, William Barnett, Jr., 1912-1975.
    Pastor; professor of theology; seminary administrator.
    2954. The Bible Enlightens Our Lives. 1968.
    2955. The Challenge of Christian Unity. Bethany, 1964.
    2956. The Cornerstone and the Builders. 1955.
    2957. "Disciples Worship from 1925 to the Present."
           United Christian Missionary Soc., 1966.
    2958. The Discovery of the Church. A History of Disciple
           Ecclesiology. Reed, 1966.
    2959. Encountering God [Sermons]. Bethany, 1965.
    2960. A Needy One Stands Before Thee. 1956.
    2961. Quest for Intelligence in the Ministry. 1970.
    2962. "Religious Experience in Terms of Sociological
           Behaviorism." Ph.D. diss., Univ. of Chicago, 1941.
    2963. The Renewal of the Church: The Panel Reports. 3
           vols. Bethany, 1963. (editor).
    2964. "The Revival of the Churches." In The Renewal of
           the Church. vol. 3. Bethany, 1963. (editor).
    2965. Sociological Behaviorism and Religious Personality.
           1944.

Boatman, Don Earl, 1913-.
    Professor of religion; member of Church of Christ.
    2966. Guidance from Galatians. College Pr., 1961.
    2967. Helps from Hebrews. College Pr., 1960.

Boeyink, David Earl, 1945-.
    Professor of religion.

2968.   "Religious and Non-Religious Therapies for the
        Alcoholic." Ph.D. diss., Harvard Univ., 1977.

Boles, Henry Leo.
2969.   Biographical Sketches of Gospel Preachers. Gospel
        Advocate Co., 1932.

Bonvillain, F. D.
        Pastor.
2970.   "The Thread of Unity. A Report on the Merger of
        Christ Church, Uniting Disciples and Presbyterians
        in Kailua, Hawaii." D. Min. thesis, School of
        Theology at Claremont, 1976.

Book, Morris Butler.
        Pastor.
2971.   Book-Miller Debate on Instrumental Music in Worship.
        Phillips Publishers, 1955.
2972.   Gospel Trail Blazers: 10 Positive Sermons.
        Orlando? 1954.

Book, William Henry, 1863-.
        Pastor.
2973.   The Columbus Tabernacle Sermons. 2 vols. Standard,
        1909-13.
2974.   The Indiana Pulpit [Sermons]. Standard, 1912.
        (editor).
2975.   Real Life and Original Sayings. Richmond, Ware &
        Duke, 1900.
2976.   Sermons for the People. Standard, 1918.

Booth, Osborne.
        Professor of religion.
2977.   The Chosen People: A Narrative History of the
        Israelites. Bethany, 1959.
2978.   "The Semantic Development of the Term [   ] in the
        Old Testament." Ph.D. diss., Yale Univ., 1942.

Borders, Karl, 1891-1953.
        Pastor; missionary.
2979.   Village Life under the Soviets. Vanguard Pr., 1927.

Boring, Mayard Eugene, 1935-.
        Pastor; professor of New Testament.
2980.   "Christian Prophets and the Gospel of Mark." Ph.D.
        diss., Vanderbilt Univ., 1969.
2981.   Sayings of the Risen Jesus: Christian Prophecy in
        the Synoptic Tradition. Cambridge Univ. Pr., 1982.
2982.   Truly Human/Truly Divine: Christological Language
        and the Gospel Form. CBP Pr., 1984.

Bostick, Sarah Lue (Howard) Young, 1868-1948.
        Home missionary.

2983.   <u>Beginning of the Missionary Work and Plans in
        Arkansas. 1896. 25 Years Service: Historical Sketch
        up to 1918.</u> N.d.

For works about her written by Disciple authors, see
   Fuller, Bertha Mason under THEOLOGY section.

Boswell, Ira Matthews, 1866-.
   Pastor.
   2984.   <u>Flaming Hearts and Other Sermons.</u> Standard, 1939.

Botkin, Robert Ralph, 1935-.
   College president.
   2985.   "The Contemporary Reconstruction of Theology among
           the Disciples of Christ with Special Reference to
           the Problems of Authority and Methodology." Ph.D.
           diss., Emory Univ., 1964.

Bouchard, Larry D.
   Professor of religion and philosophy.
   2986.   <u>Interpreting Disciples: Practical Theology in the
           Disciples of Christ.</u> Texas Christian Univ. Pr.,
           1987. (co-author).

Bowen, Thaddeus Hassell, 1893-1965.
   Seminary professor.
   2987.   <u>Characteristic Beliefs of the Disciples of Christ.</u>
           College of the Bible (Lexington), 1945.
   2988.   <u>Contemporary Theology and the Modern Minister.</u>
           College of the Bible (Lexington), 1958.

Bower, William Clayton, 1878-1954.
   Pastor; seminary professor.
   2989.   <u>Character through Creative Experience.</u> Univ. of
           Chicago Pr., 1930.
   2990.   <u>Christ and Christian Education.</u> Abingdon, 1943.
   2991.   <u>Church and State in Education.</u> Univ. of Chicago
           Pr., 1944. (co-author).
   2992.   <u>The Church at Work in the Modern World.</u> Univ. of
           Chicago Pr., 1935. (editor).
   2993.   <u>Curriculum of Religious Education.</u> Scribner, 1925.
   2994.   <u>The Disciples and Religious Education.</u> Bethany,
           1936. (editor).
   2995.   <u>Educational Task of Local Church.</u> Bethany, 1921.
   2996.   <u>History of Central Christian Church. Lexington.</u>
           Bethany, 1962.
   2997.   <u>The Living Bible.</u> Harper, 1936. (co-author).
   2998.   <u>Moral and Spiritual Values in Education.</u> Univ. of
           Kentucky Pr., 1952.
   2999.   <u>Protestantism Faces Its Educational Task Together.</u>
           Nelson, 1949.
   3000.   <u>Religious Education in the Modern Church.</u> Bethany,
           1929.

3001. <u>Robert M. Hopkins: Christian Statesman.</u> College of
       the Bible (Lexington), 1963.
3002. <u>Survey of Religious Education in Local Church.</u>
       <u>Univ. of Chicago Pr.</u>, 1919.
3003. <u>Through the Years: Personal Memoirs.</u> Transylvania
       College Pr., 1957.

Bradney, Leta Vera, 1913-.
   Pastor; church official.
3004. <u>Christian Women's Fellowship.</u> 1966. (co-author).
3005. <u>Every Time I Feel the Spirit.</u> 1960. (co-author).

*Bradshaw, Marion John, 1886-.
   Pastor; college and seminary professor.
3006. <u>Baleful Legacy, a Faith without Foundations: An</u>
       <u>Examination of Neo-Orthodoxy.</u> Modern Publishers,
       1955.
3007. <u>Free Churches and Christian Unity.</u> Beacon Pr.,
       1954.
3008. <u>The Maine Land.</u> Bradshaw, 1941.
3009. <u>The Maine Scene: A Portrait of the State of Maine.</u>
       1947.
3010. <u>The Nature of Maine as Seen by a Teacher of</u>
       <u>Philosophy.</u> Bradshaw, 1944.
3011. <u>Philosophical Foundations of Faith, a Contribution</u>
       <u>toward a Philosophy of Religion.</u> Columbia Univ.
       Pr., 1941.
3012. <u>The War and Religion: A Preliminary Bibliography of</u>
       <u>Material in English, Prior to January 1, 1919.</u>
       Association Pr., 1919. (compiler).

Bradshaw, Vinton D.
   Professor of religion.
3013. "Supervised Concurrent Field Education at Christian
       Theological Seminary." Ph.D. diss., Boston Univ.,
       1972.

Bragg, Joseph H., Jr., 1935?-.
3014. <u>God Plans for Friends.</u> Judson, 1976.

Brandt, John Lincoln, 1860-.
   Pastor.
3015. <u>Soul Saving: Revival Sermons.</u> Christian Publishing
       Co., 1907.

Branson, Gene N., 1926-.
3016. <u>Joy Beyond Sorrow.</u> Christopher, 1962.

Brenneman, Lyle Eugene, 1934-.
   Missionary to Zaire.
3017. "Conflict and Change in the Republic of Zaire."
       Ph.D. diss., American Univ., 1976.

Brewer, Grover Cleveland, 1884-1956.
   3018. <u>Contending for the Faith.</u> Gospel Advocate Co.,
        1941.
   3019. <u>A Story of Toil and Tears, Of Love and Laughter:</u>
        <u>Being the Autobiography of G. C. Brewer, 1884-1956.</u>
        Dehoff, 1957.

Brewer, Urban C., 1825-.
   3020. <u>The Bible and American Slavery.</u> Gould, 1863.

Bricker, Luther Otterbein, 1874-1942.
   Pastor.
   3021. <u>Sermons in the Sanctuary.</u> Donaldson-Woods, 1943.

*Briney, John Benton, 1839-1927.
   Pastor; editor of <u>Briney's Monthly.</u>
   3022. <u>Instrumental Music in Christian Worship.</u> Standard,
        1914.
   3023. <u>The Relation of Baptism to the Remission of Alien</u>
        <u>Sins.</u> Briney Publishing Co., 1902.
   3024. <u>Sermons and Addresses.</u> Standard, 1922.
   3025. <u>The Temptation of Christ.</u> Christian Publishing Co.,
        1892.

Broadus, Loren A., Jr.
   Professor of religion.
   3026. <u>From Loneliness to Intimacy: Help for the Golf</u>
        <u>Widow and Other Lonely People.</u> John Knox Pr., 1976.
        (co-author).
   3027. <u>How To Stop Procrastinating and Start Living.</u>
        Augsburg, 1983.

Brokaw, George Lewis.
   Pastor.
   3028. <u>Doctrine and Life [Sermons].</u> Christian Index
        Publishing Co., 1898. (editor).

Brown, Alberta Z.
   Educator; youth worker.
   3029. <u>For Students and Others Fed Up.</u> Bethany, 1970.
   3030. <u>The Seven Teen Years.</u> Bethany, 1954.
   3031. <u>Teens to 21.</u> Bethany, 1957.

Brown, Henry Clay, 1840-.
   Pastor.
   3032. <u>Memorial Sermons.</u> Tewksbury, 1893.
   3033. <u>Reason of Christian Doctrines.</u> Winona, 1904.
   3034. <u>A Successful Life.</u> Tewksbury, 1893.

Brown, John Thomas, 1869-1926.
   3035. <u>Churches of Christ.</u> Morton, 1904.
   3036. <u>Who's Who in Churches of Christ.</u> Standard, 1929.

Brown, Leslie C.
    Pastor.
    3037. "New Dimensions in Discipleship." D.Min. thesis,
         Phillips Univ. Graduate Seminary, 1982.

Brown, Leta May.
    Missionary to India.
    3038. Hira Lal of India. Bethany, 1954.
    3039. Little Brown Babe: A Christian Marriage in India.
         Revell, 1937.

*Browning, Don Spencer, 1934-.
    Pastor; seminary professor.
    3040. Atonement and Psychotherapy. Westminster, 1966.
    3041. Care of the Souls in the Classic Tradition.
         Fortress, 1984. (editor).
    3042. The Family and Pastoral Care. Fortress, 1984.
         (editor).
    3043. Generative Man: Psychoanalytic Prospectives.
         Westminster, 1973.
    3044. Life Cycle Theory and Pastoral Care. Fortress,
         1983. (editor).
    3045. The Moral Context of Pastoral Care. Westminster,
         1976.
    3046. Pastoral Care and Hermeneutics. Fortress, 1984.
         (editor).
    3047. Pastoral Theology in a Pluralistic Age. Harper,
         1983.
    3048. Pluralism and Personality: William James and Some
         Contemporary Cultures of Psychology. Associated
         Univ. Pr., 1980.
    3049. Practical Theology. Harper & Row, 1983. (editor).
    3050. Professionalism and Pastoral Care. Fortress, 1985.
         (editor).
    3051. Religious Ethics and Pastoral Care. Fortress, 1983.
    3052. Religious Thought and the Modern Psychologies: A
         Critical Conversation in the Theology of Culture.
         Fortress, 1986.
    3053. Ritual and Pastoral Care. Fortress, 1987. (editor).
    3054. Spirituality and Pastoral Care. Fortress, 1985.
         (editor).
    3055. Toward a Practical Theology of Aging. Fortress,
         1985. (editor).

*Bruner, Benjamin Harrison, 1888-.
    Pastor.
    3056. The Evangelistic Message. Christian Bd. of
         Publication, 1922.
    3057. Evenings with the Master. Christian Bd. of
         Publication, 1920.
    3058. Great Choices of the Last Week [Sermons].
         Cokesbury, 1937.

3059.　Great Days of the Last Week [Sermons].　R. R. Smith, 1931.

3060.　Great Questions of the Last Week [Sermons]. Cokesbury, 1934.

3061.　The Meaning of Church Membership.　Bethany, 1930.

3062.　Pentecost: A Renewal of Power.　Doubleday, Doran & Co., 1928.

3063.　This Sacred Hour:　Communion Meditation and Prayers. Bethany, 1953.

3064.　Toward the Sunrising [Sermons].　Cokesbury, 1935.

3065.　Which Gospel Shall I Preach?　R. R. Smith, 1930.

Buckner, George Walker Jr., 1893-1981.
　　Pastor; editor of World Call; church official.
3066.　Concerns of a World Church.　Bethany, 1943.
3067.　The Winds of God.　1947.

Burch Brown, Frank, 1948-.
3068.　Transfiguration:　Poetic Metaphor and the Languages of Religious Belief.　Univ. of North Carolina Pr., 1983.

Burgess, O. A.
3069.　A Debate on Total Depravity, Election, the Polity or Church Government of the Regular Baptist Church, Free Moral Agency, Water Baptism a Condition of Salvation...between Elder G. M. Thompson... of the Regular Baptist Church, and Elder O. A. Burgess, of Indiana, of the Reformer Church....　Sentintel Printing and Binding Establishment (Indianapolis), 1868.

Burner, Willis Judson, 1870-1957.
　　Pastor; missionary to Argentina; professor.
3070.　"The Attitudes of Contemporary Spanish-American Authors towards the U. S."　Ph.D. diss., Ohio State Univ., 1930.
3071.　"Our Mission in Argentina."　Christian Woman's Bd. of Missions, 191-?

Burnett, Thomas R., 1842-1916.
3072.　Hezekiah Jones:　A Dialogue between a Methodist and a Christian.　Gospel Advocate Publishing Co., 1895.

Burnham, Frederick William, 1871-1960.
　　Pastor; church official.
3073.　A Missionary Tour of Alaska, 1919.　Unification, 1927.

Burns, Robert Whitehall, 1904-.
　　Pastor.

3074.   The Art of Staying Happily Married.   Prentice-Hall,
        1963.
3075.   The Christian Life.   1930.

*Butler, Ovid, 1801-1881.
    Attorney; founder of Butler Univ.; editor.
    3076.   Is Slavery Sinful?   Dodd, 1863.   (contributor).

Butler, Pardee, 1816-1888.
    Evangelist; abolitionist.
    3077.   Personal Recollections of Pardee Butler....
            Standard, 1889.

See also, Harrell, David F. in GENERAL section.

Cadwell, Merrill Lorenzo, 1911-.
    Pastor; church official.
    3078.   In Spirit and with Honesty.   1973.
    3079.   "Membership."   National Church Program Coordinating
            Council, 1966.
    3080.   "Property."   National Church Program Coordinating
            Council, 1966.
    3081.   The Work of Elders in the Christian Church.   1968.
    3082.   Worship in the Christian Church.   1969.   (editor).

Calhoun, Hall Laurie, 1863-1935.
    Pastor; professor of Hebrew and Old Testament; seminary
    dean.
    3083.   "The Remains of the Old Latin Translation of
            Leviticus."   Ph.D. diss., Harvard Univ., 1904.

For works about him written by Disciple authors, see
    Doran, Adron under THEOLOGY section and
    Haymes, Don in GENERAL section.

Camp, Claudia.
    Professor of religion.
    3084.   Wisdom and the Feminine in the Book of Proverbs.
            Eisenbrauns, 1985.

*Campbell, George Alexander, 1869-1943.
    Pastor; editor of Christian Oracle and Christian Century.
    3085.   Chores and the Altar.   Bethany, 1931.
    3086.   Friends Are My Story.   Bethany, 1944.
    3087.   My Dad, Preacher, Pastor, Person: Thirty-Four
            Disciples of Christ Ministers Interpreted by a Son
            and Daughter.   Christian Bd. of Publication, 1938.
            (co-editor).

Campbell, Horace Wilbert, 1903-.
    Pastor.
    3088.   Can You Help Me?   Sermons Addressed to Individuals.
            Dorrance, 1945.

Cardwell, Sue Webb, 1915-.
    Professor of pastoral care.
    3089.   "Development of Persistence Scales Using Items of
             the Theological School Inventory." Ph.D. diss.,
             Indiana Univ., 1978.
    3090.   "The MMPI as a Predictor of Success among Seminary
             Students." Sp. Ed. thesis, Butler Univ., 1965.
    3091.   Theological School Inventory Manual for the Use of
             the TSI in Vocational Guidance of Theological
             Students. 2d. ed. Ministry Studies Bd., 1976. (co-
             author).

Carpe, William Donald, 1938-.
    Professor of church history.
    3092.   "The Vita Canonica in the Regula Canonicorum of
             Chrodegang of Metz." Ph.D. diss., Univ. of Chicago,
             1975.

*Carpenter, Homer Wilson, 1880-1964.
    Pastor.
    3093.   The Future is Now. Bethany, 1951.

Carpenter, James A.
    3094.   "Equipping the Laity for Pastoral Minstry." D.Min.
             thesis, Phillips Univ. Graduate Seminary, 1982.

Carpenter, William Whitney.
    College administrator.
    3095.   "Relationship: The Foundation of a Team Ministry."
             Ph.D. diss., School of Theology, Claremont, 1965.

Carr, James Bottorff.
    3096.   The Foreign Missionary Work of the Christian Church.
             Swift, 1946.

Carstensen, Roger Norwood, 1920-.
    Professor of Old Testament; college administrator.
    3097.   Job: Defense of Honor. Abingdon, 1963.
    3098.   "The Persistence of the 'Elihu' Point of View in
             Later Jewish Literature." Ph.D. diss., Vanderbilt
             Univ., 1960.
    3099.   Professor's Story Book. Phillips Univ. Science Pr.,
             1963.

Cartwright, Lin Dorwin, 1886-.
    Pastor; editor.
    3100.   Evangelism for Today. Bethany, 1934.
    3101.   The Great Committment: The Meaning of the
             Confession of Faith. Bethany, 1962.

*Carty, James William, Jr., 1925-.
    Pastor; journalist; professor of communications.

3102.   Advertising in the Local Church. Augsburg
         Publishing House, 1965.

Caskey, Thomas W., 1816-1896.
    Pastor.
    3103.   Caskey's Book, Lectures on Great Subjects Selected
             from the Numerous Efforts of that Powerful Orator
             and Noble Veteran of the Cross. Burns, 1884.
    3104.   Caskey's Last Book, Containing an Autobiographical
             Sketch of His Ministerial Life with Essays and
             Sermons. Messenger, 1896.

Castleberry, John Jackson, 1877-1937.
    Pastor.
    3105.   The Soul of Religion, and Other Addresses. Revell,
             1926.

Castleman, William James, 1908-.
    Pastor; editor of Garden City News.
    3106.   Beauty and the Mission of the Teacher: The Life of
             Gabriela Mistral of Chile, Teacher, Poetess, Friend
             of the Helpless, Nobel Laureate. Exposition Pr.,
             1982.
    3107.   A Historical Literary Biography of the Early Life of
             Samuel Guy Inman: Herald of Christian Cooperation,
             Advocate of Inter-American Friendship, Worker for
             World Peace, and Pioneer in Social Action. Bethany,
             1966.
    3108.   On This Foundation: Samuel Guy Inman, 1873-1904.
             Vol. 1, 1964; vol. 2, 1969.

Cave, Robert Catlett, 1843-1923.
    Pastor.
    3109.   Dedication of the Soldiers and Sailors Monument.
             1894?
    3110.   A Manual for Home Devotions. Standard, 1919.
    3111.   A Manual for Ministers. Standard, 1918.
    3112.   The Men in Gray. Confederate Veteran, 1911.

See also, Howley, Monroe E.,
    McCauley, Lynn, and
    Pearson, S. C. in GENERAL section.

Cayce, Edgar, 1877-1945.
    Psychic.
    3113.   "Auras: An Essay on the Meaning of Colors." Cayce,
             1945.
    3114.   What I Believe. A.R.E. Pr., 1946.

*Centerwall, Siegried Achorn, 1925-.
*Centerwall, Willard R., 1924-.
    Medical missionaries.

3115. <u>Phenylketonuria: An Inherited Metabolic Disorder</u>
        <u>Associated with Mental Retardation.</u> U.S. Dept. of
        Health, Education and Welfare, 1961.

Cerbin, Dwaine Edward, 1910?-.
    Pastor.
    3116. "An Analysis of the Prophetic Orientation as It
            Developed from Samuel through Second Isaiah." Th.M.
            thesis, Univ. of Southern California, 1956.

Challen, James, 1802-1878.
    Pastor; editor; poet.
    3117. <u>The Cave of Machpelah and Other Poems.</u> 1854.
    3118. <u>Christian Evidences.</u> 1857.
    3119. <u>Frank Eliott: Or, Wells in the Desert.</u> 1859.
    3120. <u>The Gospel and Its Elements.</u> 1856.
    3121. <u>Igdrasil: Or, the Tree of Existence.</u> 1859.
    3122. <u>Island of the Giant Fairies.</u> 1868.

Champie, Ting R.
    Pastor.
    3123. "A Critical Study of the Place of the Lord's Supper
            in the Worship of the Christian Church (Diciples of
            Christ)." Ph.D. diss., San Francisco Theological
            Seminary, 1978.

Chaney, Marvin Lee.
    Professor of religion.
    3124. "HDL II and the Song of Deborah: Textual,
            Philological and Sociological Studies in Judges
            5...." Ph.D. diss., Harvard Univ., 1976.

Channels, Lloyd V., 1920?-.
    Pastor.
    3125. <u>The Layman Learns To Pray.</u> Bethany, 1957.

Cheverton, Cecil Frank, 1889-1953.
    College president; professor of religious education and Old
    Testament.
    3126. <u>The Bible and Social Living.</u> 4 vols. Christian Bd.
            of Publication, 1941.
    3127. <u>A Help for the Day.</u> Mason-Springs Corp., 1933.
    3128. <u>The Old Testament for New Students.</u> Bethany, 1951.
    3129. <u>Social Teachings of the Bible.</u> 1929.
    3130. <u>When Kings and Prophets Held the Stage.</u> Bethany,
            1930.

Christensen, James Lee, 1922-.
    Pastor.
    3131. <u>Before Saying "I Do."</u> Revell, 1983.
    3132. <u>Communion Reflections and Prayers.</u> CBP Pr., 1984.
    3133. <u>The Complete Funeral Manual.</u> Revell, 1967.
    3134. <u>The Complete Handbook for Ministers.</u> Revell, 1985.

3135. Contemporary Worship Services. Revell, 1971.
3136. Creative Ways To Worship. Revell, 1974.
3137. Difficult Funeral Services. Revell, 1985.
3138. Don't Waste Your Time in Worship. Revell, 1978.
3139. Funeral Services. Revell, 1959.
3140. Funeral Services for Today. Revell, 1977.
3141. How To Increase Church Attendance. Revell, 1961.
3142. The Minister's Church, Home, and Community Services
       Handbook. Revell, 1980.
3143. The Minister's Marriage Handbook. Revell, 1966,
       1985.
3144. The Minister's Service Handbook. Revell, 1960.
3145. The Minister's Wedding Handbook.
3146. New Ways To Worship. Revell, 1973.
3147. The Pastor's Counseling Handbook. Revell, 1963.
3148. Personal Daily Prayers.
3149. Reaching Beyond Your Pulpit.

Clark, Warren Malcolm, 1936-.
    Professor of religion.
    3150. Commitment without Ideology. SCM Pr., 1973.
    3151. "The Origin and Development of the Land Promise
           Theme in the Old Testament." Ph.D. diss., Yale
           Univ., 1964.

Clawson, Bertha Fidelia, 1868-1957.
    Missionary.
    3152. Bertha Fidelia, Her Story [As Told to Jessie M.
           Trout]. Bethany, 1957.

Clingan, Donald Frank, 1926-.
    Pastor; church official.
    3153. Aging Persons in the Community of Faith. New rev.
           ed. Institute on Religion and Aging and the Indiana
           Commission on the Aging and Aged, 1980.

*Coats, George W., Jr., 1936-.
    Professor of Old Testament.
    3154. Canon and Authority: Essays in Old Testament
           Religion and Theology. Fortress, 1977. (co-editor).
    3155. From Canaan to Egypt: Structural and Theological
           Context for the Joseph Story. Catholic Biblical
           Assoc. of America, 1976.
    3156. Genesis, With an Introduction to Narrative
           Literature. Eerdmans, 1983.
    3157. Rebellion in the Wilderness: The Murmuring Motif in
           the Wilderness, Traditions of the Old Testament.
           Abingdon, 1968.
    3158. "The Rebellion of Israel in the Wilderness." Ph.D.
           diss., Yale Univ., 1966.

Cobb, William Daniel, 1937-.
    College administrator.

3159.   "Moral Relativity and Christian Ethics: A Study in
        Response to the Theology of Emil Brunner and
        Reinhold Niebuhr." Ph.D. diss., Univ. of Chicago,
        1966.

Cochran, Bess (White), 1899-.
    3160.   _Without Halos._ Bethany, 1963, c1947.

Cole, Clifford Adair, 1915-.
    Pastor.
    3161.   _The Christian Churches (Disciples of Christ) of
            Southern California. A History._ Christian
            Missionary Soc. of Southern California, 1959.
    3162.   _Faith for New Frontiers._ Herald, 1956.
    3163.   _The Mighty Act of God._ Herald, 1984.
    3164.   _Modern Women in a Modern World._ Herald, 1965.
    3165.   _The Priesthood Manual._ Herald, 1982. (compiler).
    3166.   _The Prophets Speak._ Herald, 1954.
    3167.   _The Revelation in Christ._ Herald, 1963.
    3168.   _Studies in Exodus._ Herald, 1986.

Cole, Myron C., 1909-.
    Pastor.
    3169.   _Myron Here._ Mills, 1983.
    3170.   _The Nature of the Christian Ministry._ Bethany,
            1956.

Coler, George P., d.1915.
    Professor of religion.
    3171.   _Claims of Pedagogy in Colleges and Universities._
            Hann & Adair, 1894.
    3172.   _From the Birth to the Galilean Ministry._ Ann Arbor
            Bible Chairs, 19?.

Colston, Lowell G.
    Pastor; professor of pastoral care.
    3173.   _The Context of Pastoral Counseling._ Abingdon, 1961.
            (co-author).
    3174.   "The Function of Judgment in Pastoral Counseling."
            Ph.D. diss., Univ. of Chicago, 1961.
    3175.   _Judgment in Pastoral Counseling._ Abingdon, 1969.
    3176.   _Pastoral Care with Handicapped Persons._ Fortress,
            1978.
    3177.   _Personality and Christian Faith._ Abingdon, 1972.
    3178.   _Wake Up. Self._ Christian Bd. of Publication, 1969.

Combs, George Hamilton, 1864-1951.
    Pastor.
    3179.   _The Call of the Mountains, and Fourteen Other
            Sermons._ Christian Bd. of Publication, 1914.
    3180.   _The Christ in Modern English Literature._ Christian
            Publishing Co., 1903.
    3181.   _Himmler...Nazi Spider-Man._ McKay, 1942.

3182. Homilies in Homespun. Country Club Christian Church
       (Kansas City), 1962.
3183. I'd Take This Way Again. An Autobiography. Bethany,
       1944.
3184. Some Latter-Day Religions. Revell, 1899.
3185. These Amazing Moderns. Bethany, 1933.

Compton, John Richard, 1930- .
   Church official.
   3186. "The Preparation, Production and Evaluation of an
          Orientation and Training Film for Pastoral Field
          Education Supervisors." D.Min. thesis, Lancaster
          Theological Seminary, 1977.

Conner, Americus Wood, 1854-1932.
   Pastor; editor and publisher of Boy's Friend.
   3187. The Boggs Boys: Or Corralling the Kids of
          Kiddville. Boys' Friend Library, 1899.

Conrad, Rufus.
   Pastor; founder of American Christian Evangelizing and
   Educational Association.
   3188. Historical Sermon Preached on the Occasion of the
          Thirtieth Anniversary of the Christian or Disciple
          Church. Spencer & Craig, 1876.

Cook, Gaines Monroe, 1897- .
   Pastor; church official.
   3189. Around the World with the Cooks. 1957.
   3190. The Educational Committee of the Local Church.
          Christian Bd. of Publication, 1930.

Cook, Virginia D.
   Writer.
   3191. Guideposts for Worship. Bethany, 1964.

Cooley, Harris Reid, 1857-1936.
   Pastor.
   3192. The Chicago Exposition and the Living Question: Or.
          The Problem of the Unemployed.... 1894.
   3193. Funeral Services of Henry C. Muckley. Born 1850.
          Died 1925.

Coombs, James Vincent, 1849-1920.
   Pastor.
   3194. The Christ of the Church. Sermons. Lectures and
          Illustrations. Standard, n.d.

*Cooper, David Lipscomb, 1886-1965.
   Pastor.
   3195. An Exposition of the Book of Revelation. Biblical
          Research Soc., 1972.

3196. Future Events Revealed: An Exposition of the Olivet
       Discourse. Biblical Research Soc., 1983.
3197. Man, His Creation, Fall, Redemption, and
       Glorification. Biblical Research Soc., 1948.
3198. Messiah: His Final Call to Israel. Biblical
       Research Soc., 1962.
3199. Messiah: His Glorious Appearance Imminent.
       Biblical Research Soc., 1961.
3200. Messiah: His Historical Appearance. Biblical
       Research Soc., 1958.
3201. Messiah: His Redemptive Career. Cooper, 1942.
3202. The Shepherd of Israel Seeking His Own. Biblical
       Research Soc., 1962.

Copeland, Warren Rush, 1943-.
   Professor of religion.
3203. "The Politics of Welfare Reform: An Inquiry into
       the Possible Moral, Political, and Religious
       Importance of Welfare Policy in the United States."
       Ph.D. diss., Univ. of Chicago, 1977.

Corder, David E.
   Pastor.
3204. "Exploring the Doctrine of Ministry through
       Preaching and Dialogue at First Christian Church,
       Windsor, Missouri." D.Min., Brite Divinity School,
       1983.

Corey, Stephen Jared, 1873-1962.
   Pastor; college president.
3205. Among Asia's Needy Millions. Foreign Christian
       Missionary Soc., 1915.
3206. Among Central African Tribes. Foreign Christian
       Missionary Soc., 1912.
3207. Among South American Friends. Powell & White, 1925.
3208. As I Look Back. College of the Bible (Lexington),
       1958.
3209. Beyond Statistics, Or the Wider Range of World
       Missions. Bethany, 1937.
3210. Fifty Years of Attack and Controversy: The
       Consequences among Disciples of Christ [1900-1950].
       Committee on Publication of the Corey Manuscript,
       1953.
3211. Missions in the Modern Sunday School. Christian Bd.
       of Publication, 1911.
3212. Missions in the Sunday School. 1910.
3213. Missions Matching the Hour. Cokesbury, 1931.
3214. The Preacher and His Missionary Message. Cokesbury,
       1930.

Cory, Abram Edward, 1873-1952.
    Pastor; missionary to China; church official; professor of
    missions.
    3215. Out Where the World Begins: A Story of a Far
           Country. Doran, 1921.
    3216. Think Peace. 1916.
    3217. The Trail to the Hearts of Men: A Story of East and
           West. Revell, 1916.
    3218. Voices of the Sanctuary. 1930.

Cotten, Carroll Cresswell.
    3219. "The Imperative Is Leadership: A Study of Education
           for the Professional Ministry of the Christian
           Church (Disciples of Christ)." Ph.D. diss.,
           Standford Univ., 1975.

Cotto, Pablo, 1910?-.
    Pastor; missionary.
    3220. Alicio Garcitoral: His Life and Work. T. Gaus,
           1978. (co-editor).
    3221. Antologia Religiosa y Humanista Moderna. Torres,
           1979.
    3222. Deep in the Heart [translation of Corazon Adentro].
           Carlton, 1967.
    3223. Vista Christian Church of Brownsville, Texas. 1959.

Cottrell, James J., 1877-.
    Pastor.
    3224. We Have Found the Christ. Greenwich, 1959.

Cowden, William F., 1837-.
    Pastor.
    3225. Poems: Patriotic, Descriptive and Miscellaneous. W.
           K. Bayle, 1888.

Cox, James Arthur.
    Pastor.
    3226. "Incidents in the Life of Philip Slater Fall." B.D.
           thesis, College of the Bible (Lexington), 1951.

Craddock, Fred Brenning, 1928-.
    Seminary professor.
    3227. As One without Authority: Essays on Inductive
           Preaching. Phillips Univ. Pr., 1971.
    3228. "Christology and Cosmology: An Investigation of
           Colossians 1:15-20." Ph.D. diss., Vanderbilt Univ.,
           1964.
    3229. Finding Our Place in God's Order. Christian Bd. of
           Publication, 1972.
    3230. The Gospels. Abingdon, 1981.
    3231. John. John Knox, 1982.
    3232. Overhearing the Gospel. Abingdon, 1978.
    3233. Philippians. John Knox, 1985.

3234. Preaching. Abingdon, 1985.
3235. Preaching the New Common Lectionary: Commentary.
       Abingdon, 1984. (co-author).
3236. Preaching the Common Lectionary Year A. Advent.
       Christmas. Epiphany. Abingdon, 1986.
3237. Preaching the New Common Lectionary Year A. After
       Pentecost. Abingdon, 1986.
3238. Preaching the New Common Lectionary Year A. Lent.
       Holy Week. Easter. Abingdon, 1986.
3239. Preaching the New Common Lectionary Year B. Advent.
       Christmas. Epiphany. Abingdon, 1984. (co-author).
3240. Preaching the New Common Lectionary Year B. After
       Pentecost. Abingdon, 1985.
3241. Preaching the New Common Lectionary Year B. Lent.
       Holy Week. Easter. Abingdon, 1984.
3242. Preaching the New Common Lectionary Year C. Advent.
       Christmas. Epiphany. Abingdon, 1985.
3243. Preaching the New Common Lectionary Year C. After
       Pentecost. Abingdon, 1986.
3244. Preaching the New Common Lectionary Year C. Lent.
       Holy Week. Easter. Abingdon, 1985.
3245. The Pre-Existence of Christ in the New Testament.
       Abingdon, 1968.

Crain, James A., 1886-1971.
   Church official.
3246. American Youth and the Liquor Problem. Christian
       Bd. of Publication, 1931.
3247. The Development of Social Ideas Among the Disciples
       of Christ. Bethany, 1969.

Crawford, Cecil Clement, 1893-.
   Pastor.
3248. The American Faith: A Discussion of the Theology of
       the Declaration of Independence. 1955.
3249. Calling Bible Things by Bible Names. Publishers of
       the King, n.d.
3250. Commonsense Ethics. Brown, 1966.
3251. The Crawford-Mustgrave Debate.
3252. Genesis. College Pr., 1966.
3253. The Passion of Our Lord: Sermons for the
       Resurrection Week. College Pr., 1968.
3254. Sermon Outlines. Restoration, 1927.
3255. Sermon Outlines on Acts. DeHoff, 1956.
3256. Sermon Outlines on the Cross of Christ. McQuiddy,
       1933.
3257. Sermon Outlines on the Restoration Plea.
       Restoration, 1927.
3258. Survey Course in Christian Doctrine. College Pr.,
       1962.
3259. The Transliteration Folly. Publishers of the King,
       n.d.

3260. Types and Antitypes: A Series of Bible Studies....
       Albia? Iowa, 191-.

Creasy, William Charles.
    Pastor.
    3261. "A Study of the Development of the Popular Motives
           of Health, Wealth, Power, and Success in Practical
           Theology of the Early Disciples of Christ, As it
           Appeared in Their Periodicals through 1850, With
           Some Consideration of Their Meaning for Today's
           Preacher." D. Div. diss., Vanderbilt Univ. Divinity
           School, 1971.

Creath, Jacob, Jr., 1799-1886.
    Pastor.
    3262. "An Abstinence Lecture." Winchell & Ebert, 1872.
    3263. Biographical Sketches of Elder Wm. Creath. a
           Calvinist Baptist Preacher.... Ustick, 1866.
    3264. "A Chronological Table of Important Events, From the
           Commencement of the Christian Era to the Year
           Eighteen Hundred and Twenty-Five." Spectator
           Office, 1868.
    3265. "A Tract on the Use and Abuse of Tobacco." Sosey,
           1871.

See also, Disciples of Christ Historical Society in GENERAL
Section.

Creel, James Cowherd.
    3266. The Plea to Restore the Apostolic Church. Standard,
           1902.

Crossfield, Richard Henry, 1868-1951.
    Pastor; college president.
    3267. Pilgrimages of a Parson. Owensboro, Ky., 1901.

Crow, Paul Abernathy, Jr., 1931-.
    Pastor; professor of church history; church official;
    editor of Mid-Stream.
    3268. Baptism and Christian Unity. Hartford Seminary
           Foundation, 1961.
    3269. A Bibliography of the Consultation on Church Union.
           Consultation on Church Union, 1967.
    3270. COCU - The Potential of a Decade. 1970 or 1.
    3271. Christian Unity. Friendship Pr., 1982.
    3272. Church Union at Midpoint. Association Pr., 1972.
           (co-editor).
    3273. "The Concept of Unity in Diversity in Faith and
           Order Conversations from Lausanne (1927) to the
           Oberlin (1957) Conferences." Ph.D. diss., Hartford
           Seminary Foundation, 1962.

3274.   The Consultation on Church Union, the Christian
        Church (Disciples of Christ) and Their Future. 1968
        or 9.
3275.   The Ecumenical Movement in Bibliographical Outline.
        National Council of Churches of Christ in the
        U.S.A., 1965.
3276.   Ecumenism and the Consultation on Church Union.
        1967 or 8.
3277.   Education for Church Union: A Plea for Encounter.
        Consultation on Church Union, 1970.
3278.   First Kentucky Faith and Order Conference. N.d.
3279.   Foundations for Ecumenical Commitment. New York,
        1980.
3280.   "Impulses toward Christian Unity in Nineteenth
        Century America." In Studies of the Church in
        History, pp. 183-206. Edited by H. Davies. 1983.
3281.   No Greater Love: Conferee's Source Book. Christian
        Bd. of Publication, 1966.
3282.   No Greater Love: Curriculum Area Guide. Christian
        Bd. of Publication, 1966.
3283.   A Plan of Church Union and the Church. 1970 or 1.
3284.   The Third Meeting of the Consultation on Church
        Union. 1964?
3285.   Unity, Division and Diversity in the Church.
        Hartford Seminary Foundation, 1960.
3286.   Where We Are in Church Union: A Report on the
        Present Accomplishments of the Consultation on
        Church Union. Association Pr., 1965. (co-editor).

Crowl, Howard A., 1926-.
    Missionary.
    3287.   "The Bashi: A Church Growth Study of an
            Interlacustrine Bantu People." Ph.D. diss., Fuller
            Theological Seminary, 1975.

Cullumber, Norman.
    Professor of religion.
    3288.   Please Lead Us in Prayer. Bethany, 1980.

Cunningham, Earl Harold, 1930-.
    College administrator.
    3289.   "Religious Concerns of Southern Appalachian Migrants
            in a North Central City." Ph.D. diss., Boston
            Univ., 1962.

Cutbirth, Jack Wallace.
    Pastor.
    3290.   "On Facing the Question of Decline: An Analysis of
            Decline in the Iowa Christian Church (Disciples of
            Christ) and a Program to Address the Decline."
            D.Min. thesis, Drew Univ., 1981.

Cutlip, Randall Brower, 1916-.
    College president.
    3291. In Faith and History. Bethany, 1965.

Darnell, David Rancier, 1931-.
    Professor of religion and philosophy.
    3292. "Rebellion, Rest, and the Word of God (An Exegetical
           Study of Hebrews 3:1 - 4:13)." Ph.D. diss., Duke
           Univ., 1973.

*Daugherty, Edgar Fay, 1874-1957.
    Pastor.
    3293. A Hoosier Parson: His Boosts and Bumps (An Apologia
           Pro Mea Vita). Meador, 1951.

David, William E.
    Professor of religion; missionary.
    3294. "A Comparative Study of the Social Ethics of Walter
           Rauschenbusch and Reinhold Niebuhr." Ph.D. diss.,
           Vanderbilt Univ., 1958.

Davies, Caleb, 1848-1935.
    Businessman.
    3295. The United States in Relation to the Messiah's
           Return. Knox, 1898.

*Davis, Lew Arter.
    Pastor; missionary to India.
    3296. The Layman Views World Missions. Bethany, 1964.

Davis, Morrison Meade, 1850-1926.
    3297. The Eldership. Standard, 1912.
    3298. Elijah. Christian Publishing Co., 1900.
    3299. First Principles. Standard, 1904.
    3300. How the Disciples Began and Grew. Standard, 1915.
    3301. How To Be Saved. Standard, 1914.
    3302. Queen Esther. Christian Bd. of Publication, 1898.
    3303. The Restoration Movement of the Nineteenth Century.
           Standard, 1913.

Davison, Frank Elon, 1887-1960.
    Pastor; journalist.
    3304. I Would Do It Again: Sharing Experiences in the
           Christian Ministry. Bethany, 1948.
    3305. Let's Talk It Over: Questions on Church Work and
           Church Problems Asked by Ministers and Lay People.
           Bethany, 1953.
    3306. Thru the Rear-View Mirror. Bethany, 1955.

Debbins, William, 1927-.
    Professor of philosophy.
    3307. Aphorism of Oswald Spengler. Regnery, 1967.

3308. Constructive Ethics. Prentice-Hall, 1961. (co-author).

Deen, Edith Alderman, 1905-.
     Journalist.
     3309. All of the Women of the Bible. Harper, 1955.
     3310. Family Living in the Bible. Harper, 1963.
     3311. Great Women of the Christian Faith. Harper, 1959.

Deer, Lewis H.
     Pastor.
     3312. Many Races, One Brotherhood. United Christian
            Missionary Soc., 1958. (compiler).

Denny, Robert
     3313. Memorial Tributes of Respect to Dr. Ryland Thomas
            Brown, Eminent and Profound as a Preacher of the
            Gospel.... Carlon & Hollenbeck, 1981.

Depew, Arthur McKinley, 1896-1976.
     Pastor; missionary to Africa.
     3314. Cokesbury Game Book. Abingdon, 1939.
     3315. Cokesbury Party Book. Abingdon, 1932.
     3316. Cokesbury Question Book. Abingdon, 1973.
     3317. Cokesbury Stunt Book. Abingdon, 1934.

Devitt, Thomas Kirkland.
     Pastor.
     3318. "A Study of the Use of the Lectionary and Liturgy in
            the Christian Church (Disciples of Christ)." D.Min.
            thesis, School of Theology at Claremont, 1978.

*DeWelt, Don Finch, 1919-.
     Pastor; college professor.
     3319. Acts Made Actual. College Pr., 1958.
     3320. The Church in the Bible. College Pr., 1958.
     3321. If You Want To Preach. Baker Book House, 1957.
     3322. Sacred History and Geography: A Workbook and
            Teaching Manual on the Seventeen Historical Books of
            the Old Testament. Baker Book House, 1955.
     3323. What the Bible Says about Praise and Promise.
            College Pr. Publishing Co., 1980. (co-author).

Dewey, Joanna, 1936-.
     Professor of religion.
     3324. "Markan Public Debate: Literary Technique,
            Concentric Structure and Theology in Mark 2:1-3:6."
            Ph.D. diss., Graduate Theological Union, 1977.

Dickinson, Hoke S.
     3325. The Cane Ridge Reader. Cane Ridge Preservation
            Project, 1972.

Dickinson, Richard Donald Nye, Jr.
   3326. "A Comparison of Concepts of the State in Roman
         Catholicism and the Ecumenical Movement." Ph.D.
         diss., Boston Univ., 1959.

Digweed, Marilyn.
   Editor; Christian educator; missionary.
   3327. <u>Worry and Tension.</u> Daystar Pr. (Nigeria), 1969.

Dodson, James Richard.
   Missionary to Zaire.
   3328. "Some Proposals for the Development of the
         Educational Program of a Theological School in the
         Belgian Congo." Ph.D. diss., Columbia Univ., 1957.

Donovan, Daryl G.
   Pastor.
   3329. "A Fresh Look at Baptism for the Christian Church
         (Disciples of Christ)." D.Min. thesis, San
         Francisco Theological Seminary, 1986.

Doran, Adron.
   3330. <u>The Christian Scholar: A Biography of Hall Laurie</u>
         <u>Calhoun, Protege of John William McGarvey.</u> Gospel
         Advocate Co., 1985. (co-author).

Douglass, H. Paul.
   3331. <u>The Witness of the Churches of the Congregational</u>
         <u>Order.</u> General Council of Congregational Churches,
         1940. (editor).

Douthitt, Ira Arthur.
   Pastor.
   3332. <u>Apostolic Sermons...A Series of Gospel Sermons</u>
         <u>Delivered at Many Places during the Past Twenty</u>
         <u>Years of Evangelistic Work.</u> Memphis, 1937.

Dowdy, Barton Alexander.
   College president.
   3333. "The Meaning of Kauchasthai in the New Testament."
         Ph.D. diss., Vanderbilt Univ., 1956.

Dowling, Enos Everett, 1905-.
   Professor of religion.
   3334. <u>An Analysis and Index of the Christian Magazine,</u>
         <u>1848-1853.</u> Lincoln Bible Institute Pr., 1958.
   3335. <u>Hymn and Gospel Song Books of the Restoration</u>
         <u>Movement: A Preliminary Bibliography.</u> Dowling,
         1975.
   3336. <u>The Literature of the Disciples of Christ.</u> Hustler
         Print, 1933. (co-author).
   3337. <u>Matthew.</u> Standard, 1967. (co-author).

3338. The Restoration Movement: Study Course for Youth
      and Adults. Standard, 1964.
3339. Second Annual B. D. Phillips Memorial Lectureship on
      the Restoration Movement. Lincoln Christian College
      Pr., 1972.
3340. Standard Bible Commentary: Mark. Standard, 1968.
      (co- author).

Dowling, William Worth, 1834-1920.
   Publisher of the Little Sower, Morning Watch and Little
   Chief.
3341. The Bible Hand-Book. Old Paths Publishers, 1887.
3342. The Christian Lesson Commentary. Christian
      Publishing Co., n.d.
3343. The Helping Hand: A Manual of Instruction for the
      Y.P.S.C.E. [Young People's Society of Christian
      Endeavor]. Christian Publishing Co., 1891.
3344. The Lesson Helper: An Aid for Sunday School
      Scholars.... Christian Publishing Co., 1888.
3345. The Lesson Primer: A Book of Easy Lessons for
      Little Learners.... Christian Publishing Co., 1888.
3346. The Names and Titles of Our Lord and Savior Jesus
      Christ.... Macintosh, 1866.
3347. The Normal Instructor: A Series of Normal Bible
      Studies. Christian Publishing Co., 1895.

Dugan, Herschel C.
3348. "An Adult Church Membership Based on a Model of
      Process Theology." D.Min. thesis, Phillips Univ.
      Graduate Seminary, 1981.

Dungan, David Roberts, 1837-1920.
   Pastor; college professor and president.
3349. Chang Foo or The Latest Fashions in Religion. 1885.
3350. Hermeneutics: A Text Book. Standard, 1888.
3351. Ingersoll's Mistake about Moses. 1879.
3352. Is There Sufficient Reason for Our Existence as a
      Separate Religious Body? 1876.
3353. Modern Phases of Skepticism. 1877.
3354. Modern Revivalism. 1875.
3355. Moses, The Man of God. Christian Publishing Co.,
      1899.
3356. On the Rock. 1910.
3357. Our Plea and Our Mission. 1876.
3358. Outline Studies in the Life of Christ. Des Moines,
      Iowa, 1909.
3359. Prohibition vs. License. Central Book Concern,
      1875.
3360. Rum and Ruin: The Remedy Found. Central Book
      Concern, 1879.
3361. Tour through Bible. 1908.

Eames, Samuel Morris, 1916-.
    Professor of philosophy.
    3362. Guide to the Works of John Dewey. Southern Illinois
           Univ. Pr., 1972. (co-editor).
    3363. John Dewey: The Early Works, 1882-1898. (co-
           editor).
    3364. The Leading Principles of Pragmatic Naturalism.
           Bruges, 1962. (co-author).
    3365. Logical Methods: A Workbook for a General Education
           Course in Logic. Stipes, 1966. (co-author).
    3366. The Philosophy of Alexander Campbell. Bethany,
           1966.
    3367. Pragmatic Naturalism: An Introduction. Southern
           Illinois Univ. Pr., 1977.

*Eckstein, Stephen Daniel, Jr., 1922-.
    Professor of religion.
    3368. History of the Churches of Christ in Texas, 1824-
           1950. Firm Foundation Publishing House, 1963.

Edens, Ambrose, 1920-.
    Professor of religion.
    3369. "A Study of the Book of Zephaniah as to the Date,
           Extent, and Significance of the Genuine
           Writings...." Ph.D. diss., Vanderbilt Univ., 1954.

Eikner, Allen Van Dozier, 1919-.
    Professor of religion and philosophy.
    3370. "The Nature of the Church among the Disciples of
           Christ." Ph.D. diss., Vanderbilt Univ., 1962.
    3371. Religious Perspectives and Problems: An
           Introduction to the Philosophy of Religion. Univ.
           Pr. of America, 1980. (editor).

Ellis, Dale, 1893-.
    Missionary; educator.
    3372. Disciples of Christ and Indian Americans. United
           Christian Missionary Soc., n.d.

Ellis, Joe Scott, 1928-.
    3373. The Church on Purpose: Keys to Effective Church
           Leadership. Standard, 1982.
    3374. "Factors Related to the Incorporation of the
           Principles of the Indiana Plan for Adult Education
           in Church Programs." Ph.D. diss., Indiana Univ.,
           1971.
    3375. Let Yourself G-R-O-W! Standard, 1973.
    3376. Ready, Set, Grow: Sermons on Church Growth for
           Growing Christians. Standard, 1972.

Ellmore, Alfred.
    3377. Which Is the True Church? Mathes, 1873.

Elmore, Robert Emmet, 1878-1968.
    3378. <u>Christian Unity: A Text-Book for Promoting the</u>
        <u>Fulfillment of the Lord's Prayer.</u> Standard, 1924.

Ely, Lois Anna, 1888-1972.
    Missionary to China.
    3379. <u>Disciples of Christ in China.</u> United Christian
        Missionary Soc., 1948.

*Eminhizer, Earl Eugene, 1926-.
    Professor of religion and philosophy.
    3380. <u>The Rise and the Fall of the Triennial Convention.</u>
        Chester ?, Pa., 1956.

England, Stephen Jackson, 1895-.
    College president; professor of church history.
    3381. <u>The Apostolic Church: Some Aspects of Its Faith and</u>
        <u>Life.</u> Northwest Christian College, 1947.
    3382. <u>The Christian Church and Family Life.</u> Phillips
        University, 1961. (editor).
    3383. <u>Oklahoma Christians.</u> Bethany, 1975.
    3384. <u>The One Baptism: Baptism and Christian Unity, with</u>
        <u>Special Reference to Disciples of Christ.</u> Bethany,
        1960.
    3385. <u>One Faith: Its Biblical, Historical and Ecumenical</u>
        <u>Dimensions; A Series of Essays in Honor of Stephen</u>
        <u>J. England on the Occasion of His Seventieth</u>
        <u>Birthday.</u> edited by Robert L. Simpson. Phillips
        Univ. Pr., 1966.
    3386. <u>A Report on Theological Education in the Church of</u>
        <u>Christ in Congo (Disciples of Christ).</u> United
        Christian Missionary Soc., 1967?
    3387. <u>We Disciples, a Brief View of History and Doctrine.</u>
        Christian Bd. of Publication, 1946.

*Epler, Stephen Edward, 1909-.
    College president.
    3388. <u>Honorary Degrees: A Survey of Their Use and Abuse.</u>
        American Council on Public Affairs, 1943.
    3389. <u>Six-Man Football, the Streamlined Game: Principles</u>
        <u>of Six-Man Football for Players, Coaches and</u>
        <u>Spectators.</u> Harper, 1938.
    3390. <u>The Teacher, the School, and the Community: An</u>
        <u>Annotated Directory and Bibliography.</u> American
        Council on Education, 1941.

*Errett, Isaac, 1820-1888.
    Pastor; editor of the <u>Christian Standard</u>; college
    president.
    3391. <u>Autobiography of Samuel K. Hoshour.</u> John Burns
        Publishing Co., 1884. (co-author).
    3392. <u>The Disciple</u>. 6 vols. Standard, 1884-1887. (co-
        editor).

3393. Evenings with the Bible. 3 vols. Standard, 1884-
       1889.
3394. Fifty-Nine Years of History. Standard, 1886.
3395. Letters to a Young Christian. 1877.
3396. The Life and Writings of George Edward Flower.
       Standard, 1885.
3397. Linsey-Woolsey and other Adresses. 1893.
3398. Our Position: A Brief Statement of the Distinctive
       Features of the Plea for Reformation Urged by the
       People Known as Disciples of Christ. Central Book
       Concern, 1880-1889.
3399. Standard Commentary on the International Sunday-
       School Lessons....Standard, 1883. (co-editor).
3400. Talks to Bereans. Cincinnati, 1872.
3401. Why Am I a Christian? 1889.

For works about him by Disciple authors, see
    Jefferson, Samuel Mitchell and
    Lamar, James Sanford under THEOLOGY section.

Eubanks, John Bunyan, 1913-.
    Professor of religion.
    3402. "Modern Trends in the Religion of the American
           Negro." Ph.D. diss., Univ. of Chicago, 1947.

Fairhurst, Alfred, 1843-1921.
    Pastor; attorney; natural scientist.
    3403. Atheism in Our Universities. Standard, 1923.
    3404. My Good Poems. Christian Publishing Co., 1899.
    3405. Organic Evolution Considered. Christian Publishing
           Co., 1897.
    3406. Theistic Evolution. Standard, 1919.

Fall, Philip Slater, 1798-1890.
    Pastor.
    3407. The Responsibility of the Disciples of Christ as
           Stewards of God. N.d.

For works about him by Disciple authors, see
    Cox, James Arthur under THEOLOGY section and
    Norton, Herman Albert in GENERAL section.

Fanning, Tolbert, 1810-1874.
    College founder and president; editor of the Agriculturist
    and Journal of the State and County Societies; founder of
    The Naturalist and Christian Review.
    3408. "True Methods of Searching the Scriptures."
           Christian Publishing Co., n.d.

For works about him by Disciple authors, see
    Wilburn, James R. under HISTORY section.

Farrell, James E.
    Pastor.
    3409.   "A Critical Analysis of the Life and Work of O. L.
            Shelton. Including an Anthology of His Devotional
            Writing." D.Min. thesis, San Francisco Theological
            Seminary, 1977.

Farris, Ellsworth E., 1874-1953.
    Missionary to Zaire.
    3410.   Bekolo bi' Ampaka ba Nkundo. Bolenge, 1904.

*Fee, John Gregg, 1816-1901.
    Pastor; founder of Berea College; abolitionist.
    3411.   An Anti-Slavery Manual. Printed at the Herald
            Office, 1848.
    3412.   Autobiography of John G. Fee, Berea, Kentucky.
            National Christian Assoc., 1891.
    3413.   Christian Baptism. 1878.
    3414.   The Sinfulness of Slaveholding Shown by Appeals to
            Reason and Scriptures. J. A. Gray, 1851.

Felty, David Nando, 1949-.
    Pastor.
    3415.   "Phenomenology and the Crisis of Tradition." D.Min.
            thesis, Lexington Theological Seminary, 1974.

Ferre, Gustave Adolph.
    Professor of philosophy and religion.
    3416.   Basic Philosophical Issues. Educational Publishers,
            1962. (co-author).
    3417.   "A Concept of Higher Education and Its Relation to
            the Christian Faith as Evidenced in the Writings of
            Alexander Campbell." Ph.D. diss., Vanderbilt Univ.,
            1958.
    3418.   The Layman Examines His Faith. Bethany, 1960.
    3419.   The Upper Room Chapel Talks. The Upper Room, 1957.
            (compiler).

Ferren, Iris.
    Christian educator.
    3420.   The Church's School: A Handbook. Christian Bd. of
            Publication, 1968.
    3421.   Creating the Congregation's Educational Ministry.
            Brethren Pr., 1976. (co-author).
    3422.   Pupil's Classbook for Understanding the Bible.
            Christian Bd. of Publication, 1958.
    3423.   Study Guide for Why the Church Teaches. Bethany,
            1964.

Fey, Harold Edward, 1898-1990.
    Pastor; editor of Christian Century, Fellowship, In Common,
    World Call; seminary professor.

3424. <u>The Christian Century Reader.</u> Association Pr.,
      1962. (co-compiler).
3425. <u>The Churches and a Just and Durable Peace.</u>
      Christian Century Pr., 1942.
3426. <u>Cooperation in Compassion.</u> Friendship Pr., 1966.
3427. <u>Disarmament or Obliteration.</u> H. Regnery Co., 1948.
3428. <u>History of the Ecumenical Movement.</u> 2 vols.
      Pennsylvania, 1967-1970.
3429. <u>How I Read the Riddle: An Autobiography.</u> Bethany,
      1982.
3430. <u>How My Mind Has Changed.</u> Meridian Books, 1961.
      (editor).
3431. <u>Indians and Other Americans: Two Ways of Life Meet.</u>
      Harper, 1959. (co-author).
3432. <u>The Lord's Supper: Seven Meanings.</u> Harper, 1948.
3433. <u>With Sovereign Reverence.</u> Roger Williams Pr., 1974.
3434. <u>World Peace and Christian Missions.</u> Friendship Pr.,
      1937.

*Fiers, Alan Dale, 1906-.
    Pastor.
    3435. <u>The Christian World Mission.</u> Bethany, 1966.
    3436. <u>This is Missions: Our Christian Witness in an</u>
          <u>Unchristian World.</u> Bethany, 1953.

For works about him by Disciple authors, see
    Walker, Granville Thomas under THEOLOGY section.

Fife, Clyde Lee.
    Pastor.
    3437. <u>Fife's Revival Sermons.</u> Pentecostal Publishing Co.,
          1923.

Fife, Earl Hanson.
    Pastor; author.
    3438. <u>Building a Successful Men's Bible Class.</u> Standard,
          1940.

Fillmore, Charles Millard.
    3439. <u>Fillmore's Easter Recitations and Exercises for</u>
          <u>Children and Young Folks.</u> Fillmore Bros., 1901.
          (compiler).
    3440. <u>Fillmore's Prohibition Songs.</u> Fillmore Bros., 1900.
          (editor).
    3441. <u>Songs of Night to Cheer the Fight Against the Blight</u>
          <u>of Liquordom.</u> Fillmore Music House, 1912. (editor).
    3442. <u>Tell Mother I'll Be There.</u> Fillmore Bros., 1898.
    3443. <u>Tobacco Taboo.</u> Meigs Publishing Co., 1930.

Finegan, Jack, 1908-.
    Professor of archeology.
    3444. <u>Archeological History of the Ancient Middle East.</u>
          Westview, 1979.

3445. The Archeology of the New Testament: The Life of
       Jesus and the Beginning of the Early Church.
       Princeton Univ. Pr., 1969.
3446. The Archeology of the New Testament: The
       Mediterranean World of the Early Christian Apostles.
       Westview, 1981.
3447. The Archeology of World Religions. Princeton Univ.
       Pr., 1952.
3448. At Wit's End. John Knox Pr., 1963.
3449. Beginnings in Theology. Association Pr., 1956.
3450. Book of Student Prayers. Association Pr., 1946.
3451. The Christian Church (Disciples of Christ).
       Cathedral, 1973.
3452. Christian Theology. English Univs. Pr., 1956.
3453. Clear of the Brooding Cloud. Abingdon-Cokesbury,
       1953.
3454. Discovering Israel: An Archeological Guide to the
       Holy Land. Eerdmans, 1981.
3455. Encountering New Testament Manuscripts: A Working
       Introduction to Textual Criticism. Eerdmans, 1974.
3456. First Steps in Theology. Association Pr., 1960.
3457. 40 Questions and Answers on Religion. Association
       Pr., 1960.
3458. Handbook of Biblical Chronology: Principles of Time
       Reckoningin the Ancient World and Problems of
       Chronology in the Bible. Princeton Univ. Pr., 1964.
3459. Hidden Records of the Life of Jesus: An
       Introduction to the New Testament Apocrypha.
       Pilgrim Pr., 1969.
3460. A Highway Shall Be There. Bethany, 1946.
3461. In the Beginning: A Journey through Genesis.
       Harper, 1962.
3462. India Today! Bethany, 1955.
3463. Jesus, History, and You. John Knox Pr., 1964.
3464. Let My People Go: A Journey through Exodus. Harper
       & Row, 1963.
3465. Light from the Ancient Past: The Archeological
       Background of Judaism and Christianity. Princeton
       Univ. Pr., 1959.
3466. Light from the Ancient Past: The Archeological
       Background of the Hebrew-Christian Religion.
       Princeton Univ. Pr., 1946.
3467. Like the Great Mountains. [Sermons]. Bethany, 1949.
3468. Mark of the Taw. John Knox Pr., 1972.
3469. The Orbits of Life. Bethany, 1954.
3470. Rediscovering Jesus. Association Pr., 1952.
3471. Space, Atoms, and God: Christian Faith and the
       Nuclear-Space Age. Bethany, 1959.
3472. Step by Step in Theology. Association Pr., 1962.
3473. The Three R's of Christianity. John Knox Pr., 1964.
3474. Tibet, A Dreamt of Image. Wiley Eastern, 1986.
3475. Die Ueberlieferung der Leidens- und
       Auferstehungsgeschichte Jesu. A. Topelmann, 1934.

3476. <u>Wanderer upon Earth.</u> Harper, 1956.
3477. <u>Youth Asks about Religion.</u> Association Pr., 1949.

Fitch, Alger Morton, 1919-.
   Professor of religion.
   3478. <u>Afterglow of Christ's Resurrection.</u> Standard, 1975.
   3479. "Alexander Campbell and the Hymnbook." <u>Christian
          Standard</u>, 1965.
   3480. <u>Alexander Campbell, Preacher of Reform and Reformer
          of Preaching.</u> Sweet, 1970.
   3481. <u>Claiming God's Promises.</u> Standard, 1984.
   3482. <u>Revelation.</u> Standard, 1986.

Flanagan, James M.
   3483. <u>What We Believe.</u> Bethany, 1956. (editor)

*Flowers, Ronald Bruce, 1935-.
   Professor of religion.
   3484. "The Bible Chair Movement in the Disciples of Christ
          Tradition: Attempts To Teach Religion in State
          Universities." Ph.D. diss., Univ. of Iowa, 1967.
   3485. <u>Religion in Strange Times: The 1960's and 1970's.</u>
          Mercer Univ. Pr., 1984.
   3486. <u>Toward Benevolent Neutrality: Church, State, and
          the Supreme Court.</u> Baylor Univ. Pr., 1977. (co-
          author).

Fogle, Maurice W.
   Pastor.
   3487. <u>The Bible Speaks, Evangelize: Preparatory Devotions
          for Evangelistic Callers.</u> United Christian
          Missionary Soc., 196.
   3488. <u>Christians Together: Reflections on the Book of
          Acts.</u> Bethany, 1957.

Ford, Wesley P.
   Pastor.
   3489. <u>Gift of Hope.</u> Bethany, 1963.
   3490. <u>Gift of Life.</u> Bethany, 1958.
   3491. <u>The Moments at the Lord's Table.</u> Bethany, 1962.

*Forrest, Albertina May Allen, 1872-1964.
   Laywoman.
   3492. <u>Essays on Philosophy and Life.</u> 1904.

Forrest, William M.
   Pastor.
   3493. <u>Centennial Sermon, Macedonia Christian Church,
          Orange County, Virginia, August Eleventh, 1935.</u>
          1935.

Forstman, H. Jackson.
   Seminary administrator.

3494. Christian Faith and the Church. Bethany, 1965.
3495. Christology and Human Understanding. Palo Alto,
       Calif., 1962.
3496. A Romantic Triangle: Schleiermacher and Early
       German Romanticism. Scholars Pr., 1977.
3497. Word and Spirit: Calvin's Doctrine of Biblical
       Authority. Stanford Univ. Pr., 1962.

Fortune, Alonzo Willard, 1873-1950.
    Pastor; college professor and administrator.
    3498. Adventuring with Disciple Pioneers. Bethany, 1942.
    3499. Central Christian Church, Lexington, Ky., 1816-1941.
           A. W. Fortune, 1941.
    3500. The Church of the Future. Bethany, 1930.
    3501. "The Conception of Authority in the Pauline
           Writings." Ph.D. diss., Univ. of Chicago, 1918.
    3502. The Disciples in Kentucky. Convention of the
           Christian Churches in Kentucky, 1932.
    3503. The Fountain of Life. American Bible Soc., 1937.
    3504. Origin and Development of the Disciples. Bethany,
           1924.
    3505. Thinking Things Through with E. E. Snoddy. Bethany,
           1940.

See also, Shelton, Gentry A. in GENERAL section.

Foster, Rupert Clinton, 1888-.
    Pastor; professor of religion.
    3506. The Battle of the Versions. Cincinnati Bible
           Seminary, 1953.
    3507. Chronological Outline of the Life of Christ.
           Standard, 1941.
    3508. Class Notes on the Epistle to the Hebrews and the
           Epistle of James. Standard, 1925.
    3509. The Everlasting Gospel. Standard, 1929.
    3510. An Introduction to the Life of Christ. Standard,
           1938.
    3511. The Revised Standard Version of the New Testament,
           An Appraisal. Standard, 1946.
    3512. Studies in the Life of Christ. 3 vols. Rowe, 1938-
           1968.

Fowler, George P., 1909-.
    Professor of religion.
    3513. Fundamentals of Grammar of the Greek New Testament.
           Fort Worth, Texas, 1967.
    3514. "The Meaning of Torah in the Prophetic Books of the
           Old Testament." Ph.D. diss., Yale Univ., 1954.
    3515. Our Religious Heritage: A Guide to the Study of the
           Bible. Brown, 1969.

Fowler, Newton Belnap, Jr., 1931-.
    Professor of religion.

3516. "The Faculty Christian Fellowship as a Lay
        Theological Movement." Ph.D. diss., Boston Univ.,
        1968.

Fox, William K., 1917-.
     Pastor; college professor and administrator; editor of
     Christian Plea.
     3517. Effective Discipleship for Blacks in the Christian
            Church (Disciples of Christ). Central Publishing
            Co., 1982. (editor).

Francis, Fred Owens.
     Professor of religion.
     3518. Biblical Literature: 1974 Proceedings. American
            Academy of Religion, 1974. (compiler).
     3519. Conflict at Colossae: A Problem in the
            Interpretation of Early Christianity, Illustrated by
            Selected Modern Studies. Soc. of Biblical
            Literature, 1973. (compiler).
     3520. Pauline Parallels. Fortress, 1975. (co-author).
     3521. "A Re-Examination of the Colossian Controversy."
            Ph.D. diss., Yale Univ., 1966.
     3522. Traditions as Openness to the Future. Univ. Pr. of
            America, 1984. (co-editor).

Franklin, Benjamin, 1812-1878.
     Pastor; editor; publisher.
     3523. Ability and Accountability, a Book for the Times:
            Containing the Travels of Robert Thinkwell and James
            Cautious. Christian Publishing Co., n.d.
     3524. Biographical Sketch and Writings of Elder Benjamin
            Franklin. 9th ed. Somers, 1889-.
     3525. A Book of Gems, or Choice Selections from the
            Writings of Benjamin Franklin. Burns, 1879.
     3526. Christian Experience: Or Sincerity Seeking the Way
            to Heaven. Chase & Hall, 1875.
     3527. The Gospel Preacher: A Book of Twenty Sermons.
            Franklin & Rice, 1869.
     3528. The Gospel Preacher: A Book of Twenty-One Sermons.
            G. W. Rice, 1877.
     3529. An Oral Debate. Franklin & Rice, 1874.

For works about him by Disciple authors, see
     Franklin, Joseph under THEOLOGY section;
     Castleberry, Ottis L. under HISTORY section; and
     West, Earl Irvin in GENERAL section.

Franklin, Joseph, 1834-1912.
     3530. The Life and Times of Benjamin Franklin. Burns,
            1879. (co-author).

Frederickson, Craig.
     Pastor; missionary.

3531. The Employer's View: Is There a Need for a
        Guestworker Program? Community Research Assocs.,
        1982. (co-author).

Frost, Adelaide Gail, d. 1928.
    Missionary to India.
    3532. By Waysides in India. Christian Woman's Bd. of
            Missions, 1902.
    3533. A Few Sonnets from India. Christian Woman's Bd. of
            Missions, n.d.
    3534. Raghuwar Dayal, Sometime Priest of Vishnu. 1910.

Fudge, Bennie Lee.
    Christian educator.
    3535. Can A Christian Kill for His Government? Christian
            Education Institute Store, 1943?
    3536. Mrs. Lee's Stories about Jesus. Christian Education
            Institute Store, 1956. (illustrator).

Fuller, Bertha Mason.
    Pastor; editor of The Woman's Pulpit.
    3537. The Life Story of Sarah Lue Bostick, a Woman of the
            Negro Race. 1949.

Funk, Robert Walter, 1926-.
    Professor of religion.
    3538. Apocalyptism. Herder & Herder, 1969. (editor).
    3539. A Beginning-Intermediate Grammar of Hellenistic
            Greek. Soc. of Biblical Lit., 1972.
    3540. Bultmann School of Biblical Interpretation. Gannon,
            1965. (co-editor).
    3541. Christopher Isherwood: A Reference Guide. Hall,
            1979.
    3542. Distinctive Protestant and Catholic Themes
            Reconsidered. Gannon, 1967. (co-editor).
    3543. Early Christian Miracle Stories. Scholars Pr.,
            1978. (editor).
    3544. Faith and Understanding. Harper, 1969-. (editor).
    3545. God and Christ. Gannon, n.d. (co-editor).
    3546. A Greek Grammar of the New Testament and Other Early
            Christian Literature. Univ. of Chicago Pr., 1961.
            (editor and translator).
    3547. History and Hermeneutic. Harper, 1967. (editor).
    3548. Jesus as Precursor. Fortress, 1975.
    3549. "The Kerygma, the Church, and the Ministry." Drew
            Univ., 1960.
    3550. Language, Hermeneutic and Word of God. Harper,
            1966.
    3551. New Gospel Parallels. 2 vols. Fortress, 1985-1986.
    3552. Parables and Presence: Forms of the New Testament
            Tradition. Fortress, 1982.
    3553. Religion and the Humanizing of Man. Council on the
            Study of Religion, 1972. (editor).

3554. <u>Schleiermacher as Contemporary.</u> Herder & Herder, 1970. (editor).

3555. <u>Semeia Eight: Literary Critical Studies of Biblical Texts.</u> Scholars Pr., 1977.

3556. "The Syntax of the Greek Article." Ph.D. diss., Vanderbilt Univ., 1953.

3557. <u>Translating Theology into the Modern Age.</u> Harper, 1965. (editor).

3558. "The Watershed of the American Biblical Tradition: The Chicago School, First Phase, 1892-1920." 1969.

Gardner, Fred Irvin, 1900-.
    Pastor.
3559. <u>What is Expected of Me, as a Member of the Church of Christ?.</u> Standard, 1929.

Garriott, Christopher T.
    Pastor.
3560. <u>Making the Most of the Time</u>. Bethany, 1959.

Garrison, James Harvey, 1842-1931.
    Pastor; editor of <u>Gospel Echo and Christian</u>.
3561. <u>Christian Union: A Historical Study.</u> Christian Publishing Co.,1891.

3562. <u>Helps to Faith: A Contribution to Theological Reconstruction.</u> Christian Publishing Co., 1903.

3563. <u>The Holy Spirit: His Personality, Mission and Modes of Activity.</u> Christian Publishing Co., 1905

3564. <u>A Modern Plea for Ancient Truths</u>. Christian Publishing Co., 1902.

3565. <u>The Old Faith Restated, Being a Restatement, by Representative Men, of the Fundamental Truths and Essential Doctrines of Christianity, as Held and Adovated by the Disciples of Christ, in the light of experience and Biblical Research</u>. Christian Publishing Co., 1891. (editor).

3566. <u>Our First Congress</u>. Christian Publishing Co., 1900.

3567. <u>The Reformation of the Nineteenth Century: A Series of Historical Sketches Dealing with the Rise and Progress of the Religious Movement Inaugurated by thomas and Alexander Campbell, from its Origin to the Close of the Nineteenth Century</u>. Christian Publishing Co., 1901. (editor).

3568. <u>The Story of a Century...1809-1909</u>. Christian Publishing Co., 1909.

For works about him by Disciple authors, see
    Tucker, William E. under THEOLOGY section;
    Howlet, Monroe E., and
    "James Harvey Garrison" in GENERAL section.

Garrison, Winfred Ernest, 1874-.
  College president; professor of church history, philosophy
  and religion.
  3569. <u>Affirmative Religion</u>. Harper, 1928.
  3570. <u>Alexander Campbell's Theology, Its Sources and</u>
         <u>Historical Setting</u>. Christian Publishing Co.,1900.
  3571. <u>An American Religious Movement, A Brief History of</u>
         <u>the Disciples of Christ</u>. Christian Bd. of
         Publication, 1945.
  3572. <u>Catholicism and the American Mind</u>. Willett, Clark &
         Colby, 1928.
  3573. <u>Christian Unity and Disciples of Christ</u>. Bethany,
         1955.
  3574. "Disciples of Christ." In Nature of the Church;
         Papers Presented to the Theological Commission
         Appointed by the Continuation Committee of the World
         Conference on Faith and Order, pp.283-88. Edited by
         R. Newton Flew. Harper, 1952.
  3575. <u>The Disciples of Christ, a History</u>. Christian Bd.
         of Publication, 1948. (co-author).
  3576. <u>Faith of the Free</u>. Willett, Clark & Co., 1940.
         (editor).
  3577. <u>Heritage and Destiny: An American Religious</u>
         <u>Movement Looks Ahead</u>. Bethany, 1961.
  3578. <u>Intolerance</u>. Round Table Pr., 1931.
  3579. <u>Invitation to Philosophy</u>. Univ. of Houston, 1970.
  3580. <u>The March of Faith: The Story of Religion in</u>
         <u>America since 1865</u>. Harper, 1933.
  3581. <u>One Hundred Poems of Immortality: An Anthology</u>.
         Willett, Clark & Co., 1935. (co-compiler).
  3582. <u>One Hundred Poems of Peace: An Anthology</u>. Willett,
         Clark & Co., 1934. (co-compiler)
  3583. <u>A Protestant Manifesto</u>. Abingdon-Cokesbury, 1952.
  3584. <u>The Quest and Character of United Church</u>. Abingdon,
         1957.
  3585. <u>Religion Follows the Frontier: A History of the</u>
         <u>Disciples of Christ</u>. Harper, 1931.
  3586. "The Social and Cultural Factors in the Church
         Divisions." In The Third World Conference on Faith
         and Order, p. 192. Edited by Oliver S. Tomkins.
         SCM Pr., 1953.
  3587. <u>The Sources of Alexander Campbell's Theology</u>.
         Christian Publishing Co., 1900.
  3588. <u>20 Centuries of Christianity: A Concise History</u>.
         Harcourt, Brace 1959. (co-author).
  3589. <u>Whence and Whither Disciples of Christ?</u> Christian
         Bd. of Publication, 1948.

See also, Short, Howard E. in GENERAL section.

*Gates, Errett, 1870-1951.
  Pastor; professor of church history.
  3590. <u>The Disciples of Christ</u>. Baker & Taylor, 1905.

3591. The Early Relation and Separation of Baptists and
       Disciples. R. R. Donnelly, 1904.

*Gaventa, Beverly Roberts, 1948-.
    Seminary professor.
3592. From Darkness to Light: Aspects of Conversion in
       the New Testament. Fortress, 1986.

*Gilkey, Langdon Brown, 1919-.
    Professor of religion.
3593. Catholicism Confronts Modernity: A Protestant View.
       Seabury, 1975.
3594. The Contemporary Explosion of Theology: Ecumenical
       Studies in Theology. Scarecrow, 1975. (co-author).
3595. How the Church Can Minister to the World without
       Losing Itself. Harper, 1964.
3596. "Maker of Heaven and Earth: A Thesis on the
       Relation between Metaphysics and Christian Theology
       with Special Reference to the Problem of Creation as
       That Problem Appears in the Philosophies of F. H.
       Bradley and A. N. Whitehead and in the Historic
       Leaders of Christian Thought." Ph.D. diss.,
       Columbia Univ., 1954.
3597. Maker of Heaven and Earth: A Study of the Christian
       Doctrine of Creation. Doubleday, 1959.
3598. Message and Existence: An Introduction to Christian
       Theology. Harper, 1979.
3599. Naming the Whirlwind: The Renewal of God-Language.
       Bobbs-Merrill, 1969.
3600. Reaping the Whirlwind: A Christian Interpretation
       of History. Seabury, 1976.
3601. Religion and the Scientific Future: Reflections on
       Myth, Science, and Theology. Mercer Univ. Pr.,
       1981, c1970.
3602. Shantung Compound: The Story of Men and Women under
       Pressure. Harper, 1975, c1966.
3603. Society and the Sacred: Toward a Theology of
       Culture in Decline. Crossroad, 1981.

Gilpin, W. Clark.
    Professor of religion.
3604. The Millenarian Piety of Roger Williams. Univ. of
       Chicago Pr., 1979.

Glenn, Max Eugene.
    Pastor.
3605. Appalachia in Transition. Bethany, 1970. (editor).
3606. "The Unrelated Church in Selected States/Areas."
       1968. (compiler).

Gobar, Ash.
    Professor of philosophy.

3607. "Abstract Entities." Ph.D diss., Univ. of
       Wisconsin, 1960.
3608. A Lamp in the Forest: Natural Philosophy in
       Transylvania University, 1979-1859. Transylvania
       Univ. Pr., 1982. (co-author).
3609. Philosophic Foundations of Genetic Psychology and
       Gestalt Psychology. A Comparative Study of the
       Empirical Basis, Theoretical Structure and
       Epistemological Groundwork of European Biological
       Psychology. Nijhoff, 1968 [1969].

Goodnight, Cloyd, 1881 or 1882-1932.
    Pastor; professor of religion.
    3610. Home to Bethpage, a Biography of Robert Richardson.
           Christian Bd. of Publication, 1949. (co-author).

Goodwin, Elijah, 1807-1879.
    Pastor; editor of the Christian Record.
    3611. The Family Companion: Or, A Book of Sermons.
           Cincinnati, 1866.
    3612. The Life of Elijah Goodwin, the Pioneer Preacher.
           J. Burns, 1880.

Grafton, Warren, 1901-1960.
    Pastor.
    3613. "Orientation of the City Pastor." United Christian
           Missionary Soc., 1958?
    3614. A Saturday Night Talk with God and Other Editorials.
           Bethany, 1961.

Graham, Robert, 1822-1901.
    3615. Autobiography of Frank G. Allen, Minister of the
           Gospel, and Selections from His Writings. Guide,
           1887. (editor).
    3616. The English Bible as a Text-Book in Theological
           Seminaries. N.d.

Graham, Ronald William.
    Professor of New Testament.
    3617. "The Idea of the Church in the Writings of C. H.
           Dodd." Ph.D. diss., Univ. of Iowa, 1966.
    3618. Charles Harold Dodd, 1884-1973: A Bibliography of
           His Published Writings. Lexington Theol. Sem. Lib.,
           1974.
    3619. Women in the Ministry of Jesus and in the Early
           Church. Lexington Theol. Sem., 1983.

Grant, Brian W., 1939- .
    Professor of pastoral care and counseling.
    3620. From Sin to Wholeness. Westminster, 1982.
    3621. "A Process View of Schizophrenia as Revelatory."
           Ph.D. diss., Univ. of Chicago, 1971.

3622. Reclaiming the Dream: Marriage Counseling in the
       Parish Context. Abingdon, 1986.
3623. Schizophrenia, a Source of Social Insight.
       Westminster, 1975.
3624. "The Teaching and Learning of Pastoral Counseling
       for the Next Ten Years." American Assoc. of
       Pastoral Counsellors, 1977.

Gravenstein, Monte L.
  Pastor.
  3625. "A Program for the Formation of a Singles Group at
         First Christian Church in Baton Rouge, Louisiana."
         D. Min. thesis, Brite Divinity School, 1983.

Gray, Archie W.
  3626. Preaching That Builds Churches: A Survey of
         Effective Evangelistic Preaching in the Mountains of
         East Tennessee. Trident Pr., 1940. (compiler).

Green, Francis Marion, 1836-1911.
  Pastor; historian.
  3627. The Christian Ministers' Manual. Burns, 1883.
  3628. Christian Missions, and Historical Sketches of
         Missionary Societies among the Disciples of Christ.
         Burns, 1884.
  3629. Hiram College and Western Reserve Electric
         Institute:...1850-1900. Hubbell, 1901.
  3630. The Life and Times of John Franklin Rowe. Rowe,
         1899.
  3631. A Royal Life, or, the Eventful History of James A.
         Garfield. Central Book Concern, 1882.
  3632. The Standard Manual for Sunday School Workers.
         Chase & Hall, 1878.

Greene, Wayne A.
  Pastor.
  3633. Christian Men's Fellowship. Indianapolis, 1966.

Greer, Virginia Lou.
  Educator; missionary.
  3634. Give Them Their Dignity. John Knox Pr., 1968.

Gresham, Charles R.
  Professor of Christian education.

  3635. "Independent Disciple Colleges Face the Eighties."
         KCC Pr., 1981.
  3636. Report of the Addresses, Discussion Group Reports
         and Summations of the 1st Consultation on Internal
         Unity of Christian Churches, Wichita, Kansas, 1959.
         (editor).

Gresham, Perry Epler.
   College president.
   3637. <u>Abiding Values</u>. Simpson Print, 1972.
   3638. <u>Answer to Conformity</u>. Bethany, 1961.
   3639. <u>Campbell and the Colleges</u>. Disciples of Christ
        Hist. Soc., 1973.
   3640. <u>Disciplines of the High Calling</u>. Bethany, 1954.
   3641. <u>Proud Heritage of West Virginia</u>. Standard, 1966 or
        7. (co-author).
   3642. <u>The Sage of Bethany: A Pioneer in Broadcloth</u>.
        Bethany, 1960. (compiler).
   3643. <u>What's Past Is Prologue</u>. Foundation for Economic
        Education, 1968.
   3644. <u>With Wings as Eagles</u>. Anna, 1980.

Griffeth, Ross John, 1896-.
   3645. <u>The Bible and Rural Life</u>. Standard Publishing Co.,
        1937.
   3646. <u>Building the Church of Christ</u>. Standard Publishing
        Co., 1931.
   3647. <u>Crusaders for Christ</u>. Northwest Christian College,
        1971.
   3648. <u>The Intermediate Bible Teacher and Leader</u>.
        Standard, 1949.
   3649. <u>It Began Thus: The Good News in New Testament Life
        and Literature</u>. Bethany, 1937.

*Griffin, David Ray, 1939-.
   Professor of philosophy of religion.
   3650. <u>God and Religion in the Postmodern World: Essays in
        Postmodern Theology</u>. State Univ. of New York Pr.,
        1989. (editor).
   3651. <u>Physics and the Ultimate Significance of Time:
        Bohm, Prigogine, and Process Philosophy</u>. State
        Univ. of New York Pr., 1986. (editor).
   3652. <u>The Reenchantment of Science: Postmodern Proposals</u>.
        State Univ. of New York Pr., 1988. (editor).
   3653. <u>Spirituality and Society: Postmodern Visions</u>.
        State Univ. of New York Pr., 1988. (editor).
   3654. <u>Process Theology: An Introductory Exposition</u>.
        Westminster, 1976. (co-author).

Gruenler, Royce Gordon.
   Pastor; professor of religion.
   3655. <u>The Inexhaustible God: Biblical Faith and the
        Challenge of Process Theism</u>. Baker, 1983.
   3656. <u>Jesus, Persons and the Kingdom of God</u>. Bethany,
        1967.
   3657. <u>New Approaches to Jesus and the Gospels</u>. Baker,
        1982.

Haggard, Forrest DeLoss, 1925-.
   Pastor.

3658. The Clergy and the Craft. Missouri Lodge of
      Research, 1970.

Hailey, Homer.
   3659. Attitudes and Consequences in the Restoration
         Movement. Citizen Print Shop, 1945.

Hale, Evelyn Faye.
   Pastor.
   3660. Prayer, A Way of Life. Christian Bd. of
         Publication, 1984.

*Haley, Jesse James, 1851-1924.
   Pastor; editor of the The Christian Century, and the
   Australian Christian Watchman: Missionary to England.
   3661. Debates That Made History. Christian Bd. of
         Publication, 1920.

*Hall, George F., 1864-.
   Pastor; evangelist.
   3662. Chicago Tabernacle Talks. Chicago, 1895.
   3663. How To Be Happy No Matter What Happens: Fifty-Four
         Essays. Temple Book Co., 1924.
   3664. The Lords Exchequer. Cincinnati, 1891.
   3665. Plain Points on Personal Purity. Columbian Book
         Co., 1892.
   3666. Revivals and How To Have Them. Columbian Book Co.,
         1898.
   3667. Some American Evils and Their Remedies. Cincinnati,
         1889.
   3668. Updike's Sermons: A Series of Sermons Delivered in
         the Christian Tabernacle at Emporia, Kansas.
         Standard, 1891.

Hall, Keith B., 1914-.
   Pastor; missionary.
   3669. A Missionary Speaks His Mind about Missions. United
         Christian Missionary Soc., 1959.

Hall, William D.
   Professor of religion; missionary.
   3670. Beliefs and Consequences. Bethany, 1964.
   3671. World Outreach, a Guidance Manual for the Dept. of
         World Outreach of the Local Church. St. Louis,
         1957.

Halley, Henry Hampton, 1874-.
   3672. Best Bible Verses. Halley, 1949. (compiler).
   3673. Bible Handbook. Chicago, 1924-. (compiler).

Hamilton, Clarence Herbert, 1886-.
   Missionary; college professor.

3674. <u>Buddhism, a Religion of Infinite Compassion</u>.
       Liberal Arts Pr., 1952.
3675. <u>Buddhism in India, Ceylon, China and Japan: a
       Reading Guide</u>. Univ. of Chicago, 1931.
3676. "A Psychological Interpretation of Mysticism."
       Ph.D. diss., Univ. of Chicago, 1914.
3677. <u>Wei Shih er Shih Lun, by Vasu-Bandhu</u>. American
       Oriental Soc., 1938. (translator).

Hamilton, Lulu (Snyder).
    Christian educator; missionary.
    3678. <u>Doorway to a Happy Home</u>. Bobbs-Merrill, 1950.
    3679. <u>God Lives in Homes: Meditations for Mothers</u>.
           Bethany, 1942.
    3680. <u>Our Children and God</u>. Bobbs-Merrill, 1952.
    3681. <u>Your Rewarding Years</u>. Bobbs-Merrill, 1955.

Hamlin, Griffith Askew, 1919-.
    Professor of religion.
    3682. <u>A Community and Its Schools</u>. Fulton Public Schools,
           1984.
    3683. "Educational Activities of the Disciples of Christ
           in North Carolina, 1852-1902." North Carolina State
           Dept. of Archives and History, 1956.
    3684. <u>A Heritage of Frontier Discipleship: The First One
           Hundred Fifty Years of the First Christian Church
           (Disciples of Christ), Fulton, Missouri, 1833-1983</u>.
           First Christian Church, 1983.
    3685. <u>In Faith and History: The Story of William Woods
           College</u>. Bethany, 1965.
    3686. <u>Monticello: The Biography of a College</u>. William
           Woods College, 1976.
    3687. <u>The New Testament, Its Intent and Content</u>. Carolina
           Print Co., 1959.
    3688. <u>The Old Testament, Its Intent and Content, Including
           the Apocrypha</u>. Christopher, 1958.
    3689. <u>William Woods College: The Cutlip Years, 1960-1980</u>.
           William Woods College, 1980.

Hammond, Guyton B.
    3690. <u>The Power of Self Transcendence: An Introduction to
           the Philosophical Theology of Paul Tillich</u>.
           Bethany, 1966.

Haney, Thomas N.
    Pastor; musician.

    3691. "Motivation Factors for Spiritual Growth Group
           Participation at Indian Creek Christian Church." D.
           Min. thesis, Christian Theological Seminary, 1988.

Hanlin, Harold F.
    Pastor; missionary.

3692. God's Purpose for His People. Pacific Islands Christian Education Council, 1972.

Hanna, William Herbert, 1872-1948.
Missionary to Philippines.
3693. Thomas Campbell, Seceder and Christian Union Advocate. Standard, 1935.

Hanson, Howard Elvin.
Pastor.
3694. "Preparing Lay Leadership in First Christian Church, Endicott, New York, and Endicott United Church of Christ, To Decide for or Against Local Church Merger." D. Min. thesis, Drew Univ., 1981.

Harbison, Stanley Lincoln, 1925-.
Professor of religion and social science.
3695. "The Social Gospel Career of Alva Wilmot Taylor." Ph.D diss., Vanderbilt Univ., 1975.

Hargis, Billy James, 1925-.
Pastor; evangelist; founder of "Christian Crusade."
3696. Abortion on Trial. Americans Against Abortion, 1982.
3697. Christ and His Gospel, as Preached by Billy James Hargis. Christian Crusade Publications, 1969.
3698. "Communist America: Must It be?": Mid-Eighties Update. New Leaf Pr., 1986.
3699. The Cross and the Sickle Superchurch: "The World-National Councils of Churches Infamous Story." Crusader Books, 1982. (co-author).
3700. The Death of Freedom of Speech in the U.S.A. Christian Crusade Publications, 1967.
3701. The Depth Principle. Crusader Books, 1978, c1977.
3702. The Disaster File: A Trilogy of Books on Crisis Themes: Unilateral Disarmament, Suicidal Foreign Policy, Our Biased National News Media. Crusader Books, 1978. (co-author).
3703. The Facts about Communism and Our Churches. Christian Crusade, 1962.
3704. The Federal Reserve Scandal. New Leaf Pr., 1984. (co-author).
3705. Forewarned: "Fore-Warned Fore-Armed". Christian Crusade Books, 1988.
3706. My Great Mistake. New Leaf Pr., 1985.
3707. The National News Media: America's Fifth Column. Crusader Books, Christian Crusade, 1980.
3708. Our Vietnam Defeat! What Happened? Christian Crusade, 1975.
3709. Riches and Prosperity through Christ: The Power of Christian Belief. Church of the Christian Crusade, 1978.

3710. A Satanic Conspiracy Undermines the U.S.A.
        Christian Crusade Publications, 1972.
3711. Should Protestants Support the "Vietcong"?
        Christian Crusade, 1969.
3712. That Chicago Revolution! Christian Crusade, 1968.
3713. Thou Shalt Not Kill...My Babies. Christian Crusade
        Publications, 1977.
3714. The Total Revolution. Christian Crusade
        Publications, 1972.
3715. Why I Fight for a Christian America. Nelson, 1974.

See also, Seaman, John in GENERAL section.

Harms, John W.
    Pastor.
    3716. Prayer in the Market Place. Bethany, 1958.

Harrell, David Edwin, Jr., 1930-.
    Professor of history; member of Church of Christ.
    3717. All Things Are Possible: The Healing & Charismatic
           Revivals in Modern America. Indiana Univ. Pr.,
           1975.
    3718. "A Decade of Disciples of Christ Social Thought,
           1875-1885." M.A. thesis, Vanderbilt Univ., 1958.
    3719. Disciples and the Church Universal. Disciples of
           Christ Historical Soc., 1967. (co-author).
    3720. "Emergence of the "Church of Christ" Denomination."
           C.E.I. Publishing Co., 1972.
    3721. Minorities in Modern America. Indiana Univ. Pr.,
           19__. (co-editor)
    3722. Oral Roberts: An American Life. Indiana Univ. Pr.,
           1985.
    3723. Pat Robertson: A Personal, Religious, and Political
           Portrait. Harper, 1987.
    3724. Quest for a Christian America: A Social History of
           the Disciples of Christ. 2 vols. Disciples of
           Christ Historical Soc., 1973.
    3725. The Roots of the Moral Majority: Fundamentalism
           Revisited. Institute for Ecumenical and Cultural
           Research, 1981.
    3726. "A Social History of the Disciples of Christ to
           1866." Ph.D. diss., Vanderbilt Univ., 1962.
    3727. The Social Sources of Division in the Disciples of
           Christ, 1865-1900. Publishing Systems, 1973.
    3728. Varieties of Southern Evangelicalism. Mercer Univ.
           Pr., 1981. (editor).
    3729. White Sects and Black Men in the Recent South.
           Vanderbilt Univ. Pr., 1971.

Harrelson, Walter Joseph.
    Professor of religion; Baptist.
    3730. The Bible in American Culture. Fortress, 1982-.
           (co-editor).

3731. <u>From Fertility Cult to Worship</u>. Doubleday, 1969.
3732. <u>Genesis</u>. 2 vols. Graded Pr., 1981.
3733. <u>Interpreting the Old Testament</u>. Holt, 1964.
3734. <u>Israel's Prophetic Heritage: Essays in Honor of
        James Muilenberg</u>. Harper, 1962. (co-editor).
3735. <u>Jeremiah, Prophet to the Nations</u>. Judson, 1959.
3736. <u>The Ten Commandments and Human Rights</u>. Fortress,
        1980.
3737. <u>Tradition and Theology in the Old Testament</u>.
        S.P.C.K. (London), 1977. (contributor).

Harris, Alton Louis, 1918-.
    Pastor; missionary.
    3738. "A United Ministry for a United Church in Congo."
            Ph.D. diss., Lexington Theological Seminary, 1966.

Harrison, Ida (Withers), 1851-1927.
    Political activist.
    3739. <u>Beyond the Battle's Rim: A Story of the Confederate
            Refugees</u>. Neale Publishing Co., 1918.
    3740. <u>Four Little Bridges</u>. Alden, 1890.
    3741. <u>Forty Years of Service: A History of the Christian
            Woman's Board of Missions, 1874-1914</u>. N.d.
    3742. <u>Gardens all the Year</u>. Stratford Co., 1927.
    3743. <u>History of the Christian Woman's Board of Missions</u>.
            1920.
    3744. <u>Memoirs of William Temple Withers</u>. Christopher
            Publishing House, 1924.

Harrison, Russell F., 1918-.
    Pastor; Christian educator.
    3745. <u>Brief Prayers for Bread and Cup: For Elders at the
            Communion Table</u>. Bethany, 1976.
    3746. <u>Called To Mission and Unity</u>. United Christian
            Missionary Soc., 1965. (co-author).
    3747. <u>Concern That Makes a Difference</u>. Indianapolis,
            1962.
    3748. <u>Southeast Asia Kaleidoscope</u>. United Christian
            Missionary Soc., 1968.
    3749. <u>This is CYF</u>. Christian Bd. of Publication, 1954.
    3750. <u>World Outreach</u>. Indianapolis, 1966.

Harrison, Traverce.
    3751. <u>The Christian's Life and Program</u>. Standard, 1923.

Hasker, William, 1935-.
    Professor of philosophy.
    3752. <u>Metaphysics: Constructing a World View</u>.
            InterVarsity, 1983.

 Hatt, Harold E.
    Pastor; professor of religion.

3753. "A Comparative Inquiry into Two Modes of
       Revelation." Ph.D. diss., Vanderbilt Univ., 1963.
3754. Cybernetics and the Image of Man. Abingdon, 1968.
3755. Encountering Truth: A New Understanding of How
       Revelation, as Encounter, Yeilds Doctrine.
       Abingdon, 1966.
3756. Man, What a World! Christian Bd. of Publication,
       1970.

Hawkins, Elza Meredith.
    Professor of religion.
    3757. "Theological and Political Aspects in the
           Development of Religious Heterogeneity in England:
           A Study of Sixteenth and Seventeenth Century
           England." Ph.D. diss., Univ., of Nebraska, 1957.
    3758. From Now To Pentecost: A Mirrored View of
           Developments in Christianity. New Day, 1982.
    3759. A Many-Faceted Jewel: The Church in New Testament
           Images. Carlton, 1978.

Hay, David M., 1935-.
    Professor of religion.
    3760. "The Use of Psalm 110 in the Early Church." Ph.D.
           diss., Yale Univ., 1965.
    3761. Glory at the Right Hand: Psalm 110 in Early
           Christianity. Abingdon, 1973.

Hay, Lawrence Cord.
    Professor of religion.
    3762. "The Oracles against the Foreign Nations in Jeremiah
           46-51." Ph.D. diss., Vanderbilt Univ., 1960.

Hayden, Amos Sutton., 1813-1880.
    Pastor; historian; musician.
    3763. Christian Hymn and Time Book. Root & Cady, 1870.
    3764. Early History of the Disciples in the Western
           Reserve, Ohio. Chase & Hall, 1875.
    3765. The Hymnist: Heart Hymns and Home Melodies. 3d ed.
           Bosworth, 1862.

Hayden, Morgan Parritt, 1873-1928.
    Pastor.
    3766. The Bible and Woman. Standard, 1902.
    3767. The Bible Key. 1891.
    3768. The Higher Criticism: Its Meaning, History, Kinds
           and Characteristics. N.d.

Haynes, Titus.
    Professor of religion.
    3769. Fundamentalism in Black Inner City Storefront
           Churches. Vantage, 1978.
    3770. "An Inquiry into the Attitudes of Black Christian
           Laymen of the Disciples of Christ Church: Toward

Beliefs and Practices in the Ministries of Older
Established, Newly Established, and Storefront
Churches." Ph.D. diss., New York Univ., 1978.

Heath, Donald Floyd.
    Professor of religion.
    3771. <u>Our Christian Heritage</u>. Phillips Univ. Pr., 1967-.
          (co-editor).
    3772. "The Presidential Campaign of 1928: Protestant's
          Opposition to Alfred E. Smith as Reflected in
          Denominational Periodicals." Ph.D. diss.,
          Vanderbilt Univ., 1973.

Heaton, Charles Huddleston.
    Church organist; choir director.
    3773. "The Disciples of Christ and Sacred Music." Ph.D.
          diss., Union Theol. Sem., 1956.
    3774. <u>A Guidebook to Worship Services of Sacred Music</u>.
          Bethany, 1962.
    3775. <u>How To Build a Church Choir</u>. Bethany, 1958.

Hedley, George Percy.
    3776. "Where the Scriptures Speak." In Christian Heritage
          in America, pp.116-27. Macmillan, 1946.

Heimer, Haldor Eugene.
    Missionary.
    3777. "The Kimbanguists and the Bapostolo: A Study of Two
          African Independent Churches in Luluabourg, Congo,
          in Relation to Similar Churches and in the Context
          of Lulua Traditional Culture and Religion." Ph.D.
          diss., Hartford Seminary Foundation, 1971.

Helseth, Donald Lawrence.
    Pastor; missionary.
    3778. "Preaching from the Lectionary." D.Min thesis, Iliff
          School of Theology, 1980.

Hempfling, Robert James, 1930-.
    Pastor; church official.
    3779. "The Gospel of Truth and Its Affinity with the
          Hermetic Corpus and the Fourth Gospel." Th.D. diss.,
          Iliff School of Theology, 1961.

Hendricks, Grace.
    Missionary.
    3780. <u>Lonesome Trial</u>. Saulsbury Publishing Co., 1918.

Hendryx, Warren B., 1836-1905.
    Pastor.
    3781. <u>Analytic and Synthetic Bible Lessons</u>. Indianapolis,
          1879.

3782. The Teacher, the Class and the Book: A Series of
       Fifty-Two Sunday School Lessons.... Bosworth, Chase
       & Hall, 1872-.

Henson, Elmer D., 1901-.
    Pastor; professor of religion.
    3783. The Word We Preach: Sermons in Honor of Dean Elmer
           D. Henson. Texas Christian Univ. Pr., 1970.

Herod, William David.
    Missionary.
    3784. Lands of Faith and Ferment: South America.
           Christian Bd. of Publication, 1976. (co-author).

Heron, Frances (Dunlap).
    Editor; Christian educator.
    3785. Betty Ann, Beginner, Lines from Her Diary. Bethany,
           1930.
    3786. The Busy Berrys. Friendship Pr., 1950.
    3787. A Century Beckons: One Hundred and Ninety-Two
           Christian Citizens Plead for Extension and
           Intensification of Religious Education.
           International Council of Religious Education, 1946.
           (editor).
    3788. Here Comes Elijah. Bethany, 1959.
    3789. Kathy Ann, Kindergartner. Abingdon, 1955.
    3790. With My Whole Heart. Westminster, 1950.

Heron, Laurence Tunstall.
    Journalist.
    3791. ESP in the Bible. Doubleday, 1974.
    3792. One Heron Line and Its Origins. The Author, 1988.

Higdon, Elmer Kelso, 1887-1961.
    Missionary to Philippines.
    3793. The Christian Use of Money. National Christian
           Council of the Philippine Islands, 1937.
    3794. Faith Triumphant in the Philippines. Friendship
           Pr., 1946.
    3795. From Carabao to Clipper. Friendship Pr., 1941.
           (co-author).
    3796. How to Find God: Some Suggestions for Public
           Worship. National Christian Council of the
           Philippine Islands, 1937.
    3797. Jesus and National Aspirations. Philippines
           Christian Institute, 1929.
    3798. New Missionaries for New Days. Bethany, 1956.
    3799. The Sun Returning. United Christian Missionary
           Soc., 1947.
    3800. Why Protestantism in the Philippines? Ilocano Print
           Co., 1937.

Higdon, Idella Eleanor (Wilson), 1889-.
    Missionary.
    3801. From Carabao to Clipper. Friendship Pr., 1941.
           (co-author).

High, Dallas M.
    Professor of philosophy and religion.
    3802. Medical Treatment of the Dying Moral Issues.
           Schenkman, 1978. (co-editor).
    3803. New Essays on Religious Language. Oxford Univ. Pr.,
           1969. (compiler).

Hill, Claude Eugene, 1874-.
    Pastor.
    3804. Keeping the Faith: A Book of Sermons. Bethany,
           1929.

Hill, John Louis.
    3805. As Others See Us, and As We Are. Standard, 1908.

Hill, Marilynne, 1920-.
    Missionary; educator.
    3806. Called to Mission and Unity. United Christian
           Missionary Soc., 1965.
    3807. Clear Voices above the Clamor. United Christian
           Missionary Soc., 1955.
    3808. Common Concerns, a Common Hope. Christian Bd. of
           Publication, 1958.
    3809. Long Forks. United Christian Missionary Soc., 1966.
    3810. Southeast Asia Kaleidoscope. United Christian
           Missionary Soc., 1968. (co-author).
    3811. They Went to India: Biographies of Missionaries of
           the Disciples of Christ. United Christian
           Missionary Soc., 1954.

Hinman. George Warren, 1869-.
    Missionary; Christian educator.
    3812. The American Indian and Christian Missions. Revell,
           1933.
    3813. Christian Activities among American Indians.
           Society for Propagating the Gospel among the Indians
           and Others in North America, 1933.
    3814. Community Responsibility for Oriental Immigrants.
           American Missionary Assoc., 192-.
    3815. "Congregational Missions among Indians." New York,
           1930.
    3816. Directory of Oriental Missions. Home Missions
           Council and Council of Women for Home Missions,
           1923?
    3817. Facing the Future in Indian Missions. Council of
           Women for Home Missions, and Missionary Education
           Movement, 1932.

3818. "The Fifty-Fourth Year of the Foochow Mission of the
American Board." Foochow, 1901.

3819. The Oriental in America. Missionary Education
Movement of the United States and Canada, 1913.

3820. Our Caribbean Neighbors. Missionary Education
Movement and Council of Women for Home Missions,
193-.

*Hocking, William Earnest, 1873-1966.
Professor of philosophy.

3821. The Church and the New World Mind. Bethany, 1944.

3822. The Coming World Civilization. Greenwood, 1973,
c1956.

3823. Experiment in Education. Regnery, 1954.

3824. Freedom of the Press, a Framework of Principle. Da
Capo Pr., 1972, c1947.

3825. The Immortality of Man. Lancaster, Pa., 1945.

3826. Living Religions and a World Faith. Macmillan,
1940.

3827. Man and the State. Archon Books, 1968, c1926.

3828. The Meaning of Immortality in Human Experience,
Including Thoughts on Death and Life, Revised.
Harper, 1957.

3829. Preface to Philosophy: Textbook. Macmillan, 1946.
(co-author).

3830. Present Status of the Philosophy of Law and of
Rights. Rothman, 1986, c1926.

3831. Science and the Idea of God. Univ. of North
Carolina Pr., 1944.

3832. Strength of Men and Nations: A Message to the
U.S.A. Vis-a-Vis the USSR. Harper, 1959.

3833. Types of Philosophy. Scribner, 1959.

3834. What Man Can Make of Man. Harper, 1942.

Hoffman, Dan Clayton.
Pastor; missionary.

3835. "Re-Imaging the Missionary: A Study in Ministry and
Power." D.Min thesis, Christian Theological
Seminary, 1981.

Hoffman, Gustavus Adolphus, 1847-1937.

3836. What Shall I Do To Be Saved? American Christian
Missionary Soc., n.d.

Holt, Basil Fenelon, 1902-.
Missionary to South Africa.

3837. Christian Nurture. Standard, 1943.

3838. The Disciples of Christ in South Africa.
Indianapolis, n.d.

3839. The Divine Call to Mission and the Church's
Response. 1963?

3840.   Greatheart of the Border: A Life of John Brownlee,
        Pioneer Missionary in South Africa.   South African
        Missionary Museum, 1976.
3841.   An Hour with General Dobbie. Zondervan, 1945.
3842.   Joseph Williams and the Pioneer Mission to the
        Southeastern Bantu. Lovedale, 1954.
3843.   Old Testament Types of New Testament Christians.
        Zondervan, 1940.
3844.   Place-Names in the Transkeian Territories. Africana
        Museum (Johannesburg), 1959.
3845.   They Came Our Way: A Miscellany of Historical Tales
        and Sketches of the Old Cape Colony. Hale, 1974.
3846.   Visions from the Vaal: Sermons and Addresses.
        Standard, 1929.
3847.   What Time Is It? The Second Coming of Christ...
        Standard, 1936.
3848.   Where Rainbirds Call, a Record of the Transkei.
        Timmins, 1972.

Hoover, Guy Israel, 1872-1943.
     Pastor; professor of religion.
3849.   The Annual County Mass Meeting of Churches in the
        Plan of Work Employed by the Churches of Christ in
        Indiana. Indianapolis, 1920.
3850.   The Butler College Ministerial Student Aid Fund.
        Indianapolis, 1920.
3851.   "The Disciples of Christ and Their Educational Work
        in Indiana." Butler College, 1916.
3852.   Indiana for Christ...Christ for the World. Indiana
        Christian Missionary Assoc., 1931.
3853.   An Informational Statement as to the Indiana
        Christian Missionary Association. Indiana Christian
        Missionary Assoc., 1930s?
3854.   A State Wide Program of Evangelism. 1937.

Hoover, Harvey Daniel.
     Pastor.
3855.   Living the Liturgy. Gettysburg, Pa., 1946.

Hopkins, Alexander Campbell.
     Musician; hymn writer.
3856.   Specimen Pages of Christian Music for Evangelists
        Selected from Revised Christian Hymnal and Christian
        S.S. Hymnal. Christian Publishing Co., n.d.

Hopkins, Robert Milton, 1878-1955.
     Pastor; church official.
3857.   The Disciples and Religious Education. Christian
        Bd. of Publication, 1936. (co-editor)
3858.   Dr. Robert M. Hopkins and International
        Christianity. William-Frederick Pr., 1956.

For works about him written by Disciple authors, see
    Bower, William Clayton under THEOLOGY section.

Hopkins, William W.
    Pastor.
    3859.   Public and Private Rights.   Christian Pub. Co.,
            1900.

Hopper, Myron Taggart, 1903-1960.
    Pastor; professor of religion.
    3860.   The Candle of the Lord.   Bethany, 1948.
    3861.   New Testament Life and Literature: A Course for
            Students of High School Age in Weekday Church
            Schools.   Bethany, 1950.
    3862.   Young People's Work in Protestant Churches in the
            United States.   Univ. of Chicago, 1941.   [Excerpted
            from Ph.D. diss.]

Hopson, Winthrop Hartly, 1823-1889.
    Pastor; physician; college president.
    3863.   Sermons of....   Standard, 1889.

Horton, Roy F., 1902-.
    Pastor; naturalist.
    3864.   Inspiration Point and Its Personalities.   Bethany,
            1961.

Hoven, Ard, 1906-.
    Pastor.
    3865.   Christ Is All!   [Sermons].   Standard, 1954.

Hoven, Victor Emanuel, 1871-.
    Professor of religion.
    3866.   The New Testament Epistles: Analysis and Notes.
            Baker, 1959.
    3867.   Notes on the Revelation.   Northwest Christian
            College, 1949.
    3868.   Outlines of Biblical Doctrine.   1948.
    3869.   The Purpose and Progress in Prophecy.   E.B.U. Pr.,
            1929.
    3870.   Shadow and Substance.   Bethany, 1934.

Howe, Henry, 1811-1868.
    Evangelist.
    3871.   The Diary of a Circuit Rider.   Voyageur, 1933.

Howell, Robert Lee.
    Pastor.
    3872.   The Fish - A Ministry of Love.   Jarrow, 1973.

    3873.   Fish for My People.   Morehouse-Barlow Co., 1968.
    3874.   Lost Mountain Days.   Jarrow, 1973.

Hudson, Charles Rollin, 1865-1941.
    Pastor.
    3875. <u>Forty Years a Minister of the Gospel</u>. Los Angeles,
           1930.

Hudson, L. Richard.
    3876. <u>Westside Christian Church: A Study of Church and
           Community</u>. Association of the Christian Churches in
           Indiana, 1966.

Huegel, Frederick Julius, 1889-.
    Pastor; professor of philosophy and history; missionary.
    3877. <u>Bone of His Bone</u>. Marshall, Morgan & Scott
           (London), 1933.
    3878. <u>Calvary's Wondrous Cross</u>. Zondervan, 1949.
    3879. <u>The Cross of Christ, the Throne of God</u>. Marshall,
           Morgan & Scott, (Edinburgh), 1936.
    3880. <u>Fairest Flower</u>. Zondervan, 1945.
    3881. <u>Forever Triumphant</u>. Zondervan, 1955.
    3882. <u>High Peaks in Redemption</u>. Marshall, Morgan & Scott
           (London), 1939.
    3883. <u>John Looks at the Cross</u>. Marshall, Morgan & Scott
           (London), 1957.
    3884. <u>The Mystery of Iniquity: Keys to Victorious
           Christian Living</u>. Bethany, 1968.
    3885. <u>Prayer's Deeper Secrets</u>. Zondervan, 1959.
    3886. <u>That Old Serpent, the Devil</u>. Marshall, Morgan &
           Scott (London), 1939.

Huff, Howard F.
    Professor of religion.
    3887. <u>Breakthrough to Life: A Guidebook for Use with
           Small Groups Participating in the Breakthrough to
           Life Education Program of the Christian Church in
           Oklahoma</u>. Oklahoma City, 1975. (co-author).
    3888. <u>Hakone Communique', Being the Official Report of the
           Second... Conference, Held..Under the Joint Auspices
           of the Japan Christian Literature Commission and the
           East Asia Christian Conference</u>. Japan Christian
           Literature Commission, 1959. (editor).

Hughes, Jasper Seaton, 1843-.
    Pastor.
    3889. <u>The King's Trumpet</u>. The Author, 1921.
    3890. "Lessons in the Revelation." Holland, Mich., n.d.
    3891. <u>Mystery of the Golden Cloth, the Story of the
           Christ</u>. Star, 1895.
    3892. <u>The Revelation</u>. The Author, 1910.
    3893. <u>The Seer of Patmos: Or, John's Place in the
           Christian Economy</u>. Scofield, 1899.
    3894. "Sweet as Honey." N.d.

Humbert, John O.
    Pastor, church official.
    3895. A House of Living Stones. CBP Pr., 1987.

Humbert, Royal.
    Professor of religion and philosophy.
    3896. A Compend of Alexander Campbell's Theology.
           Bethany, 1961. (editor).

Hume, Theodore Carswell, 1904-1943.
    Pastor.
    3897. Flight to Destiny. An Interpretation for Youth of
           the Life of Theodore Carswell Hume. Association
           Pr., 1945.
    3898. The Immediate Origins of the War (28th June - 4th
           August 1914). Yale Univ. Pr., 1928. (translator).

Hunt, Julian O.
    3899. Christian Is the Name of the Church. Harrisonburg,
           Va., 1962.

Hunter, Barton.
    Pastor; professor of religion.
    3900. The Big Difference. Bethany, 1957.
    3901. Building Peace: Suggestions for Church and
           Community. Friendship, Pr., 1976. (co-author).
    3902. Christian Action and Community Service.
           Indianapolis, 1966.

Hurd, Della.
    3903. The Way of This General Practitioner [Harry Hurd].
           The Author, 1968.

Huston, Frank Claude, 1871-1959.
    Pastor; evangelist; composer; singer.
    3904. Nineteen Sacred Songs. Huston, 1937.
    3905. One Hundred Hymns and Gospel Songs. The Author,
           1955.
    3906. When Our Boys Come Home Again. Huston, 1918.
    3907. Write a Letter Home to Mother. Huston, 1917.

Idleman, Finis Schuyler, 1875-1941.
    Pastor; assistant editor of Christian Union Quarterly.
    3908. "The Alpine Glow." Dobbs Ferry, N.Y., 1930.
    3909. Peter Ainslie, Ambassador of Good Will. Willett
           Clark & Co., 1941.

Illingworth, Alfred Scott, 1919-.
    Professor of religion.
    3910. "The Text of Luke in the Menologion of the Greek
           Lectionary." Ph.D. diss., Univ. of Chicago, 1957.

Irelan, Elma C. 1880-.
  Missionary to Mexico.
    3911. <u>Fifty Years with Our Mexican Neighbors</u>. Bethany,
          1944.

Jacobs, James Vernon, 1898-.
  Pastor; Christian educator, editor.
    3912. <u>Bible Quiz Book</u>. Standard, 1939.
    3913. <u>Bible Quizzes for Everyone</u>. Standard, 1961.
    3914. <u>Bible Story-Lessons for Parents to Teach</u>. Christian
          Family Books, 1962.
    3915. <u>Church Handbook: Basic Helps for Lay and Student
          Ministers</u>. Standard, 1961.
    3916. <u>81 Short Speeches for 44 Occasions</u>. Standard, 1954.
    3917. <u>Everyday Stories</u>. Standard, 1943.
    3918. <u>500 Plans and Ideas for Church Officers</u>. Standard,
          1957.
    3919. <u>450 True Stories from Church History</u>. Eerdmans,
          1955.
    3920. <u>Fun with Bible Quizzes</u>. Standard, 1961.
    3921. <u>How to Increase Your Sunday School Attendance</u>.
          Zondervan, 1960.
    3922. <u>How to Plan and Conduct Sunday School Worship
          Services</u>. Zondervan, 1964.
    3923. <u>How to Speak and Pray in Public</u>. Standard, 1951.
    3924. <u>Illustrations from Great Literature</u>. Higley, 1952.
    3925. <u>Inspiring Talks, for Superintendents, Youth Leaders,
          Teachers, Speakers</u>. Standard, 1962.
    3926. <u>Junior Stories for Today</u>. Standard, 1937.
    3927. <u>New Bible Quizzes</u>. Standard, 1941.
    3928. <u>1,000 Plans and Ideas for Sunday School Workers</u>.
          Zondervan, 1957.
    3929. <u>600 Doctrinal Illustrations</u>. Standard, 1941.
          (co-compiler).
    3930. <u>Starlight Talks To Youth</u>. Baker, 1961.
    3931. <u>Teaching Problems and How To Solve Them</u>. Zondervan,
          1962.
    3932. <u>Teaching the Bible through Play</u>. Standard, 1929.
    3933. <u>Teaching Tools for Sunday Schools</u>. Zondervan, 1963.
    3934. <u>Ten Steps To Leadership</u>. Standard, 1956.
    3935. <u>24 Messages for Men</u>. Standard, 1961.
    3936. <u>24 Talks for Sunday School Workers' Conferences</u>.
          Zondervan, 1961.
    3937. <u>Understanding Your Pupils</u>. Zondervan, 1959.
    3938. <u>What Makes Pupils Learn</u>. Zondervan, 1961.
    3939. <u>What We Believe</u>. Standard, 1963.

Jacobs, Norman E.
  Professor of religion.
    3940. <u>Christians Learning for Christian Living</u>. Christian
          Bd. of Publication, 1961.

3941. The Church Alive and Perking: A Workshop on
       Planning Church Programs. Christian Bd. of
       Publication, 1973.
3942. "Some Relationships Between Selected Personal
       Factors and Attitudes of Adults Toward the Church."
       Ph.d. diss., Univ. of Pittsburgh, 1963.

Jefferson, Samuel Mitchell, 1849-1914.
   Pastor.
   3943. Isaac Errett's Contribution to the Religious
          Movement of the Disciples of Christ. Rokker, n.d.
   3944. Standard Commentary on the International
          Sunday-School Lessons. Standard, 1883-. (editor).

Jenkins, Burris Atkins, Sr., 1869-1945.
   3945. American Religion as I See It Lived. Bobbs-Merrill,
          1930.
   3946. The Beauty of the New Testament. Doran, 1925.
   3947. The Bracegirdle. Lippincott, 1922.
   3948. The Drift of the Day. Willett, Clark & Colby, 1928.
   3949. Facing the Hindenburg Line: Personal Observations
          at the Fronts and in the Camps of the British,
          French, Americans and Italians, during the Campaigns
          of 1917. Revell, 1917.
   3950. Father Meany and the Fighting 69th. Fell, 1944.
   3951. Fresh Furrow. Willett, Clark & Co., 1936.
   3952. Hand of Bronze. Willett, Clark & Co., 1933.
   3953. Heroes of Faith: A Study of a Chapter from the
          Greek New Testament for Beginners. Funk & Wagnalls,
          1896.
   3954. Is Theism a Logical Philosophy? Halderman-Julius,
          1930.
   3955. It Happened "Over There.". Revell, 1918.
   3956. Let's Build a New World [Sermons]. Harper, 1934.
   3957. The Man in the Street and Religion. Revell, 1917.
   3958. My Job - Preaching: Samples for Preachers and
          Laymen. Cokesbury, 1932.
   3959. Princess Salome. Lippincott, 1921.
   3960. The Protestant: A Scrap-Book for Insurgents.
          Christian Century Pr., 1918.
   3961. Torrent. Bobbs-Merrill, 1932.
   3962. Where My Caravan Has Rested. Willett, Clark & Co.,
          1939.
   3963. The World's Debt to Protestantism. Stratford, 1930.

For works about him written by Disciple authors, see
   Svanoe, Harold C. under HISTORY section.

Jewett, Frank L., 1874-1969.
   Founder of a Bible Chair at University of Texas.
   3964. The Story of the Texas Bible Chair. United
          Christian Missionary Soc., 194__.

John, Roger.
    3965. <u>Disciples of Christ</u>. Mandeville, La., 1976.

Johnson, Ashley Sidney, 1857-1925.
    Pastor; founder and president of Johnson Bible College.
    3966. <u>Bible Readings and Sermon Outlines on the Christian</u>
            <u>Plea</u>. Old Paths Book Club, 195_.
    3967. <u>The Busy Man's Bible Encyclopedia</u>. Gospel Light
            Pub. Co., n.d.
    3968. <u>Correspondence Bible College</u>. Ogden, 1901.
    3969. <u>The Great Controversy: A Scriptural and Historical</u>
            <u>Search after the True Basis of Christian Union</u>.
            Haws, 1882.
    3970. <u>The Holy Spirit and the Human Mind</u>. Gaut-Ogden,
            1903.
    3971. <u>Johnson's Speeches</u>. Ogden, 1895.
    3972. <u>Letters to a Young Methodist Preacher</u>. College
            Pr.,19__.
    3973. <u>Opening the Book of the Seven Seals [Revelation]</u>.
            College Pr., n.d.
    3974. <u>Out of Darkness into Light</u>. Press of Guide Printing
            & Publishing Co., 1894.
    3975. <u>The Self-Interpreting New Testament</u>. Kimberlin
            Heights, Tenn., n.d.
    3976. <u>Ten Evangelistic Sermons</u>. College Pr., 196_.
    3977. <u>Ten Lessons in How To Read, How To Understand and</u>
            <u>How To Remember the Bible</u>. Gaut-Ogden, 1903.
    3978. <u>The Tennessee Evangelist: A Series of Ten Sermons</u>.
            Standard, 1886.
    3979. <u>Thirteen Expository Sermons on the Book of Hebrews</u>.
            College Pr., 196_.
    3980. <u>True Basis of Christian Union</u>. Haws, 1882.

For works about him by Disciple authors, see
    Smith, James Henry Oliver under THEOLOGY section.

Johnson, Barton W., 1833-1894.
    Pastor; educator.
    3981. <u>The Gospel of Mark: A New Commentary, Workbook,</u>
            <u>Teaching Manual</u>. College Pr., 1965.
    3982. <u>John</u>. A Commentary for the People. Christian
            Publishing Co., 1886.
    3983. <u>The Normal Instructor: A Series of Bible Studies</u>.
            2 vols. St. Louis, 1894-1895.
    3984. <u>The People's New Testament</u>.
    3985. <u>Vision of the Ages</u>. Central Book Concern, 1881.
    3986. <u>Young Folks in Bible Lands</u>.

Johnson, H. Eugene.
    Attorney; historian.
    3987. <u>The Christian Church Plea</u>. New Life Books, 1975.
    3988. <u>The Current Reformation: Thoughts from Thomas</u>
            <u>Campbell</u>. 1972.

3989.   The Declaration and Address for Today. Reed, 1971.
3990.   Duly and Scripturally Qualified: A Study of the
        Ministry of the Christian Church Movement. New Life
        Books, 1975.
3991.   Simple Principles: Robert Richardson's Reformation.
        Johnson, 1977.
3992.   Unity of Faith and Practice. Johnson, 1976.

Johnson, Harold R.
     Pastor.
3993.   Becoming a Guest of the Holy: A Guide to
        Experiencing Life in the Spirit. Christian Bd. of
        Publication, 1978.
3994.   Congregational Programming in the Christian Church
        (Disciples of Christ). Christian Bd. of
        Publication, 1976-1979. (co-author).

Jones, Allen Bailey.
3995.   The Spiritual Side of Our Plea. Christian
        Publishing Co., 1901.

Jones, Claude C. 1879-.
     Pastor.
3996.   "Reminiscences of North Carolina." Carolina
        Discipliana Library, 1954.
3997.   The Opportunities of Age: Stimulating Interviews
        with Active Retired People and Some Contemplating
        Retirement. Christopher, 1959.
3998.   The Teaching Methods of the Master. Bethany, 1957.

Jones, Edgar Dewitt, 1876-1956.
     Pastor; journalist.
3999.   The Coming of the Perfect [Sermons]. Bethany, 1946.
4000.   Lords of Speech: Portraits of Fifteen American
        Orators. Willett, Clark & Co., 1937.
4001.   A Man Stood Up to Preach: And Fifteen Other
        Sermons. Bethany, 1943.
4002.   The Pulpit Stairs [Sermons]. Bethany, 1934.
4003.   Sermons I Love to Preach. Harper, 1953.

For works about him written by Disciple authors, see
Cartwright, George Washington under THEOLOGY section.

Jones, George Curtis, 1911-.
     Pastor; writer.
4004.   Candles in the City. Word, 1973?
4005.   Christian Stewardship: What Are You Worth?
        Bethany, 1954.
4006.   The Church Parking Lot. Fortress, 1967.
4007.   Handbook of Church Correspondence. MacMillan, 1962.
4008.   How Come We're Alive. Word, 1976.
4009.   I Met a Man: Imagined Remembrances of Jesus. Word,
        1971.

4010. In Their Light We Walk. Bethany.
4011. A Man and His Religion. Bethany, 1967.
4012. March of the Year: Especial Sermons for Special
       Days. Bethany, 1959.
4013. On Being Your Best [Addresses]. Macmillan, 1950.
4014. Parents Deserve To Know. Macmillan, 1960.
4015. Patterns of Prayer. Bethany, 1964.
4016. Repairing Our Religion. Christopher, 1945.
4017. Strongly Tempted. World Pub. Co., 1968.
4018. What Are You Doing? Bethany, 1956.
4019. Which Way is Progress [Sermons]. Bethany, 1953.
4020. Youth Deserves To Know. Macmillan, 1958.

Jones, Joe Robert, 1936-.
    College president.
    4021. "Analytic Philosophy and Religious Language: A
           Bibliography." Southern Methodist Univ., 1970.

Jones, Myrddyn William, 1913-.
    Pastor; librarian.
    4022. "The Function of the Gospel of Mark." Ph.D diss.,
           Univ. of Chicago, 1945.

Jordan, Robert L.
    Pastor.
    4023. Two Races in One Fellowship. United Christian
           Church, 1944.

Joyce, James Daniel, 1921-.
    Pastor; college professor and administrator.
    4024. The Living Christ in Our Changing World [Sermons].
           Bethany, 1962.
    4025. The Place of the Sacraments in Worship. Bethany,
           1967.

*Keck, Leander Earl, 1928-.
    Seminary professor and administrator.
    4026. The Bible in the Pulpit: The Renewal of Biblical
           Preaching. Abingdon, 1978.
    4027. A Future for the Historical Jesus: The Place of
           Jesus in Preaching and Theology. Abingdon, 1971.
    4028. Mandate to Witness: Studies in the Book of Acts.
           Judson, 1964.
    4029. The New Testament Experience of Faith. Bethany,
           1976.
    4030. Paul and His Letters. Fortress, 1979.
    4031. The Pauline Letters. Abingdon, 1984. (co-author).
    4032. Studies in Luke-Acts: Essays Presented in Honor of
           Paul Schubert. Abingdon, 1966. (co-editor).
    4033. Taking the Bible Seriously: An Invitation to Think
           Theologically. Association, 1962.

Keckley, Weldon.
  Pastor.
  4034. The Church School Superintendent: The Person and
         the Job. Bethany, 1963.

Keith, Noel Leonard.
  Professor of religion.
  4035. The Brites of Capote. Texas Christian Univ. Pr.,
         1950.
  4036. "Glossolalia." Texas Assoc. of Christian Churches,
         196_.
  4037. The Green Horse. Rowdy: A Christmas Story. Stewart
         & Keith, 1949.
  4038. The Human Rift: Bridges to Peace and Understanding.
         Bethany, 1963.
  4039. Paul's Message for Today: Echoes from William C.
         Morro and Granville T. Walker. Texas Christian
         Univ. Pr., 1970.
  4040. Religion: An Introduction and Guide to Study. 2d
         ed. Brown, 1967.
  4041. The Story of D.S. Burnet. Bethany, 1954.
  4042. Worship Highways. Bethany, 1943. (co-compiler).

Kellems, Jesse Randolph, 1892-.
  Pastor.
  4043. Alexander Campbell and the Disciples Lectures...
         Smith, 1930.
  4044. The Deity of Jesus and Other Sermons. Christian Bd.
         of Publication, 1919.
  4045. Glorying in the Cross. and Other Sermons. Christian
         Bd. of Publication, 1914.
  4046. New Testament Evangelism: A Series of Addresses on
         Evangelistic Preaching. Music and Methods.
         Standard, 1922.
  4047. Pentecosts under the Southern Cross. Standard,
         1925.
  4048. The Resurrection Gospel. and Other Sermons.
         Standard, 1924.
  4049. Studies in the Forgiveness of Sins. Doran, 1926.

Keller, William Edward, 1922-.
  Pastor; missionary.
  4050. Stewards of a Lifetime: A Guide to the
         Responsibility of the Board of Stewards for Local
         Church Finance. United Church of Christ in the
         Philippines, 1964.

Kellett, James Roy, 1939-.
  College administrator.
  4051. "Toward an Explication of Man." Ph.D. diss., School
         of Theology at Claremont, 1977.

Kelley, James Patrick.
  Professor of religion.
  4052. "Revelation and the Secular in the Theology if
       Dietrich Bonhoeffer." Ph.D. diss., Yale Univ.,
       1980.

Kelly, Mary Frances E., 1875?-.
  Missionary to China.
  4053. Some Chinese Friends of Mine. Powell & White, 1924.

Kemp, Charles F., 1912-.
  Pastor; professor of religion.
  4054. The Caring Pastor: An Introduction to Pastoral
       Counseling in the Local Church. Abingdon, 1985.
  4055. Christian Dimensions of Family Living. Christian
       Bd. of Publication, 1964.
  4056. The Church and Community Resources. Bethany, 1977.
       (co-author).
  4057. The Church: The Gifted and the Retarded Child.
       Bethany, 1957.
  4058. Counseling with College Students. Prentice-Hall,
       1964.
  4059. Guidance for Church Vocations. United Christian
       Missionary Soc., n.d.
  4060. Guidebook of Pastoral Counseling. Abingdon, 1971.
  4061. Learning about Pastoral Care. Abingdon, 1970.
  4062. Life-Situation Preaching. Bethany, 1956.
  4063. The Pastor and Community Resources. Bethany, 1960.
  4064. The Pastor and Vocational Counseling. Bethany,
       1961.
  4065. Pastoral Care and Poverty. Abingdon, 1973.
  4066. Pastoral Care with the Poor. Abingdon, 1972.
  4067. Pastoral Preaching. Bethany, 1963.
  4068. A Pastoral Triumph: The Story of Richard Baxter and
       His Ministry at Kidderminster. Macmillan, 1948.
  4069. Physicians of the Soul, a History of Pastoral
       Counseling. Macmillan, 1947.
  4070. Prayer-Based Growth Groups. Abingdon, 1974.
  4071. The Preaching Pastor. Bethany, 1966.
  4072. Preparing for the Ministry. Bethany, 1959.
  4073. Smart Golf: A Study of the Mental and Emotional
       Side of the Game of Golf. Branch-Smith, 1974.
  4074. Student's Guidebook: Theological School Study
       Habits Inventory. Texas Christian Univ., 1963.
  4075. Theological School, Check List of Study Skills and
       Attitudes. Bethany, 1965. (co-author).
  4076. Thinking and Acting Biblically. Abingdon, 1976.
  4077. The World of Golf and the Game of Life. Bethany,
       1978.
  4078. You and Your Life-Style: A Personal Guide to
       Christian Living. Bethany, 1980.

Kenney, Richard Bruce.
    Professor of religion.
    4079. "Ante-Nicene Greek and Latin Patristic Uses of the
           Biblical Manna Motif." Ph.D. diss., Yale Univ.,
           1968.

Kepple, Ella Huff.
    Pastor; missionary.
    4080. Balti. Bethany, 1959.
    4081. Fun and Festival from Latin America. Friendship
           Pr., 1961.
    4082. Mateo of Mexico. Friendship Pr., 1961.
    4083. Three Children of Chili. Friendship Pr., 1961.

Kerr, Paul Edward.
    Pastor.
    4084. Dr. Cy-Losanganya: A Biography of Cyrus McNeely
           Yocum. Bethany, 1973.

Kershner, Bruce Lesher, 1871-1949.
    Pastor; seminary professor; missionary.
    4085. The Head Hunter and Other Stories of the
           Philippines. Powell & White, 1921.
    4086. A Twentieth Century Apocalypse. Exposition Pr.,
           1951.

*Kershner, Frederick Doyle, 1875-1953.
    Seminary professor and dean.
    4087. How to Promote Christian Union, an Historical and
           Practical Handbook. Standard, 1916.
    4088. Pioneers of Christian Thought. Bobbs-Merrill, 1930.
    4089. The Religion of Christ: An Interpretation. Revell,
           1911.
    4090. The Restoration Handbook, Studies in the History and
           Principles of the Movement to Restore New Testament
           Christianity. Standard, 1920.
    4091. Sermons for Special Days. Doran, 1922.
    4092. The Spiritual Message of Great Art. Meigs, 1928.
    4093. Those Gay Middle Ages. Willett, Clark & Co., 1938.

See also, Osborn, Ronald E. in GENERAL section.

Kesler, Benjamin E.
    4094. The Kesler and Ellmore Debate: Held at Jasonville,
           Indiana, September 29 to October 6, 1915. Covering
           the Leading Differences between the Church of the
           Brethren and the Church of Christ (Disciples).
           Brethren Publishing House, 1916.

Kilgore, Charles Franklin.
    Missionary.
    4095. The James O'Kelly Schism in the Methodist Episcopal
           Church. Casa Unida de Publicaciones, 1963.

King, Joseph, 1831-1890.
    Pastor.
    4096. Sanctification: An Address.... Millennial
        Harbinger, 1866.
    4097. Sermons, With Memoir. Standard, 1893.

Kingsbury, Leslie Lyall.
    Professor of philosophy.
    4098. "The Philosophical Influences Bearing on Alexander
        Campbell and the Beginnings of the Disciples of
        Christ Movement." Ph.D. diss., Univ. of Edinburgh,
        1954?

Kingsolver, Mary.
    Pastor.
    4099. Teacher's Guide for Wondering about God. American
        Baptist Bd. of Education & Publication, 1969.
    4100. Wondering about God. American Baptist Bd. of
        Education & Publication, 1969.

Kinnamon, Michael K., 1949-.
    Professor of theology.
    4101. Baptism, Eucharist and Ministry: A Guide for Study.
        Council on Christian Unity of the Christian Church
        (Disciples of Christ), 1984.
    4102. The Cry of the Cuckoo: Literature and Evil in the
        Contemporary Age. Ph.D. diss., Univ. of Chicago,
        1980.
    4103. In God's Image: Reflections on Identity, Human
        Wholeness, and the Authority of Scripture. World
        Council of Churches, 1983. (co-editor).
    4104. Towards Visible Unity. World Council of Churches,
        1982. (editor).
    4105. Unity, in Each Place--In All Places--: United
        Churches and the Christian World Communions. World
        Council of Churches, 1983. (editor).

Kirsch, Augustin Paul.
    4106. Christianity: Or, Why I Became a Non-Sectarian.
        Standard, 1913.

Klein, Theodore Ernest, 1934-.
    Professor of philosophy.
    4107. "The World as Horizon: Husserl's Constitutional
        Theory of the Objective World." Ph.D. diss., Rice
        Univ., 1967.

Klemme, Huber F.
    Pastor.
    4108. The Bible and Our Common Life. Christian Education
        Pr., 1953.
    4109. Poverty and Plenty in Our Time: A Coursebook for
        Leaders of Adults. United Church Pr., 1966.

4110. <u>Your Church and Your Community</u>. Christian Education
Pr., 1957.

Klingman, Charles Christopher, 1881-.
Pastor.
4111. <u>Christianity Through the Centuries</u>. Taylor, Texas,
1936.
4112. "From Feud to Fraternity: Preaching an Unbiased
Analysis of Three Major Experiments in Christian
Unity." Electra, Texas, 1930.
4113. "The Function of the Pulpit [Address]." 1936?
4114. <u>My Yesterdays. August, 1881-August, 1971: The
Autobiography of Charles Christopher Klingman</u>.
Banner Print Co., 1971.

Kuntz, Kenneth A.
Pastor.
4115. <u>The Congregation as Church</u>. Bethany, 1971.
4116. <u>The Minister and the Christian Life Curriculum</u>.
Christian Bd. of Publication, 1968.
4117. <u>The Pilgrim</u>. Bethany, 1957.
4118. <u>The Pioneer</u>. Bethany, 1960.
4119. <u>Wooden Chalices. New Ideas for Stewardship</u>.
Bethany, 1963.

Kuroiwa, Wallace Hisashi Ryan.
Professor of religion.
4120. "The Internment of the Japanese in America during
World War II: An Interpretation According to Ethics
of Character." Ph.D diss., Emory Univ., 1983.

Kuykendall, William Henry Frazer, 1934-.
Librarian.
4121. "Egyptian Religious Activity in Palestine and Syria
during the Third and Second Millennia before
Christ." Ph.D. diss., Johns Hopkins Univ., 1966.

Ladd, James Earl, 1901-1951.
Pastor.
4122. "As Much As In Me Is..." and Other Sermons.
Portland: Printed by Beattie, 1951.

Lahutsky, Nadia M.
Professor of religion.
4123. "Wilfred Ward, English Catholicism and the Modernist
Controversy, 1890-1912." Ph.D. diss., Vanderbilt
Univ., 1984.

Lair, Loren E.
Pastor.
4124. <u>The Christian Church (Disciples of Christ) and Its
Future</u>. Bethany, 1971.

4125. The Christian Churches and Their Work. Bethany, 1963.

4126. From Restoration to Reformation: The Story of the Beginning. Growth and Development of the Christian Church (Disciples) in Iowa. 1970.

Lamar, James Sanford, 1829-1908.
   Pastor.
4127. "Baptist Baptism vs. Christian Baptism: A Sermon..." Chronicle & Constitutionalist Job Print., 1878.

4128. "A Discourse Delivered in Christian Church...." Office of the Constitutionalist, 1861.

4129. First Principles: Or. The Birth of a Christian. Standard, 1891.

4130. Luke. Chase & Hall, 1878.

4131. Memoir of Isaac Errett with Selections from His Writings. 2
vols. Standard 1893.

4132. The Organon of Scripture: Or. The Inductive Method of Biblical Interpretation. Lippincott, 1860.

4133. Recollections of Pioneer Days in Georgia. Augusta? Ga., 1898?

4134. "What is the Christian Church? Or Who Are the Disciples of Christ?" Christian Missionary Convention, 1883.

Lappin, Samuel Strahl, 1870-1960.
   Evangelist.
4135. The Church at Our Place: Songs. Recitations and Suggestions for an Evening's Entertainment. Designed for Use in Local Churches... Standard, 1929.

4136. Communion Manual. Standard, 1935.

4137. The Home and Family in the Light of Bible Teaching. Standard, 1923.

4138. Lappin's Sermon Outlines. Standard, 1925.

4139. Run. Sammy. Run: Sixty-Five Years a Preacher Man. Bethany, 1958.

4140. The Training of the Church. Standard, 1911.

4141. Where the Long Trail Begins. Standard, 1913.

4142. Wren's Nest. Christian Bd. of Publication, 1919.

4143. Zachary Taylor Sweeney. Christian Commoner. N.d.

Lawrence, Kenneth.
4144. Classic Themes of Disciples Theology: Rethinking the Traditional Affirmations of the Christian Church (Disciples of Christ). Texas Univ. Pr., 1986. (editor).

Ledbetter, Carl Scotius, 1910-.
   Army chaplain; college professor and administrator.
4145. "The History of Open Membership in the Churches of Christ." M.A. thesis, Butler Univ., 1940.

Lee, Allan W.
  Pastor.
  4146. One Great Fellowship: Travels of a Global Minister.
         Exposition Pr., 1974.

Leggett, Marshall.
  4147. Introduction to the Restoration Ideal. Standard,
         1986.

Lehman, Joel Baer, 1866-1942.
  Church official.
  4148. Some Results in the Negro Work. Christian Woman's
         Bd. of Missions, 1917?

*Lemmon, Clarence Eugene, 1888-1963.
  Pastor; editor of World Call.
  4149. The Art of Church Management. Bethany, 1933.
  4150. The Disciples of Christ in Missouri. Centennial
         Commission, 1937. (co-author).
  4151. Preaching on New Testament Themes: Sermons by
         Active Pastors of Present-Day Christian Churches
         (Disciples of Christ). Bethany, 1964. (editor).
  4152. Preaching on Old Testament Themes: Sermons by
         Active Pastors of Present-Day Christian Churches
         (Disciples of Christ). Bethany, 1963. (editor).
  4153. Religion Helps. Bethany, 1942.

Lentz, Richard E.
  Pastor; church official.
  4154. Adult Education in Christian Churches. Christian
         Bd. of Education, 1961.
  4155. Christian Growth in Family Life. Bethany, 1959.
  4156. Christian Worship by Families. Bethany, 1957.
  4157. Making the Adult Class Vital. Bethany, 1954.
  4158. Our Teaching Ministry. Christian Bd. of
         Publication, 1967.
  4159. Solving Leadership Problems. Christian Bd. of
         Publication, 1964?

Leslie, Ruth Rebecca.
  Missionary to Mexico.
  4160. Mi Iglesia: Curso para Escuelas Biblicas de
         Vacaciones. Departamento Primario [Course for
         Primary Dept. of Vacation Bible School]. Casa Unida
         de Publicaciones, 1950.

*Lester, Hiram Jefferson, 1933- .
  College professor and administrator.
  4161. Inasmuch--The Saga of NBA. National Benevolent
         Assoc., 1987. (co-author).
  4162. "Relative Clauses in the Pauline Homologoumena and
         Antilegomena." Ph.D. diss., Yale Univ., 1973.

Lewis, Benjamin Franklin, 1918- .
  Professor of philosophy and religion.
  4163. "The Concept of 'Meaning in History.'" Ph.D. diss.,
         Univ. of Cincinnati, 1961.
  4164. The Moral and Religious Predicament of Modern Man.
         Poseidon, 1972. (editor).

Lewis, Grant K., 1868-1938.
  Church official.
  4165. The American Christian Missionary Society and the
         Disciples of Christ. Christian Bd. of Publication,
         1937.

*Lewis, Hazel Asenath, 1886- .
  Children's worker.
  4166. Bethany Junior Department Manual. Christian Bd. of
         Publication, 1945. (editor).
  4167. Knowing Children Better. Westminster, 1941.
  4168. Methods for Primary Teachers. Front Rank Pr., 1921.
  4169. Planning for Children in the Local Church. Bethany,
         1933.
  4170. Programs for Teachers' Conferences, Beginners' and
         Primary. Pilgrim, 1922.
  4171. Vacation Church School, Manual for the Teacher. 4
         vols. Bethany, 1924. (co-editor).

Lewis, Jack P.
  4172. The Last Things: Essays Presented by His Students
         to Dr. W. B. West, Jr. upon the Occasion of His 65th
         Birthday. Sweet, 1972. (editor).

Lhamon, William Jefferson, 1855-1955.
  Evangelist; Bible college president, evangelist.
  4173. "An Address to the Members of the Commission for the
         Restudy of the Disciples of Christ..." Columbia,
         Mo., n.d.
  4174. The Character of Christ Fact or Fiction. Revell,
         1914.
  4175. Heroes of Modern Missions. Revell, 1899.
  4176. Missionary Fields and Forces of the Disciples of
         Christ. Bethany, 1898.
  4177. Studies in Acts. Christian Publishing Co., 1897.
  4178. "Syllabi: Studies in the Christ Character, and in
         New Testament Introduction." N.d.

*Liggett, Thomas Jackson, 1919- .
  Seminary president, missionary to Argentina.
  4179. Where Tomorrow Struggles To Be Born: The Americas in
         Transition. Friendship Pr., 1970.

Lindley, Denton Ray.
    College president.
    4180. Apostle of Freedom [Alexander Campbell]. Bethany,
           1957.

Linn, Jan
    Pastor.
    4181. Christians Must Choose: The Lure of Culture and the
           Command of Christ. CBP Pr., 1985.
    4182. Living Out God's Love: Mission Groups in Action.
           Judson, 1981.
    4183. Two Are Better Than One: The Ministry of John and
           Hazel Suttenfield. The Author, 1973.

Lipscomb, David, 1831-1918.
    Pastor; editor of Gospel Advocate; educator.
    4184. A Commentary on the Gospel According to John.
           Gospel Advocate Co., 1971, c1939.
    4185. A Commentary on the New Testament Epistles. 5 vols.
           Gospel Advocate Co., 1933-58.
    4186. David Lipscomb: Journalist in Texas, 1872. Nortex,
           1973.
    4187. Queries and Answers by David Lipscomb, Editor of the
           Gospel Advocate. McQuiddy Printing Co., 1910.
    4188. Queries and Answers by Lipscomb and Sewell: Being a
           Compilation of Queries with Answers by D. Lipscomb
           and E. G. Sewell. Covering a Period of Forty Years
           of their Joint Editorial Labors on the Gospel
           Advocate. McQuiddy Printing Co., 1921.
    4189. Salvation from Sin. McQuiddy Printing Co., 1913.

For works about him written by Disciples authors, see
    Hooper, Robert E. and
    Robinson, John L. under HISTORY section;
    West, Earl in GENERAL section.

Lobingier, John Leslie, 1884-.
    Pastor.
    4190. The Better Church School. Pilgrim, 1952.
    4191. Business Meetings That Make Business. Collier,
           1969.
    4192. Colonial Education under the Dutch Reformed Church.
           Chicago, 1916.
    4193. Educating for Peace. Pilgrim, 1930. (co-author).
    4194. How Big Is Your World? A Course Plan For Young
           People of High School Age. Pilgrim, 1931.
    4195. How To Use "Great Is the Company." Friendship Pr.,
           1947.
    4196. If Teaching Is Your Job. Pilgrim, 1956.
    4197. Instructor's Guide Book, for Use with The
           Organization and Administration of the Church
           School. Boston, 1924.

4198. <u>Is War the Way? A Six Session Course...</u> Pilgrim,
       1935.
4199. <u>The Master's Way: Studies for Men in the Navy</u>.
       YMCA, 1918.
4200. <u>The Missionary Education of Adults</u>. Missionary
       Education Movement of the United States and Canada,
       1938.
4201. <u>Our Church: A Course of Study for Young People of
       the High-School Age</u>. Univ. of Chicago Pr., 1927.
4202. <u>Pilgrims and Pioneers in the Congregational
       Christian Tradition</u>. United Church Pr., 1965.
4203. <u>Projects in World-Friendship</u>. Univ. of Chicago Pr.,
       1925.
4204. <u>What Shall We Do about Missions</u>? A Six Session
       Course for Young People. Pilgrim, 1933.
4205. <u>World-Friendship through the Church School: A
       Training Course for Church Workers</u>. Univ. of
       Chicago Pr., 1923.
4206. <u>Youth and the World Outlook for Young People's
       Classes and Societies</u>. Pilgrim, 1929.

*Lockhart, Clinton, 1858-1951.
   Pastor; college president; professor of Bible.
   4207. <u>The Messianic Message of the Old Testament</u>. Des
          Moines? Iowa, 1905.

Lockhart, William S.
   4208. <u>The Ministry of Worship: A Study of the Need,
          Psychology and Technique of Worship</u>. Christian Bd.
          of Publication, 1927.

Loftis, Zenas Sanford, 1881-1909.
   Medical missionary to Tibet.
   4209. <u>A Message from Batang: The Diary of Z. S. Loftis,
          M.D. Missionary to Tibetans</u>. Revell, 1911.

Lollis, James A., 1909-.
   Church official.
   4210. <u>Christian Action and Community Service</u>.
          Indianapolis, 1966.
   4211. "Love Never Quits." Unified Promotion, 196_.

Longan, George W., 1819-1891.
   Pastor.
   4212. <u>Origin of the Disciples of Christ: A Review of
          Prof. W.H. Whitsitt's Volume Entitled "Origin of the
          Disciples of Christ</u>." Christian Publishing Co.,
          1889.
   4213. <u>A Symposium on the Holy Spirit</u>. Burns, 1879.
          (co-author).

Lord, Dick.
   Pastor.

4214.   "Developing Programs around the Theme of 'Peace' at Rush Creek Christian Church, Arlington, Texas." D. Min. thesis, Brite Divinity School, 1984.

Lord, James A., 1849-1922.
   Editor of the Christian Standard.
   4215.   From Darkness to Light: A Series of Autobiographical Sketches Relating to Religious Experiences, by Eminent Ministers of the Christian Church. Standard, 1907.

Lowe, Frank Melville.
   4216.   The Pastorate among the "Disciples of Christ: A Study in Vocational Guidance. Bethany, 1923.

Lucas, Daniel R., 1840-1907.
   Pastor; chaplain.
   4217.   Apostolic Hymns and Songs. Chase & Hall, 1875.
   4218.   History of the 99th Indiana Infantry. Rosser & Spring, 1865.
   4219.   New History of the 99th Indiana Infantry. Horner, 1900.
   4220.   Paul Darst: Or, A Conflict between Love and Infidelity. Central Book Concern, 1877.

Lunger, Alberta (Huff).
   Pastor.
   4221.   Roadside Tables. Bethany, 1960.

Lunger, Harold Lehman.
   Professor of Christian ethics.
   4222.   Being Christian in Our Time. 2 vols. Christian Bd. of Publication, 1963.
   4223.   The Bible and Our Social Responsibility. Bethany, 1958.
   4224.   A Citizen under God. Christian Bd. of Publication, 1973.
   4225.   Descendants of Jacob Lunger of Derrs (1811-1896) with a Discussion of His Ancestry. The Author, 1981.
   4226.   Finding Holy Ground [Sermons]. Bethany, 1957.
   4227.   A Pocket Full of Seeds, and Other Sermons. Bethany, 1954.
   4228.   The Political Ethics of Alexander Campbell. Bethany, 1954.

Lunger, Irvine Eugene, 1912-.
   College president.
   4229.   "Protestantism and the Problem of the Individual in Modern Society." Ph.D. diss., Univ. of Chicago, 1939.
   4230.   The Real Task of Institutions of Higher Education. Univ. of Kentucky, 1960.

4231. <u>Worship, a Guidance Manual for the Dept. of Worship</u>
<u>of the Local Church</u>. St. Louis, 1957.

Lynn, Robert Charles.
4232. <u>The Church Faces the Problem of Juvenile</u>
<u>Delinquency</u>. Carlton, 1965.

Lyon, K. Brynolf.
Professor of pastoral care.
4233. "Practical Theology and Human Fulfillment:" An
Essay on the Relio-Ethical Structure of Old Age."
Ph.D. Diss., Univ. of Chicago, 1982.

McBride, Neal Fletcher.
4234. "A Conceptual Diagnostic Model for Adult Christian
Education in Congregational Forms of Church
Structure." Ed.D. diss., Indiana Univ., 1975.

McCallum, William Cecil.
4235. <u>The Graded Church</u>. Bethany, 1930.

*McCash, Isaac Newton, 1861-1953.
Pastor; college president; editor of <u>American Home</u>
<u>Missionary</u>.
4236. <u>Horizon of American Missions</u>. Revell, 1913.
4237. <u>Ten Plagues of Modern Egypt</u>. Personal Help
Publishing Co., 1905.

McCasland, Selby Vernon, 1896-1970.
College professor.
4238. <u>The Bible in Our American Life...A High School Text</u>
<u>for Student Use</u>. Virginia Council of Religious
Education, 1942.
4239. <u>By the Finger of God: Demon Possession and Exorcism</u>
<u>in Early Christianity in the Light of Modern Views</u>
<u>of Mental Illness</u>. Macmillan, 1951.
4240. "The Genesis of the New Testament Narratives of the
Resurrection of Jesus." Ph.D. diss., Univ. of
Chicago, 1926.
4241. <u>The Pioneer of Our Faith: A New Life of Jesus</u>.
McGraw-Hill, 1964.
4242. <u>The Religion of the Bible</u>. Crowell, 1960.
4243. <u>Religions of the World</u>. Random House, 1969.
(co-author).
4244. <u>The Resurrection of Jesus</u>. Nelson, 1932.
4245. <u>Syllabus for Religion 1 and 2. The Literature and</u>
<u>Religion of the Bible</u>. Crowell, 1960.

McCaw, John Emory.
Professor of religion.
4246. "Formula and Freedom among the Disciples of Christ."
D. B. thesis, Univ. of Chicago, 1949.

4247. "Spiritual Motivations for Decade of the Sixties;
       Lectures..." College of Churches of Christ in
       Canada, 1960. McCaw, Mabel (Niedermeyer), 1899-.
       Writer.
4248. Bible Friends: A Cooperative Vacation Church School
       Text for Use with Children 4-8 Years Old. Bethany,
       1954.
4249. My Indian Picture Story Book. Friendship Pr., 1944.
4250. My Story Book about the Bible. Friendship Pr.,
       1947.
4251. Some Time Every Day, a Devotional Book for Junior
       Boys and Girls. Bethany, 1948.
4252. Then I Think of God, a Book of Devotional Readings
       for Children. Bethany, 1942.
4253. This is God's World: A Book on Christian
       Stewardship for Boys and Girls. Bethany, 1946.
4254. What God Can Do. Broadman Pr., 1982.

McCoy, Jerry Dan.
    Professor of religion and philosophy.
    4255. "The Doctrine of the Incarnation in a Whiteheadian
           Perspective." Ph.D. diss., Columbia Univ., 1973.

McCutchen, William N.
    Pastor.
    4256. Ministry to, with, and through Volunteers: Toward a
           Theology of Volunteerism for the Christian Church
           (Disciples of Christ)." D. Min. thesis, San
           Francisco Theological Seminary, 1984.

McDonald, Claude C., Jr.
    4257. There's Comfort in His Love. Revell, 1970.

McGarvey, John William, 1829-1911.
    Pastor; college professor and president; editor.
    4258. The Authorship of the Book of Deuteronomy, With Its
           Bearings on the Higher Criticism of the Pentateuch.
           Standard, 1902.
    4259. Autobiography. College of the Bible, Lexington,
           1960.
    4260. Chapel Talks Delivered before the Student Body of
           The College of the Bible in 1910 and 1911. Lufkin,
           Texas: Gospel Guardian, 1956.
    4261. Class Notes on Sacred History. 3 vols. 1893-1894.
    4262. A Commentary on Acts of Apostles. Wrightson, 1863.
    4263. Evidences of Christianity. 2 vols. 1891.
    4264. The Fourfold Gospel: Or, A Harmony of the Four
           Gospels. Standard, 1914. (co-author).
    4265. A Guide to Bible Study. 1897.
    4266. The J.W. McGarvey Sesquicentennial Lecture Series,
           1978-1979. Lexington Theol. Seminary, 1981.
    4267. Jesus and Jonah. 1896.
    4268. Lands of the Bible. Standard, 1880.

4269. McGarvey's Letters to Bishop McIlvaine, on "Christian Union." Holman, 18__.
4270. Matthew and Mark. Chase & Hall, 1875.
4271. New Commentary on Acts of Apostles. Standard, n.d.
4272. New Testament Evidences. College Pr., 1975.
4273. Sacred Didactics. De Hoff Publications, 1954.
4274. A Series of Fifty-Two Bible Lessons, for the Use of Intermediate and Advanced Classes in the Sunday-School. Guide, 1889.
4275. Sermons Delivered in Louisville, Kentucky, June-September, 1893. 1894.
4276. Short Essays in Biblical Criticism. Standard, 1910.
4277. Standard Bible Commentary. Standard, 1904-.
4278. Standard Commentary on the International Sunday-School Lessons. Standard, 1883.
4279. Thessalonians, Corinthians, Galatians, and Romans. Standard, 1916.
4280. What Shall We Do about the Organ? F. L. Rowe, n.d.

For works about him written by Disciple authors, see
Trimble, John Clifton under HISTORY section;
Bennett, Weldon,
Graham, Ronald W.,
Leggett, Marshall J.,
Lexington Theological Seminary and,
Stevenson, Dwight F. in GENERAL section.

McGavran, Donald Anderson, 1897-.
Missionary.
4281. The Bridges of God: A Study in the Strategy of Missions. World Dominion Pr., 1955.
4282. Church Growth and Christian Mission. Harper, 1965. (editor).
4283. "Church Growth and Mission in Jamaica." United Christian Missionary Soc., 1958.
4284. Church Growth in Jamaica. Lucknow Publishing House (India), 1962.
4285. Church Growth in Mexico. Eerdmans, 1963. (co-author).
4286. "Church Growth in West Uktal [India]." United Christian Missionary Soc., 1956.
4287. "The Church in a Revolutionary Age." Christian Board of Publication, 1955.
4288. Crucial Issues in Missions Tomorrow. Moody, 1972. (editor).
4289. "Do Churches Grow?" World Dominion Pr., 1963.
4290. "Education and the Beliefs of Popular Hinduism." Ph.D. diss., Columbia Univ., 1936.
4291. Eye of the Storm: The Great Debate in Mission. Word, 1972. (editor).
4292. God's Messengers to Mexico's Masses. Institute of Church Growth, 1962. (co-author).

4293. How Churches Grow: The New Frontiers of Mission.
       World Dominion Pr., 1959.
4294. Multiplying Churches in the Philippines. United
       Church of Christ in the Philippines, 1958.
4295. A Study of the Life and Growth of the Church of the
       Disciples of Christ in Puerto Rico.... United
       Christian Missionary Soc., 19__ .
4296. Understanding Church Growth. Eerdmans, 1970.

McKiernan-Allen, Linda.
4297. "Colleagues in Marriage and Ministry." In Women
       Ministers, pp. 169-82. Edited by J. Weidman. 1981.
       (co-author).

Macklin, W.E., 1886-1927.
   Missionary to China.
4298. "Life of Thomas Jefferson." Christian College Pr.
       (Nanking), 1903. (co-author).

*McLean, Archibald, 1850-1920.
   Pastor; college president; church official.
4299. Alexander Campbell as a Preacher: A Study. Revell,
       1908.
4300. Epoch Makers of Modern Missions. Revell, 1912.
4301. Handbook of Missions. 1897.
4302. The History of the Foreign Christian Missionary
       Society. Revell, 1921.
4303. Missionary Addresses. 1895.
4304. Where the Book Speaks, or Mission Studies in the
       Bible. Revell, 1907.

For works about him written by Disciple authors, see
Warren, William Robinson under THEOLOGY section.

McLellan, Hugh, 1870- .
   Pastor.
4305. Hugh McLellan's Sermons. Bethany, 1928.

McNeill, Robert Hayes, 1946- .
   Church official.
4306. "Historical Address...Delivered July 3, 1949 at
       Beaver Creek, North Carolina: In Celebration of the
       Founding of the Beaver Creek Baptist Church, Wilkes
       County, North Carolina." 1949.

McQuiddy, J. Clayton, 1858-1924.
4307. The Profitable Word. Gospel Advocate, 1925.

Madearis, Dale W.
4308. Facts about Our Churches and a Changing America.
       United Christian Missionary Soc., 1956.
       (co-author).

Manire, Benjamin F., 1828-1911.
 Pastor.
 4309. <u>Conversion: A Series of Sermons</u>. Messenger, 1895.

Mankamyer, Orlin Le Roy, 1903-.
 4310. <u>The Holy Spirit, His Office and His Work</u>. 1951?
 4311. <u>Personal Worker's Hand-Book</u>. Rowe, 1934.

Marshall, Frank Hamilton, 1868-1956.
 College administrator.
 4312. "The Judaizing Faction at Corinth." Ph.D. diss.,
         Yale Univ., 1927.
 4313. <u>Phillips University's First Fifty Years (October 9,
         1906 - October 9, 1956)</u>. Phillips Univ., 1957-.
 4314. <u>The Religious Backgrounds of Early Christianity</u>.
         Bethany, 1931.

For works about him written by Disciple authors, see
Myers, Oma Lou under HISTORY section.

Marshall, Levi, 1856-1927.
 Pastor.
 4315. <u>Rivets for Truth</u>. Christian Publishing Co., 1909.

Martin, J. Lemuel, 1810-1871.
 4316. <u>The Voice of the Seven Thunders: Or, Lectures on
         the Apocalypse</u>. Bosworth, 1870.

*Martin, Sylvester Mitchell, 1857-1937.
 Pastor; evangelist; educator.
 4317. <u>Thirty Years on the Firing-Line, Shots from the
         Battery of Truth Which Have Been Somewhat Effective
         against the Entrenchment of Sin, the Follies of Our
         Days, and the Errors of the Religious World</u>.
         Standard, 1920.

Martindale, Elijah, 1793-1874.
 4318. <u>Autobiography and Sermons of Elder Elijah
         Martindale, also Pioneer History of the Boyd Family</u>.
         Carlton & Hollenbeck, 1892.

Maschke, Ruby.
 4319. <u>Disciples of Christ Story-N-Puzzle Book</u>. Standard,
         1983.

Mason, David V.
 Pastor.

 4320. "A Critical Study of Friendship in Single Life and
         Its Relationship to Church Singles Groups and the
         General Fellowship of the Church." D. Min. thesis,
         San Francisco Theol. Seminary, 1984.

Mathes, James Madison, 1808-1892.
    4321. <u>The Western Preacher</u>. Bedford, Ind., 1865.
    4322. <u>Debate on Baptism and Kindred Subjects</u>... Bosworth,
           1868.

Matthews, William R.
    Pastor.
    4323. <u>Autobiography</u>. 1950.

Maus, Cynthia Pearl, 1880-1970.
    Christian educator.
    4324. <u>Christ and the Fine Arts: An Anthology of Pictures,
           Poetry, Music, and Stories Centering in the Life of
           Christ</u>. Harper, 1938.
    4325. <u>Great Paintings of the Life of Jesus</u>. Pulpit Book
           Club, 1951.
    4326. <u>The Old Testament and the Fine Arts: An Anthology
           of Pictures, Poetry, Music, and Stories Covering the
           Old Testament</u>. Harper, 1954. (compiler).
    4327. <u>Puerto Rico in Pictures and Poetry</u>. Caxton
           Printers, 1941. (compiler).
    4328. <u>Teaching the Youth of the Church</u>. Doran, 1925.
    4329. <u>Time to Remember: The Memoirs of Cynthia Pear Maus</u>.
           Exposition, 1964.
    4330. <u>The World's Great Madonnas: An Anthology of
           Pictures, Poetry, Music, and Stories Centering in
           the Life of the Madonna and Her Son--Music Section</u>.
           Harper, 1947. (co-author).
    4331. <u>Youth and Creative Living: A Practical Guide-Book
           for Youth and Leaders of Youth in the Field of
           Character Growth</u>. Long & R. R. Smith, 1932.
    4332. <u>Youth and the Church: A Manual for Teachers and
           Leaders of Intermediates, Seniors and Young People</u>.
           Standard, 1919.
    4333. <u>Youth Organized for Religious Education</u>. Bethany,
           1925.

Medbury, Charles Sanderson, 1865-1932.
    4334. <u>From Eden to the Jordan: A Series of Lessons in the
           Pentateuch</u>. Standard, 1909.
    4335. <u>From the Jordan to the Throne of Saul</u>. Standard,
           1910.
    4336. <u>From the Throne of Saul to Bethlehem</u>. Standard,
           1911.
    4337. <u>Mobilizing the Mind of America</u>. League To Enforce
           Peace, 1918.

For works about him written by Disciple authors, see
    Miller, Raphael Harwood under THEOLOGY section.

Medearis, Dale W.
    Church official.

4338. The Congregation Plans for Action. Indianapolis,
        1966.
4339. Disciples of Christ in Town and Country. United
        Christian Missionary Soc., 1959.
4340. Facts about Our Churches and a Changing America.
        United Christian Missionary Soc., 1956.

Merrell, James L.
    4341. They Live Their Faith: Portraits of Men and Women
            with a Mission. Bethany, 1965.

Merritt, George W.
    Pastor.
    4342. Truth for Today [Five Minute Radio Sermons]. Gospel
            Advocate, 1976.

Metze, Mabel.
    Christian educator.
    4343. Christian Education. Indianapolis, 1966.
    4344. Christian Education, a Guidance Manual for the Dept.
            of Christian Education of the Local Church. St.
            Louis, 1957.

Meyer, Marvin W.
    Professor of religion.
    4345. The Institute for Antiquity and Christianity Report,
            1972-80. The Institute, 1981. (editor).
    4346. The Letter of Peter to Philip: Text, Translation,
            and Commentary. Scholars Pr., 1981.
    4347. "The Mithras Liturgy." Scholars Pr., 1976. (editor
            and translator).
    4348. The Secret Teachings of Jesus: Four Gnostic
            Gospels. Random House, 1984. (translator).
    4349. Who Do People Say I Am?: The Interpretation of
            Jesus in the New Testament Gospels. Eerdmans, 1983.

Miles, John and Sara.
    Missionaries to Congo.
    4350. Bible Ethics. International Correspondence
            Institute (Brussels), 1979.

Miller, Dale, 1923-.
    Professor of religion.
    4351. The Adult Son. Wallace-Homestead, 1974.
    4352. Death Penalty Update. Drake Univ., 1977. (editor).
    4353. Let Us Break Bread Together. Bethany, 1971.
            (co-author).
    4354. "Protestantism and Politics in Rhode Island:
            1636-1657." Ph.D. diss., Univ. of Chicago, 1955.
    4355. A Special Kind of Mother. Wallace-Homestead, 1974.
    4356. The Termination of Age: A Conference on Death and
            Dying. Des Moines, Ia., 1975. (editor).

Miller, James Blair, 1916- .
    Professor of Christian education.
    4357. Our Church's Story: Teacher's Edition. Christian
           Bd. of Publication, 1961.
    4358. "Patterns of Disagreement Concerning Religion in
           Relation to Public Education in the United States."
           Ed.D. diss., Indiana Univ., 1955.
    4359. Teacher's Book: Year Six, Fall. Judson, 1952.

Miller, Raphael Harwood, 1874-1963.
    Pastor; editor of Christian Evangelist.
    4360. "Augustus O Thomas." In Addresses and Proceedings.
           National Education Association of the United States,
           1935.
    4361. Charles S. Medbury, Preacher and Master Workman for
           Christ. Christian Bd. of Publication, 1932.
    4362. Who Lives in You [Sermons]. Bethany, 1935.

*Milligan, Robert, 1814-1875.
    College president and professor; editor of Millennial
    Harbinger.
    4363. Analysis of the New Testament. 1874.
    4364. The Divine Scheme of Redemption. Bethany, 1957,
           c1868.
    4365. Epistle to the Hebrews. Chase & Hall, 1876.

Minard, Herbert Leslie, 1908- .
    4366. Christian Youth in Wartime Service. Chicago, 1943.
    4367. A Manual for Leaders of Intermediates. Christian
           Bd. of Publication, 1937.
    4368. We Learn about the Church: The Meaning of Church
           Membership. Christian Bd. of Publication, 1941.

Minck, Franklin Henry, 1904- .
    4369. Christian Stewardship. Indianapolis, 194_.
           (co-author).

Moeller, Harold Carl, 1945- .
    4370. "Toward a Post-Revolutionary Theological Foundation
           for the Overseas Ministries Enterprise of the
           Christian Church (Disciples of Christ)." D. Min.
           thesis, School of Theology at Claremont, 1977.

Moffett, Robert, 1835-1908.
    Church official; evangelist.
    4371. Seeking the Old Paths and Other Sermons. Cleveland,
           1899.
Moninger, Herbert, 1876-1911.
    4372. The Adult Bible Class in Training for Service.
           Standard, 1910.
    4373 Bible Drills. Standard, 1908.
    4374. Fifty Lessons in Training for Service. Standard,
           1907.

4375. Forty-Two Lessons in Training for Service.
       Standard, 1909.
4376. Matthew's Gospel at the Point of a Question.
       Standard, 1909.
4377. The New Testament Church. Standard, 1908.
4378. 101 Things for Adult Bible Classes To Do. Standard,
       1911.
4379. Preparatory Training Course for Children between the
       Ages of Eight and Fifteen. Standard, 1909.
4380. Standard Commentary on the International
       Sunday-School Lessons. Standard, 1883-19__.
4381. Studies in the Gospels and Acts. Standard, 1908.
4382. What's the Answer? For Use in Intermediate and
       Adult Classes, Class Socials, etc. Standard, 1908.

Monroe, Herald B.
    Christian educator.
4383. The Christian Youth Fellowship: Recreation and
       Social Life Manual. Christian Bd. of Publication,
       1942.

Monser, John Waterhaus.
4384. The Literature of the Disciples: A Study.
       Christian Publishing Co., 1906.

Montgomery, John Dexter, 1891-.
    Missionary to Jamaica and Mexico.
4385. Disciples of Christ in Argentina, 1906-1956: A
       History of the First Fifty Years of Mission Work.
       Bethany, 1956.
4386. "Recent Tendencies in Religious Idealism in South
       America." Ph.D. diss., Univ. of Chicago, 1933.
4387. Teaching Adults: In-Service Leader's Guide."
       United Christian Missionary Soc., n.d.

Montgomery, Riley Benjamin, 1895-.
    Bible college president.
4388. The Education of Ministers of Disciples of Christ.
       Bethany, 1931.
4389. The Living God Calls [Sermons]. Lexington, 1965.
4390. The Ministry of All Believers: The Pastoral Role of
       the Christian Ministry. College of the Bible
       (Lexington), 1962.
4391. The Newspaper Story of Lynchburg College, Session
       1947-1948. Lexington, 1972.
4392. Reminiscences. Lexington, 1974.

Moore, George Voiers, 1897-.
    Professor of pastoral theology.
4393. The Art of Church Membership. Bethany, 1942.
4394. Better Church Leaders. Bethany, 1950.
4395. Centennial Directory of the College of the Bible.
       College of the Bible (Lexington), 1965. (editor).

4396. Improving the Small Church School. Bethany, 1932.
4397. In All Things: The Perfecting of the Pastoral
       Minister. College of the Bible (Lexington), 1956.
4398. Interchurch Cooperation in Kentucky, 1865 to 1965.
       Keystone Printery, 1965.
4399. "Values Discovered in the Supervision of College and
       University Student Leaders in Religious Education."
       Ph.D. diss., Univ. of Chicago, 1934.

Moore, Paul L.
   Pastor.
4400. Seven Words of Men around the Cross. Abingdon,
       1963.

Moore, William Joseph, 1903-.
   Pastor; professor of religion.
4401. New Testament Concept of the Ministry. Bethany,
       1956.
4402. "A Study of the Concept of the Mighty Word in
       Ancient Hebrew Literature." Ph.D. diss., Univ. of
       Chicago, 1940.

Moore, William Thomas, 1832-1926.
   Pastor; college professor.
4403. At Seventy-Five, and Other Poems. Christian
       Publishing Co., 1907.
4404. Biographies and Sermons of Pioneer Preachers.
       Goodpasture, 1954. (co-editor).
4405. A Comprehensive History of the Disciples of Christ.
       Revell, 1909.
4406. The Fundamental Error of Christendom. Christian
       Publishing Co., 1902.
4407. Heroes and Heroes; Or, The Triumphs of Faith, Hope
       and Love [Poem]. Foreign Christian Missionary Soc.,
       1900.
4408. Inaugural Service Held on Tuesday Evening, January
       21, 1896. Columbia, Mo., 1896.
4409. The Life of Timothy Coop. Christian Commonwealth
       Publishing Co, (London), 1889.
4410. The Living Pulpit of the Christian Church. Carroll,
       1868. (editor).
4411. Losing Life and Finding It. A Memorial Sermon on
       the Life & Character of the Christian Statesman,
       James Abram Garfield... Partridge (London), 188_?
4412. Man Preparing for Other Worlds...A Study of Man in
       the Light of the Bible, Science and Experience.
       Christian Publishing Co., 1904.
4413. The New Living Pulpit of the Christian Church.
       Christian Bd. of Publication, 1918.
4414. "Our Strength and Our Weakness. An Address before
       the American Christian Missionary Society..."
       Cincinnati, 1865.

4415. The Plea of the Disciples of Christ. Christian
       Century Co., 1906.
4416. Preacher Problems. Revell, 1907.
4417. Supremacy of the Heart Life. Revell, 1908.
4418. Views of Life: Addresses on the Social and
       Religious Questions of the Age. Cincinnati, 1869.

*Morehouse, Daniel Walter, 1876-1941.
   Astronomer; college president.
   4419. International Convention, Disciples of Christ, San
          Antonio, Texas, October 15-20, 1935: Sermons, and
          Addresses. Christian Bd. of Publication, 1936.
   4420. International Reference Work. Holst Publishing Co.,
          1927. (co-editor).
   4421. The New Teachers' and Pupils' Cyclopedia. 8 vols.
          Holst Publishing Co., 1927.

Morris, Donald Bryan.
   Pastor.
   4422. "Ministering to the Needs of Our People." D. Min.
          thesis, Andover Newton Theological School, 1983.

*Morrison, Charles Clayton, 1874-1966.
   Pastor; editor of Christian Century, Pulpit, Christendom.
   4423. The Meaning of Baptism. Disciples Publication Soc.,
          1914.
   4424. The Outlawry Of War: A Constructive Policy for
          World Peace. Willett, Clark & Colby, 1927.
   4425. The Unfinished Reformation. Books for Libraries
          Pr., 1968, c1953.

See also, Deloff, Linda-Marie in GENERAL section.

Morrison, Hugh Tucker, 1877-.
   4426. Logan Place. Springfield, Ill., 1938.
   4427. Mysterious Omissions: An Interpretation of Certain
          Unresolved Issues in the New Testament Church. Univ.
          of Chicago, 1969.
   4428. "Religion." W. B. Blakemore, 1971.
   4429. A Theory of Pitch and Range in Voice Production.
          Annals of American Research, 1953.
   4430. The Unrecorded Biographical Years. Springfield,
          Ill., 1966.

*Morton, Clement Manly, 1884-1976.
   Pastor; evangelist; missionary; seminary professor.
   4431. Adventures in Prayer. Revell, 1966.
   4432. Isle of Enchantment: Stories and People of Puerto
          Rico. Bethany, 1970.
   4433. Paraguay, the Inland Republic. Powell & White,
          1926.

Moseley, Joseph Edward, 1910-1973.
    Church official.
      4434. The Concern for Benevolence Among Disciples of
            Christ, a Study Course for Older Young People and
            Adults. Christian Bd. of Publication, 1957.
      4435. Disciples of Christ in Georgia. Bethany, 1954.
      4436. Evangelism - Commitment and Involvement. Bethany,
            1965. (editor).
      4437. My Dad, Preacher, Pastor, Person: Thirty-Four
            Disciples of Christ Ministers Interpreted by a Son
            or Daughter. Christian Bd. of Publication, 1938.
            (co-editor).
      4438. "Open Wide and Say Ahhhh! Immersed in History
            [Address]." Disciples of Christ Historical Soc.,
            1966.
      4439. The Spanish-Speaking People of the Southwest.
            Council on Spanish-American Work, 1966. (editor).
      4440. "Unfair to Wastebaskets [Address]." Disciples of
            Christ Historical Soc., 1965.
      4441. Using Drama in the Church. Bethany, 1939.
            (co-author).

Moses, Helen Elizabeth (Turney), 1853-1908.
    President of Christian Woman's Board of Missions.
      4442. Helen E. Moses, of the Christian Woman's Board of
            Missions: Biographical Sketch, Memorial Tributes,
            Missionary Addresses By Mrs. Moses, Sonnets and
            Other Verses. Revell, 1909.

Moss, J. J., 1806-1895.
      4443. Criticism, Exegesis and Interpretation of Scripture,
            and Scripture References. Cincinnati, 1887.

Mullendore, William.
      4444. The Urge of the Unrational in Religion. Stratford,
            1930.

Mullins, George Gatewood.
    Pastor.
      4445. My Life Is an Open Book [Sermons]. J. Burns, 1883.

Munnell, Thomas, 1823-1898.
    Pastor; college professor.
      4446. The Care of All the Churches. Christian Publishing
            Co., 1888.
      4447. Discussion, Shall Christians Go To War? Bosworth,
            Chase & Hall, 1872.

      4448. Evangelists and Their Work in the Churches.
            Christian Publishing Co., 1887.
      4449. Setting Churches in Order: How To Do It. Christian
            Publishing Co., n.d.

4450. A Symposium on the Holy Spirit. Burns, 1879.
       (co-author).

Munro, Harry Clyde, 1890-1962.
    Pastor; missionary; editor; college professor.
    4451. Agencies for the Religious Education of Adolescents.
           Bethany, 1925.
    4452. "As Protestants We Believe." United Christian
           Missionary Soc., 19__.
    4453. Be Glad You're a Protestant! Bethany, 1948.
    4454. Christian Education in Your Church. Bethany, 1933.
    4455. The Church as a School. Bethany, 1929.
    4456. The Director of Religious Education. Westminster,
           1930.
    4457. The Effective Adult Class. Bethany, 1934.
    4458. Fellowship Evangelism through Church Groups.
           Bethany, 1951.
    4459. How To Increase Your Sunday School. Bethany, 1926.
    4460. The Pastor and Religious Education. Abingdon, 1930.
    4461. Protestant Nurture: An Introduction to Christian
           Education. Prentice-Hall, 1956.
    4462. Vacation Church School Manual for the Teacher.
           Bethany, 1924.
    4463. Why Should I Teach? Bethany, 1946.

*Murch, James DeForest, 1892-1973.
    Pastor; journalist; seminary president.
    4464. Adventuring for Christ in Changing Times: An
           Autobiography of James DeForest Murch. Restoration
           Pr., 1973.
    4465. B. D. Phillips: Life and Letters. Standard, 1969.
    4466. Christian Education and the Local Church: History,
           Principles, Practice. Standard, 1943.
    4467. Christian Minister's Manual. Standard, 1937.
    4468. Christians Only, a History of the Restoration
           Movement. Standard, 1962.
    4469. Cooperation without Compromise. Eerdmans, 1956.
    4470. The Free Church. Restoration Pr., 1966.
    4471. God Still Lives: A Testimony and a Challenge by a
           Latter-Day Christian. Christian Action, 1941.
    4472. The Protestant Revolt: Road to Freedom for American
           Churches. Crestwood Books, 1967.
    4473. 600 Doctrinal Illustrations. Standard, 1941.
           (co-author).
    4474. Studies in Christian Living. Christian Action,
           1937.
    4475. The Sword and the Trowel: Exile and Restoration.
           Regal Books, 1968.
    4476. Teach Me To Pray. Standard, 1958.
    4477. Teach or Perish! An Imperative for Christian
           Education at the Local Church Level. Eerdmans,
           1961.

Murphy, Frederick Ira, 1933-.
    Pastor.
    4478.   "The American Christian Press and Pre-War Hitler's
             Germany, 1933-1939." Ph.D. diss., Univ. of Florida,
             1970.

Murphy, Paul D., 1913-.
    Pastor.
    4479.   Heart Pricking Sermons. Murphy, 1975.

Murrell, Arthur Van, 1929-.
    Pastor; journalist; seminary professor.
    4480.   "The Effects of Exclusivism in the Separation of the
             Churches of Christ from the Christian Church."
             Ph.D. diss., Vanderbilt Univ., 1972.

*Myers, Robert Edward, 1932-.
    Professor of philosophy.
    4481.   C. S. Lewis and Religious Knowledge. Angora,
             1975-76.
    4482.   "The Elusive Self and the Intimidating Other." In
             Philosophers Look at Science Fiction. Nelson-Hall,
             1982.
    4483.   The Intersection of Science Fiction and Philosophy:
             Critical Studies. Greenwood, 1983. (editor).
    4484.   "Jack Williamson." In Science Fiction Writers.
             Scribner's, 1982.
    4485.   Jack Williamson, a Primary and Secondary
             Bibliography. Hall, 1980.
    4486.   "Philosophic Insight through Science Fiction." In
             Teaching Science Fiction. Owlswick, 1980.

Nakarai, Toyozo Wada, 1898-1984.
    Professor of religion.
    4487.   Biblical Hebrew. Bookman, 1951.
    4488.   An Elder's Public Prayers. Carlton, 1968.
    4489.   Notes on the Revised Standard Version. 1954.
    4490.   Shin Tossa Nikki. Indiana Lincoln Foundation, 1962.
             (co-author).
    4491.   A Study of the Impact of Buddhism upon Japanese Life
             as Revealed in the Odes of the Kokin-Shu. Mitchell,
             1931.

Nance, Ellwood Cecil.
    4492.   Florida Christians, Disciples of Christ. College
             Pr., 1941.
    4493.   From Dust to Divinity. Tribune Pr., 1935.

Nation, Carry Amelia Moore, 1846-1911.
    Temperance activist.
    4494.   The Use and Need of the Life of Carry A. Nation.
             Steves & Sons, 1904.

Needleman, Jacob.
    Professor of philosophy.
    4495. The Heart of Philosophy. Knopf, 1982.
    4496. Lost Christianity. Doubleday, 1980.
    4497. The New Religions. Crossroad, 1984, c1970.
    4498. On the Way To Self Knowledge. Knopf, 1976.
            (co-editor).
    4499. Religion for a New Generation. Macmillan, 1977.
            (co-editor).
    4500. Speaking of My Life: The Art of Living in the
            Cultural Revolution. Harper & Row, 1979.
    4501. The Sword of Gnosis: Metaphysics. Cosmology.
            Tradition. Symbolism: Essays. Penguin Books, 1974.
            (compiler).
    4502. Understanding the New Religions. Seabury, 1978.
            (co-editor).

Nelson, John Robert, 1920-.
    Missionary to Tunisia.
    4503. The Changing Face of Methodism. Cathedral, 1972.
    4504. Christian Unity in North America. A Symposium.
            Bethany, 1958.
    4505. Church Union in Focus: Guide for Adult Group Study.
            United Church Pr., 1968.
    4506. Crisis in Unity and Witness. Geneva, 1968.
    4507. Criterion for the Church. Abingdon, 1963.
    4508. Fifty Years of Faith and Order. National Student
            Christian Federation, 1963. (co-author).
    4509. The Lawson-Vanderbilt Affair: Letters to Dean
            Nelson. Nashville, 1960.
    4510. Let Us Pray for Unity. Upper Room, 1963.
    4511. No Man Is Alien: Essays on the Unity of Mankind.
            Brill, 1971. (editor).
    4512. One Lord. One Church. Association Pr., 1958.
    4513. The Realm of Redemption: Studies in the Doctrine of
            the Nature of the Church in Contemporary Protestant
            Theology. 4th ed. Epworth, 1957.
    4514. "A Theology to Match the Church's Opportunity."
            Vanderbilt Univ. Pr., 1958.

Nelson, Joseph Lee, 1923-.
    Professor of religion.
    4515. "The Groaning of Creation: An Exegetical Study of
            Romans 8:18-27." Ph.D. diss., Union Theology
            Seminary, Richmond, Va., 1969.

Nelson, Robert Gilbert.
    Church official; missionary.
    4516. The Centennial of Disciples of Christ in Jamaica
            [Address]. 1958?
    4517. Congo Crisis and Christian Mission. Bethany, 1961.
    4518. Disciples of Christ in Jamaica. 1858-1958. Bethany,
            1958.

Nelson, William Verner.
 4519. <u>Vacation Bible School Handbook</u>. Standard, 1942.

Neth, John Watson.
 Pastor; journalist.
 4520. <u>Walter Scott Speaks: A Handbook of Doctrine</u>.
   Emmanuel School of Religion, 1967.

Nichols, Rodney Ralph.
 Professor of philosophy.
 4521. "Being and Symbol in Paul Tillich." Ph.D. diss.,
   Univ. of Missouri, 1974.

Nixon, Ray L.
 4522. "An Order of Mission in the Local Church." D. Min.
   thesis, Phillips Univ. Graduate Seminary, 1981.

Nooe, Roger Theophilus, 1881-.
 4523. "Prayers." Disciples of Christ Historical Soc.,
   1968.

Nordgulen, George.
 Professor of religion.
 4524. <u>Perspectives in World Religious</u>. 2 vols. P. Lal
   (Calcutta), 1981.
 4525. <u>A Witness to God: A History of the Mt. Zion</u>
   <u>Christian Church [Madison County, Kentucky]</u>. 1982.

Norton, Herman Albert.
 Seminary administrator; pastor; historian.
 4526. "The Organization and Function of the Confederate
   Military Chaplaincy, 1861-1865." Ph.D. diss.,
   Vanderbilt Univ., 1965.
 4527. <u>Prayers Offered by the Chaplain, Reverend Herman A.</u>
   <u>Norton at the Opening of the Daily Sessions of the</u>
   <u>Senate of Tennessee during the Seventy-Seventh</u>
   <u>General Assembly</u>. Nashville? 1951?
 4528. <u>Rebel Religion: The Story of Confederate Chaplains</u>.
   Bethany, 1961.
 4529. <u>Religion in Tennessee, 1777-1945</u>. Univ. of
   Tennessee Pr., 1981.
 4530. <u>Struggling for Recognition</u>. Dept. of the Army,
   1977.
 4531. <u>Tennessee Christians: A History of the Christian</u>
   <u>Church (Disciples of Christ) in Tennessee</u>. Reed,
   1971.

Nottingham, William Jesse, 1927-.
 Pastor; missionary to France; church official.
 4532. <u>Christian Faith and Secular Action: An Introduction</u>
   <u>to the Life and Thought of Jacques Maritain</u>.
   Bethany, 1968.
 4533. <u>God's Underground</u>. Bethany, 1970. (translator).

4534. The Practice and Preaching of Liberation. CBP Pr.,
       1986.
4535. Prayer at the Heart of Life, by Pierre-Yves Emery.
       Obis, 1975. (translator).

O'Neall, Kelly, 1890-.
4536. I Have Called You Friends. Bethany, 1954.
4537. Paths the Master Trod, Lenten Meditations. Bethany,
       1951.
4538. Rhyme, Rhythm, and Reason: Poems With a Punch.
       Bethany, 195_.

Osborn, George Edwin, 1897-1965.
Professor of practical theology.
4539. Christian Worship, a Service Book. Christian Bd. of
       Publication, 1953.
4540. "The Disciples of Christ and Worship." 1952.
4541. A Faith To Live By. Christian Bd. of Publication,
       1945.
4542. The Glory of Christian Worship. Christian
       Theological Seminary Pr., 1960.
4543. "The Psychology of Christian Public Worship." Ph.D.
       diss., Univ. of Edinburgh, 1932.
4544. "Training the Devotional Life." United Christian
       Missionary Soc., 19__.

*Osborn, Ronald Edwin, 1917-.
Pastor; editor; professor of church history; seminary
administrator.
4545. Christian Ministry in Today's World. Bethany, 1967.
4546. A Church for These Times. Abingdon, 1965.
4547. "Disciples of Christ." In The American Church of
       the Protestant Heritage, pp. 387-412. Edited by
       Vergilius Ture Anselm Ferm. Greenwood, 1972, c1953.
4548. Disciples and the Church Universal. Disciples of
       Christ Historical Soc., 1967.
4549. The Education of Ministers for the Coming Age. CBP
       Pr., 1987.
4550. Experiment in Liberty: The Ideal of Freedom in the
       Experience of the Disciples of Christ. Bethany,
       1978.
4551. The Faith We Affirm: Basic Beliefs of Disciple of
       Christ. Bethany, 1979.
4552. In Christ's Place: Christian Ministry in Today's
       World. Bethany, 1967.
4553. A Man Who Wrote Scripture. Christian Bd. of
       Publication, 1945. (editor).
4554. "The Reformation of Tradition." In The Renewal of
       the Church, vol. 1. Bethany, 1963. (editor).
4555. Restructure...Toward the Christian Church (Disciples
       of Christ). Christian Bd. of Publication, 1966.
4556. The Spirit of American Christianity. Harper, 1958.

See also, McAllister, Lester G. in GENERAL section.

Owen, George Earle.
    Missionary; church official.
    4557.   A Century of Witness, 1875-1975 [A History of Downey
            Avenue Christian Church]. Christian Church
            Services, 1975.
    4558.   Faith and Freedom: The Problem of Religious Freedom
            and the Christian Answer. Philippine Federation of
            Christian Churches, 1953.
    4559.   The Nature of Prayer: As Reflected and Interpreted
            by Selected Poems. The Author, 1975.
    4560.   Voices: Selected Poetry from the Writings of George
            Earle Owen, edited by Margaret Richards Owen.
            Margaret Richards Owen, 1982.

Owens, Robert J.
    Professor of religion.
    4561.   The Genesis and Exodus Citations of Aphrahat, the
            Persian Sage. E.J. Brill, 1983.

Page, Kirby, 1890-1957.
    Pastor; evangelist.
    4562.   The Abolition of War. Doran, 1924. (co-author).
    4563.   An American Peace Policy. Doran, 1925.
    4564.   Capitalism and Its Rivals. Eddy & Page, 1936?
    4565.   Christianity and Economic Problems, Facts,
            Principles, Programs: A Discussion Group Text-Book.
            Association Pr., 1922.
    4566.   Christianity and Industry. Doran, 1921-22.
            (co-author).
    4567.   Collective Bargaining: An Ethical Evaluation....
            Doran, 1921.
    4568.   Creative Pioneers. Association Pr., 1937.
            (co-author).
    4569.   Danger Zones of the Social Order. Doran, 1926.
            (co-author).
    4570.   Dollars and World Peace. Doran, 1927.
    4571.   France and the Peace of Europe. Doran, 1923.
    4572.   How To Find the Will of God? Tidings, 1954.
            (co-author).
    4573.   How To Keep America Out of War. Fellowship of
            Reconciliation (New York), 1939.
    4574.   How To Pray. Source, 1952.
    4575.   Imperialism and Nationalism: A Study of Conflict in
            the Near East and of the Territorial and Economic
            Expansion of the United States. Doran, 1925.
    4576.   Incentives in Modern Life: Are the Motives of Jesus
            Practicable in Modern Business and Professional
            Life? Doran, 1922.
    4577.   Individualism and Socialism: An Ethical Survey of
            Economic and Political Forces. Farrar & Rinehart,
            1933.

4578. <u>Industrial Facts</u>. Doran, 1921.
4579. <u>Is Mahatma Gandhi the Greatest Man of the Age? A</u>
<u>Biographical Interpretation and an Analysis of the</u>
<u>Political Situation in India</u>. K. Page, 1930.
4580. <u>Jesus or Christianity: A Study in Contrasts</u>.
Doubleday, Doran, 1929.
4581. <u>Kirby Page and the Social Gospel: An Anthology</u>.
Garland, 1976.
4582. <u>The Light Is Still Shining in the Darkness; 30</u>
<u>Complete Services of Worship</u>. La Habra, Calif.,
1946.
4583. <u>Living Abundantly: A Study of Creative Pioneer</u>
<u>Groups through Twenty-Seven Centuries of Exploration</u>
<u>of Pathways to Joyous and Abundant Life</u>. Farrar &
Rinehart, 1944. (editor).
4584. <u>Living Courageously</u>. Farrar & Rinehart, 1936.
4585. <u>Living Creatively</u>. Farrar & Rinehart, 1932.
4586. <u>Living Joyously: An Anthology of Devotional</u>
<u>Readings for 365 Days</u>. Rinehart, 1950.
4587. <u>Living Prayerfully: How to Experience Life's</u>
<u>Deepest Satisfactions and Serve Mankind Most</u>
<u>Effectively</u>. Farrar & Rinehart, 1941.
4588. <u>Living Triumphantly</u>. Farrar & Rinehart, 1936.
4589. <u>Makers of Freedom: Biographical Sketches in Social</u>
<u>Progress</u>. Books for Libraries Pr., 1970, c1926.
4590. <u>Must We Go To War</u>? Farrar & Rinehart, 1937.
4591. <u>National Defense: A Study of the Origins, Results</u>
<u>and Prevention of War</u>. Farrar & Rinehart, 1931.
4592. <u>A New Economic Order</u>. Harcourt, 1930.
4593. <u>Now Is the Time To Prevent a Third World War</u>.
Garland, 1972, c1946.
4594. <u>Pamphlets and Essays</u>. 5 vols. 1923-53.
4595. <u>Pamphlets on War and Peace</u>. Doran, 1923-27.
4596. <u>The Personality of Jesus</u>. Association Pr., 1932.
4597. <u>Power from the Bible. Selected Devotional Readings</u>.
K. Page, 195_.
4598. <u>Property</u>. Eddy & Page, 1936?
4599. <u>Recent Gains in American Civilization</u>. Harcourt,
1928. (editor).
4600. <u>Religious Resources for Personal Living and Social</u>
<u>Action</u>. Farrar & Rinehart, 1939.
4601. <u>The Renunciation of War</u>. Doubleday, 1928.
4602. <u>Something More, a Consideration of the Vast,</u>
<u>Undeveloped Resources of Life</u>. Association Pr.,
1920.
4603. <u>The Sword or the Cross, Which Should Be the Weapon</u>
<u>of the Church Militant</u>? Christian Century Pr.,
1921.
4604. <u>The Sword or the Cross: An Examination of War in</u>
<u>the Light of Jesus' Way of Life</u>. 2d ed. Doran,
1922.
4605. <u>20,870 Clergymen on War and Economic Injustice</u>. K.
Page, 1934.

4606. <u>The United States Steel Corporation: An Analysis of the Social Consequences of Modern Business Policies</u>. Doran, 1922.
4607. <u>War: Its Causes, Consequences and Cure</u>. Doran, 1923.
4608. <u>What Shall We Do about War</u>? Eddy & Page, 1935.
4609. <u>The Will of God for These Days</u>. La Habra, Calif., 1945.

Painter, J. H.
4610. <u>The Iowa Pulpit of the Church of Christ, Its Aim and Work</u>. J. Burns, 1884. (editor).

Palmer, Ralph T.
4611. "A Project to Provide Marriage Enrichment in a Christian Context." D. Min. thesis, Phillips Univ., 1973.
4612. <u>Some Problems in Modern Missionary Recruitment</u>. United Christian Missionary Soc., 1960.

Paregien, Stanley, 1941-.
4613. <u>The Day Jesus Died [Sermons]</u>. Firm Foundation, 1970.
4614. <u>Twenty-Six Lessons on the Gospel of John</u>. College Pr., 1984, c1977.

Parrott, Rodney L.
Seminary administrator.
4615. "Paul's Political Thought: Romans 13:1-7 in the Light of Hellenistic Political Thought." Ph.D. diss., Claremont Graduate School, 1980.

Parry, Wilbur Clyde, 1900-.
Pastor, Christian educator.
4616. <u>Christian Education for Adults</u>. Bethany, 1946.

Partin, Harry Baxter, 1925-.
Professor of history of religions.
4617. "The Muslim Pilgrimage." Ph.D. diss., Univ. of Chicago, 1967.
4618. <u>Religious and Spiritual Groups in Modern America</u>. 2d. ed. Prentice Hall, 1988. (co-author).

Paternoster, Ira A.
Church official.
4619. <u>The Disciples of Christ in South Africa</u>. Indianapolis, n.d.
4620. <u>Latin American "Consulta</u>." Indianapolis, 1970.

*Patrick, Dale Alfred, 1938-.
Professor of Old Testament and religious thought.
4621. <u>Arguing with God: The Angry Prayers of Job</u>. Bethany, 1977.

4622. Old Testament Law. John Knox, 1985.
4623. The Rendering of God in the Old Testament.
       Fortress, 1981.

Paul, Charles Thomas, 1869-1940.
    Pastor; college professor; editor.
    4624. The Call of China: New Missionaries for the New Era
           in the New Republic. College of Missions
           (Indianapolis), 1919.
    4625. Missionary Mountain Peaks: Outline Studies in
           Christian Expansion. Standard, 1913-.
    4626. Somewhere in All the World: Latest Call to
           Christian Students from Foreign Fields of Disciples
           of Christ. College of Missions (Indianapolis),
           1920.

For works about him written by Disciples authors, see
Inman, Samuel Guy under INTERNATIONAL AFFAIRS section.

*Paulsell, William Oliver, 1935-.
    Pastor; seminary professor and administrator.
    4627. Taste and See: A Personal Guide to the Spiritual
           Life. Upper Room, 1976.

Payne, A. B.
    4628. Poems. 1947.

Pellett, David Claude, 1911-.
    Professor of religion.
    4629. "The Holy Week Lectures in the Greek Gospel
           Lectionary." Ph.D. diss., Univ. of Chicago, 1954.

Perdue, Leo.
    Professor of religion.
    4630. A Prophet to the Nations: Essays in Jeremiah
           Studies. Eisenbrauns, 1984. (co-editor).
    4631. Scripture in Context II: More Essays on the
           Comparative Method. Eisenbrauns, 1983.
           (co-editor).
    4632. Wisdom and Cult: A Critical Analysis of the Views
           of Cult in the Wisdom Literatures of Israel and the
           Ancient Near East. Scholars Pr, 1977.

*Peters. Eugene Herbert, 1929-1983.
    Professor of philosophy.
    4633. The Creative Advance: An Introduction to Process
           Philosophy as Context for Christian Faith. Bethany,
           1966.
    4634. Faith and Creativity: Essays in Honor of Eugene H.
           Peters. CBP Pr., 1987.
    4635. "Form, Unity and the Individual." Ph.D. diss.,
           Univ. of Chicago, 1960.

4636.   Hartshorne and Neoclassical Metaphysics: An
        Interpretation. Univ. of Nebraska Pr., 1970.

Peters, Gerald L.
4637.   "Training Members of First Christian Church,
        Harlingen, Texas, In the Art of Christian Caring."
        D. Min. thesis, Brite Divinity School, 1983.

Peterson, Orval Douglas, 1902-.
4638.   The NBA [National Benevolent Association of the
        Christian Churches]-What It Is and What It Does.
        St. Louis, 1966.
4639.   Stewardship in the Bible. Christian Bd. of
        Publication, 1952.
4640.   That We Might Know Him. Zondervan, 1941.
4641.   Washington-Northern Idaho Disciples. Christian Bd.
        of Publication, 1945.

Peterson, Raleigh J., Jr.
Professor of religion.
4642.   Christian Ethics and Current Issues. Lincoln, Neb.,
        1965? (co-author).
4643.   The Interrelation Between Theology and Science.
        Univ. of Nebraska, 1966 or 7. (co-author).

Petrie, Peter Albert.
4644.   "Ye Shall Know the Truth, and the Truth Shall Make
        You Free." Standard, 1903.

Phillips, Mildred Welshimer.
Pastor.
4645.   Addresses. Standard, 1967.

Phillips, Thomas Wharton, Sr., 1835-1912.
Company president; congressman; publisher; founder of
Phillips University; philanthropist.
4646.   The Church of Christ. Funk & Wagnalls, 1905.
4647.   The Tariff Speech...." Washington, 1894.

Philputt, Allan Bearden, 1856-1925.
Pastor.
4648.   American Etiquette and Rules of Politeness. Davis,
        1882.

*Philputt, James McBride, 1860-1832.
Pastor.
4649.   "That They May All Be One": Autobiography and
        Memorial of James M. Philputt, Apostle of Christian
        Unity. Christian Bd. of Publication, 1933.

For works about him written by Disciple authors, see
    Willett, Herbert Lockwood under THEOLOGY section.

Pickett, Frank.
    Missionary to Paraguay.
    4650. Miguel de Unamuno's Theology of Encounter." D. Div.
           diss., Vanderbilt Univ., 1969.

Plantteburg, George, 1828-1904.
    4651. A Book of Sermons, Practical and Controversial, by
           John Tomline Walsh. Walsh, 1870. (editor).

Polk, David Patrick.
    Professor of religion.
    4652. "On the Way to God: An Exploration into the
           Theology of Wolfhart Pannenberg." Ph.D. diss.,
           Claremont Grad. School, 1983.

Pontius, Myron Lee.
    Pastor.
    4653. The Resurrection of the Unknown Soldier [Sermons].
           Cokesbury, 1935.

Pope, Richard Martin, 1916-.
    Professor of church history.
    4654. The Church and Its Culture: A History of the Church
           in Changing Cultures. Bethany, 1965.
    4655. The College of the Bible. College of the Bible
           (Lexington), 1951.
    4656. "Drury College: An Interpretation." Ph.D. diss.,
           Univ. of Chicago, 1955.
    4657. The Man Who Responds. Christian Bd. of Publication,
           1969.
    4658. Our Changing and Changeless Faith. Christian Bd. of
           Publication, 1974.

Porter, Calvin Lewis, 1933-.
    Professor of New Testament.
    4659. Emmanuel: God With Us. World Convention of
           Churches of Christ, 1974?
    4660. "A Textual Analysis of the Earliest Greek
           Manuscripts of the Gospel of John." Ph.D. diss.,
           Duke Univ., 1961.

Pounds, John Edward, 1864-1925.
    4661. Efficiency: A Study of the Why and How of Adult
           Class Work. Christian Bd. of Publication, 1912.

Pounds, Mattie, d. 1917.
    Laywoman; youth worker.
    4662. "Views from the Mission Fields of the Christian
           Woman's Board of Missions, 190_."

Powell, Edward Lindsay, 1860-.
    Pastor.

4663. Perils of the Church in the World of To-Day.
       Louisville, Ky., 1891.
4664. Savonarola: Or, The Reformation of a City.
       Sheltman, 1903.
4665. The Victory of Faith. Sermons and Addresses.
       Christian Publishing Co., 1905.

Powell, Wilfred Evans, 1893-.
     Seminary professor.
4666. Education for Life with God: A Discussion of the
       Meaning of Religious Education. Abingdon, 1934.
4667. The Growth of Christian Personality: A Study of the
       Pupil for Teachers of Religion in Home and School.
       Bethany, 1929.
4668. "Note Book Containing Outline of the History of
       Religious Education." Ann Arbor, Mich., 1927.
4669. Scattered Seed: The Story of the Oswald Coulters,
       Missionaries in China 1922-51. Bethany, 1969.
4670. The Understanding of Adult Ways. Bethany, 1941.
4671. Vacation Church School, Manual for the Teacher. 3d
       Ser. Bethany, 1924.

Power, Frederick Dunglison, 1851-1911.
     Pastor; editor.
4672. Bible Doctrine for Young Disciples. Christian
       Publishing Co., 1889.
4673. Life of William Kimbrough Pendleton. Christian
       Publishing Co., 1902.
4674. Sketches of Our Pioneers. Bethany, 1898.
4675. Thoughts of Thirty Years. United Society of
       Christian Endeavor, 1905.

Poyser, George K.
4676. Orthodoxy in the Civil Courts... In Which Was
       Involved the Orthodoxy of the Christian Church....
       Edited by J. H. Edwards. Standard, 1891.

Priest, Doug, Jr.
4677. Unto the Uttermost: Missions in the Christian
       Churches - Churches of Christ. William Carey Lib.,
       1984. (editor).

Procter, Alexander, 1825-1900.
     Pastor.
4678. The Witness of Jesus and Other Sermons. Christian
       Publishing Co., 1901.

Pugh, Samuel Frank, 1904-.
     Pastor; church official; editor of World Call.
4679. Between - Time Meditations: 20th Century Psalms.
       Bethany, 1954.
4680. The Church's Ministry to the Homebound. United
       Christian Missionary Soc., 1960.

4681. <u>How To Select and Call a Minister</u>. United Christian
     Missionary Soc., 1953.
4682. <u>Membership, a Guidance Manual for the Dept. of</u>
     <u>Membership of the Local Church</u>. St. Louis, 1957.
4683. <u>The NonResident Member</u>. United Christian Missionary
     Soc., n.d.
4684. <u>Primer for New Disciples</u>. United Christian
     Missionary Soc., 1963.

Pyatt, Charles Lynn, 1886-1960.
    4685. "The Moral Teachings of the Jews at the Time of
       Christ." Ph.D. diss., Harvard Divinity School,
       1916.

For works about him written by Disciples authors, see
    Pierson, Roscoe Mitchell under LIBRARY SCIENCE section; and
    Lexington, Ky. College of the Bible in GENERAL section.

*Radford, Benjamin Johnson, 1838-1933.
    Pastor; college president.
    4686. <u>The Disciple</u>. 6 vols. Standard, 1884-1887.
       (co-editor).
    4687. <u>History of Woodford County</u>. W. T. Dowdall Printer,
       1877.
    4688. <u>The Place of the Gospel in the Development of</u>
       <u>Humanity</u>. Standard, 1923.

Rains, Paul Boyd.
    Evangelist.
    4689. <u>Francis Marion Rains</u>. Christian Bd. of Publication,
       1922.

Rambo, Victor Clough.
    Missionary to India.
    4690. "The Curable Blind: A Guide for Establishing Mobile
       Eye Hospitals Based on Eye Departments of General
       Hospitals in Developing Countries." Novelty
       Printing Co., 1974. (co-author).
    4691. <u>Glorious Words of Salvation: Selections from the</u>
       <u>King James Version of the Holy Bible</u>. Lucknow
       Publishing House, 1974.

Rector, Franklin E.
    Seminary professor.
    4692. <u>Facts about Our Churches and a Changing America</u>.
       United Christian Missionary Soc., 1956.
       (co-author).

Reed, William LaForest, 1912-.
    Professor of Old Testament.
    4693. <u>Ancient Records from North Arabia</u>. Univ. of Toronto
       Pr., 1970. (co-author).

4694. <u>The Asherah in the Old Testament</u>. Texas Christian
       Univ. Pr., 1949.
4695. <u>The Excavations at Dibon in Moab</u>. American Schools
       of Oriental Research, 1954.
4696. "The Nature and Function of the Asherah in Israelite
       Religion." Ph.D. diss., Yale Univ., 1942.
4697. <u>A Selected Bibliography on Biblical Theology</u>.
       College of the Bible (Lexington), 1960.
       (co-author).
4698. <u>Translating and Understanding the Old Testament</u>.
       Abingdon, 1970. (editor).

Reese, William Lewis, 1921-.
   Professor of philosophy.
   4699. "The Aristotelian Concept of an Absolute God as
          Evaluated in the Categories of Process Philosophy."
          Ph.D. diss., Univ. of Chicago, 1947.
   4700. <u>The Ascent from Below: An Introduction to
          Philosophical Inquiry</u>. Houghton Mifflin, 1959.
   4701. <u>Dictionary of Philosophy and Religion: Eastern and
          Western Thought</u>. Humanities Pr., 1980.
   4702. <u>Philosophers Speak of God</u>. Univ. of Chicago Pr.,
          1953. (co-editor).
   4703. <u>Process and Divinity: The Hartshorne Festchrift</u>.
          Open Court Publishing Co., 1964. (co-editor).

Reeve, Jack V.
   Church official; editor.
   4704. <u>A God to Glorify through Christian Stewardship</u>.
          Bethany, 1964. (editor).
   4705. <u>Mirror for the Chief Oikonomos</u>. Council Pr., 1967.
   4706. <u>Stewardship and Church Finance</u>. Indianapolis, 1966.

Renner, R. Richard, 1896-.
   Writer.
   4707. <u>Savonarola, the First Great Protestant</u>. Greenwich,
          1965.

Reynolds, Ira Hubert, 1914-.
   4708. "Chinese Acculturation in Ilocos: Economic,
          Political, Religious." Ph.D. diss., Hartford
          Seminary Foundation, 1964.

Reynolds, John Clopton, 1825-1906.
   Publisher of <u>Gospel Echo</u>.
   4709. <u>The Moberly Pulpit, A Book of Sermons</u>. Christian
          Publishing Co., 1881.

Reynolds, Mildred.
   Missionary to India.
   4710. <u>We Lived in Tiger Jungle</u>. Bell, 1970?

Rhee, Song Nai, 1935-.
    Professor of religion.
    4711.   "Emerging Complex Society in Prehistoric Southwest
           Korea." Ph.D. diss., Univ. of Oregon, 1984.

Rice, Perry James, 1867-1948.
    President of Campbell Institute.
    4712.   Conditions in the Congo Free State. Foreign
           Christian Missionary Soc., 19__?
    4713.   The Disciples of Christ in Chicago and Northeastern
           Illinois, 1839-1939. 194_.

Richardson, Robert, 1806-1876.
    Physician; college professor.
    4714.   Communings in the Sanctuary. Transylvania Print. &
           Publishing Co., 1872.
    4715.   Memoirs of Alexander Campbell.... 2 vols.
           Lippincott, 1767-70.
    4716.   A Scriptural View of the Office of the Holy Spirit.
           Chase & Hall, 1873.

For works about him written by Disciple authors, see
    Goodnight, Cloyd,
    Johnson, H. Eugene,
    Stevenson, Dwight E. under THEOLOGY section; and
    Berry, Stephen Pressley in GENERAL section.

Richardson, William Judson, 1921-.
    Professor of religion.
    4717.   "Alexander Campbell's Use of History in His
           Apologetical Theology." Ph.D. diss., Univ. of
           Oregon, 1962.
    4718.   Christian Doctrine: "The Faith, Once Delivered."
           Standard, 1983. (editor).
    4719.   Heidegger. Nijhoff, 1963.
    4720.   "The Historiography of Alexander Campbell with
           Reference to the Problem of Christian Apologetics."
           1955.
    4721.   Social Action vs. Evangelism: An Essay on the
           Contemporary Crisis. W. Carey Lib., 1977.
    4722.   "Value Judgements in History and the Restoration
           Movement." In Essays on New Testament Christianity,
           pp. 103-14. Edited by C. R. Wetzel. 1978.
    4723.   Where the Action Is: The Role of Evangelism in
           God's Purpose for the Church Today. Emmanuel School
           of Religion, 1976.

Riggs, Graham F.
    Pastor.
    4724.   "Discovering the Church's Mission through Fellowship
           Groups in Three Congregational Settings." D. Min.
           thesis, Phillips Univ., 1976.

Rijnhart, Susie (Carson), 1868-1908.
  Missionary physician to Tibet.
  4725. With the Tibetan's in Tent and Temple. Revell,
         1901.

Rivera, Juan Marcos.
  Missionary to Venezuela.
  4726. Cartas a Jesus. Consejo Latinoameri-cano de
         Iglesias, 1982.

Roberts, Price.
  4727. Studies for New Converts. Standard, 1939.

Robinson, William, 1777-1963.
  Theologian.
  4728. The Biblical Doctrine of the Church. Bethany, 1948.
  4729. Christianity Is Pacifism. Allen & Unwin, 1933.
  4730. A Companion to the Communion Service. Oxford Univ.
         Pr., 1942.
  4731. Completing the Reformation: The Doctrine of the
         Priesthood of All Believers. College of the Bible
         (Lexington), 1955.
  4732. The Devil and God. Abingdon-Cokesbury Pr., 1945.
  4733. Holy Baptism and Holy Communion: Being a Brief
         Course of Scriptural Instruction for Those About to
         Solemnly Dedicate Their Lives to the Service of
         Jesus Christ. Berean Pr., 1945.
  4734. The Shattered Cross: The Many Churches and the One
         Church. Berean Pr., 1945.
  4735. "The View of the Disciples or Churches of Christ."
         In The Ministry and the Sacraments, pp.253-68.
         Edited by Robert Dunkerley. SCM Pr., 1937.
  4736. What Churches of Christ Stand For. Berean Pr.,
         1959.

Rodriguez Casco, Eusebio.
  Missionary to South America.
  4737. Los Perros del 9 y Otros Relatos. Nuevas Ediciones
         Argentinas, 1978.

Rogers, Donald B., 1931-.
  Professor of Christian education.
  4738. In Praise of Learning. Abingdon, 1980.
  4739. The Way of the Teacher. Discipleship Resources,
         1984.

Rogers, Samuel, 1789-1877.
  4740. Autobiography of Elder Samuel Rogers. Standard,
         1980.

Rose, Davis Glenn, 1928-.
  Professor of Old Testament.

4741. The Old Testament's Understanding of the New. N. W.
       Preachers Parliament, 1967.
4742. Seeking God's Word for Our Day. Christian Bd. of
       Publication, 1963.
4743. Teaching the Bible in the Church. Christian Bd. of
       Publication, 1969.

*Ross, Emory, 1877-1973.
   Pastor; missionary to Africa.
4744. Africa Disturbed. Friendship Pr., 1959.
       (co-author).
4745. African Heritage. Friendship Pr., 1952.

Ross, Mabel Hughes, 1909-.
   Missionary to Zaire.
4746. On Another Day...": Tales Told among the Nkundo of
       Zaire. Archon, 1979.

Ross, Roy George, 1898-1978.
   Christian educator.
4747. The Disciples and Religious Education. Christian
       Bd. of Publication, 1936. (co-editor).
4748. Disciples of Christ Silver Anniversary of Religious
       Education. 193_.

Ross, William Gordon, 1900-.
   Professor of philosophy and religion.
4749. Companion of Eternity. Abingdon, 1961.
4750. "Human Nature and Utility in Howe's Social
       Philosophy." Ph.D. diss., Columbia Univ., 1942.
4751. Meditations of Elton Trueblood. Harper, 1975.
       (editor).
4752. Nothing Happens in Small Towns. Christopher, 1973.
4753. Why... to Okinawa? Christopher, 1971.

Rossman, Vern J.
   Missionary to Japan.
4754. Between Yesterday and Tomorrow: A One-Act Play
       about Japan. Friendship Pr., 1957.
4755. Called To Mission and Unity. United Christian
       Missionary Soc., 1965. (co-author).
4756. Drum, Hammer and Cross, a One-Act Play. Friendship
       Pr., 1967.

Rothenburger, Leila (Avery), 1874-1942.
   Laywoman.
4757. Candlelights at Dusk. Commercial Service Co., 1939.

Rothenburger, William Frederick, 1874-1959.
   Pastor.
4758. "Alexander Campbell's View of the Scriptures." B.D.
       thesis, Univ. of Chicago, 1907.

4759. The Cross in Symbol, Spirit and Worship. Stratford
        Co., 1930.
4760. International Convention, Disciples of Christ, Des
        Moines, Iowa, October 16-21, 1934: Sermons and
        Addresses. Christian Bd. of Publication, 1935.

Rowe, Frederick Louis, 1886-.
    Missionary to Congo.
    4761. The Bible in Questions and Answers. F. L. Rowe,
           1916. (co-author).
    4762. Duties and Beauties of Life, a Book for the Home.
           F. L. Rowe, 1908. (editor).
    4763. Letters to an Orphan. F. L. Rowe, 1911.
    4764. Our Savior's Prayer for Unity: A Symposium on the
           Seventeenth Chapter of John. F. L. Rowe, 1918.
           (compiler).
    4765. Pioneer Sermons and Addresses. F. L. Rowe, 1908.
           (compiler).
    4766. "Systematic Study." In Outlines of Bible Study. F.
           L. Rowe, 1914.

*Rowe, John Franklin, 1827-1897.
    Editor of American Christian Review.
    4767. The Apostolic Church Restored. Sommer, 1889.
    4768. The Gospel in Type and Antitype. Cincinnati, 1892.
    4769. History of Reformatory Movements Resulting in a
           Restoration of the Apostolic Church. Cincinnati,
           1890.

For works about him written by Disciple authors, see
    Green, Francis Marion under THEOLOGY section.

Rowell, Joseph Cy, 1934-.
    Professor of religion.
    4770. The Choice Is Yours. Christian Bd. of Publication,
           1970. (co-author).
    4771. "Foundational Aims of Christian Education for the
           Christian Church (Disciples of Christ)." Christian
           Bd. of Publication, 1984?
    4772. The Senior High Conference. Christian Bd. of
           Publication, 1962.
    4773. "A Theory of Lay Leadership for Adult Study Groups
           in the Church." Th.D. diss., Princeton Theological
           Seminary, 1965.
    4774. To Be a Person, Teacher's Guide for Grades 9 and
           10. American Baptist Bd. of Education and
           Publication, 1969.

Rudd, James.
    Pastor.
    4775. "Preparing Some Members of Highland Heights
           Christian Church for Volunteer Work with Interfaith

Ministries." D. Min. thesis, Brite Divinity School, 1983.

Rush, Michael Gerald.
   Pastor.
   4776. "Dialogue between the Congregations of the Roman Catholic Church and the Christian Church (Disciples of Christ)... in Logan, West Virginia." D. Min. thesis, Drew Univ., 1980.

Russell, Jerry Max, 1936-.
   Missionary to India.
   4777. "Coordinating Agencies as Interorganizational Linkage Mechanisms: An Analysis of North Carolina's Regional Family Planning Programs." Ph.D. diss., Univ. of North Carolina, 1976.

Rutherford, Mark.
   Church Official.
   4778. The Christian Layman and His Church. Bethany, 1958.

Rutherford, Roy Meyers.
   4779. "An Examination of American Study Procedures for Three International Missionary Conferences... With Implications for Missionary Education in Local Christian Churches (Disciples of Christ)." Ed.R.D. diss., Hartford Seminary Foundation, 1962.

Ryan, Matthias Bishop, 1855-.
   4780. New Testament Names, A Study of Various Scriptural Apellations Used to Designate the Followers of Christ. Standard, 1917.

Sadler, McGruder Ellis, 1896-1966.
   Pastor; chancellor of Texas Christian University.
   4781. "Texas Christian University: The Recent Developments [Address]." Newcomen Soc., 1965.

Saenz, Michael, 1925-.
   College president; missionary to Puerto Rico.
   4782. "Economic Aspects of Church Development in Puerto Rico: A Study of the Financial Policies and Procedures of the Major Protestant Church Groups in Puerto Rico from 1898-1957." Ph.D. diss., Univ. of Pennsylvania, 1961.

Salmon, Donald M.
   Church official.
   4783. The Bible Speaks, Evangelize. Indianapolis, 196_. (co-author).
   4784. "Evangelism." United Christian Missionary Soc., 196-?

4785.   The Minister-Evangelist. United Christian
        Missionary Soc., 1962.
4786.   "Symbolism in the Christian Church at Eureka,
        Illinois."   Eureka? Ill., 1942.

Sanders, Joseph Enloe.
4787.   "Major Theological Beliefs of the Churches of Christ
        and Their Implications for Christian Education
        [1800-1956]." Ph.D. diss., Boston Univ., 1957.

Sanderson, Eugene Claremont, 1859-1940.
    Pastor; college president; founder of World Evangel.
4788.   Bible and History Studies. Church and School
        Publishing Co., 1912.
4789.   Our English Bible. 1912.

Sandlin, James Lee.
    Pastor.
4790.   Musings of a Parson. Naylor Publishing.

Sarvis, Guy W.
    Missionary to China.
4791.   Maude Operation at One. 1935.
4792.   The Word for Christmas: A Christmas Play in One
        Act. United Christian Missionary Soc., n.d.

Saunders, Joseph S.
4793.   "Black Disciples are Moving: Out of the Balcony,
        into the Main Auditorium." 198_.

Scheen, Jerry S.
4794.   "A Study in Self-Concept Ratings of Christian Church
        (Disciples of Christ) Ministers Serving
        Congregations of Two Hundred and Forty or More
        Members." Ph.D. diss., Univ. of Utah, 1976.

Sewell, Elisha Granville, 1830-1824.
4816.   Christian Hymns. Gospel Advocate Publishing Co.,
        1889.
4817.   Gospel Lessons and Life History. McQuiddy, 1908.
4818.   Proper Division of the Word of God. Gospel Advocate
        Publishing Co., 1891.
4819.   Queries and Answers, by Lipscomb and Sewell.
        McQuiddy, 1921.

Sexson, William Mark, 1877-1953.
4820.   History and Purpose of Rainbow. A. J. Holman Co.,
        1929.
4821.   Little Boy Bo. Christopher Publishing House, 1939.
4822.   The Power of Color. Christopher Publishing House,
        1939.
4823.   Rainbow Building. McAlester? Okla., 1944.

4824. Ritual. Order of the Rainbow for Girls. Office of
       Supreme Assembly, 1946.

Shackleford, John, 1834-1821.
   4825. Life. Letters and Addresses of Dr. L. L. Pinkerton.
          Chase & Hall, 1976. (editor).

Shae, Gam Seng.
   Missionary to Indonesia.
   4826. Biblical Basis of the Christian Family. Baptist
          Council on World Mission, 1982. (co-author).

Sharp, Allan Rhinehart, 1925-.
   Professor of religion.
   4827. "A Study of Protestant Undergraduate Pre-Theological
          Education in the United States." Ed.D. diss., Duke
          Univ., 1963.

Shaw, Knowles, 1834-1878.
   4828. The Golden Gate: A Collection of New Songs for the
          Sunday-School. Prayer Meetings and Social Circle.
          J. Church, 1874. (compiler).
   4829. The Golden Gate for the Sunday School. J. Church,
          18__.
   4830. The Gospel Trumpet. J. Church, 1875.
   4831. Knowles Shaw's Memorial Songs. Hungerford, 1939.
   4832. The Morning Star: A Collection of New Sacred
          Songs... Chase & Hall, 1878.
   4833. Shining Pearls. A Collection of Choice Music for
          Revivals and Sunday Schools. J. Church, 1868.
          (compiler)
   4834. Sparkling Jewels for the Sunday School. A New
          Collection of Choice Music. J. Claude, 1871.

For works about him written by Disciple authors, see
   Baxter, William under THEOLOGY section.

Shaw, Roud.
   Pastor.
   4835. Pentecost and God's Hurry [Sermons]. Christopher,
          1856.

Shelton, Albert Leroy, 1875-1922.
   Physician; missionary to China and Tibet.
   4836. Pioneering in Tibet: A Personal Record of Life and
          Experience in Mission Fields. 1921.
   4837. Tibetan Folk Tales. Doran, 1925.

Shelton, Flora Beal, 1871-1966.
   Missionary to Tibet.
   4838. Chants from Shangri-la. Palm Springs, Calif., 1939.
   4839. Folk Tales of Tibet. Story Book Pr., 1951.
   4840. Shelton of Tibet. Doran, 1923.

4841. <u>Sunshine and Shadow on the Tibetan Border</u>. Foreign
      Christian Missionary Soc., 1912.
4842. <u>Tibetan Folk Tales. Translated by A. L. Shelton,
      M.D.</u> Doran, 1925. (editor).

Shelton, Gentry Allen, 1911-.
    Professor of religion.
    4843. "A Study of Directors of Religious Education in
          Churches of the Disciples of Christ in the United
          States." Ph.D. diss., Univ. of Kentucky, 1954.

Shelton, Orman Leroy, 1895-1959.
    Pastor; seminary president; editor of <u>National Stewardship</u>.
    4844. <u>The Church Functioning Effectively</u>. Christian Bd.
          of Publication, 1946.

For works about him written by Disciple authors, see
    Farrell, James E. under THEOLOGY section; and
    Osborn, Ronald E. in GENERAL section.

Shepard, Darrell Royce.
    Professor of philosophy.
    4845. "The Sensibility of 'Holy Spirit'." Ph.D. diss.,
          Univ. of Nebraska, 1967.

Shields, James Leroy, 1942-.
    Professor of education.
    4846. "Alexander Campbell: A Synthesis of Faith and
          Reason (1823-1860)." Ph.D. diss., Syracuse Univ.,
          1874.

Shifflet, Stephen Thomas.
    Pastor.
    4847. "The Christian Nurture of Children through the
          Sacraments." D. Min. thesis, United Theological
          Seminary of the Twin Cities, 1982.

Shirts, Sheldon Vincent.
    Professor of Greek and New Testament.
    4848. "The Fourth Gospel, with Canonical and Noncanonical
          Parallels, Variant Readings, and Manuscript
          Support." Th.D. diss., Pacific School of Religion,
          1967.

Shoemaker, George Curtiss.
    Professor of religion.
    4849. "Colloquium in Practice of Ministry." D. Min.
          thesis, Phillips Univ. Graduate Seminary, 1973.

Shorrock, Hallam Carey, 1923-.
    4850. <u>Is the Emergency Over? A Report about Korea and the
          Programs of Korea Church World Service during 1958</u>.
          Seoul, Korea, 1960.

Short, Howard Elmo, 1907-.
    Pastor; professor of church history; editor of <u>Christian
    Evangelist</u>.
    4851. "Bucer and Church Organization." Ph.D. diss.,
          Harford Theol. Seminary, 1942.
    4852. <u>Christian Unity Is Our Business: Disciples of
          Christ within the Ecumenical Fellowship</u>. Bethany,
          1953.
    4853. <u>Doctrine and Thought of the Disciples of Christ</u>.
          Christian Bd. of Publication, 1951.
    4854. <u>Education for the Christian Ministry for Tomorrow's
          Church</u>. College of the Bible (Lexington), 1953.
          (editor).
    4855. "The Literature of the Christian Church (Disciples
          of Christ)." In The Christian Church (Disciples of
          Christ), pp. 285-307. Edited by G. Beazley. 1973.
    4856. "President Garfield's Religious Heritage and What He
          Did With It." Hiram College? 1981.
    4857. <u>Reformation, Restoration, and Renewal: Lectures
          Delivered in Emmanuel College, the University of
          Toronto, January, 1956</u>. Toronto? 1956.

Shrout, Thomas Reuben.
    Professor of philosophy and religion.
    4858. <u>Lighting Up Life: An Exploration of Selected Verses
          from the Sermon on the Mount</u>. Christian Bd. of
          Publication, 1972.
    4859. "The Personality of Paul." Ph.d. diss., Harvard
          Univ., 1954.

Sibley, Jack Raymond, 1930-.
    Professor of philosophy.
    4860. "The Concept of Depth in the Thought of Bernard E.
          Meland As It Illuminates His Understanding of Faith
          and Reason." Ph.D. diss., Univ. of Chicago, 1967.
    4861. <u>Logic for Life: A Comparison Notebook</u>. Ginn, 1980.
    4862. <u>Process Philosophy: Basic Writings</u>. Univ. Pr. of
          America, 1978. (co-editor).

Sikes, Walter W., 1896-1966.
    Professor of ethics and theology.
    4863. <u>Christian Faith and Experience</u>. Christian Bd. of
          Publication, 1962.
    4864. <u>On Becoming the Truth: An Introduction to the Life
          and Thought of Soren Kierkegaard</u>. Bethany, 1968.
    4865. <u>Renewing Higher Education from Within</u>. Jossey-Bass,
          1974.
    4866. <u>Revolution and Renewal: Christian Response to the
          Technological and Social Revolutions of Our Time</u>.
          Commission on Church and Society of the Christian
          Churches (Disciples of Christ), 1965.
    4867. <u>The Stranger in My House</u>. Bethany, 1957.

Sillars, Chester Archibald, 1909-.
    4868. <u>Preliminary Research (Northeastern Association of</u>
          <u>Christian Churches)</u>. Schenectady, 1962.
    4869. "A Chat with Chet, in Verse and Rhyme." Bethany,
          1971.

Simpson, Robert L.
    Professor of religion.
    4870. <u>The Interpretation of Prayer in the Early Church</u>.
          Westminster, 1965.
    4871. <u>One Faith: Its Biblical, Historical, and Ecumenical</u>
          <u>Dimensions</u>. Phillips Univ. Pr., 1966. (editor).
    4872. <u>Our Christian Heritage</u>. Phillips Univ. Pr., 1967-.
          (co-compiler).

Six, Ray L.
    Missionary to China.
    4873. <u>Road Log: Geology Field Trip No. 1</u>. Oklahoma A. &
          M. College, 1931.

Sizemore, Roger.
    Seminary administrator.
    4874. <u>Keeping in Touch</u>. Christian Bd. of Publication,
          1973.

Sly, Florence M.
    Writer.
    4875. <u>Your Family and Christian Stewardship</u>. Bethany,
          1958.

Sly, Virgil Adolph, 1901-.
    Pastor; church official.
    4876. <u>The Congo Mission of Disciples of Christ</u>. United
          Christian
          Missionary Soc., 1950?
    4877. <u>Report on the Congo Mission</u>. United Christian
          Missionary Soc., 1946.
    4878. <u>To the Ends of the Earth</u>. Nebraska School of
          Religion, 1970.
    4879. <u>Today the Kingdom Comes, the Story of Christian</u>
          <u>Missions and Education for the Year 1934-35</u>. United
          Christian Missionary Soc., 19__. (editor).
    4880. "The Virgil A. Sly Lectures to the Council of
          Agencies, Chapman College, Orange, California..."
          United Christian Missionary Soc., 1968.

Smith, Benjamin Lyon, 1859-1833.
    4881. <u>Alexander Campbell</u>. Bethany, 1930.

    4882. <u>A Manual of Forms for Ministers for Special</u>
          <u>Occasions and for the Work and Worship of the</u>
          <u>Church</u>. Christian Bd. of Publication, 1919.

Smith, Butler Kennedy, 1807-1875.
 4883. An Earnest Inquiry into the True Scriptural
    Organization of the Churches of God in Jesus Christ.
    Indianapolis Printing and Publishing House, 1871.
 4884. A Series of Discourses on Various Subjects.
    Printing and Publishing House Printers, 1874.

Smith, Clayton Chaney, 1845-1919.
 Naturalist; missionary.
 4885. Jamaica: Sketches of Jamaica and the Mission Work
    Done There by the Christian Woman's Board of
    Missions. Christian Woman's Bd. of Missions, 19__.
 4886. The Life and Work of Jacob Kenoly. Methodist Book
    Concern, 1912.
 4887. A Little Story Concerning Jacob Kenoly's Life and
    Work. Christian Woman's Bd. of Missions, 1911?

Smith, Dennis Edwin, 1944-.
 Professor of religion.
 4888. "Social Obligation in the Context of Communal Meals:
    A Study of the Christian Meal in I Corinthians in
    Comparison with Graeco-Roman Communal Meals." Ph.D.
    diss., Harvard Univ., 1980.

Smith, Elsie Higdon.
 Dietician.
 4889. Potwin Christian Church. Mennonite Pr., 1969.

Smith, George Thomas, 1843-1920.
 Pastor; missionary to Japan.
 4890. Critique on Higher Criticism. Industrial Free Pr.,
    1900.

Smith, Harry Denman, 1866-1933.
 4891. "In Memory of Frank A. Parkinson: A Report of His
    Funeral..." Corey Pr., 1929.
 4892. A Preacher's First Books. Standard, 1933.

Smith, James Henry Oliver, 1857-1935.
 Pastor; evangelist.
 4893. "Ashley S. Johnson Still Speaks." Kimberlin
    Heights? Tenn., n.d.
 4894. What Think Ye of Christ? and Other Sermons.
    Standard, 1927.
 4895. The World's Need of a Non-Sectarian Church.
    Mountaineer, 1909.

Smith, John "Raccoon", 1784-1868.
 Evangelist.
 4896. Sectarian Stratagem Exposed: Or, the Correspondence
    between Bishop John Smith, of the Church of Jesus
    Christ... According to the New Testament, and the

Rev. Edward Stevenson...a Teacher of Methodism....
Prosser, 1936.

For works about him written by Disciples authors, see
Cochran, Louis under ENGLISH section;
Pierson, Roscoe Mitchell under LIBRARY SCIENCE section; and
Williams, John Augustus under HISTORY section.

Smith, Joseph Martin, 1912-.
    Seminary administrator; missionary to China and the
    Philippines.
    4897. Called to Mission and Unity. United Christian
           Missionary Soc., 1965. (co-author).
    4898. "A Strategy of World Mission: The Theory and
           Practice of Mission As Seen in the Present World
           Mission Enterprise of The Disciples of Christ."
           Ph.D. diss., Union Theol. Seminary, 1961.
    4899. The World Christians Live In. Christian Bd. of
           Publication, 1964.

Smith, Leslie R., 1904-.
    4900. Four Keys To Prayer. Bethany, 1962.
    4901. From Sunset to Dawn, a Book of Meditations to Help
           Those in Grief. Craw & Craw, 1944.
    4902. This Love of Ours. Abingdon-Cokesbury, 1947.
    4903. Two Sides of the Disciple Coin. Bethany, 1958.

Smith, Marvin E.
    Seminary administrator.
    4904. The Bible and Our Social Responsibility. Bethany,
           1958. (co-author).
    4905. C. H. 302 (Christianity and the European Nations -
           A.D. 800-1600). Univ. of Chicago, 1941.
           (co-author).
    4906. "Leader's Guide for the New Testament Experience of
           Faith." 1977.

Smith, Samuel D., III, 1923-.
    Professor of religion and philosophy.
    4907. "A Study of the Relation between the Doctrine of
           Creation and the Doctrine of Revelation through the
           Created Universe in the Thought of John Calvin,
           Friedrich Schleiermacher and Paul Tillich." Ph.D.
           diss., Vanderbilt Univ., 1965.

Smith, William Fountain.
    4908. A Death Shot at Campbellism. Highland, Tenn., 1899.

Smith, William Martin, 1916-.
    Church official.
    4909. For the Support of the Ministry: A History of
           Ministerial Support, Relief, and Pensions among

Disciples of Christ. Pension Fund of Disciples of
Christ, 1956.

4910. Lessons in Daniel. Newby Book Room, 1972.

4911. Servants Without Hire: Emerging Concepts of the
Christian Ministry in the Campbell-Stone Movement.
Disciples of Christ Historical Soc., 1968.

Smythe, Lewis Strong Casey.
Missionary to China.

4912. "Changes in the Christian Message for China by
Protestant Missionaries." Ph.D. diss., Univ. of
Chicago, 1928.

4913. Experimental Design in the Silliman University
Community Development Program. Silliman University
(Philippines), 1958.

4914. Southern Churches and Race Relations. Lexington,
1960.

4915. War Damage in the Nanking Area. December. 1937 to
March. 1938. Mercury, 1938.

Snodgrass, R.C.
Pastor.

4916. "Trustees of Our Heritage; A Series of Five
Lectures...." Northwest Christian College Pr.,
1948.

Sommer, Daniel, 1850-1940.
Pastor; editor of American Christian Review.

4917. Appeal for Unity. Apostolic Review [193_].

4918. Concerning Church Government. Octographic Review,
1910.

4919. Correspondence of Daniel Sommer with Nathan H.
Shepherd. J.B. Briney. J. H. Garrison. and K. A.
Lord. 1900.

4920. Daniel Sommer 1850-1940. Edited and compiled by
William E. Wallace. 1969.

4921. Questions. Answers and Remarks Concerning the Text
and Teaching of the New Testament. Apostolic
Review, n.d.

4922. A Record of My Life. Disciples of Christ Historical
Soc., 1955.

4923. Sectarianism. Analyzed. Defined and Exposed. 2d ed.
D. Sommer, 18__.

For works about him written by Disciple authors, see
Wright, James Roy under THEOLOGY section;
Morrison, Matthew C.,
Wallace, William E. under HISTORY section; and
Miller, Robert Henry in GENERAL section.

Spaulding, Helen F.
Church official.

4924. <u>Audio-Visual Research</u>. National Council of the
       Churches of Christ in the U.S.A., 1952?
4925. <u>A Study of Weekday Kindergartens and Nursery Schools
       under Church Auspices</u>. Committee on Children's
       Work, 1955. (co-author).
4926. <u>A Study of Youth Work in Protestant Churches</u>.
       Chicago, 1956? (co-author).
4927. <u>Youth Look at the Church</u>. New York, 1956.

Spencer, Claude Elbert, 1898-.
4928. <u>An Author Catalog of Disciples of Christ and Related
       Religious Groups</u>. Disciples of Christ Historical
       Soc., 1946. (compiler).
4929. <u>Educational Institutions of Disciples of Christ</u>.
       Disciples of Christ Historical Soc., 1955?
       (compiler).
4930. <u>Educational Institutions of the Disciples of Christ</u>
       (485 Institutions). Rev. Nov. 1964. Disciples of
       Christ Historical Soc., 1965. (compiler).
4931. <u>From Box to Box: Or, The Random Reminiscences of a
       Book Collector</u>. Disciples of Christ Historical
       Soc., 1965.
4932. <u>Periodicals of the Disciples of Christ and Related
       Religious Groups</u>. Disciples of Christ Historical
       Soc., 1943. (compiler).
4933. <u>Writers, and Story Tellers of the Disciples of
       Christ</u>. C. Willard, 1959.
4934. <u>Theses Concerning the Disciples of Christ and
       Related Religious Groups</u>. Disciples of Christ
       Historical Soc., 1964. (compiler).
4935. <u>Theses Concerning the Disciples of Christ, the
       Churches of Christ, and the Christian Church</u>.
       Disciples of Christ Historical Soc., 1941.
       (compiler).

Spencer, Isaac J., 1851-1922.
   Pastor.
4936. <u>The Christian Lesson Commentary, for the Use of
       Teachers and Advanced Students</u>. Multi vols.
       Christian Publishing Co., n.d. (co-author).

Sprague, William L.
   Seminary administrator.
4937. <u>A Community of Concern: A Seminary Report of the
       Clergy Training Program in Drug Abuse, McLean
       Hospital, Belmont, Massachusetts...</u> Belmont, Mass.?
       1977. (editor).
4938. <u>Our Christian Church Heritage: Journeying in Faith,
       A Resource Book for Lay Persons</u>. Christian Bd. of
       Publication, 1978. (co-editor).

Squire, Russel Nelson.
  4939. Where Is the Bible Silent: Essays on the
          Campbell-Stone Religious Restoration of America.
          Southland, 1973.

Stanley, Arthur J.
  Church official.
  4940. Christian Churches for New Times. United Christian
          Missionary Soc., 1961.
  4941. Past Is Prologue To the Future: Historical Summary
          of 53 Churches. Lake Grove Printing Co., 1977.

Steckel, Clyde James, 1928-.
  Professor of religion.
  4942. "Oskar Pfister's Methodology and Its Implications
          for Pastoral Theology." Ph.D. diss., Univ. of
          Chicago, 1965.
  4943. Theology and Ethics of Behavior Modification. Univ.
          Pr. of America, 1979.

Stelzle, Charles, 1869-1941.
  4944. American Social and Religious Conditions. Revell,
          1912.
  4945. Boys of the Street: How To Win Them. Revell, 1904.
  4946. The Call of the New Day To the Old Church. Revell,
          1915.
  4947. Christianity's Storm Center: A Study of the Modern
          City. Revell, 1907.
  4948. The Church and Labor. Houghton Mifflin, 1910.
  4949. The Church and the Labor Movement. American Baptist
          Publication Soc., 1910.
  4950. The Gospel of Labor. Revell, 1912.
  4951. If I Had Only One Sermon To Preach: Sermons by
          Twenty-One Ministers. Harper, 1927. (editor).
  4952. "Leaflets on Liquor Problem." Westerville, Ohio,
          1914.
  4953. Letters from a Workingman. Revell, 1908.
  4954. Liquor and Labor: A Survey of the Industrial
          Aspects of the Liquor Problem in New Jersey.
          Anti-Saloon League of New Jersey, 1917.
  4955. Messages to Workingmen. Revell, 1906.
  4956. Principles of Successful Church Advertising.
          Revell, 1908.
  4957. The Right To Drink: A Discussion of Personal
          Liberty. New York City, 1920.
  4958. The Social Application of Religion. Eaton & Mains,
          1908.
  4959. The Social Ideals of the Churches and the Social
          Program by the Government. Good Neighbor League,
          1936.
  4960. A Son of the Bowery: The Life Story of an East Side
          American. Doran, 1926.
  4961. Why Prohibition! Doran, 1918.

4962. The Working Man and Social Problems. Revell, 1903.
4963. Yearbook of American Churches. Round Table Pr.,
      1916-. (editor).

Stephenson, James M.
     4964. A Report of a Public Discussion... Subject: The
           Kingdom of God upon Earth... As Taught by the
           Prophets, Christ and His Apostles... Downey &
           Brouse, 1866.

Stevenson, DeLoris.
     Writer.
     4965. Land of the Morning [Philippines]. Bethany, 1956.

*Stevenson, Dwight Eshelman, 1906-.
     Pastor; seminary professor and administrator.
     4966. The Bacon College Story: 1836-1865. College of the
           Bible (Lexington), 1962.
     4967. Christianity in the Philippines. College of the
           Bible (Lexington), 1955.
     4968. Disciples Preaching in the First Generation: An
           Ecological Study. Disciples of Christ Historical
           Soc., 1969.
     4969. Dwight E. Stevenson: A Tribute by Some of His
           Former Students. Edited by William R. Barr.
           Lexington Theol. Seminary, 1975.
     4970. Faith Takes a Name. Harper, 1954.
     4971. The False Prophet. Abingdon, 1965.
     4972. The Fourth Witness. Bethany, 1954.
     4973. The History of the Bethany Church of Christ.
           Bethany, W. Va. 1940.
     4974. Home to Bethphage, a Biography of Robert Richardson.
           Christian Bd. of Publication, 1949. (co-author).
     4975. In the Biblical Preacher's Workshop. Abingdon,
           1967.
     4976. Lexington Theological Seminary, 1865-1965: The
           College of the Bible Century. Bethany, 1964.
     4977. Monday's God. Bethany, 1976.
     4978. On Holy Ground: Meditations Written in Jerusalem.
           Bethany, 1963.
     4979. Preaching on the Books of the New Testament.
           Harper, 1956.
     4980. Preaching on the Books of the Old Testament.
           Harper, 1961.
     4981. Reaching People from the Pulpit: A Guide to
           Effective Sermon Delivery. Harper, 1958.
           (co-author).
     4982. Walter Scott: Voice of the Golden Oracle, a
           Biography. Christian Bd. of Publication, 1946.
     4983. A Way in the Wilderness: Holy Land Meditations.
           Bethany, 1968.

For works about him written by Disciple authors, see
    Barr, William Richard under THEOLOGY section; and
    White, Richard C. in GENERAL section.

Stevenson, Paul Huston, 1890-1971.
    Physician; anthropologist; missionary to China.
    4984. "Detailed Anthropocentric Measurements of the
           Chinese of the North China Plain." Commercial Pr.,
           1938.
    4985. "Human Types in Peking." Peking Leader Pr., 1927.

Stewart, David, 1938-.
    Professor of philosophy.
    4986. Exploring Phenomenology. American Library Assoc.,
           1974. (co-author).
    4987. Exploring the Philosophy of Religion.
           Prentice-Hall, 1980.
    4988. Fundamentals of Philosophy. Macmillan, 1982.
    4989. The Meaning of Humanness in a Technological Era.
           Ohio Univ., 1978.
    4990. The Philosophy of Paul Ricoeur. Beacon, 1978.
    4991. Social and Political Essays by Paul Ricoeur. Ohio
           Univ., 1974. (co-editor).

Stewart, John William.
    Professor of Old Testament.
    4992. "Doctrinal Influence upon the New Testament of
           Clement of Alexandria." Ph.D. diss., Duke Univ.,
           1966.

Stewart, Oliver Wayne, 1867-1937.
    Pastor; politician; editor.
    4993. "Prohibition Issues." In The Bottle of 1900.
           Monarch, 1900.
    4994. Speeches of the Flying Squadron. Hanly & Stewart,
           1915. (co-editor).

Stinnette, Charles Roy, 1914-.
    Professor of pastoral care.
    4995. "Anxiety and Christian Faith." Ph.D. diss.,
           Columbia Univ., 1949.
    4996. Anxiety and Faith: Toward Resolving Anxiety in
           Christian Community. Seabury, 1955.
    4997. Faith, Freedom and Selfhood: A Study in Personal
           Dynamics. Seabury, 1959.
    4998. Grace and the Searching of Our Heart. Association
           Pr., 1962.
    4999. Learning in Theological Perspective. Association
           Pr., 1965.

Strain, Dudley.
    5000. The Measure of a Minister. Bethany, 1964.

Strain, John Paul, 1928- .
  Professor of philosophy.
  5001. <u>Modern Philosophies of Education</u>. Random House,
        1971. (compiler).

Streator, Martin Lyman.
  Pastor.
  5002. <u>The Anglo-American Alliance in Prophecy</u>
        <u>[Anglo-Israelism]</u>. Our Race Publishing Co., 1900.

Stuckenbruck, Earl Roy.
  5003. <u>Sine qua non</u>. European Evangelistic Soc., 1965?

Suggs, James C.
  5004. <u>This We Believe</u>. Bethany, 1977. (editor).

*Suggs, Marion Jack, 1924- .
  Pastor; seminary professor and administrator.
  5005. <u>The Gospel Story</u>. Bethany, 1960.
  5006. <u>The Layman Reads His Bible</u>. Bethany, 1957.
  5007. <u>The New English Bible with the Apocrypha</u>. Oxford
        Univ. Pr., 1976. (co-editor).
  5008. <u>Studies in the History and Text of the New Testament</u>
        <u>in Honor of Kenneth Willis Clark</u>. Univ. of Utah
        Pr., 1967. (co-editor).
  5009. <u>Wisdom, Christology, and Law in Matthew's Gospel</u>.
        Harvard Univ. Pr., 1970.

Sutton, Jack A.
  Church official.
  5010. <u>Witness Beyond Barriers</u>. Bethany, 1968.

Swander, Clarence F., 1874-1959.
  Church official.
  5011. <u>Introduction to Religious Education</u>. Multigraph
        Print., 1934.
  5012. <u>Making Disciples in Oregon</u>. St. Louis, 1928.

Swann, George Betts, 1882- .
  Pastor.
  5013. <u>Sermons</u>. Progress Printing Co., (Owensboro, Ky.).

Swearingen, Tilford Tippett, 1902- .
  Pastor; college president.
  5014. <u>The Community and Christian Education</u>. Bethany,
        1950.
  5015. <u>Must a Man Live</u>? Bethany, 1941.
  5016. <u>Planning for Young People in the Local Church</u>.
        Bethany, 1933.
  5017. <u>Planning for Young People in Your Church</u>. Bethany,
        1944.

Sweeney, Elsie Irwin.
   Philanthropist.
   5018. "A Layman's View of Baptism in Relation to Its
          Authority, Importance, and Value in a Christian Life
          and also, Its Bearing on the Present Trend towards
          Ecumenicity." 196-.
   5019. "A Re-Study of Baptism in Relation to Its Authority,
          Importance, and Value in a Christian Life, and also
          Its Bearing on the Present Trend toward
          Ecumenicity." Columbus, Ind., 1966.

Sweeney, John S.
   Pastor.
   5020. Sweeney's Sermons. Gospel Advocate, 1892.

*Sweeney, Zachary Taylor, 1849-1926.
   Pastor; lecturer.
   5021. Bible Readings. 2 vols. Standard, 1903-1904.
          (co-editor).
   5022. New Testament Christianity. Columbus, Ind., 1923.
          (editor).
   5023. The Spirit and the Word: A Treatise on the Holy
          Spirit in the Light of a Rational Interpretation of
          the Word of Truth. Standard, 1919.
   5024. Under Ten Flags. An Historical Pilgrimage.
          Standard, 1888.

For works about him written by Disciple authors, see
   Lappin, Samuel Strahl; and
   Welshimer, Pearl Howard under THEOLOGY section; and
   McAllister, Lester under HISTORY section.

Sweeten, Robert W.
   Pastor.
   5025. "Interpreting the Letter to the Ephesians for First
          Christian Church of Marshall, Missouri." D. Min.
          thesis, Phillips Univ. Graduate Seminary, 1983.

Swinney, Oram Jackson, 1899-.
   Pastor.
   5026. Restoration Readings. Old Paths Book Club, 1949.
          (compiler).

Tade, George Thomas, 1923-.
   College administrator.
   5027. "A Rhetorical Analysis of the Spiritual Exercises of
          Ignatius Loyola." Ph.D. diss., Univ. of Illinois,
          1955.

Tate, John T.
   Pastor.

5028.   "Organizing Shepherding Support Groups for First
        Christian Church, Mineral Wells, Texas." D. Min.
        thesis, Brite Divinity School, 1983.

Tatlock, Lloyd E., 1925-.
Tatlock, Janice Ruth, 1928-.
    Missionaries to Mexico.
    5029.   Born To Be Free: Christian Concern for Human
            Rights. Christian Bd. of Publication, 1979.

Taylor, Alva Wilmot, 1871-1957.
    5030.   Christianity and Industry in America. Friendship,
            1933.
    5031.   Mexico, 1926, 1926?
    5032.   Social Evangelism, n.d.
    5033.   The Social Work of Christian Missions. Foreign
            Christian Missionary Soc., 1912.

For works about him by Disciple authors, see
Wasson, Woodrow Wilson under HISTORY section.

Taylor, C. Richard.
    Pastor.
    5034.   "The Contribution of the Disciples of Christ and
            Their Periodical Literature to the Cause of
            Christian Union." B. D. thesis, College of the
            Bible, Lexington, 1954.

Taylor, William Brooks, 1865-1941.
    5035.   "The Contribution of the Christian College to the
            Restoration Movement: An Address...." Christian
            College Assoc., 1912.
    5036.   Studies in the Epistles and Revelation. Standard,
            1910.

Teegarden, Kenneth Leroy, 1921-.
    Pastor; church official.
    5037.   We Call Ourselves Disciples. Bethany, 1975.

Thomas, Cecil K., 1911-.
    College professor.
    5038.   Alexander Campbell and His New Version. Bethany,
            1958.

Thomas, James David, 1910-.
    Religious writer.
    5039.   A Descriptive Catalogue of the Greek Papyri in the
            Collection of Wilfred Merton, vol. III. Univ. of
            London, 1967.
    5040.   Facts and Faith. 2 vols. Biblical Research Pr.,
            1965.
    5041.   Great Preachers of Today. Biblical Research Pr.,
            1960-. (editor).

5042. "The Greek Text of Tobit." Ph.D. diss., Univ. of
       Chicago, 1957.
5043. Spiritual Power: Great Single Sermons. Biblical
       Research Pr., 1972.
5044. "We Be Brethren": A Study in Biblical
       Interpretation. Biblical Research Pr., 1958.

Thomas, Robert Arthur Dr., 1919-.
     Church official.
     5045. "A Program of Personal Religious Counseling for
            Churches in Small Cities." D. B. thesis, Univ. of
            Chicago, 1944.
     5046. "A Sketch of the History of University Christian
            Church [1890-1965]." 1965.

Thompson, Robert O'Hair, 1925-.
     College administrator.
     5047. "The Function and Limits of Faith and Reason, A
            Critique of Emil Brunner's Methodology." Ph.D.
            diss., Univ. of Chicago, 1970.

Thorton, Edwin William.
     5048. Lord's Day Worship Services for the Aid of the
            Smaller Churches. Standard, 1930. (editor).
     5049. Special Sermons for Special Occasions. College Pr.,
            1967, c1921. (editor).

Thorp, Roy L.
     5050. Stewardship and Finance, a Guidance Manual for the
            Dept. of Stewardship and Finance of the Local
            Church. St. Louis, 1957.

Thurston, Burton Bradford, 1920-.
     College administrator.
     5051. "Alexander Campbell's Principles of Hermeneutics."
            Ph.D diss., Harvard Univ., 1958.

Tiffin, Gerald Clay.
     5052. "The Interaction of the Bible College Movement and
            the Independent Disciples of Christ Denomination."
            Ph.D. diss., Stanford Univ., 1968.

Timmons, Millard Gregory.
     Pastor.
     5053. "Lay Ministry for Fellowship and Involvement." D.
            Min. thesis, United Theol. Seminary (Dayton), 1981.

Titus, Charles Buttz, 1863-.
     Missionary to China.
     5054. Christ's One Church Forever: A China-African
            Mission Story. Cherokee, Okla., 1933.
     5055. The Greatest Work in the World: Or, the Mission of
            Christ's Disciples. Harper? Kansas., 1906.

5056. <u>Sam Wang's College: Or, China Won</u>. Christopher,
       1925.
5057. <u>Who Governs the Church</u>? 2 vols. Standard, 1919.

Tobias, Robert, 1919-.
     Seminary professor; church official.
5058. <u>Communist-Christian Encounter in East Europe</u>.
       School of Religion Pr., (Indianapolis), 1956.
5059. <u>Preaching on Christian Unity</u>. Bethany, 1958.
       (editor).

Todd, Joseph Clinton, 1879-1962.
     Seminary professor.
5060. <u>Politics and Religion in Ancient Israel: An
       Introduction to the Study of the Old Testament</u>.
       Macmillan, 1904.
5061. <u>Prescribed Biblical and Religious Courses in
       American Colleges and Universities</u>. Bloomington?
       Ind., 1934.

Toler, Thomas W.
     Pastor.
5062. <u>The Elder at the Lord's Table</u>. Bethany, 1954.
5063. "Teaching the Christian Way." Bethany, 1965.

Tomlinson, Lee Glenn.
5064. <u>Churches of Today in the Light of Scripture</u>.
       Christian Leader Corp., Printers, 1927.

Torres, Lucas, 1933-.
5065. <u>Dignidad: Hispanic Americans and Their Struggle for
       Dignity</u>. Christian Bd. of Publication, 1975.
5066. <u>Struggle for Dignity: Hispanic Americans and Their
       Relationship to the Churches in the United State</u>s.
       Indianapolis, 1974.

Travers, Libbie Miller.
5067. <u>Sectarian Shackles</u>. Macmillan, 1926.

Trout, Jessie M.
     Missionary to Japan; church official.
5068. <u>Berthe Fidelia. Her Story As Told to Jessie M.
       Trout</u>. Bethany, 1957.
5069. <u>Forward in Missions and Education: Disciples of
       Christ Help Build the Kingdom</u>. United Christian
       Missionary Soc., 195_?
5070. <u>Kagawa, Japanese Prophet</u>. United Soc. for Christian
       Literature (London), 1959. (editor).
5071. <u>Like a Watered Garden [Devotions]</u>. Bethany, 1954.
5072. <u>The Two Kingdoms</u>, by Toyohiko Kagawa. Lutterworth
       (London), 1941. (translator).

Trudinger, Leonhard Paul, 1930-.
    Professor of music.
    5073. New Meanings for Old. Graphicopy, 1972.

Tubman, Emily Harvie (Thomas), 1794-1885.
    Philanthropist; laywoman.
    5074. In Memoriam: Mrs. Emily H. Tubman, Born March 21st,
           1794, Died June 9th, 1885. 188_?

For works about her written by Disciple authors, see
Bennett, Joseph R. under THEOLOGY section.

Tucker, Robert Preston, 1949-.
    Professor of religion and philosophy.
    5075. "The Christology of John B. Cobb, Jr." Ph.D. diss.,
           Univ. of Chicago, 1984.

Tupper, Charles B.
    Pastor.
    5076. Called, in Honor: Ethics of the Christian Ministry
           Creatively Interpreted. Bethany, 1949.

Turner, Dean.
    Pastor; professor of philosophy of education.
    5077. The Autonomous Man: An Essay in Personal Identity
           and Integrity. Bethany, 1970.
    5078. Classrooms in Crisis: Parents' Rights and the
           Public School. Accent Books, 1986. (co-author).
    5079. Commitment To Care: An Integrated Philosophy of
           Science, Education, and Religion. Devin-Adair,
           1978.
    5080. The Einstein Myth and the Ives Papers: A Counter
           Revolution in Physics. Devin-Adair, 1979.
           (co-editor).
    5081. Krinkle Nose: A Prayer of Thanks. Devin-Adair,
           1979.
    5082. Lonely God, Lonely Man: A Study in the Relation of
           Loneliness to Personal Development, with a
           Re-Evaluation of Christian Tradition. Philosophical
           Lib., 1960.

*Tyler, Benjamin Bushrod, 1840-1922.
    Pastor; journalist.
    5083. Concerning the Disciples of Christ. 1897.
    5084. History of the Disciples of Christ. New York,
           1893-1897.

Underwood, Charles Eugene.
    College president; professor of Old Testament.
    5085. The Church College: Inaugural Address...on the
           Occasion of His Installation as President of Eureka
           College. Eureka College Pr., 1912.

Updike, Jacob Van, 1850-1907.
  Pastor; evangelist.
  5086. Bible Readings and Drills. P. O. Updike, 1899.
  5087. Sermons and Songs. Christian Publishing Co., 1889.
          (co-author).
  5088. Updike's Sermons. Standard, 1891.

Updike, Phyllis Ann.
  Missionary to Zaire; nurse.
  5089. "Physiological Circadian Rhythmicity in Human
          Preterm Infants." Ph.D. diss., Indiana Univ., 1982.

Vaca, Victor Hugo.
  Missionary to Paraguay.
  5090. Financing Primary Health Care Programs. World
          Council of Churches, 1987.

Van Buren, James Geil, 1914-.
  Pastor; professor of religion and humanities.
  5091. "Cults Challenge the Church: Study Course for Youth
          and Adults." Standard, 1965.
  5092. A Forgotten Scotsman: George MacDonald. 1959.
  5093. Increase in Learning: Essays in Honor of James G.
          Van Buren. Edited by Robert J. Owens, Jr. and
          Barbara E. Hamm. Manhattan Christian College, 1979.
  5094. The Lord of the Early Christians. Manhattan Bible
          College, 1955.
  5095. The Search: The Living God Seeks Man. Standard,
          1974.
  5096. Ten Thousand Listened. 1959.
  5097. What the Bible Says about Praise and Promise.
          College Pr. Publishing Co., 1980. (co-author).

Wagers, Charles Herndon, 1910-.
  Professor of religion.
  5098. Christian Faith and Philosophical Inquiry. College
          of the Bible (Lexington), 1961.

Wake, Arthur N.
  Professor of music.
  5099. Companion to Hymnbook for Christian Worship.
          Bethany, 1970.

Wakefield, Edmund Burritt, 1846-1921.
  Pastor; professor; soldier.
  5100. International Sunday School Lessons: Uniform Lesson
          Commentary. Muhlenburg, 1954-.
  5101. Standard Commentary on the International
          Sunday-School Lessons... Standard, 1883-19__.
          (editor).

Waldrop, W. Earl.
  5102. How To Combat Communism. Bethany, 1962.

5103. <u>What Makes America Great</u>. Bethany, 1957.
5104. <u>You've Got a Problem</u>. Naylor, 1962.

Walk, David.
    5105. "Lindon Street Christian Pulpit?...a Sermon...June
          21, 1874." N.d.

*Walker, Dean Everest, 1898-.
    Pastor; professor of religion; historian; college
    president.
    5106. <u>Adventuring for Christian Unity: A Survey of the
          History of Churches of Christ (Disciples)</u>. Berean
          Pr., 1935.
    5107. "An Approach to Reconciliation." In <u>Increase in
          Learning</u>, pp. 107-16. Edited by R. Owens. 1979.
    5108. "The Authority of the Word." Kentucky Christian
          College Pr., 1981.
    5109. <u>Essays on New Testament Christianity: A Festschrift
          in Honor of Dean E. Walker</u>. Standard, 1978.
          (editor).
    5110. "Renewal through Recovery." Kentucky Christian
          College Pr., 1981.

*Walker, Granville Thomas, 1908-.
    Pastor.
    5111. <u>Four Faces of Christian Ministry: Essays in Honor
          of A. Dale Fiers</u>. Bethany, 1973. (co-author).
    5112. <u>Go Placidly amid the Noise and Haste: Meditations
          on the "Desiderata."</u> Texas Christian Univ. Pr.,
          1973.
    5113. <u>The Greatest of These</u>. Bethany, 1963.
    5114. <u>Paul's Message for Today: Echoes from William C.
          Morro & Granville T. Walker</u>. Texas Christian Univ.
          Pr., 1970.
    5115. <u>Preaching in the Thought of Alexander Campbell</u>.
          Bethany Pr., 1954.

For works about him written by Disciple authors, see
Keith, Noel Leonard under THEOLOGY section.

Walker, John Byron, 1939-.
    Missionary to Japan; radio show host.
    5116. "Telling Others about New Life in Christ for the
          Space Age." Central Christian Church (Lexington),
          1965.
    5117. "Theory and Practice in a Boston Parents' Movement."
          D. Min. thesis, Boston Univ., 1977.

Walker, Virgil Reziah, 1883-.
    5118. <u>Glory Trail</u>. Vantage, 1956.

Wallace, Ray W.
    Pastor.

5119. Christian Youth Fellowship: CYF Handbook.
        Christian Bd. of Publication, 1945.

Ward, James Keith.
    Pastor.
    5120. "Introducing Disciples of Christ Lay Ministers in
           Central Alabama to Clinical Pastoring." D. Min.
           thesis, Brite Divinity School, 1983.

Ward, Mae (Yoho).
    Church official.
    5121. "Christian Action in Argentina." United Christian
           Missionary Soc., 194_?
    5122. "Disciples of Christ in Latin America." United
           Christian Missionary Soc., 1942.
    5123. "Disciples of Christ in Latin America and Jamaica."
           United Christian Missionary Soc., 1951?
    5124. Latin America: Witness and Risk. Christian Bd. of
           Publication, 1980.
    5125. "Mexico Looks Forward." United Christian Missionary
           Soc., 194_?
    5126. "Report from Paraguay." United Christian Missionary
           Soc., 1948?
    5127. The Seeking Heart: The Prayer Journal of Mae Yoho
           Ward. CBP Pr., 1985.

Ware, James, 1913-.
    5128. Peep into a Chinaman's Library: Being a Popular
           View of Chinese Literature. Shanghai Mercury
           Office, 1896.

Warford, Malcolm L.
    Seminary president.
    5129. Colloquy: Conversations with the Faculty, Union
           Theological Seminary, 1976-1977. Office of
           Educational Research, 1977. (editor).
    5130. The Education of the Public. Pilgrim Pr., 1980.
    5131. The Necessary Illusion: Church Culture and
           Educational Change. United Church Pr., 1976.
    5132. "Piety, Politics, and Pedagogy, an Evangelical
           Protestant Tradition in Higher Education at Lane,
           Oberlin, and Berea, 1984-190_? Ed.D diss., Teachers
           College, Columbia Univ., 1973.

*Warren, William Robinson, 1868-1947.
    Pastor; editor.
    5133. The Life and Labors of Archibald McLean. Bethany,
           1923.
    5134. Program of the International Centennial
           Celebration... of the Disciples of Christ...
           Pittsburgh, 1909.

5135.   Survey of Service: Organizations Represented in
        International Convention of Disciples of Christ.
        Christian Bd. of Publication, 1928.

Wassenick, Paul G.
    Professor of religion.
    5136.   Aids to Christian Learning.   Christian Bd. of
            Publication, n.d.

*Watkins, Keith, 1931-.
    Pastor; professor of worship.
    5137.   The Breaking of Bread: An Approach to Worship for
            the Christian Churches (Disciples of Christ).
            Bethany, 1966.
    5138.   Faithful and Fair: Transcending Sexist Language in
            Worship. Abingdon, 1981.
    5139.   The Feast of Joy: The Lord's Supper in Free
            Churches. Bethany, 1977.
    5140.   Liturgies in a Time When Cities Burn. Abingdon,
            1969.
    5141.   Thankful Praise: A Resource for Christian Worship
            Prepared for the Use of the Christian Church
            (Disciples of Christ). CBP Pr., 1987. (editor).

Watson, Keene Arnold, 1924-.
    Missionary to Congo.
    5142.   "The Evaluation of Practices in Preventive and
            Curative Medicine through Medical Records and
            Special Study." Ph.D. diss., Univ. of California,
            Berkeley, 1967.

Watters, Archibald Clark, 1887-1970.
    Professor of missions.
    5143.   "A Century of Churches of Christ." Berean Pr.,
            193_?
    5144.   History of British Churches of Christ. Butler
            Univ., 1948.

Wells, Goldie Ruth.
    Missionary to Congo.
    5145.   Sila, Son of Congo. Bethany, 1945.

Welsh, Wiley A.
    Seminary president.
    5146.   Villains on White Horses: Sermons on Passages from
            Paul. Bethany, 1964.

*Welshimer, Pearl Howard, 1873-1957.
    Pastor; editor.
    5147.   A Bible-School Vision. Standard, 1909.
    5148.   Concerning the Disciples: A Brief Resume of the
            Movement to Restore the New Testament Church.
            Standard, 1935.

5149. The Great Salvation. Standard, 1954.
5150. Welshimer's Sermons. Standard, 1927.
5151. Zachary Taylor Sweeney: Appreciation Regret. N.d.

For works about him written by Disciple authors, see
Arant, Francis M. under THEOLOGY section.

Wertz, Spencer Kiefer.
   Professor of philosophy.
   5152. "Humean Models of Historical Discourse." Ph.D.
          diss., Univ. of Oklahoma, 1970.

West, John William, 1871-1958.
   5153. Sketches of Our Mountain Pioneers. J. W. West,
          1939.
   5154. Sketches of Three Pioneer Preachers: Elder Ezekiel
          Evans, Elder Cyrus Holt, Elder P. D. West and the
          Religious Work of Their Descendants. J. W. West,
          1955?
   5155. A Totalitarian Church, a Menace To Liberty and
          Democracy. 3d ed. J. W. West, 1945.

West, Robert Frederick, 1916-.
   Pastor; professor of religion.
   5156. Alexander Campbell and Natural Religion. Yale Univ.
          Pr., 1948.
   5157. Christian Decision and Action. Herder, 1968.
   5158. The Church and Organized Movements. Harper, 1946.
          (co-author).
   5159. God's Gambler. Prentice-Hall, 1964.
   5160. Light Beyond Shadows: A Minister and Mental Health.
          Macmillan, 1949.
   5161. Preaching on Race. Bethany, 1962.
   5162. "Who Are the Christian Churches and What Do We
          Believe?" West, 1954. (co-author).

West, William Garrett, 1913-.
   Pastor; seminary professor.
   5163. "Annotated Bibliography of Children's Stories,
          Selected from Volumes Available in the Yale Divinity
          School Library." 1938.
   5164. Barton Warren Stone: Early American Advocate of
          Christian Unity. Disciples of Christ Historical
          Soc., 1954.
   5165. Goal To Go. Bethany, 1974.
   5166. Staff Relationships in a Church. Home and State
          Missions Planning Council, 1958.
   5167. Who Are the Christian Churches and What Do We
          Believe? W. G. West, 1954. (co-author).

Wharton, Emma Virginia (Richardson), d.1922.
   5168. Life of G. L. Wharton. Revell, 1913.

Wheeler, Joseph Clyde.
    Pastor.
    5169. <u>Claim These Victories [Sermons]</u>. Bethany, 1956.
    5170. <u>Here Lies Our Hope</u>. Christopher, 1955.
    5171. <u>Light for Dark Days</u>. Bethany, 1965.
    5172. <u>This Way, Please</u>! Bethany, 1972.
    5173. <u>Winning What You Want</u>. Bethany, 1960.

*White, Richard Clark, 1916- .
    Pastor; professor of homiletics.
    5174. <u>Being the Church Universal</u>. Christian Bd. of
          Publication, 1971.
    5175. <u>Biblical Preaching: How To Find and Remove Barriers</u>.
          CBP Pr., 1988.
    5176. <u>Melito of Sardis Sermon "On the Passover": A New</u>
          <u>English Translation with Introduction and</u>
          <u>Commentary</u>. Lexington Theol. Seminary Lib., 1976.
          (translator).
    5177. <u>The Vocabulary of the Church: A Pronunciation</u>
          <u>Guide</u>. Macmillan, 1960.

Whitley, Oliver Read.
    Professor of sociology of religion.
    5178. <u>The Church: Mirror or Windows? Images of the</u>
          <u>Church in American Society</u>. Bethany, 1969.
    5179. <u>Religious Behavior: Here Sociology and Religion</u>
          <u>Meet</u>. Prentice Hall, 1964.
    5180. <u>Trumpet Call of Reformation</u>. Bethany, 1959.

Wickizer, Willard Morgan, 1899-1974.
    Pastor; church official.
    5181. <u>Constitutions and By-Laws for Local Churches</u>.
          United Christian Missionary Soc., n.d.
    5182. <u>The Derelict Saint and Other Sermons</u>. Bethany,
          1936.
    5183. <u>From Frontier to Frontiers in Home Missions</u>. United
          Christian Missionary Soc., 1960.
    5184. "Guidance Manual for Disciples of Christ." Rev. ed.
          Christian Bd. of Publication, 1957.
    5185. <u>Making Public Worship Meaningful</u>. United Christian
          Missionary Soc., 19__.

Wiggs, L. D., 1888- .
    5186. <u>Thirty-Nine Years with the Great I Am</u>. Chapel Hill?
          N.C., 1952.

Wilburn, Ralph Glenn, 1909- .
    Seminary dean.
    5187. <u>The Historical Shape of Faith</u>. Westminster, 1966.
    5188. "The Interrelation between Theology and Science."
          Nebraska School of Religion, 1966 or 7.
    5189. <u>Notes in the Course: History of the Church</u>. Enid,
          Okla., 1952.

5190. The Prophetic Voice in Protestant Christianity.
       Bethany, 1956.
5191. "The Reconstruction of Theology." In The Renewal of
       the Church, vol. 1. Bethany, 1963. (editor).
5192. "Schleiermacher's Conception of Grace, in the Light
       of the Historical Development of the Doctrine of
       Grace." Ph.D. diss., Univ. of Chicago, 1945.

Wilfred, Harvey O.
    Pastor.
5193. "The Creating Word: A Theological Approach To
       Preaching." D. Min. thesis, Phillips Univ., 1972.

*Willett, Herbert Lockwood, 1864-1944.
    Pastor; seminary professor; associate editor of Christian
    Century.
5194. Basic Truths of the Christian Faith. Christian
       Century Co., 1903.
5195. The Bible through the Centuries. Willett, Clark &
       Colby, 1929.
5196. The Call of the Christ. Revell, 1912.
5197. Finding God through the Beautiful. American
       Institute of Sacred Literature, 1929. (co-author).
5198. The Jew through the Centuries. Willett, Clark and
       Co., 1932.
5199. Life and Teachings of Jesus. Bethany, 1898.
5200. The Message of the Prophets of Israel to the
       Twentieth Century. Univ. of Chicago Pr., 1916.
5201. Our Bible: Its Origin, Character and Value.
       Christian Century Pr., 1917.
5202. Our Plea for Union and the Present Crisis.
       Christian Century Co., 1901.
5203. The Popular and Critical Bible Encyclopedia and
       Scriptural Dictionary. 2 vols. Howard-Severance
       Co., 1901. (co-editor).
5204. Progress: Anniversary Volume of the Campbell
       Institute on the Completion of Twenty Years of
       History. Christian Century Pr., 1917. (co-editor).
5205. The Prophets of Israel. Revell, 1899.
5206. The Ruling Quality: A Study of Faith as the Means
       of Victory in Life. Revell, 1902.
5207. Studies in the First Book of Samuel, for the Use of
       Classes in Secondary Schools and in the Secondary
       Division of the Sunday School. Univ. of Chicago
       Pr., 1909.
5208. The Teachings of the Books. Revell, 1899.
       (co-author).
5209. "That They May All Be One"; Autobiography and
       Memorial of James M. Philputt, Apostle of Christian
       Unity. Christian Bd. of Publication, 1933.
       (co-editor).
5210. The World's Great Religious Poetry. Macmillan,
       1923.

*Williams, John Augustus, 1824-1903.
  College professor and president.
  5211. In Memoriam: Remarks on the Life and Character of
         General Samuel L. Williams. R. Clarke & Co., 1872.
  5212. Rosa Emerson. Christian Publishing Co., 1897.

*Williams, Raymond Brady, 1935-.
  Pastor; professor of religion.
  5213. A New Face of Hinduism: The Swaminarayan Religion.
         Cambridge Univ. Pr., 1984.
  5214. "Origen's Interpretation of the Gospel of John."
         Ph.D. diss, Univ. of Chicago, 1966.
  5215. Religions of Immigrants from India and Pakistan:
         New Threads in the American Tapestry. Cambridge
         Univ. Pr., 1988.

*Williamson, Clark Murray, 1935-.
  Seminary president; professor of theology.
  5216. God Is Never Absent. Bethany, 1977.
  5217. Has God Rejected His People?: Anti-Judaism in the
         Christian Church. Abingdon, 1982.

Willis, John T., 1922-.
  Professor of religion.
  5218. My Servants, the Prophets. Biblical Research Pr.,
         1971.
  5219. "The Structure, Setting and Inter-Relationships of
         the Periscopes in the Book of Micah." Ph.D. diss.,
         Vanderbilt Univ., 1966.

Willyard, Warren Hastings.
  5220. The Divine Creed: Or, The Only Ground of Union.
         Stephens & Bedaine Printers, 1899.

*Wilson, Bert, 1878-1943.
  College president and professor.
  5221. The Christian and His Money Problems. Doran, 1922.
  5222. Dad's Letters on a World Journey. Powell & White,
         1921.
  5223. In the Land of the Salaam. Powell & White, 1921.
  5224. Know Your Local Church. Standard, 1922.
  5225. Progressive Stewardship. Unified Promotion, 1941.

Wilson, George Hugh.
  5226. "Unity and Restoration in the Ecumenical Thought of
         the Disciples of Christ: With Special Reference to
         the Disciples' Part in the Evolution of the World
         Council of Churches." Ph.D. diss., Hartford
         Seminary Foundation, 1962.

Wilson, Louis Charles.
  5227. Twentieth Century Sermons and Addresses. Standard,
         1902. (editor).

Wilson, Robert Allen.
    5228.   "An Evaluation of the Christian Education Curricula
        of Bible Colleges Supported by Christian Churches."
        D. R. E. diss., Southern Baptist Theol. Seminary,
        1972.

*Wilson, Robert Rutherford, 1942-.
    Professor of Old Testament.
    5229.   Canon, Theology, and Old Testament Interpretation:
        Essays in Honor of Brevard S. Childs. Fortress Pr.,
        1988. (co-editor).
    5230.   Genealogy and History in the Biblical World. Yale
        Univ., 1977.
    5231.   Prophecy and Society in Ancient Israel. Fortress
        Pr., 1980.
    5232.   Sociological Approaches to the Old Testament.
        Fortress Pr., 1984.

Winquist, Charles Edwin, 1944-.
    Professor of religion.
    5233.   Abstracts: [Annual Meeting], 1980, American Academy
        of Religion, Society of Biblical Literature, Dallas,
        Texas, 5-9 November, 1980. Scholars Pr., 1980.
        (co-editor).
    5234.   Abstracts: [Annual Meeting], American Academy of
        Religion, Society of Biblical Literature, San
        Francisco, December 1981. Scholars Pr., 1981.
    5235.   Annual Meeting, New York, New York, 15-18 November
        1979: [American Academy of Religion] Abstracts.
        Scholars Pr., (editor).
    5236.   The Archaeology of the Imagination. Scholars Pr.,
        1981. (editor).
    5237.   The Communion of Possibility. New Horizons Pr.,
        1975.
    5238.   Homecoming: Interpretation, Transformation, and
        Individuation. Scholars Pr., 1978.
    5239.   "Knowing and Being: An Inquiry into the Ontological
        Significance of Language." Ph.D. diss., Univ. of
        Chicago, 1970.
    5240.   Practical Hermeneutics: A Revised Agenda for the
        Ministry. Scholars Pr., 1980.
    5241.   The Transcendental Imagination: An Essay in
        Philosophical Theology. Nijhoff, 1972.

Wismar, Donald Roy, 1926-.
    Professor of psychology and religion.
    5242.   "A Sacramental View of Preaching, As Seen in the
        Writings of John Calvin and P. T. Forsyth and
        Applied to the Mid-Twentieth Century." Th.D. diss.,
        Pacific School of Religion, 1963.

Wolfe, Michael Craig.
    Pastor.

5243. "The Growth and Decline of the Christian Church
       (Disciples of Christ) in Los Angeles County: What
       Could Our Future Be?" D. Min. thesis, School of
       Theol. at Claremont, 1982.

Wood, Thomas E.
    Church official.
    5244. "Another Stewardship." Unified Promotion, 196_.
    5245. Worship. Indianapolis, 1966.

Works, Herbert Melvin, 1931-.
    Professor of religion.
    5246. "The Church Growth Movement to 1965: An Historical
           Perspective." D. Miss. diss., Fuller Theol.
           Seminary, 1974.

Worrell, John Edward, 1933-.
    Professor of religion.
    5247. "Concepts of Wisdom in the Dead Sea Scrolls." Ph.D.
           diss., Claremont Grad. School, 1968.

Wright, James Roy, 1888-.
    5248. The Wright-Sommer Debate.... Questions Discussed:
           "Instrumental Music" and "The Societies."
           Unionville (Mo.) Republican Printing Co., 1916.

Wyker, James D.
    Educator.
    5249. Program of the Rural Church: A Manual for
           Developing the Rural Church Community. Bible
           College at the Univ. of Missouri, 195_.

Wyker, Mossie Allman, 1902-.
    Laywoman.
    5250. Church Women in the Scheme of Things. Bethany,
           1953.

Yocum, Cyrus McNeely, 1883-1958.
    Church official.
    5251. "The Disciples of Christ Congo Mission in Africa."
           1928.
    5252. "Disciples of Christ in Japan." United Christian
           Missionary Soc., 1949.

For works about him written by Disciple authors, see
    Kerr, Paul Edward under THEOLOGY section.

*Zollars, Ely Vaughan, 1847-1916.
    Pastor; college president and professor; founder of
    Phillips University.
    5253. The Abrahamic Promises Fulfilled. Standard, 1913.
    5254. Baccalaureate and Convocation Sermons. Standard,
           1912.

5255. The Commission Executed. Standard, 1912.
5256. The Great Salvation. Standard, 1896.
5257. Hebrew Prophecy. Standard, 1907.
5258. The Word of Truth. Standard, 1910.

AUTHOR INDEX

Boring, Mayard Eugene, 2980-2982.
Born, Jerry Lynn, 2490.
Bortz, Walter Raymond, 693.
Boschke, Friedrich Ludwig, 2491-2516.
Bostick, Sarah Lue (Howard) Young, 2983.
Boswell, Ira Matthews, 2984.
Botkin, Robert Ralph, 2985.
Bouchard, Larry D., 2986.
Bowdler, George A., 2208-2210.
Bowen, Thaddeus Hassell, 2987-2988.
Bower, William Clayton, 38, 2989-3003.
Bowman, Alden Elbert, 694.
Boyd, Maurice, 1548-1555.
Boyd, Robin, 39.
Boyd, Wade M.F., 511.
Boyer, John Elvin, 2114.
Braden, Gayle Anderson, 1556.
Bradney, Leta Vera, 3004-3005.
Bradshaw, Marion John, 3006-3012.
Bradshaw, Vinton D., 3013.
Bragg, Joseph H., Jr., 3014.
Brandt, John Lincoln, 3015.
Branson, Gene N., 3016.
Breen, Quirinus, 1557-1559.
Brenneman, Lyle Eugene, 2211, 3017.
Brenton, Charles L., 2517.
Brewer, Marion Carey, 2212-2213.
Brewer, Thomas Bowman, 1560-1562.
Brewer, Urban C., 3020.
Bricker, Luther Otterbein, 3021.
Briggs, Eugene Stephen, 695-696.
Briney, John Benton, 3022-3025.
Brinson, Marion B., 40.
Britton, Joseph C., 2518-2519.
Britton, Rollin J., 41.
Bro, Margueritte (Harmon), 42, 1089-1106.
Broadus, Loren A., Jr., 43-44, 3026-3027.
Broce, Thomas E., 697-698.
Brokaw, George Lewis, 3028.
Brooks, Wayne Maurice, 2520.
Brothers, Barbara, 1107.
Brown, Alberta Z., 3029-3031.
Brown, Caroline, 46.
Brown, David Francis, 2521.
Brown, Ella Lees, 1108.
Brown, Francis Robert, 2115-2117.
Brown, G., 47.
Brown, Genevieve, 48.
Brown, Henry Clay, 3032-3034.
Brown, Hilton Ultimus, 699-700.
Brown, Homer A., 552-553.
Brown, John Thomas, 3035-3036.
Brown, Leslie C., 3037.

Carmon, J.N., 60.
Carpe, William Donald, 61-63, 3092.
Carpenter, Homer Wilson, 3093.
Carpenter, James A., 3094.
Carpenter, Kenneth Halsey, 2529.
Carpenter, Leewell Hunter, 1574.
Carpenter, William Whitney, 3095.
Carr, A., 64.
Carr, James Bottorff, 3096.
Carstensen, Roger Norwood, 3097-3099.
Cartwright, Colbert S., 65.
Cartwright, George Washington, 1575.
Cartwright, Lin Dorwin, 3100-3101.
Carty, James W., Jr., 1109-1116, 3102.
Casey, Mike, 66.
Caskey, Thomas W., 3103-3104.
Cassell, R.B., 67.
Castle, Conan Jennings, 1471.
Castleberry, Ottis L., 1576-1578.
Castleman, William James, 3106-3108.
Cauble, Commodore Wesley, 1579.
Cave, Robert Catlett, 3109-3112.
Caves, Thomas Courtney, 2530.
Cayce, Edgar, 3113-3114.
Cecil, Levi Moffitt, 1117.
Centerwall, Siegried Achorn, 3115.
Cerbin, Dwaine Edward, 3116.
Challen, James, 69, 3117-3122.
Chamberlin, Gary D., 716.
Chambers, W., 70.
Champie, Ting R., 3123.
Chandler, R., 71.
Chaney, Marvin Lee, 3124.
Channels, Lloyd V., 3125.
Channels, Vera Grace, 1958-1962, 2405-2410.
Chapin, David A., 648.
Charles, Searle Franklin, 1580-1582.
Chase, Ira Joy, 2216.
Cheatham, Richard Beauregard, 2411.
Cheek, William Henry, 2679-2680.
Chen, Kuo-Tsai, 2119-2120.
Cheverton, Cecil Frank, 3126-3130.
Chrisman, James Riley, 1583.
Christensen, James Lee, 3131-3149.
Church, Samuel Harden, 1584-1596.
Clague, James G., 76.
Clark, Champ, 2217.
Clark, Elmer Talmage, 77.
Clark, Randolph, 717.
Clark, Sara Graves, 78.
Clark, Stephen Lee, 1472.
Clark, Thomas Curtis, 1118-1143.
Clark, Warren Malcolm, 3150-3151.

Clawson, Bertha Fidelia, 3152.
Clay, Comer, 2218-2221.
Cleaver, Charles, 2121.
Cliett, Charles B., 1007.
Clingan, Donald Frank, 3153.
Coats, George W., Jr., 3154-3158.
Cobb, William Daniel, 3159.
Cochran, Bess (White), 1597-1599, 3160.
Cochran, Louis, 1144-1154.
Coffey, Carole, 79.
Coffland, Jack Arthur, 718.
Coggins, James Caswell, 80.
Cole, Clifford Adair, 3161-3168.
Cole, Myron C., 81, 3169-3170.
Cole, Steven George, 2412-2414.
Coler, George P., 3171-3172.
Collias, Eugene E., 2531-2541.
Collier, Robert Eugene, 2542
Collins, Johnnie Andrew, 1600.
Colquitt, Landon Augustus, 2122.
Colston, Lowell G., 3173-3178.
Coltharp, Forrest Lee, 2123.
Combs, George Hamilton, 3179-3185.
Compton, John Richard, 3186.
Conner, Americus Wood, 3187.
Conrad, Rufus, 3188.
Cook, Billy Cy, 1008-1009.
Cook, Gaines Monroe, 87, 3189-3190.
Cook, Joseph Lee, 2023-2037.
Cook, Robert Edward, 2543.
Cook, Virginia D., 3191.
Cooley, Harris Reid, 3192-3193.
Coombs, James Vincent, 1155-1161, 3194.
Cooper, David Lipscomb, 3195-3202.
Cooper, Guy LeRoy, 1162.
Cooper, Myers Young, 2222.
Copeland, Warren Rush, 3203.
Corbett, Robert G., 2544.
Corder, David E., 3204.
Corey, Stephen Jared, 3205-3214.
Corwin, Betty Jane, 2415-2416.
Cory, Abram Edward, 88, 3215-3218.
Costello, Lawrence F., 719.
Cotten, Carroll Cresswell, 720, 3219.
Cotto, Pablo, 3220-3223.
Cottrell, James J., 3224.
Cowden, William F., 3225.
Cox, Blanche, 721.
Cox, Charles Leonard, 2417.
Cox, Claude, 90.
Cox, Harold Glenwood, 2714.
Cox, James Arthur, 3226.
Craddock, Fred Brenning, 91, 3227-3245.

Dickinson, Hoke S., 3325.
Dickinson, Richard Donald Nye, Jr., 3326.
Dietze, C.E., 116.
Digweed, Marilyn, 3327.
Doane, Joseph William, 2546-2547.
Dobbs, Ralph Cecil, 725-726.
Dobkins, Betty Eakle, 1627.
Dodson, James Richard, 3328.
Donley, Carol Cram, 1164-1165.
Donovan, Daryl G., 3329.
Doolen, Richard M., 1628-1629.
Dooley, Donald, 2548-2549.
Doran, Adron, 3330.
Douglas, Crerar, 1630-1631.
Douglas, H. Paul, 3331.
Douthitt, Ira Arthur, 3332.
Dowdy, Barton Alexander, 3333.
Dowling, Enos Everett, 3334-3340.
Dowling, William Worth, 3341-3347.
Downing, Glenn Dale, 561.
Doyle, B., 160.
Drake, Ralph, 161.
Draper, John Daniel, 2550.
Dreisbach, Dale Alson, 2551-2552.
Dugan, Herschel C., 3348.
Duke, James Oliver, 163, 1632-1633.
Dungan, David Roberts, 3349-3361.
Duns, Donald Frederick, 1166-1167.
Dyble, John E., 261.

Eames, Samuel Morris, 3362-3367.
Eckstein, Stephen Daniel, Jr., 3368.
Edens, Ambrose, 3369.
Edmunds, Russell David, 1634-1637.
Ehlers, Glenn Leroy, 1012.
Eikner, Allen Van Dozier, 3370-3371.
Eller, David B., 166.
Ellis, Dale, 3372.
Ellis, Joe Scott, 3373-3376.
Ellis, John William, 1168-1170.
Ellis, William E., 167.
Ellmore, Alfred, 3377.
Elmore, Robert Emmet, 3378.
Else, John F., 2715-2716.
Ely, Lois Anna, 3379.
Eminhizer, Earl Eugene, 3380.
England, Stephen Jackson, 168, 3381-3387.
Epler, Stephen Edward, 3388-3390.
Epperson, Kenneth Boyd, 727.
Erisman, Fred Raymond, 1171-1173.
Erlewine, Walter William, 1638.
Ernst, F. Gene, 1473.
Errett, Isaac, 3391-3401.

Gobar, Ash, 3607-3609.
Goff, Lewin A., 1177.
Goodloe, Nancy Ruth, 2191.
Goodnight, Cloyd, 3610.
Goodpasture, Albert Virgil, 1652-1654.
Goodrich, Howard Bruce, 734.
Goodwin, Donald Francis, 1178.
Goodwin, Elijah, 3611-3612.
Goodwin, Marcia Melissa Bassett, 1179-1183.
Gordon, George Newton, 735-752.
Gorsuch, Arthur Bennette, 1184.
Gorsuch, Richard Lee, 2433-2437.
Gosnell, Jack Leslie, 2124.
Grafton, Warren, 3613-3614.
Graham, Lorenz B., 1185-1204.
Graham, Robert, 3615-3616.
Graham, Ronald William, 219, 3617-3619.
Granberg, Charles Boyd, 2564-2565.
Grant, Brian W., 3620-3624.
Gravenstein, Monte L., 3625.
Gray, Archie W., 3626.
Gray, James, 220.
Green, Edith, 753-755.
Green, Francis Marion, 3627-3632.
Green, Jerry, 2192.
Greene, Wayne A., 3633.
Greer, Virginia Lou, 3634.
Greisch, J.R., 221.
Gresham, Charles R., 3635-3636.
Gresham, Perry Epler, 222, 3637-3644.
Griffeth, Ross John, 223, 3645-3649.
Griffin, Charles Hudson, 2253-2255.
Griffin, David Ray, 224, 3650-3654.
Griffin, Jean, 1963.
Grigg, Neil Sadler, 2566-2574.
Griggs, Harry Hubert, 1205.
Grimes, Larry Edward, 1206.
Grosse, Fay Wiseman, 2040.
Gruenler, Royce Gordon, 3655-3657.
Grupp, Stanley E., 2718-2722.
Gugler, Carl Wesley, 2575.
Guldenzopf, E. Charles, 2576-2577.
Gulick, Dennis, 2125-2126.
Gulick, Frances, 2127.
Gustafson, Paul Moody, 2723.
Gwinn, Mary Jane, 2041.

Hackleman, William Edward Michael, 1488-1494.
Haddox, Benjamin Edward, 2724-2725.
Hagee, Gale Lee, 515.
Haggard, Forrest DeLoss, 3658.
Hailey, Homer, 3659.
Haldiman, Jerrold T., 2153.

Higdon, Elmer Kelso, 256, 3793-3800.
Higdon, Idella Eleanor (Wilson), 3801.
High, Dallas M., 3802-3803.
Highlander, James Lee, 1233.
Hilgedick, Lorraine, 764.
Hill, Claude Eugene, 3804.
Hill, Edwin S., 2438.
Hill, John Louis, 3805.
Hill, Marilynne, 3806-3811.
Hine, William C., 2257.
Hinman, George Warren, 3812-3820.
Hinsdale, Burke Aaron, 765-828.
Hinton, Maxine Armstrong, 2155.
Hoagland, Bruce D., 1497.
Hocking, William Earnest, 3821-3834.
Hockman, Daniel Mack, 1686.
Hodge, Frederick Arthur, 1687.
Hoffman, Dan Clayton, 3835.
Hoffman, Gustavus Adolphus, 3836.
Hoffman, William Michael, 568-573.
Hoffman, Wilson Jesse, Jr., 1688.
Hogan, Bernice Harris, 1234-1245.
Hoge, Dean R., 261.
Hohman, John Terrill, 829.
Holland, Harold E., 263.
Holman, C.T., 264.
Holstead, Roland Edward, 265.
Holstrom, Eric C., 266.
Holt, Basil Fenelon, 3837-3848.
Honey, Richard David, 2439.
Hoover, Guy Israel, 267, 3849-3854.
Hoover, Harvey Daniel, 3855.
Hopkins, Alexander Campbell, 3857-3858.
Hopkins, William W., 3859.
Hooper, Robert E., 1689-1691.
Hooper, Myron Taggart, 3860-3862.
Hopper, Rex D., 2735.
Hopson, Ella (Lord), 1692.
Hopson, Winthrop Hartley, 3863.
Hopwood, Josephus, 830.
Hornaback, Joseph Hope, 2131.
Horton, Roy F., 3864.
House, Charles T., 1693.
Houser, David John, 1246.
Housley, Carl Blair, 574.
Houts, Larry Lee, 2588.
Hoven, Ard, 3865.
Hoven, Victor Emanuel, 3866-3870.
Howard, Guy, 1247-1249.
Howe, Henry, 3871.
Howell, Robert Lee, 3872-3874.
Howenstine, Lydia (Kimmel), 1694.
Howland, William C., 268.

John, Roger, 3965.
Johnson, Ashley Sidney, 3966-3980.
Johnson, Barton W., 3981-3986.
Johnson, Daniel Thomas, 1721-1722.
Johnson, Douglas, 392.
Johnson, Frank P., 2442.
Johnson, Gordon Verle, 2595-2597.
Johnson, H. Eugene, 3987-3992.
Johnson, Harold R., 3993-3994.
Johnson, Lyndon Baines, 2291-2313.
Johnson, Tom Lofton, 2314-2316.
Johnson, Wendell Gilbert, 2134-2136.
Johnston, Francis E., 2681-2693.
Johnston, Glenn Eric, 2137.
Jones, Alexander Elvin, 1250-1252.
Jones, Allen Bailey, 3995.
Jones, Charles Thomas, Jr., 1723-1724.
Jones, Claude C., 3996-3998.
Jones, Edgar Dewitt, 284, 3999-4003.
Jones, George Curtis, 4004-4020.
Jones, Joe Robert, 285, 4021.
Jones, Millard Lawrence, Jr., 1021.
Jones, Myrddyn William, 4022.
Jones, Richard Bruce, 838.
Jones, Willis Rumble, 1725-1727.
Jordan, Orvis F., 286.
Jordan, Robert L., 4023.
Jorgenson, Dale Alfred, 1498-1499.
Jouett, Edward Stockton, 1990-1992.
Joyce, James Daniel, 4024-4025.
Judah, J. Stillson, 2049-2053.

Kane, Charles P., 287.
Kaufman, Harold Frederick, 2745-2758.
Keaton, Marjorie, 577.
Keck, Leander Earl, 4026-4033.
Keckley, Weldon, 4034.
Keefer, Gary Bruce, 1022.
Keene, Laurence C., 288, 2759-2761.
Keith, Noel Leonard, 4035-4042.
Kellems, Jesse Randolph, 4043-4049.
Keller, William Edward, 4050.
Kellett, James Roy, 4051.
Kelly, Dolores Goodwin, 1728.
Kellogg, Donald Homer, 839-841.
Kelly, Charles Robert, 2694.
Kelly, Emma Chenault, 1253.
Kelly, James Patrick, 4052.
Kelly, Mary Frances E., 4053.
Kelly, William W., 842.
Kemp, Charles F., 4054-4078.
Kemp, Robert A., 578.
Kenderdine, James Marshall, 579-580.

McPherson, Chalmers, 1770.
McQuiddy, J. Clayton, 4307.
McWhiney, Grady, 1771-1778.
McWhirter, David Ian, 320, 2055-2057.
Madearis, Dale W., 4308.
Major, James Brooks, 1779.
Malehorn, Harold Arthur, 869-875.
Manchester, Harland Frank, 1030-1031.
Mancil, Ervin, 2697.
Maness, Dale Dwayne, 2139.
Manire, Benjamin F., 4309.
Mankamyer, Orlin LeRoy, 4310-4311.
Mann, Russell A., 1300.
Margot, Louis, III, 650.
Markham, Edwin, 1301-1320.
Markus, Franklin William, 876.
Marshall, David Franklin, 1321-1323.
Marshall, Frank Hamilton, 4312-4314.
Marshall, Levi, 4315.
Martin, Edwin W., 2318.
Martin, Henry G., 1324-1325.
Martin, J. Lemuel, 4316.
Martin, Randel Odell, 877.
Martin, Sylvester Mitchell, 4317.
Martin, Warren Bryan, 878-883.
Martindale, Elijah, 4318.
Maschke, Ruby, 4319.
Mason, David V., 4320.
Mather, Kirtley Fletcher, 2614-2636.
Mathes, James Madison, 4321-4322.
Matthews, William R., 4323.
Maus, Cynthia Pearl, 4324-4333.
Maxwell, Ross A., 2637-2642.
Mead, Frank Spencer, 321-322.
Medbury, Charles Sanderson, 4334-4337.
Medearis, Dale W., 4338-4340.
Meeking, Basil, 323.
Meenen, Henry John, 586.
Mees, John Paul, 884.
Megginson, Robert Eugene, 2140.
Meldau, Elizabeth Uzzle, 522.
Mell, Galen Palmer, 2643.
Menges, Paul F., 587.
Merrell, James L., 4341.
Merritt, George W., 4342.
Messmer, Victor C., 588.
Metze, Mabel, 4343-4344.
Meyer, Marvin W., 4345-4349.
Miculka, Jean H., 1326.
Milano, Duane R., 589.
Miles, John, 4350.
Miles, Sara, 4350.
Miller, Dale, 4351-4356.

Miller, James Blair, 885-887, 4357-4359.
Miller, Joseph Irwin, 590.
Miller, Merl Eldon, 888.
Miller, Phillip V., 327.
Miller, Raphael Harwood, 4360-4362.
Miller, Robert Henry, 328.
Miller, Timothy, 329.
Miller, Victor J., 2644.
Miller, Wilbur C., 2462.
Miller, William Lee, 889-898.
Milligan, Robert, 4363-4365.
Mills, Dorothy Hurst, 2180.
Minard, Herbert Leslie, 4366-4368.
Minck, Franklin Henry, 4369.
Minniear, Deloris Jeanne, 1780.
Mitchell, Irvine Eugene, 2765.
Mix, Clarence Rex, 899-901.
Moeller, Harold Carr, 4370.
Moffett, Robert, 330, 4371.
Moninger, Herbert, 4372-4382.
Monroe, Herald B., 4383.
Monser, John Waterhaus, 4384.
Montgomery, John Dexter, 4385-4387.
Montgomery, Riley Benjamin, 4388-4392.
Moomaw, Donn D., 331.
Moore, George Voiers, 4393-4399.
Moore, Jerome Aaron, 1327-1328.
Moore, Paul L., 4400.
Moore, William Joseph, 4401-4402.
Moore, William Thomas, 332, 4403-4418.
Moorhouse, William Mervin, 1781.
Morehouse, Daniel Walter, 4419-4421.
Morgan, Sarah, 1966-1970.
Morgan, Philip, 333.
Morison, William James, 1782-1783.
Morrill, Milo True, 334, 1784.
Morris, Donald Bryan, 4422.
Morris, Philip D., 335.
Morrison, Charles Clayton, 336-337, 4423-4425.
Morrison, Hugh Tucker, 4426-4430.
Morrison, John L., 338.
Morrison, Matthew C., 1785.
Mort, F.L., 339.
Morton, Clement Manly, 4431-4433.
Morton, Raymond Clark, 902.
Moseley, Joseph Edward, 340, 4434-4441.
Moses, Helen Elizabeth (Turney), 4442.
Moss, David Billy Ross, 2645.
Moss, J.J., 4443.
Moudy, James M., 903-904.
Moyer, Robert E., 2141.
Muir, Kenneth Arthur, 1329-1350.
Mullendore, William, 4444.

Osborn, George Edwin, 4539-4544.
Osborn, Ronald Edwin, 357-371, 4545-4556.
Ossman, Albert John, 2319.
Osterberg, Myron Levi, 1501.
Overman, Ralph Theodore, 2160-2163.
Overton, Patrick Miles, 1366.
Owen, Dan Kelly, 2463.
Owen, George Earle, 4557-4560.
Owens, Barbara L., 1971.
Owens, Robert J., 4561.
Oxley, Theron D., Jr., 2142.

Paddock, W., 372.
Page, Kirby, 4562-4609.
Painter, J.H., 4610.
Palmer, Ralph T., 4611-4612.
Parady, William Harold, 524-526.
Paregien, Stanley, 4613-4614.
Parker, J.M., 375.
Parrish, Margaret Ware, 2196.
Parrott, Rodney L., 4615.
Parry, Wilbur Clyde, 4616.
Parshall, Clyde Joseph, 2464.
Partin, Harry Baxter, 4617-4618.
Paternoster, Ira A., 4619-4620.
Patrick, Dale Alfred, 4621-4623.
Paul, Charles Thomas, 4624-4626.
Paulin, Philip Edwin, 910.
Paulsell, William Oliver, 377, 4627.
Payne, A.B., 4628.
Payne, John Barton, 1791.
Payne, Ronald Glenn, 911.
Pearson, Samuel Campbell, Jr., 378-381, 1792-1793.
Peck, Lawrence Keith, 2143.
Pellett, David Claude, 4629.
Pelworth, Thomas Formalt, 912.
Pendergrass, Webster, 527.
Pendleton, William Kimbrough, 2707.
Pendleton, Winston K., 1367-1376.
Pennington, Sam N., 2652.
Peoples, Robert Hayes, 1794.
Perdue, Leo, 4630-4632.
Peskin, Allan, 382.
Peters, Eugene Herbert, 4633-4636.
Peters, George Llewellyn, 913, 1795.
Peters, Gerald L., 4637.
Peterson, Larry, 1502.
Peterson, Orval Douglas, 4638-4641.
Peterson, Oscar William, 1796.
Peterson, Raleigh J., Jr., 4642-4643.
Petrie, Peter Albert, 4644.
Pettengill, Frederick B., 594.
Petty, John Edward, 914.

Phelps, Mrs. John U., 1797.
Phillips, Marion Carl, 595-596.
Phillips, Mary Kathryn, 1503.
Phillips, Mildred Welshimer, 4645.
Phillips, Thomas Wharton, Jr., 2320-2324.
Phillips, Thomas Wharton, Sr., 4646-4647.
Phillips, William Louis, 1377-1379.
Philputt, Allan Bearden, 4648.
Philputt, James McBride, 4649.
Pickett, Frank, 4650.
Pierce, Lee C., 383.
Pierce, Linda Lou, 915.
Pierson, Roscoe Mitchell, 384, 2058-2069.
Pinkerton, Lewis Letig, 1798.
Pippin, Frank Johnson, 1380-1384.
Pittman, Riley Herman, 2766.
Plantteburg, George, 4651.
Platt, Robert Martin, 2767-2774.
Plowman, E.E., 385.
Plummer, Mark A., 1799-1803.
Polk, David Patrick, 4652.
Pollard, Lucille Addison, 2465.
Pontius, Myron Lee, 4653.
Pope, Richard Martin, 386-389, 4654-4658.
Porter, Calvin Lewis, 4659-4660.
Porter, Jack R., 2144-2145.
Potter, Marguerite, 1804-1809.
Pounds, John Edward, 4661.
Pounds, Mattie, 4662.
Powell, Edward Lindsay, 4663-4665.
Powell, Wilfred Evans, 4666-4671.
Powell, William Ray, 916-918.
Power, Frederick Dunglison, 4672-4675.
Powers, Wanda C., 919.
Poyser, George K., 4676.
Presler, Elizabeth Pettit, 2164.
Preusz, Gerald Clyde, 920.
Price, David Eugene, 2325-2330.
Price, Sharon, 921.
Priest, Doug, Jr., 4677.
Pritchard, Mary Hanson, 2653-2654.
Procter, Alexander, 4678.
Proctor, Ben Hamill, 1810-1813.
Pruitt, Elaine, 1385.
Pugh, Charles Ray, 597-599.
Pugh, Samuel Frank, 4679-4684.
Pyatt, Charles Lynn, 391, 4685.

Quinn, Bernard, 392.

Radford, Benjamin Johnson, 4686-4688.
Ragan, Stephen C., 393.
Rains, Paul Boyd, 4689.

Savage, Dennis, 417.
Savage, Dennis Ben, 933.
Sayre, Cynthia Woolever, 2776.
Sayre, John Leslie, 2070-2085.
Scheen, Jerry S., 4794.
Scheer, Gladys Elizabeth, 2086-2087.
Schippers, Louis, 2467.
Schmal, Philipp, Jr., 2165-2166.
Schmalhausen, Myrtle Ruth, 1972.
Schmehl, Willard Reed, 528-529.
Schmulbach, Charles David, 2661.
Schnell, Kempes Yoder, 1827.
Schriever, Errol G., 1036.
Schroeder, Oliver Charles, Jr., 1993-2008.
Schuster, Monroe, 1828.
Schwabe, George Blaine, 2361.
Scott, Barbara Kerr, 1829.
Scott, Blair Thaw, 603-604.
Scoville, Orlin James, 530-537.
Seaman, John, 418.
Seaman, Thomas Warren, 2777.
Sears, L.C., 419.
Sechler, Earl Truman, 1830-1835.
Segler, Julius Alfred, 2662-2663.
Selleck, John Hugh, 1515.
Sessions, Will A., Jr., 1393-1396.
Sewell, Elisha Granville, 4816-4819.
Sexson, William Mark, 4820-4824.
Shackleford, John, 4825.
Shae, Gam Seng, 4826.
Sharp, Allan Rhinehart, 4827.
Sharp, Paul Frederick, 1836-1839.
Sharratt, William Bert, 1840.
Shaw, Chandler, 1841-1846.
Shaw, Henry King, 1847-1852.
Shaw, Knowles, 4828-4834.
Shaw, Roud, 4835.
Shelton, Albert Leroy, 4836-4837.
Shelton, Flora Beal, 4838-4842.
Shelton, Gentry Allen, 420, 4843.
Shelton, Orman Leroy, 421, 4844.
Shelton, William A., 1853.
Shepard, Darrell Royce, 4845.
Shepherd, James Walton, 422.
Sheppard, Sallie, 652.
Sherlock, Wallace E., 423.
Sherman, Charles, 934.
Sherwood, Henry Noble, 1854-1860.
Shields, James Leroy, 4846.
Shifflet, Stephen Thomas, 4847.
Shirley, James Clifford, 935.
Shirts, Sheldon Vincent, 4848.
Shoemaker, George Curtiss, 4849.

Waldrop, W. Earl, 2379-2381, 5102-5104.
Walk, David, 5105.
Walker, Dean Everest, 5106-5110.
Walker, Granville Thomas, 5111-5115.
Walker, James Lynwood, 2469.
Walker, John Byron, 5116-5117.
Walker, Virgil Reziah, 5118.
Wall, Sandy A., 977-978.
Wallace, Ray W., 5119.
Wallace, William E., 1897.
Walstrom, John, 656-657.
Walter, James Ellsworth, 979-984.
Walwik, Theodore Joseph, 1418-1419.
Ward, James Britton, 2668.
Ward, James Keith, 5120.
Ward, Mae (Yoho), 5121-5127.
Wardrep, Bruce N., 618.
Ware, Charles Crossfield, 464, 1898-1915.
Ware, James, 5128.
Ware, Ray M., 619-620.
Warford, Malcolm L., 5129-5132.
Warne, Clinton Lee, 621-624.
Warren, Louis Austin, 1916-1927.
Warren, William Robinson, 5133-5135.
Wassenick, Paul G., 5136.
Wasson, Woodrow Wilson, 465, 1928-1931.
Watkins, B.U., 466.
Watkins, Don O., 625-626.
Watkins, Keith, 467-470, 5137-5141.
Watson, George H., 1932.
Watson, Gerald Glenn, 2382.
Watson, Keene Arnold, 5142.
Watson, Roy Alvin, 1420.
Watters, Archibald Clark, 5143-5144.
Weaver, Ben H., 985.
Weaver, Gustine Nancy (Courson), 1421-1432.
Webb, Harold Quentin, 627.
Webb, Henry E., 471-472, 1933.
Webber, Percy R., 1934.
Webster, Jesse A., 1523.
Welch, Rosa Page, 1524-1525.
Wells, Carl Douglas, 473.
Wells, Goldie Ruth, 5145.
Welsh, Matthew Empson, 2383.
Welsh, Robert K., 474.
Welsh, Wiley A., 475, 5146.
Welshimer, Helen, 1433-1442.
Welshimer, Pearl Howard, 5147-5151.
Wentz, Richard E., 476.
Wertz, Spencer Kiefer, 5152.
West, Donald F., 1935.
West, Earl Irvin, 477-479.
West, John William, 5153-5155.

SUBJECT INDEX

In a bibliography of this length, even one which has broad subject categories, some kind of subject index becomes necessary. However, users will probably not find the index as specific as they would like, due to the fact that the bibliographers had to discern subject headings from book titles that are not very specific, or from broad subject categories in the indexes from which the works are taken. Users will still have to do a fair amount of "digging," but it is hoped the index will help users to narrow down the number of works they will need to examine.

Subject categories refer mainly to works which deal with the Disciples of Christ as a movement. Therefore, the main sections which have been indexed are the "Periodical and General Literature" section and the "Theology/Philosophy/ Religion" section of the "Names." Some works have been placed in one or more subject categories, and some have not been indexed at all because the title was too general.

Atlantic Christian College

1904.

Baptism

19, 61, 62, 175, 348, 2864, 2941, 3023, 3069, 3268, 3329, 3384, 3413, 4101, 4127, 4322, 4423, 4733, 4735, 4808, 4908, 5018, 5019.

Bethany College

491, 996, 4259, 4673.

Bible

4, 80, 91, 201, 255, 353, 380, 381, 1394, 1632, 2811,
2830, 2831, 2857, 2904, 2918, 2935, 2951, 2954, 2997,
3126, 3129, 3130, 3202, 3236, 3237, 3238, 3239, 3240,
3241, 3242, 3243, 3244, 3249, 3260, 3310, 3320, 3323,
3341, 3342, 3350, 3361, 3393, 3408, 3458, 3465, 3497,
3503, 3506, 3515, 3518, 3538, 3540, 3547, 3550, 3555,
3556, 3558, 3616, 3645, 3672, 3673, 3730, 3766, 3767,
3768, 3776, 3781, 3791, 3843, 3912, 3913, 3914, 3920,
3927, 3932, 3964, 3966, 3967, 3977, 3983, 4033, 4076,
4079, 4103, 4108, 4132, 4223, 4238, 4242, 4245, 4250,
4265, 4267, 4268, 4274, 4276, 4277, 4304, 4336, 4350,
4443, 4475, 4487, 4489, 4597, 4631, 4672, 4691, 4697,
4728, 4741, 4742, 4743, 4758, 4761, 4766, 4783, 4788,
4789, 4818, 4890, 4904, 4975, 5006, 5007, 5021, 5044,
5064, 5086, 5097, 5108, 5195, 5201, 5203, 5230, 5238,
5239.

Bible - New Testament

220, 445, 798, 1070, 1077, 1374, 1402, 1403, 2790, 2804,
2806, 2832, 2874, 2875, 2876, 2888, 2939, 2947, 2949,
2966, 2967, 2980, 2981, 2982, 3025, 3195, 3196, 3197,
3228, 3230, 3231, 3233, 3292, 3319, 3324, 3333, 3337,
3340, 3346, 3445, 3446, 3455, 3473, 3475, 3482, 3488,
3501, 3508, 3509, 3510, 3511, 3512, 3513, 3519, 3520,
3521, 3539, 3546, 3551, 3552, 3592, 3649, 3657, 3687,
3759, 3779, 3861, 3890, 3892, 3893, 3910, 3946, 3953,
3973, 3975, 3979, 3981, 3982, 3984, 3985, 4022, 4028,
4029, 4030, 4031, 4032, 4039, 4130, 4151, 4162, 4177,
4178, 4184, 4185, 4240, 4262, 4263, 4264, 4270, 4271,
4272, 4273, 4279, 4312, 4316, 4346, 4349, 4351, 4363,
4365, 4376, 4377, 4381, 4400, 4401, 4427, 4515, 4536,
4614, 4615, 4629, 4660, 4685, 4764, 4780, 4817, 4848,
4858, 4859, 4888, 4906, 4921, 4972, 4979, 4992, 5005,
5008, 5009, 5022, 5025, 5036, 5109, 5114, 5146, 5208,
5214.

Bible - Old Testament

11, 12, 1864, 2048, 2113, 2820, 2849, 2850, 2938, 2946,
2977, 2978, 3083, 3084, 3097, 3116, 3124, 3128, 3151,
3154, 3155, 3156, 3157, 3158, 3168, 3252, 3298, 3302,
3322, 3351, 3355, 3369, 3461, 3464, 3514, 3595, 3596,
3688, 3732, 3733, 3734, 3735, 3736, 3737, 3760, 3761,
3762, 4152, 4207, 4258, 4326, 4334, 4335, 4553, 4561,
4621, 4622, 4623, 4630, 4679, 4693, 4694, 4695, 4696,
4698, 4910, 4980, 5060, 5073, 5200, 5205, 5207, 5218,
5219, 5229, 5231, 5232, 5253, 5257, 5258.

Bibliographies

145, 149, 272, 320, 384, 1623, 1900, 2040, 2044, 2055, 2056, 2057, 2063, 2065, 2076, 2083, 2084, 2112, 2261, 3269, 3275, 3335, 3336, 3390, 3618, 4021, 4384, 4485, 4697, 4855, 4928, 4933, 4934, 4935, 5163.

Black Disciples
(See also Minorities)

65, 75, 144, 149, 858, 859, 1362, 1363, 1364, 1365, 1486, 1524, 1525, 1744, 1794, 2172, 2173, 2174, 2881, 2950, 2983, 3188, 3402, 3517, 3537, 3769, 3770, 3777, 4023, 4148, 4744, 4745, 4793, 4885, 4886, 4887, 4914.

Butler University

26, 93, 715, 1250, 3850, 3851, 3903.

Campbell, Alexander, 1788-1866

3, 146, 217, 248, 254, 273, 338, 438, 445, 1745, 1840, 1954, 3366, 3417, 3479, 3480, 3568, 3570, 3587, 3639, 3642, 3661, 3896, 4043, 4098, 4180, 4228, 4299, 4715, 4717, 4720, 4758, 4846, 4881, 4973, 5038, 5051, 5115, 5156.

Campbell, Thomas, 1763-1864

315, 3568, 3693, 3988, 3989.

Children and Youth

468, 1119, 1269, 1270, 1283, 1780, 2395, 2879, 2926, 3029, 3030, 3031, 3187, 3246, 3343, 3439, 3460, 3477, 3680, 3749, 3860, 3862, 3930, 3986, 4014, 4020, 4153, 4167, 4169, 4232, 4251, 4252, 4253, 4254, 4328, 4331, 4332, 4333, 4366, 4367, 4383, 4451, 4672, 4820, 4821, 4822, 4823, 4824, 4847, 4925, 4926, 4927, 4945, 5015, 5016, 5017, 5119, 5163.

Christian Education

231, 269, 411, 436, 662, 665, 666, 667, 669, 670, 675, 676, 678, 679, 680, 681, 682, 683, 885, 887, 1277, 1278, 1279, 1281, 1282, 1284, 1285, 1291, 1292, 1840, 2392, 2878, 2990, 2993, 2994, 2995, 3000, 3002, 3005, 3190, 3211, 3212, 3213, 3338, 3344, 3345, 3346, 3374, 3399, 3420, 3421, 3422, 3423, 3438, 3632, 3648, 3781, 3782, 3787, 3789, 3857, 3861, 3912, 3913, 3914, 3917, 3918, 3919, 3920, 3921, 3922, 3924, 3925, 3926, 3927, 3928, 3929, 3931, 3932, 3933, 3936, 3937, 3938, 3944, 4034, 4057, 4099, 4100, 4109, 4116, 4154, 4157, 4158, 4160,

4166, 4167, 4168, 4170, 4171, 4190, 4194, 4195, 4196,
4197, 4198, 4199, 4200, 4201, 4204, 4205, 4206, 4234,
4235, 4245, 4248, 4249, 4250, 4274, 4278, 4319, 4328,
4332, 4343, 4344, 4357, 4359, 4372, 4373, 4374, 4375,
4378, 4379, 4380, 4382, 4386, 4387, 4396, 4399, 4434,
4451, 4454, 4455, 4456, 4457, 4459, 4460, 4461, 4462,
4463, 4466, 4477, 4519, 4616, 4661, 4666, 4667, 4668,
4670, 4671, 4738, 4739, 4747, 4748, 4771, 4772, 4774,
4779, 4787, 4813, 4828, 4829, 4833, 4834, 4843, 4858,
4924, 4936, 5011, 5014, 5061, 5086, 5091, 5100, 5101,
5131, 5136, 5147, 5228.

Christian Life

1091, 1110, 2163, 2166, 2393, 2410, 2470, 2798, 2803,
2809, 2813, 2817, 2819, 2823, 2825, 2837, 2843, 2845,
2865, 2889, 2891, 2896, 2928, 2929, 2937, 2956, 2960,
3026, 3027, 3040, 3057, 3075, 3110, 3125, 3126, 3131,
3148, 3150, 3229, 3288, 3301, 3375, 3376, 3382, 3418,
3450, 3469, 3481, 3494, 3526, 3544, 3660, 3665, 3678,
3679, 3681, 3691, 3701, 3709, 3716, 3751, 3836, 3840,
3877, 3878, 3879, 3880, 3881, 3882, 3883, 3884, 3885,
3886, 3889, 3894, 3900, 3940, 3970, 3974, 3993, 4015,
4017, 4018, 4055, 4070, 4076, 4078, 4117, 4118, 4129,
4137, 4153, 4155, 4181, 4221, 4222, 4350, 4417, 4431,
4474, 4476, 4488, 4523, 4535, 4541, 4544, 4559, 4574,
4584, 4585, 4586, 4587, 4588, 4627, 4658, 4826, 4863,
4874, 4899, 4900, 4977, 5071, 5081, 5095, 5127, 5165,
5171, 5172, 5173, 5206, 5216.

Christian Theological Seminary

55, 164, 284, 365, 366, 430, 442, 3013.

Church and State

180.

Church Membership

38, 325, 326, 2941, 3061, 3079, 3348, 4145, 4368, 4393,
4682, 4684, 5063.

Claremont Graduate School of Theology

105.

Conferences and Conventions

2, 7, 52, 56, 86, 95, 118, 119, 123, 124, 129, 134, 135,
136, 137, 138, 139, 140, 162, 173, 177, 178, 179, 183,
184, 186, 187, 189, 191, 194, 195, 196, 212, 256, 277,
306, 307, 308, 317, 324, 333, 336, 337, 344, 356, 408,

Conferences and Conventions (cont.)

>   409, 453, 464, 487, 1743, 2879, 3278, 3281, 3282, 3566,
>   4419, 4760, 4779, 5134, 5233, 5234, 5235.

Disciples - General

>   32, 42, 53, 58, 60, 74, 76, 79, 80, 83, 87, 92, 104, 115,
>   120, 121, 126, 128, 133, 154, 157, 159, 160, 161, 165,
>   169, 170, 181, 185, 188, 215, 219, 221, 223, 230, 234,
>   262, 281, 288, 289, 300, 347, 359, 362, 363, 371, 373,
>   396, 398, 415, 417, 422, 431, 440, 441, 454, 457, 458,
>   462, 463, 481, 482, 500, 503, 504, 1174, 1529, 1599,
>   1609, 1611, 2775, 2788, 2799, 2815, 2816, 2822, 2846,
>   2847, 2848, 2920, 2921, 2927, 2930, 2933, 2934, 2958,
>   2963, 2964, 2987, 3018, 3078, 3080, 3085, 3160, 3266,
>   3290, 3331, 3370, 3381, 3407, 3415, 3451, 3483, 3559,
>   3564, 3574, 3577, 3590, 3614, 3646, 3719, 3805, 3895,
>   3899, 3939, 3943, 3965, 3987, 3992, 3994, 4008, 4010,
>   4056, 4106, 4124, 4125, 4149, 4246, 4307, 4308, 4338,
>   4339, 4340, 4341, 4415, 4440, 4441, 4493, 4545, 4551,
>   4554, 4555, 4627, 4644, 4646, 4654, 4692, 4714, 4722,
>   4727, 4814, 4844, 4889, 4918, 4940, 5004, 5022, 5037,
>   5110, 5135, 5162, 5167, 5180, 5184, 5243.

Disciples - History

>   30, 54, 64, 68, 70, 73, 77, 94, 110, 150, 171, 202, 209,
>   210, 225, 232, 239, 241, 246, 247, 252, 255, 280, 305,
>   310, 320, 321, 322, 330, 341, 353, 378, 397, 425, 452,
>   455, 459, 460, 466, 479, 480, 484, 489, 495, 502, 507,
>   1230, 1534, 1564, 1597, 1618, 1619, 1626, 1656, 1659,
>   1660, 1696, 1716, 1717, 1725, 1726, 1727, 1738, 1739,
>   1742, 1747, 1748, 1781, 1784, 1789, 1815, 1816, 1818,
>   1867, 1869, 1870, 1878, 1879, 1889, 1903, 1936, 1948,
>   1956, 2072, 2204, 2812, 2883, 2905, 3210, 3291, 3300,
>   3303, 3325, 3339, 3352, 3357, 3377, 3387, 3392, 3394,
>   3398, 3401, 3498, 3504, 3567, 3568, 3571, 3575, 3585,
>   3591, 3724, 3726, 3727, 3776, 4084, 4090, 4098, 4134,
>   4144, 4145, 4147, 4202, 4212, 4405, 4438, 4446, 4468,
>   4470, 4525, 4550, 4674, 4686, 4767, 4769, 4857, 4872,
>   4883, 4895, 4896, 4916, 4938, 4939, 5020, 5026, 5067,
>   5083, 5084, 5143, 5144, 5148, 5153, 5154, 5204, 5220.

Disciples - History - Alabama

>   1790, 1932.

Disciples - History - California

>   243, 302, 304, 363, 473, 1681, 1935, 2761, 3161, 3293,
>   5243.

Disciples - History - Vermont

334.

Disciples - History - Virginia

40, 404, 1533, 1563, 1614, 1687, 1871, 3493.

Disciples - History - Washington

4641, 5046.

Disciples - History - West Virginia

491, 1533, 1601, 4973.

Disciples - History - Wisconsin

3871.

Division

9, 24, 51, 65, 66, 90, 109, 158, 167, 191, 199, 207, 216, 232, 239, 240, 242, 249, 270, 272, 273, 293, 352, 395, 410, 435, 471, 479, 507, 1621, 1739, 1819, 1931, 1933, 1949, 1950, 1951, 2971, 3019, 3586, 3659, 3720, 3727, 4468, 4480, 4923, 5248.

Drake University

928.

Ecumenism

1, 8, 13, 18, 20, 21, 22, 29, 33, 38, 39, 45, 62, 72, 81, 82, 84, 89, 94, 95, 96, 98, 100, 101, 102, 103, 106, 107, 108, 117, 122, 141, 142, 143, 152, 155, 163, 168, 182, 193, 197, 198, 202, 203, 213, 214, 217, 218, 222, 229, 256, 264, 266, 268, 274, 290, 291, 292, 294, 296, 299, 301, 303, 307, 313, 315, 318, 319, 323, 329, 332, 333, 335, 336, 346, 357, 358, 367, 376, 383, 390, 392, 400, 401, 403, 410, 424, 426, 438, 444, 446, 447, 448, 461, 467, 472, 474, 476, 492, 497, 505, 1532, 1625, 2268, 2810, 2814, 2818, 2821, 2826, 2948, 2955, 2970, 3007, 3066, 3268, 3269, 3270, 3271, 3272, 3273, 3274, 3275, 3276, 3277, 3279, 3280, 3283, 3284, 3285, 3286, 3312, 3326, 3378, 3384, 3428, 3561, 3573, 3584, 3636, 3694, 3719, 3969, 3980, 4087, 4104, 4105, 4112, 4269, 4398, 4425, 4469, 4504, 4505, 4506, 4510, 4512, 4546, 4547, 4548, 4649, 4734, 4736, 4764, 4776, 4808, 4852, 4871, 4897, 4917, 5018, 5019, 5034, 5059, 5106, 5107, 5174. 5190, 5202, 5209, 5220, 5226.

Education

127, 227, 267, 338, 443, 488, 720, 811, 858, 859, 1691, 1788, 4879, 4929, 4930, 5130.

Education, Higher

26, 36, 47, 49, 50, 93, 201, 228, 394, 419, 427, 465, 845, 858, 868, 922, 1533, 1607, 1685, 1719, 2080, 2834, 2998, 2999, 3330, 3403, 3412, 3417, 3484, 3629, 3635, 3639, 3683, 3685, 3686, 3689, 3850, 3851, 3964, 3968, 4230, 4313, 4391, 4656, 4781, 4865, 4913, 4966, 5035, 5061, 5085, 5132.

Evangelism

34, 48, 69, 172, 295, 311, 1155, 1157, 1577, 2866, 2869, 2871, 2872, 2873, 3056, 3100, 3332, 3437, 3487, 3626, 3647, 3666, 3697, 3854, 3871, 4028, 4046, 4311, 4436, 4448, 4458, 4721, 4723, 4783, 4784, 4785, 4804, 4805, 4807, 4809, 4830, 5010, 5116, 5255.

Finances

71, 127, 164, 442, 496, 3850, 4706, 4782, 4909, 5050, 5090, 5221.

Hiram College

465, 788, 789, 2853, 3629.

Homosexuality
(See Social Justice)

Jesus Christ

23, 798, 1120, 1156, 2836, 2877, 2887, 2903, 3167, 3172, 3198, 3199, 3200, 3201, 3245, 3295, 3358, 3459, 3463, 3470, 3478, 3507, 3536, 3548, 3619, 3656, 3657, 3697, 3797, 3847, 3891, 3998, 4009, 4024, 4027, 4044, 4089, 4174, 4178, 4241, 4244, 4257, 4267, 4324, 4325, 4348, 4349, 4430, 4576, 4580, 4596, 4604, 4605, 4607, 4608, 4613, 4640, 4659, 4726, 4894, 5196, 5199.

Jones, James (Jim)

283.

Journals

55, 113, 200, 263, 316, 339, 355, 366, 406, 477, 1112, 1115, 1116, 1684, 1779, 1786, 1849, 2068, 3019, 3261, 3429, 3772, 4187, 4188, 4478, 4932, 5034.

Laity

360, 449, 469, 1962, 2410, 3081, 3094, 3125, 3297, 3305, 3306, 3373, 3418, 3516, 3625, 3633, 3692, 3694, 3770, 3902, 3915, 4115, 4140, 4159, 4256, 4320, 4394, 4422, 4637, 4680, 4683, 4724, 4773, 4775, 4778, 4938, 5006, 5028, 5053, 5120, 5250.

Lexington Theological Seminary
(Formerly College of the Bible)

43, 116, 204, 250, 297, 386, 432, 475, 3003, 3208, 3498, 4259, 4260, 4392, 4395, 4655, 4976.

Lord's Supper

85, 112, 467, 1516, 1532, 1631, 2760, 2864, 2950, 3063, 3123, 3132, 3432, 3491, 3745, 4025, 4101, 4136, 4353, 4730, 4733, 4735, 4759, 5062, 5139.

Lynchburg College

966, 976, 4391.

Minorities

385, 391, 418, 3431, 3721, 3729, 3812, 3813, 3814, 3815, 3816, 3817, 3819, 4439, 4914, 5065, 5066, 5161.

Missions

48, 88, 131, 132, 317, 340, 372, 426, 959, 1675, 1677, 1746, 1934, 2069, 2263, 2269, 2710, 2827, 2853, 2860, 2861, 2862, 2867, 2870, 2901, 2902, 2909, 2911, 2983, 3038, 3039, 3071, 3073, 3096, 3152, 3205, 3206, 3207, 3209, 3211, 3214, 3215, 3217, 3287, 3296, 3328, 3372, 3379, 3380, 3386, 3394, 3410, 3434, 3435, 3436, 3532, 3533, 3534, 3628, 3669, 3671, 3738, 3741, 3743, 3746, 3748, 3750, 3777, 3784, 3794, 3798, 3799, 3800, 3801, 3806, 3807, 3808, 3809, 3810, 3811, 3812, 3813, 3814, 3815, 3816, 3817, 3818, 3820, 3835, 3837, 3838, 3839, 3842, 3852, 3853, 3903, 3911, 4047, 4053, 4080, 4081, 4082, 4083, 4084, 4085, 4165, 4175, 4176, 4179, 4182, 4200, 4204, 4209, 4236, 4281, 4282, 4283, 4284, 4285, 4286, 4287, 4288, 4291, 4292, 4293, 4294, 4295, 4300, 4301, 4302, 4303, 4304, 4370, 4385, 4414, 4442, 4516, 4517, 4518, 4558, 4612, 4619, 4620, 4624, 4625, 4626, 4662, 4669, 4677, 4710, 4712, 4725, 4744, 4745, 4746, 4755, 4779, 4782, 4798, 4836, 4841, 4876, 4877, 4878, 4879, 4880, 4885, 4887, 4897, 4898, 4912, 4965, 4967, 5003, 5033, 5054, 5069, 5121, 5122, 5123, 5124, 5125, 5126, 5145, 5183, 5223, 5246, 5251, 5252.

Music

75, 407, 1423, 1486, 1488, 1489, 1490, 1492, 1493, 1494, 1524, 1525, 3022, 3335, 3440, 3441, 3479, 3763, 3765, 3773, 3774, 3775, 3856, 3904, 3905, 4046, 4135, 4217, 4280, 4324, 4326, 4330, 4800, 4801, 4802, 4803, 4810, 4811, 4816, 4828, 4830, 4831, 4832, 4833, 4834, 5087, 5099.

Pastoral Care

2387, 2968, 3041, 3042, 3044, 3045, 3046, 3047, 3050, 3051, 3053, 3054, 3147, 3153, 3173, 3174, 3175, 3176, 3177, 3178, 3620, 3621, 3622, 3623, 3624, 4054, 4058, 4060, 4061, 4065, 4066, 4069, 4611, 4937, 4995, 4996, 4998, 5045, 5120, 5160.

Pastors

5, 6, 25, 46, 97, 114, 140, 205, 224, 226, 237, 261, 295, 312, 316, 350, 364, 366, 405, 412, 416, 419, 420, 428, 433, 469, 477, 490, 493, 772, 1535, 1574, 1575, 1577, 1578, 1639, 1953, 2070, 2082, 2794, 2796, 2801, 2802, 2829, 2833, 2834, 2853, 2936, 2961, 2969, 2975, 3003, 3087, 3111, 3134, 3143, 3144, 3149, 3170, 3204, 3214, 3267, 3293, 3304, 3305, 3313, 3429, 3612, 3613, 3615, 3627, 3658, 3875, 3972, 3990, 4059, 4063, 4064, 4068, 4071, 4072, 4139, 4146, 4183, 4215, 4216, 4259, 4297, 4321, 4323, 4361, 4390, 4397, 4404, 4416, 4437, 4446, 4467, 4552, 4681, 4794, 4812, 4892, 4909, 4911, 5000, 5041, 5076.

Peace

52, 153, 173, 190, 192, 207, 233, 402, 408, 1600, 2268, 2275, 2277, 2795, 2808, 3012, 3215, 3216, 3425, 3427, 3434, 3901, 4038, 4193, 4198, 4203, 4205, 4214, 4337, 4424, 4447, 4562, 4563, 4570, 4571, 4573, 4590, 4591, 4593, 4595, 4601, 4603, 4604, 4729.

Phillips University

4313.

Politics

236, 279, 342, 343, 354, 377, 418, 1691, 1826, 2378, 3698, 3702, 3703, 3705, 3708, 3710, 3711, 3715, 3772, 3797, 3821, 3822, 4224, 4228, 4615, 5102, 5103.

Preaching

23, 327, 1078, 1387, 1578, 2830, 2831, 2832, 3065, 3204, 3227, 3232, 3234, 3235, 3236, 3237, 3238, 3239, 3240, 3241, 3242, 3243, 3244, 3321, 3480, 3626, 3778, 3958, 4000, 4046, 4062, 4067, 4071, 4299, 4410, 4413, 4473, 4534, 4968, 4971, 4975, 4979, 4980, 4981, 5115, 5175, 5193, 5242.

Scott, Walter, 1796-1861

2922, 4520, 4982.

Seminaries
(See Theological Education)

Sermons and Addresses

134, 136, 137, 138, 139, 140, 282, 603, 771, 1074, 1156, 2792, 2793, 2824, 2836, 2840, 2855, 2858, 2863, 2868, 2880, 2882, 2930, 2931, 2932, 2953, 2959, 2972, 2973, 2974, 2976, 2984, 3015, 3021, 3024, 3028, 3032, 3058, 3059, 3060, 3064, 3088, 3104, 3105, 3179, 3182, 3188, 3194, 3253, 3254, 3255, 3256, 3257, 3332, 3419, 3437, 3460, 3467, 3524, 3527, 3528, 3611, 3662, 3668, 3783, 3804, 3846, 3863, 3956, 3966, 3976, 3978, 3979, 3999, 4001, 4002, 4003, 4004, 4012, 4013, 4016, 4019, 4024, 4044, 4045, 4048, 4091, 4096, 4097, 4113, 4122, 4127, 4128, 4138, 4151, 4152, 4173, 4226, 4227, 4260, 4275, 4303, 4305, 4309, 4318, 4342, 4362, 4371, 4389, 4404, 4410, 4411, 4413, 4418, 4419, 4445, 4479, 4537, 4613, 4645, 4653, 4665, 4675, 4678, 4709, 4760, 4765, 4781, 4790, 4799, 4804, 4835, 4884, 4894, 4951, 5013, 5020, 5043, 5048, 5049, 5059, 5087, 5088, 5105, 5112, 5146, 5149, 5150, 5161, 5169, 5176, 5182, 5227, 5254.

Social Justice

125, 130, 156, 173, 179, 189, 206, 224, 235, 238, 240, 251, 265, 307, 343, 364, 369, 429, 3020, 3076, 3203, 3247, 3411, 3412, 3414, 3424, 3426, 3443, 3696, 3713, 3718, 3724, 4161, 4210, 4223, 4237, 4522, 4532, 4534, 4581, 4589, 4600, 4605, 4606, 4638, 4721, 4866, 4904, 5029.

Stewardship

2864, 3793, 4005, 4050, 4119, 4253, 4369, 4434, 4639, 4704, 4705, 4706, 4875, 5050, 5225, 5244.

Stone, Barton Warren, 1772-1844.

1899, 1944, 1945, 5164.

Texas Christian University

1328, 1658, 4781.

Theological Education

35, 44, 105, 116, 140, 164, 204, 250, 284, 297, 298, 314,
351, 386, 389, 391, 430, 432, 434, 442, 449, 475, 483,
486, 506, 2038, 2387, 3013, 3089, 3090, 3091, 3186, 3219,
3293, 3328, 3386, 3616, 4074, 4075, 4388, 4395, 4549,
4787, 4827, 4849, 4854, 5052, 5129, 5228.

Theology

9, 14, 15, 44, 59, 63, 93, 163, 167, 211, 222, 246, 253,
261, 269, 270, 271, 285, 297, 327, 328, 361, 370, 379,
380, 381, 387, 416, 421, 435, 461, 485, 493, 495, 498,
499, 1624, 1626, 1633, 1891, 1892, 2431, 2835, 2841,
2886, 2890, 2892, 2893, 2894, 2895, 2897, 2898, 2899,
2900, 2925, 2940, 2945, 2985, 2986, 2988, 3006, 3033,
3049, 3055, 3069, 3072, 3092, 3098, 3101, 3114, 3159,
3197, 3248, 3261, 3299, 3430, 3449, 3452, 3456, 3495,
3496, 3505, 3516, 3542, 3545, 3554, 3557, 3562, 3565,
3570, 3587, 3598, 3603, 3650, 3654, 3655, 3670, 3690,
3753, 3754, 3755, 3756, 3896, 4049, 4051, 4052, 4088,
4094, 4103, 4144, 4189, 4213, 4233, 4255, 4310, 4364,
4406, 4412, 4450, 4452, 4513, 4514, 4520, 4552, 4554,
4676, 4697, 4716, 4717, 4718, 4728, 4731, 4732, 4736,
4768, 4845, 4853, 4939, 4942, 4943, 4964, 4969, 5023,
5075, 5098, 5111, 5112, 5177, 5187, 5191, 5194, 5197,
5241, 5256.

Transylvania University

842, 1719, 3608.

University of Chicago

9, 10, 50, 351, 1527, 2834, 3003.

Women

17, 144, 176, 244, 245, 309, 345, 409, 412, 1402, 1419,
1428, 1531, 1563, 1649, 1675, 1677, 1741, 1746, 1831,
1835, 2952, 3004, 3084, 3164, 3309, 3311, 3619, 3741,
3743, 3766, 4297, 4442, 4662, 5068, 5074, 5250.

Worship

85, 99, 368, 399, 468, 469, 470, 1283, 2395, 2805, 2807,
2854, 2884, 2957, 2971, 3022, 3082, 3123, 3135, 3136,
3138, 3142, 3146, 3191, 3318, 3731, 3774, 3796, 3855,
3860, 3922, 4025, 4042, 4156, 4208, 4231, 4539, 4540,